MANAGING PERSONAL FINANCE

MANAGING PERSONAL FINANCE

Holley H. Ulbrich
Associate Professor
of Economics
Clemson University

T. Bruce Yandle, Jr.
Professor of Economics
Clemson University

1979

BUSINESS PUBLICATIONS, INC.
Dallas, Texas 75243

Irwin-Dorsey Limited
Georgetown, Ontario L7G 4B3

ISBN 0-256-02208-9
Library of Congress Catalog Card No. 78–70014

Printed in the United States of America

1 2 3 4 5 6 7 8 9 0 MP 6 5 4 3 2 1 0 9

Preface

One might reasonably ask why anyone wishes to write another textbook in an already crowded field. This text grew out of our search for a satisfactory text for our students, one that they could read for pleasure and profit, use as a guide in making personal financial decisions, and keep as a reference book after the course ended.

We wanted to incorporate a limited amount of economic analysis because we believe that a better understanding of the market system and how it works will improve the student's comprehension of the economic decision process. We wanted to cover some topics that were shortchanged in most other texts, including marginal analysis, compounding and discounting, fringe benefits and Social Security, buying a funeral, keeping records, budgeting time, bank services, nontraditional investments, and a market perspective on job search and consumerism.

We wanted to take account of the special problems faced by singles, divorcees, two-earner families, newlyweds, retired couples—all of the "nonstandard" family situations. Most important of all, we wanted to emphasize a lifestyle approach to personal decision making by providing a framework within which the student could incorporate his or her own tastes and preferences, values, habits, and career and family situation—all of the things which made her or him one of the 215 million unique consumers in our market system. And we wanted the student to see how his or her inputs change over time, so that the decisions made at 20 can be revised as the situation changes at 30, 50, or 65.

We did not want to write a "cookbook." Most consumer decisions have no pat answers, but there is a common body of information and some general decision-making procedures which every informed financial manager should understand. This book tries to provide that information and develops those step-by-step decision processes without burdening the student with "thou shalts" and "thou shalt nots."

Those who have made a contribution to this effort are numerous. And there are some to whom we are especially indebted. These include our students, who told us what they needed in a text; our spouses, Carlton Ulbrich and Dot Yandle, who listened, read, commented, put up with our many hours of writing and rewriting, but most of all, who have lived with us and shared in many financial decisions; our colleagues at Clemson University, who offered suggestions, comments, and criticisms; and our children. Christine, Carla, and Katrina Ulbrich and Kathryn, Bruce, and Eric Yandle have taught us much about how a family's needs and expenses, tastes, and choices change over time. Kathryn Yandle also performed the basic research and wrote the first draft of the final two chapters. We deeply appreciate the financial support of the Sirrine Foundation during the final stages of preparing the manuscript for publication. The excellent cartoons are the work of our friend, Kate Palmer. Finally, we are indebted to Dianne Haselton for her meticulous typing and correction of our errors. Of course, the responsibility for any remaining errors and omissions is shared equally by the authors.

December 1978

Holley H. Ulbrich
T. Bruce Yandle, Jr.

Contents

List of tables and charts

List of figures

FIGURE

PART I

These seven chapters are concerned with getting started as a consumer in our market system—choosing a job; making decisions; keeping records; drawing up budgets; using credit; buying a house; and using your power as a consumer through careful shopping, effective complaining, and through the regulatory power of government.

ESTABLISHING YOUR LIFESTYLE

Chapter 1

Introduction

You can't always get what you want. But if you try sometimes, you get what you need.

Mick Jagger

All of us have heard the fairy tales which end with the traditional words "and they got married and lived happily ever after." Somehow that short summary of what follows adolescence doesn't quite jibe with Mick Jagger's words and the experiences of many people. Some do not marry, some do and then divorce, and even into the most blissful lives some rain must fall. One of the storm clouds that follows people through adulthood and sometimes ruins their "happily ever afters" is the problem of acquiring and spending income. Money may not be the root of all evil, but money definitely has been the root of many divorces, family squabbles, emotional crises, and even an occasional suicide.

Managing money is something people learn to do rather haphazardly, beginning with that first allowance and the choice made between bubble gum and candy bars, through the teenage babysitting or yardwork money which went quickly to buy record albums, Coke, and movie tickets. Somewhere along the way quantum leaps are made to regular income, grocery and doctor bills, insurance, and mortgages. On-the-job training tends to prevail. You learn by doing, just as you learn to cook, repair bicycles, and rear children. Trial and error, a little advice from the elders, a little help from our friends, and occasionally a few books carry you through. Is there a better way?

This book is a how-to guide designed to help in the process of making the normal financial decisions that affect, even determine your lifestyle. The book is not a cookbook full of golden rules for instant success. It is a guide, a book of logic and principles which can be used even when the golden rules change. The focus is on the decisions, the choices you will make.

The ability to manage money can be acquired either haphazardly or systematically. In either case, money management is an acquired skill, like riding a bicycle, solving a quadratic equation, repairing a car, or cooking a meal. Each of these skills requires a fairly intensive learning period, after which the practice becomes second nature. With some learning, you can balance easily on a bicycle, diagnose the clunk in the engine very quickly, or whip up a balanced and appealing meal in half an hour. The increased efficiency from mastering these skills enables you to devote your time and attention to other things. Nevertheless, periodic updating of skills is necessary. For example, those who learned to ride on the old one-speeds have had to adjust to derailleurs, gearshifts, racing handlebars, and balancing on lightweight bicycles. New recipes, techniques, and tools such as the crockpot constantly change the technology of cooking.

Money management skills follow the same pattern of learning and updating. Most of what you learn about methods of organization and the techniques and content of the decision-making process can be acquired quickly. With practice money management takes less and less time and attention. These financial skills should liberate you from devoting large amounts of time and attention to getting and spending, allowing you to enjoy a wider range of choices and to devote more of your time to living, loving, learning, and doing other things which you enjoy.

YOUR LIFESTYLE IN A MARKET SYSTEM

A major emphasis of this book is the establishment of a personal *lifestyle*. A lifestyle is the visible result of your unique values, tastes, preferences, priorities, and idiosyncrasies which express the outer reaches of your personality and the inner constraint of available money and time. It includes your job or career, housing, furnishings, clothing, automobile, budget, borrowing and savings habits, and investment preferences. More broadly, it includes your choice of community, friends, marriage partner (if any), reading material, political attitudes, and leisure activities.

You have a broad range of choices in determining your own lifestyle. While you may not always get what you want, you will have choices unlike those of most people on earth. Just keeping body and soul together is a challenge for many people. Either owning a home or being able to rent an apartment or a room could be the ultimate in living for others. Very few people have the choice of seeking a simple but happy existence or a wealthy, more complex, but still happy, way of life. Americans today have that choice, a choice made possible by our market system.

Of course choosing a lifestyle doesn't make it so. That is just a first step. Seeking to achieve a lifestyle in the market system is the name of the game.

The American economy is a *market system,* a system where individuals own property including their own labor and make decisions as to how they will allow their property to be used. In a market system, individuals choose the work or careers they will follow; how, when, and where they will work; and what they will do with their earnings. In a market system, all individuals are consumers. The consumer is the central unit, the focal point of the system. Increasing consumer well-being is the sole purpose of all economic activity. Most consumers play other economic roles as well; some are primarily consumer-workers, others are consumer-managers, still others are consumer-owners, or even a combination of all four roles.

The collective action of all individual consumers in a market system determines what will be produced, who will produce it, and how production will occur.

Consumers as individuals have tremendous latitude in making decisions in our economic system. For example, a consumer can decide to wear purple tights, drive a dune buggy, live on a diet of yogurt and sunflower seeds, and fish for a living. An individual can also study law; get a diploma; wear a three-piece suit, Oxford cloth shirts with button-down collars, and fancy shoes; and advise Wall Street brokers for a living. It is also possible to mix it up—fish in purple tights on weekends and practice law in a three-piece suit during the week. These choices are made possible by the freedom and decentralization of a market economy.

No matter what your choice of lifestyles, you will face some economic realities. The most basic economic reality is that of scarce resources. In order to acquire a claim on some of those scarce resources, it is necessary to generate an income. This income may come from your own hard work, or from an inheritance (someone else's hard work). Once you have an income, you will have to make decisions about using it. How much will you allocate for fun in the sun, food and shelter, medical care, and transportation? And will you save some money or borrow more for special purposes?

If you save, you will need to decide what to do with your savings. Will you bury them in the backyard, keep the money in a cookie jar, buy U.S. savings bonds, or invest the money in McDonald's stock?

Along the way, you may want to purchase a stereo system, a car, or a boat, something which may cost more than you have in savings. How will you finance the purchase? Will you borrow from your uncle, use a credit card (if you have one), get a loan from a savings and loan association, or borrow from a bank?

Most likely you will decide to live indoors. Will you rent an apartment, buy a home, lease a condominium, or buy a mobile home? How will you decide and what are the surprises which await you when you do? And if you buy, where will you get all that money?

Of course, if you have an income and some property, you may decide to protect it. Can you insure your earnings? What about your stereo, boat, car, and house? And what are the unexpected hazards that you may forget to insure against?

These are private considerations, for the most part. And although we have referred to our economy as a market system through which most private decisions are made, we should not have to remind you that there is also a sizeable public sector. So while you may have some ideas about what you will do with your earnings, federal, state, and local governments have some ideas, too. You will pay some taxes, perhaps a substantial amount of taxes. A little time spent learning about taxes could generate large future returns.

All of the concerns mentioned change through time. Goals and objectives also change over the course of the life cycle. For example, the needs and financial responsibilities of young adults are usually large relative to their incomes. But as the years roll along both major investment decisions and higher earnings can be expected. Thoughts about retirement eventually enter the picture. Each period of life raises interesting economic questions. In fact, an astonishing number of major financial decisions can be identified as you contemplate a typical adult life.

Life would be simpler if these decisions and problems were encountered only once. If, for example, you could organize your finances, develop a budget, set down your investment plans, arrange for insurance, taxes, and retirement early in life, you could then spend your time earning a living and pursuing happiness. Unfortunately, or maybe happily, it doesn't work out that way. Two things invalidate the single-fix strategy.

First, there is a balancing of benefits and costs which has to be considered for each major decision. And the benefits and costs change. To illustrate this, consider life insurance. Very few single adults are financially responsible for other individuals. That is, if misfortune befalls a single swinger it would be sad indeed, but not likely a financial disaster for a family. Even so, the single adult may wish to have some life insurance to provide for funeral expenses, settle debts, or to provide for a favorite charity or an impoverished relative.

When a person marries and takes on new responsibilities, the benefits of insurance or costs of not having it change. What had been a perfect arrangement for managing risk will likely change, also. The person will have to get a new plan. As lifestyles change, financial planning must change also.

The one-time financial fix fails to work for a second reason. Life is filled with the unexpected. Good things (and some unpleasant things) happen which you would never have predicted. New learning, also, opens up new opportunities and new desires. In other words, life is too unpredictable to allow for a single, once and for all insurance or investment program; a single, perfect budget; or a golden rule for reducing tax liabilities. Indeed, the tax laws change so frequently that it is hardly wise to memorize the form numbers.

To a great extent, the inability to make a single, lifetime financial plan reflects the exciting possibilities offered by our market system. Individuals and families can choose. They can change careers, relocate, take risks, and make other dramatic changes in their lifestyles. If everything were planned, financial decision making might be simple. But so would life!

YOUR LIFE INCOME AND EXPENDITURES

This introduction to the financial decisions which the typical person faces over a lifetime can be thought of as the analog of the natural life cycle. Indeed, the natural and financial life cycles are closely related. But while people have not as yet learned how to shift youthful vigor to the post-65 retirement years or to transfer mature wisdom from life's later years to earlier ones, they have learned to alter their financial lifestyle. Income and expenses can be shifted backward or forward by borrowing and lending.

Consider a typical *lifetime earnings profile* which is illustrated in Figure 1–1. (An actual profile is given in Chapter 2.) Note the level of earnings at the

Figure 1–1
Lifetime income pattern

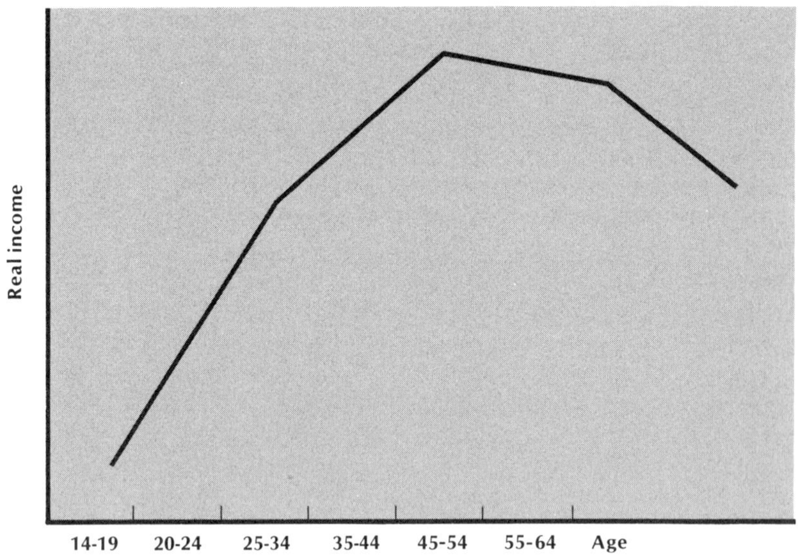

18-year-old end of the curve in the figure. Also notice the curve's steepness from 18 to 30. When the curve is very steep, earnings are increasing rapidly relative to time. The curve eventually flattens out and then turns down. While this is not shown in Figure 1–1, the curve can continue even after the individual is dead and gone through investment income or survivor annuities. That is, unlike people, earnings can be immortal (almost).

You can influence every dimension of your earnings curve. For example, you have some degree of control as to when you begin to generate income on a permanent or full-time basis. You can take more or less time in preparing yourself, investing in your *human capital* so as to increase the likelihood of earning more later. You can also invest some of your earnings in the early years and thereby add a stream of investment income to your later wage and salary income.

Certain precautions can also be taken to protect your anticipated income stream. That is, you can purchase both disability income insurance, which provides income should you become unable to work, and life insurance, which can provide either an income stream in the event of death or supplemental retirement income should you live to a healthy old age. Of course, you can select from many savings plans which allow you to shift expenditures from one period to another.

The point is this—your lifetime income profile can be managed so as to attain your personal goals and objectives as fully as possible.

Having examined the income side of the picture, let's turn to the other side. There is probably also some natural lifetime expense profile. However, expenses are far more subject to our control (or lack of control) than earnings. That is, nature limits a person's earnings capacity, since productivity is so closely related to age, experience, and inherent capacities. Expenses, on the other hand, can explode and become large at any time. Give a Master Charge card to a ten-year-old and you will see expense explosion in action. Expenses can also be held to some minimum across an entire lifetime. Occasionally, there will be a story of some wealthy millionaire who survives on soy beans, orange juice, and milk and lives in a loft. Maybe that's why some people become millionaires! Of course, income and expense must eventually balance.

The problem with expenses relates to a concept from economics known as the *insatiable wants* of the consumer. The idea is simple. People never seem to be completely satisfied. Upon finishing college, for example, a graduating senior might feel that a salary of $15,000 per year would provide everything she might want. On the basis of college expenditures, her attitude is understandable. But a typical college student has not usually coped with utility bills, big-city rent, income and property taxes, providing suitable clothes for work, and a host of other *invisible costs.* Even if these previously unseen costs become recognized, experiences and contacts with other people will lift many new items to the top of the want list. Inevitably, there are pressures and temptations to adjust your lifestyle. Goals and objectives need to be set. Then, expenses and earnings can be managed to help you achieve them.

ORGANIZING YOUR FINANCES: YOUR MANAGEMENT STYLE

Since both earnings and expenses can be managed to achieve the various styles of living you might select over a lifetime, you should consider a few management ideas.

First, in order to be successful, management styles must fit the individual.

Management techniques can include much detail, or they can be broad and simple. But whatever the case, management boils down to making a plan and carrying it out. And the first planning step is the establishing of goals and objectives.

Goals, as opposed to *objectives,* are usually rather broad. For example, you might select owning a home in ten years as a long-range goal. By considering what is involved, taking inventory of your present financial resources and commitments, and determining the requirements of home ownership, you might set some objectives so that the goal can be attained. One objective might relate to saving a down payment. Studying types of housing, locations, and methods of finance might be a second objective. Acquiring a lot could be a third. The objectives can be arrayed in a time path so that in accomplishing them you will reach the ten-year goal.

Once you have some clear goals and objectives established you can begin to manage your activities so that they will be achieved. Figure 1–2 illustrates the process just described. And Figure 1–3 gives some added perspective to the process. Housing might be a long-term goal. Buying a new car could be a short-term goal. In each case, you will want to identify specific objectives which make the goal possible. Once you have the management process organized for your goals and objectives, you then have a plan.

Figure 1–2
Setting goals and objectives

One	Establish broad goals
Two	Inventory current resources for achieving goals
Three	Identify objectives which lead to goal
Four	Establish a plan which connects resources to objectives

Plans usually are not carved in stone. They must be flexible. Both the time dimension and the elements of your plans have to be subject to change. After all, we are talking about chunks of your life. And in the case of the housing goal, an awful lot can happen in ten years.

Furthermore, plans must include ideas from those who will be affected by them. If a couple plans together and jointly makes decisions, the chances of success are greatly improved. In fact, nothing promises doom with greater certainty than plans which one person tries to impose on another.

Each of the major consumer decisions can be approached through the goal-setting and planning process. Setting aside time for dreaming, goal setting, and reviewing progress can be a fruitful and enjoyable experience. Keeping a notebook in which to jot down ideas and save clippings, goal-related pictures, and data can also help in the process. One thing is clear: in

Figure 1–3
Goals and objectives: An illustration

GOAL
Home ownership in 5 years

Objective 1 :
Save downpayment

Objective 2 :
Investigate finance plans
and types of homes

Objective 3 :
Acquire lot

thinking, dreaming, and writing up goals and plans, your mind becomes actively involved in the process. And if you commit your mind and energies to the attainment of goals, something will happen. You will begin to make progress or to learn and thereby reassess your plan. Sometimes you will learn that your plans are not realistic. In some cases, you may not have reached far enough; in others, you may have reached too far.

The process of planning in order to achieve specific goals and objectives will involve the management of your personal finances—your income and expenses. Now, you have a reason for learning about consumer finance. It is for that purpose that the contents of the remaining chapters of the book are now introduced.

A GUIDE TO THE BOOK

You have already encountered the notion of a lifetime earnings profile and the way in which expenses can change over time. In describing these concepts, it was pointed out that an individual's earnings occur somewhat predictably while expenses can go out of control at the drop of a hat. It was also suggested that both earnings and expenses were related to the individual's life cycle. This book is organized along the same lines.

The book has five major parts dealing with the consumer's lifestyle. First, we discuss those things which relate to "Establishing Your Lifestyle." In this part, we discuss jobs and careers, how the labor market operates, and the things you will want to consider when making employment decisions. We also devote a chapter to record keeping—how to organize your income and expenses to tell what and how you are doing. Details on budgeting are included, and tips on how to make a budget are offered.

Major consumer decisions enter the picture when you are getting established. Thus, part I includes two chapters on borrowing and using credit. The first chapter covers general information on credit, how it is established, what loans cost, and where to get them. The second chapter is devoted exclusively to housing, rent or buy questions, how to purchase a house, and where that decision enters your life cycle.

Part I is concluded with a discussion of the consumer's role in the market economy and how consumer power can be enhanced.

Once you begin to generate an income and make major purchases, new risks enter the picture. With an income, a house, furnishings, and a car, you have something to protect. Indeed, you can expect to spend some time and money to avoid the even higher cost of not protecting your resources. Part II of the book is devoted to "Protecting Your Lifestyle." In this part, you will find an introduction to the insurance concept and special chapters on all the major insurance decisions which consumers generally make.

Having gotten established and taken steps to protect yourself from losses, you may begin to long for even better things. How can you enhance your lifestyle? Part III of the book speaks to that question. Adding to your assets is the main topic of discussion there. A chapter is devoted to various savings instruments—how they work and what they earn. This is followed by separate chapters on stocks, bonds, mutual funds, and other investments.

Many people will congratulate you when you are successful in making money. Some will take you out for dinner, others will send flowers, but one in particular will send an annual bill. The bill collector is the government, which is very interested in your lifestyle. Part IV focuses on federal, state, and local taxes, why you must pay them, the varieties in which they are found, how they work, and how you can make them work for you.

The final part in the book examines the golden years of the life cycle. Topics on retirement planning, income sources, tax considerations, estates, and wills are included. The final topic is that last but necessary transaction—purchasing a funeral.

Each chapter in the book contains key words which will be set off by italic type. These are listed at the end of the chapters, along with questions for discussion, and problems to help you in reviewing the main concepts. An appendix on the mathematics of finance is also provided, which will be referred to at various points throughout the book. There is also an appendix to this chapter which introduces and explains the use of marginal analysis, a concept which should prove helpful in all decision making.

Remember, happiness is the ultimate goal of all economic activity. Thus, your financial success will be measured by the happiness you obtain in life. This book is intended to help.

KEY WORDS

Goals
Human capital
Insatiable wants
Invisible costs
Lifestyle
Lifetime earnings profile
Market system
Objectives

PROBLEM

Your personal style of money management depends on some of your personal characteristics. Those most relevant to money management are (1) willingness to tolerate or assume risk; (2) attentiveness to detail; (3) ability to postpone or delay consumption; (4) effort you are willing to put into gathering information for decisions; and (5) your expected income level relative to others in your community.

Rate yourself on these characteristics and discuss their relevance to money management. Save your checklist for reference in future chapters as you develop a record-keeping and budgeting system, an insurance program, a housing plan, and an investment strategy.

APPENDIX: MARGINAL ANALYSIS

Throughout this book the process by which the consumer arrives at decisions will be discussed. Some decisions involve large sums and long-term commitments, like buying a house or car or choosing a job. Most decisions however, involve small trade-offs—should I spend those extra few dollars on more life insurance or insulating the house? Can I cut a few dollars off my weekly food budget to pay for piano lessons? Is air conditioning for my car worth the extra $3 a month on my monthly car payment and the 50 cents a week it adds to my summer gasoline bill? Even a house is not either-or, but involves questions like "should I spend the extra $2,000 for a house with a deck, which will add $16 to my monthly mortgage payment?" You will be constantly weighing the gain in satisfaction from a few more dollars spent here as opposed to the loss in satisfaction from a few less dollars spent there.

The allocation of a limited income among competing uses is a question of what economists call *marginal analysis.* This is based on the notion that as more of something is acquired, the additional units give less and less additional satisfaction. The first ice-cream cone is a treat, the second pleasant, but less exciting, and the third may give you a stomachache. Conversely, as you cut back in some area of expenditure—for example, recreation—the satisfaction given up becomes more and more painful as you find you are leaving yourself with less and less. If your normal daily intake is 2,000 calories, the anguish in cutting back to a 1,500-calorie diet is far less than the anguish of a further cutback from 1,500 calories to 1,000. You must weigh the additional pain of food sacrifice against the additional benefit of accelerated weight loss.

Marginal analysis is theoretically a matter of adding, subtracting, and comparing. If it were possible to find a unit in which to make such comparisons, the consumer could compute trade-off decisions. Economists sometimes work with such an imaginary unit of utility (called *utils*) to illustrate the workings of marginal analysis. Suppose you are considering how much bread and milk to buy with $3 to spend. Bread is 50 cents a loaf, and milk is 50 cents a quart. Your evaluation of the satisfaction they give your family (in taste, hunger abatement, and nutritional value) looks something like the accompanying table:

	Bread (loaf)		***Milk (quart)***	
Units	***Total utils***	***Marginal utils***	***Total utils***	***Marginal utils***
0	0		0	
1	100	100	80	80
2	175	75	140	60
3	225	50	190	50
4	250	25	225	35
5	260	10	250	25
6	260	0	265	15
7	260	0	275	10

The marginal utils are the increase in total satisfaction resulting from the purchase of one more unit. Your first 50 cents will go to bread (100 utils), the second to milk (80 utils), the third to bread (75 utils), the fourth to milk (60 utils). The fifth and sixth can go either way; each adds 50 utils to total satisfaction. Your $3 will give you a total of 415 utils of satisfaction, with three of each. This is the most satisfaction you can attain with this set of preferences and this amount of money (415 utils). Another $1.50 would be used to buy two more quarts of milk and one more loaf of bread.

If the prices are different, it is possible to compute and compare marginal utility per dollar spent. Suppose that bread was, instead, 25 cents a loaf, and milk remained at 50 cents a quart. Then the schedule is as shown in the accompanying table:

Units	Bread (loaf)			Milk (quart)		
	Total utils	Marginal utils	MU/$	Total utils	Marginal utils	MU/$
0	0			0		
1	100	100	400	80	80	160
2	175	75	300	140	60	120
3	225	50	200	190	50	100
4	250	25	100	225	35	70
5	260	10	40	250	25	50
6	260	0	0	265	15	30
7	260	0	0	275	10	20

With $3 to spend you will start with three loaves of bread (400, 300, and 200 utils per dollar), then two milk (160 and 120), then one of each at 100 utils each. At this point you would have four loaves of bread, two quarts of milk, and one dollar left. The next dollar will go to milk since it offers more utility per dollar. The total purchase would be four bread and four milk. Total utility would be 475 utils.

In practice, the weighing of utility is highly subjective, depending on personal and cultural tastes and preferences. But the weighing process is still there. In record keeping, a trade-off is made between the additional effort (cost) involved in keeping more meticulous records against the additional benefit from planning and tax information. In budgeting, you will constantly trade off between more food and less recreation, more clothing and less heat, more spending now and less spending later (saving). In insurance, the trade-off is the benefit in protection of higher limits of liability against the dollar cost or perhaps against the savings in a larger deductible. In housing, there is a choice between some desirable features—deck, pool, family room, second bath, location, space—and the other consumption foregone in accepting a larger monthly payment, or against each other—a family room versus a deck, or a larger lot, or a better view.

In credit, the borrower weighs the larger monthly payment and shorter repayment time against the opposite, or the gain in satisfaction from having something now rather than later against the cost in terms of interest payments. In investments, you may accept a little more risk or a little less liquidity (ease of conversion to cash) for a slightly higher yield.

A decision-making technique which may sound more familiar is cost/benefit analysis, which is a practical application of marginal analysis. Two examples of this approach are given; basically, in each case a list of costs (including discounted future costs) is weighed against benefits (including discounted future benefits). (For a discussion of discounting, see the appendix on the Mathematics of Finance.)

Some cost/benefit comparisons weigh two alternatives (refrigerator A or refrigerator B, job one versus job two) but the technique is basically the same. This more systematic approach to decision making helps to clarify the issues and identify *all* of the relevant costs and benefits.

All consumer decisions are made at the margin, directly or by means of cost/benefit analysis. Consumers subjectively weigh gains and losses, benefits and costs, satisfaction and pain or displeasure or effort against each other. The housewife who says, "I don't have time to comparison shop," is really saying that the gains in dollars saved are less than the value of the time and effort which she would have to expend. Even the child agonizing over soda pop versus comic books is wrestling with a decision at the margin.

In the chapters that follow, you will be encountering the decision-making process in many different forms. Try to look at these decisions in marginal or cost/benefit terms. It may help you to sharpen your decision-making techniques, not only in financial decision making, but in all of the many day-to-day decisions you make, from when to get up in the morning to when to go to bed at night.

Decision 1
Should we buy a new refrigerator/freezer?

Costs

1. | | |
|---|---|
| Cash price .... | \$500 |
| Less trade-in .... | 50 |
| | \$450 |
| Down payment .... | \$ 50 |

Finance the balance @ 12.5% for 2 years, pay \$18.87/month.

Present value* of \$50 now plus \$18.87/month for 2 years, using a 6% discount rate, is

$$\$50 + \$18.87\text{x} \frac{[1 - (1.005)^{-24}]}{0.005}$$
$$= \$475.76$$

2. Shopping time
This dollar figure should be considered in the light of the other consumption forgone—recreation? Investments? Other household purchases?

Benefits

1. Saving in repairs over next 5 years (discounted) \$120 (est.)
2. Grocery saving† of \$5/month over next 10 years discounted at 6%.

$$\frac{\$5[1 - (1.005)^{-120}]}{0.005} = \$450.37$$

3. Savings on electricity‡ at \$2/month over next 10 years discounted at 6%

$$\frac{\$2[(1 - 0.005)^{-120}]}{0.005} = \$180.15$$

4. Convenience?
5. Improved attractiveness of kitchen?

Since the costs of \$475.76 are less than the benefits of \$750.52 (items 1–3) plus any value you might assign to the intangibles (4 and 5), you should make this purchase.

* Discounting and present value are explained in the appendix.
† Resulting from savings on specials, less spoilage, fewer trips to store, and so forth.
‡ Presumably the new model is more efficient.

Decision 2
Should wife go to work?
(a one-year comparison)

Costs			*Benefits*	
1. Child care	$800	1.	Income	$7,000
2. Clothes, transportation, etc.	$500		Less *increased* income tax* (est.)	1,600
3. Reduced level of household services	?		Less FICA	410
			Equals	$4,990
4. Loss of leisure time	?	2.	Work satisfaction of wife	?

Here the dollar comparison is fairly straightforward; $4,990 − $1,300 = $3,690. The difficulty lies in weighing the intangibles (3 and 4 on the cost side and 2 on the benefit side). If $3,690 + wife's work satisfaction is greater than the value of lost leisure and reduced household services, the decision would be yes.

* If the husband is already in the 25 percent bracket, all of her income (except work expenses and part of child care costs) is taxed at 25 and 28 percent.

Chapter 2

Getting and spending: Choosing a career and making decisions

To be or not to be; that is the question.
Shakespeare

INTRODUCTION

The question "To be or not to be" hardly seems relevant to the typical college student. But when you are asked "What will you be?" or "Which lifestyle will you seek?" the plot begins to thicken. Answers to these questions can be very clear—in hindsight. In fact, a lifetime is filled with many decisions which taken together form a career path. Perhaps by looking ahead a little, looking back will eventually become a little more pleasant. In either case, what you get from your career will determine largely how much you can spend in a lifetime. And your spending will certainly influence your lifestyle.

Economics and finance involve the study of choice, looking at alternatives and making decisions. And few decisions are more important than occupational choice. More often than not, your selection of friends, where you might live, how you dress, and even what you think about will be influenced deeply by where you work and what you do on the job. For these important reasons, we will devote this chapter to a discussion of the world of work. In the chapter you will find approaches to these questions:

- How much am I worth?
- How do I search for work?

- What is my *real income*?
- Who gets the jobs?
- Where are the jobs?
- Where do I get employment information?

Within these topics are some useful tips on decision making, comparing job offers, and using economic theory to explain job markets. Later chapters

"I find this work truly fulfilling in many ways—there's the exercise, the sense of accomplishment, and, most important, the opportunity to make lots of noise."

Reprinted by permission The Wall Street Journal

cover such topics as taxes, fringe and employment benefits, retirement, each of which is an important aspect of the world of work.

SALARIES AND WAGES: HOW MUCH AM I WORTH?

How much are you worth? Your chemistry professor may estimate the market value of the elements of your body and reply, "$75." A philosopher, a minister, or your fiancé might respond: "An infinite amount." But when you go to apply for a job, your prospective boss may say: "$2.75 per hour." What goes on here? Why the great divergence in estimates?

Like it or not, a person's value in the marketplace is determined by how much happiness he or she produces for others, that is, happiness for which others are willing to pay. So whether you weld a part or wield a pen, the amount you produce and the price the products obtain will determine how much you are paid. To do good for yourself generally requires that you produce goods for others.

It seems only logical, that the value of workers—welders or wielders—is determined in part by the value of our product. When individuals join a production process they generally add something to output. (Otherwise, they wouldn't be kept on the job!) However, the nature of most production is such that additional workers tend to add less and less to output. Each worker adds something, but the amount added tends to get smaller. Think about it this way: the capacity of machines, buildings, streets, farmland, or whatever, tends to be fixed. As more workers enter the production process these fixed components begin to become crowded, thus, the amount added by each worker begins to decline. In economics the amount added to production by each worker is called the *marginal product of labor*. And the amount a firm can pay an employee relates to the marginal product of labor, which declines as more workers are hired. Of course, an employee's product has no value unless a customer will buy it. Thus, the price of the product is surely important in determining wage and salaries. Finally, firms must generally lower price in order to sell more products. These two things taken together tend to cause firms to assign a declining value to additional workers.

It is helpful to consider this relationship in terms of a diagram. Figure 2–1 describes the declining *demand for labor* for a particular firm. Notice that the curve in the figure falls from left to right reflecting the declining value of output which would be added by additional workers. (Two quantity-price sets are described in the diagram for illustrative purposes.)

While the diagram may look rather cold and inhumane, it does in fact reflect a composite of human forces. You will recall that the value of a worker's product will be determined by how much the worker produces and how much the product is valued by the ultimate customer. Furthermore, competition among firms for good workers tends to lead to their being used in the most productive way. When a firm finds a way to be more productive,

Figure 2–1
Demand for labor

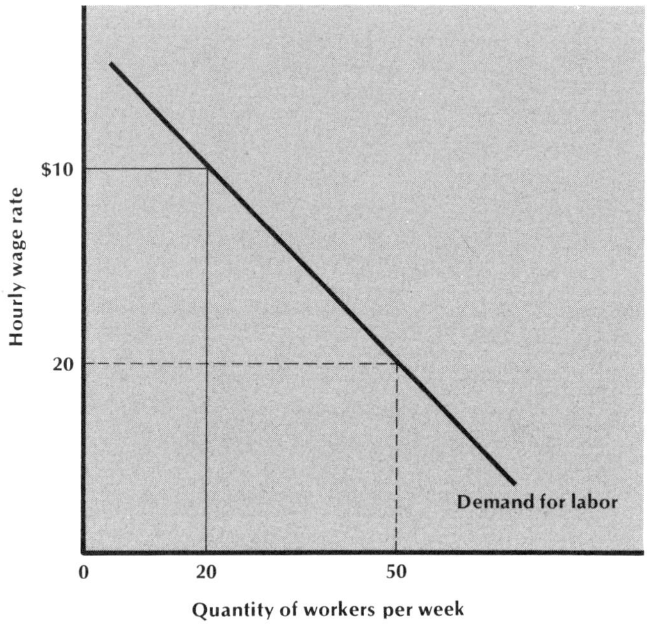

its demand for labor shifts out. Thus, each worker is worth more. The same thing happens when consumers decide that a particular product is more valuable.

Of course there is a pessimistic side also. The demand for labor's product can disappear completely carrying with it the demand for labor. Remember the Edsel?

The demand side of the labor market is half the story of salary determination. There is also supply. When you inquire about a job you are then a part of the *supply of labor*. Let's take a particular situation. You hear of a job opening at a local restaurant. Maybe you see a sign in a window or read an ad in the newspaper. The sign or ad represents demand. Since you are hard-up for cash, you search out the restaurant and talk to the manager. How many other people might do the same thing? The greater the number, the greater the supply of labor. Of course more people are generally willing to work when wages become relatively high, and some people are willing to work longer for the same reason. For these two reasons, the supply of labor is depicted in Figure 2–2 as a curve which slopes up from left to right.

When Figures 2–1 and 2–2 are brought together, as in Figure 2–3, we then can show a representative labor market. The intersection of the two curves is the point where, for a wage of $7.50 per hour, the quantity of workers

Figure 2–2
Supply of labor

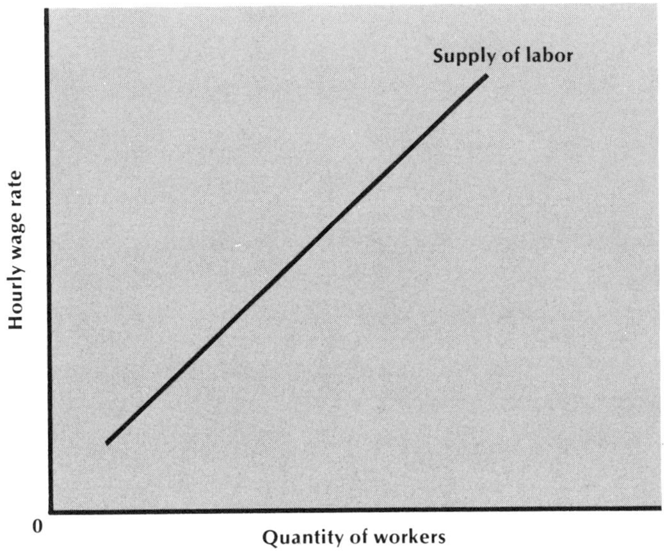

Figure 2–3
Demand and supply

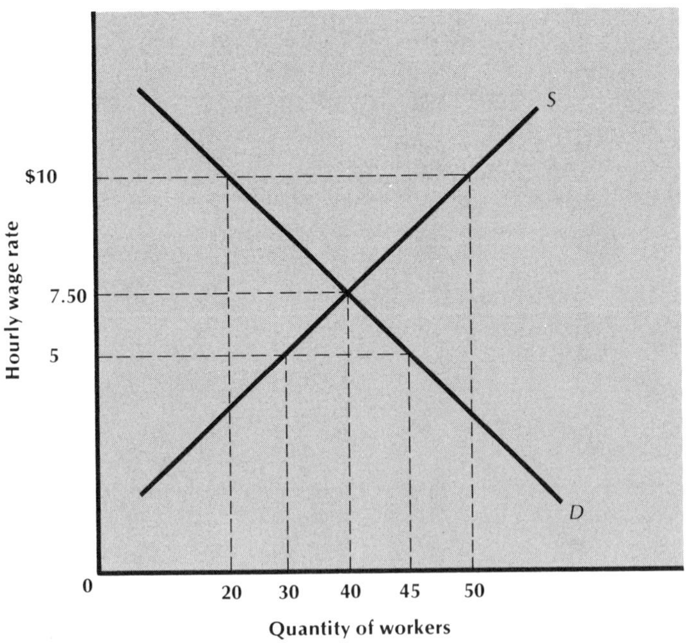

demanded equals the quantity supplied. Notice that when the wage is \$5 the quantity demanded is greater than the number willing to work at that wage. If such a wage developed, competition among firms for workers would cause the wage to rise. Also note what happens when the wage is \$10 per hour. At that wage, the number of willing workers exceeds the quantity of workers demanded by firms. In this situation, the unhired workers would tend to compete for jobs and offer their services at lower wages. Thus, the wage would tend to fall toward the *equilibrium wage level* of \$7.50 per hour. So much for the diagram. What does it say about your wage?

In our example about the restaurant, you had applied for a job which had been advertised at a particular wage. Suppose 500 people had applied for the one job. In that case, you would expect the wage rate to fall. On the other hand, suppose you had been hired at \$3.35 per hour, an equilibrium wage. Then, everything would hold so long as supply and demand remained unchanged. If, however, several other restaurants opened in the area, an increase in demand might occur. Take a look at Figure 2–4. There you see a new, higher demand curve which is labeled D_2. Notice the equilibrium wage is now \$4.35 per hour. The analysis suggests that when the wage rises more workers become attracted to the market. Of course, if you are working at the same old restaurant, your wage will tend to rise also. Otherwise, the manager

Figure 2–4
Changing labor markets

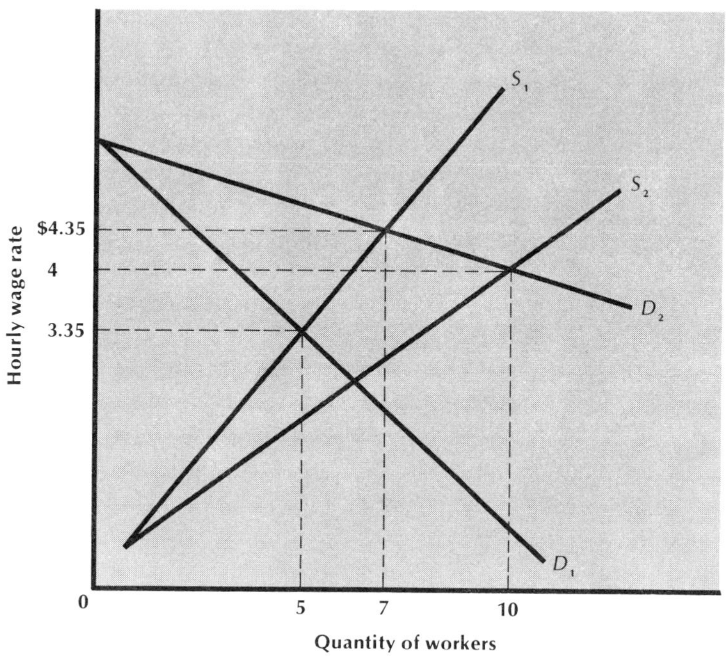

would expect to lose your services. Put differently, if the restaurant doesn't pay your *opportunity cost,* you will take off for that better opportunity. (Opportunity cost is the cost of alternatives forgone to take this job, buy this meal, or take this trip.)

Generally speaking, when wages rise in one field, people in other fields hear the news. However, they may live in other places, or they may not have all the qualifications for the job. Both situations can present problems. But each problem can be remedied at a cost. For example, if the cost of moving or training is less than the expected increase in earnings, more people will enter the higher-wage labor market. In terms of Figure 2–4, this shows up in a shift of the supply curve. Notice S_2 and the new equilibrium wage of $4. The wage rate has fallen.

In a market economy, the value of our work is determined by both demand and supply. And both demand and supply change as the world turns. For this reason, it is helpful to understand some of the elements of the market when thinking about career choice. A little knowledge about demand and supply may reduce your level of frustration when searching the job market.

LIFETIME INCOME

What you earn in a particular job becomes a component of your lifetime income profile. If you could see your future and know with certainty the earnings for each year, you could obviously construct a picture describing income and time. A typical picture would show earnings rising from age 21 to age 40. Then, earnings might reach a peak, flatten out for a few years and begin to turn down. Figure 2–5 describes this pattern.

If you had perfect foresight and could consider a number of alternative career paths, you would want to determine the *present value* of each path. Techniques for calculating present value are described in the appendix on the Mathematics of Finance at the end of the book and will be used throughout the book. However, at this point, the idea of present value needs to be introduced.

Given the choice of having $5,000 today versus $5,000 ten years from now most people would say: "Give me the money now!" That is, they place a discount on future earnings. Another approach to the concept can be taken by asking "How much money would you be willing to take today rather than waiting ten years to get $5,000?" Suppose someone said $3,850. The $1,150 difference would be the amount of the discount. It is possible to obtain the interest rate at which they discounted, the *discount rate,* by taking the $3,850 and calculating the interest rate needed for that amount to grow to $5,000 in ten years. In this case, the discount rate would be approximately 5 percent. In other words, if the person put the $3,850 in a savings account paying 5 percent interest, compounded annually, he would have $5,000 in ten years.

Figure 2–5
Real income profile

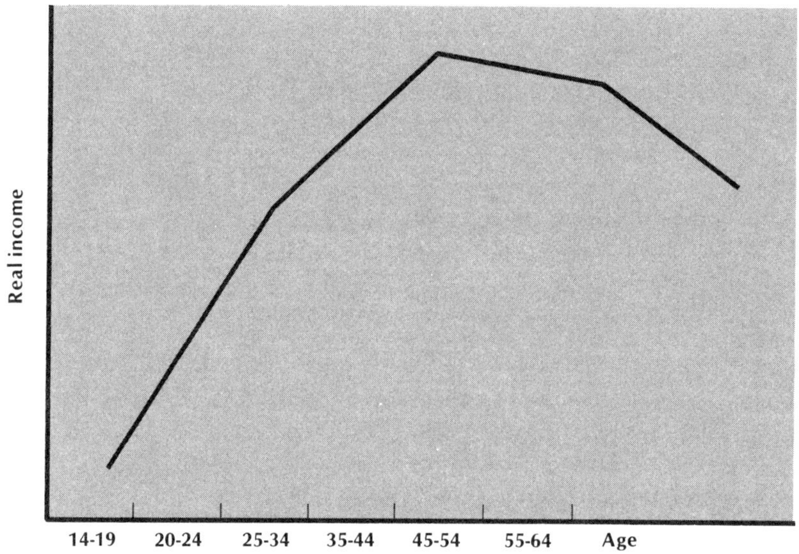

Now, back to the career choice problem. One career path might have lower earnings in the first ten years, when compared with another choice, but higher earnings in the succeeding ten years. For example, a person working toward becoming a surgeon may forego earnings for quite some time expecting to make up for the lean years when they began to practice medicine. Another individual might take a job as a machinist right out of high school. When compared with his friend the medical student, the machinist may look like a millionaire. But what about later? To compare the two careers you would discount their value, net of expense, to the present. Of course, the discount rate and relative sizes of income and expenses would determine which path had the greatest value.

An illustration may help you further to understand discounting. Suppose you are assured that if you complete a one-year night program in accounting, you will earn $500 more per year over the next four years than you would otherwise. The course will cost $1,000 payable on the first night and a lot of long nights away from home. So, you could struggle through the course, pay the tuition, and increase your life income profile. Is it worth it?

Here are the details of the problem:

Future income to gain	$500 per year for four years
Present cost of course	$1,000
Discount (interest rate)	10 percent

Figure 2–6 describes the problem. You will see that there are four equal elements of income to be considered. And as was discussed, the further away

Figure 2–6
Annuity problem

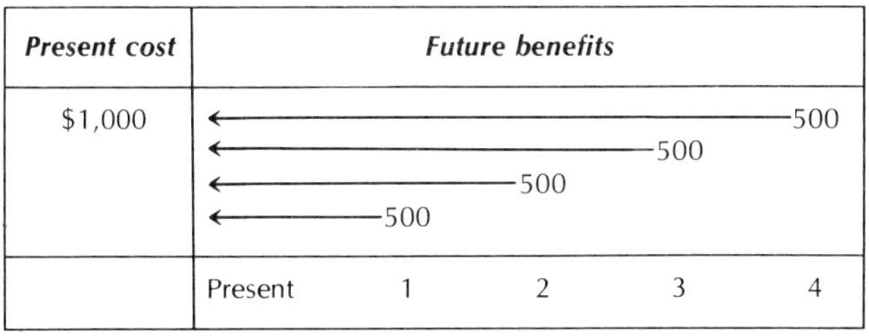

each element is in time, the less it is worth today. A stream of future annual payments is called an *annuity*. And this problem involves the calculation of the value today of a four-year annuity of $500 per year which begins one year from now. The details of this kind of problem are explained in the appendix on Mathematics of Finance. Table A–1 has various factors for making calculations and column 6 contains factors to calculate the present value of an annuity. Consider a four-year annuity at 10 percent interest. The factor in the table is 3.17. If you multiply the annuity amount, $500, by the factor you will have its present value or $1,585. That is the value of your future payments of $500 each spread over four years when the interest or discount rate is 10 percent.

Now, to get that increase you will have to give up $1,000, plus five nights per week for one year. On the basis of money alone, you might buy the deal. However, if your leisure time is worth more than $585, you will forget it.

People make decisions like this daily. Investments in human capital (education) are like those made in machinery, stocks, and bonds. Income from one source is given up in order to get more income later, and career paths are the result of intended and unintended investment. Indeed, the time you have invested in working through this section should yield a future net return.

At any given moment, each person is on a career path headed somewhere. Evaluating the choices open to you is an important part of the job search process.

THE JOB SEARCH

The search process can be an important part of getting a job which satisfies your career choice. If you have the basic qualifications—education, experience, and personality—those parts of your human capital, you will want to match them with a job opportunity. If you lack any of these qualities, you will want to find employment where they can be developed.

Search takes time and may involve other costs as well. And where there are costs, some economic considerations need to be made. Put simply, an individual should search until the added value of the next opportunity just equals the additional cost involved in gaining the opportunity. For example, your cost is low when you have no employment. That is, you only give up your leisure time when reading want ads, making telephone calls, and arranging for interviews. Of course, there can be travel costs, mailing costs, and telephone costs. This is certainly so if you organize a careful search which covers a large section of the country or world. But costs really begin to become significant when you have an opportunity to work and pass it by in order to look further. Then the opportunity cost of search involves the forgone income plus the ongoing search-related expenses.

As you will see again, income forgone has a value which increases through time. In principle, the cost is measured as if you took the salary you would have earned and invested it, or saved it in an interest-bearing savings account. The gain is compounded in each case. That is, the total value increases each day. To illustrate this, imagine that you are holding out for a job which will pay $500 per week. While searching for that goal, you pass up a position which would pay $300 per week. From that day forward, your search generates a loss of $300 per week. If you were to go on for six months you would have forfeited $7,800 plus the interest you would have earned on that money. Of course, this places a burden on the search and, in fact, diminishes sharply the net benefits of the $500 job, when you land it. Intuitively, you can see there is a net gain of $200 per week when the $500 job is obtained. But it would take almost six months on that job to regain the $7,800 of forgone income plus the interest forgone. After that point, you would begin to realize the benefits of the $500 job.

Search costs can be substantial. For this reason, it may be advantageous to gather information when you are in school, on vacation, or during other periods prior to the time of the real search. Work-study programs, internships, and summer jobs offer excellent opportunities for learning about careers and lowering the cost of search. When you think about it, you may earn more with the same pay as another person, if your search costs have been lower.

REAL VERSUS MONEY INCOME

In addition to search costs, there is another important cost to consider when comparing salaries. The subject is real versus money income. Consider two identical jobs: you can take a position as a computer programmer either in Detroit, Michigan, or in Anchorage, Alaska. Furthermore, the gross salaries are the same, which includes not only stated salary but also expected dress on the job, work-related trips, and other activities. In other words, the difference in the two positions boils down to your cost of delivering yourself ready to work each day, that is, the cost of maintaining your lifestyle. That cost can vary significantly between work locations. For example, there are differences in taxes, travel costs, heating, medical, entertainment, food, and insurance costs, just to mention some of the important items. If these things are the same in terms of real goods, yet cost more in Anchorage than in Detroit, your real income will be highest in Michigan, even though your salary is the same. These differences are shown in Table 2–1. Notice that the table shows

Table 2–1
Cost of family consumption for middle income four-person families (selected locations: Autumn 1975)

Boston, Massachusetts	$13,512
Detroit, Michigan	11,936
Austin, Texas	10,658
Atlanta, Georgia	10,972
Anchorage, Alaska	15,865
Nonmetropolitan North Central	10,043

Source: *Handbook of Labor Statistics, 1977,* pp. 272–73.

the cost of living for families in the middle income range for different locations. In assembling the data in Table 2–1, an effort was made to keep a hypothetical family at the same level of real consumption. Thus, things are on a comparable basis. Before taking a job, you should consider the real benefits, not just the monetary benefits.

While there are important differences in the cost of living among various cities, there is another more pervasive problem to consider—*inflation*. The purchasing power of the dollar has declined steadily in recent years and is still declining. Twenty dollars today won't buy the same real goods that it would five years ago. In fact, it would take approximately 30 1977 dollars to buy the same basket of goods which a $20 bill would have bought in 1972.

The *consumer price index,* a measure used to track the purchasing power of the dollar, is based on actual purchases of the same goods through time. Shoppers from the Bureau of Labor Statistics go out, buy a large array of goods, and record the prices. One month later they repeat their shopping trip, being careful to purchase the same goods. The present consumer price index (CPI) is based on 1967 as the beginning year. In other words, 1967 is equal to 100 percent. Table 2–2 and Figure 2–7 show samples of indices for the years 1950 to 1977. As the index gets larger, the purchasing power of the dollar gets smaller. Notice that the index is expressed as a percentage. That is, prices in 1977 were 1.632 times those in 1967 or 63 percent higher.

You can use the CPI to compare your real earnings through time. To illustrate, suppose you took a job in 1972 making $10,000 per year. To find

Table 2–2
Consumer price index, 1950–1977
(1967 = 100)

Year	*Index*
1950	88.4
1960	96.7
1965	98.4
1970	111.8
1972	118.9
1974	130.6
1976	154.3
1977	163.2

Source: *Economic Report of the President, 1978,* p. 315.

the 1967 dollar equivalent of your 1972 $10,000 job, you would divide the current salary by the 1972 index:

$$\frac{\$10{,}000}{1.189} = \$8{,}937 \text{ in 1967 dollars.}$$

Now suppose your income increased through time so that you are making $12,000 in 1976. Are you better off in terms of real purchasing

Figure 2–7
Consumer price index, 1950–1978

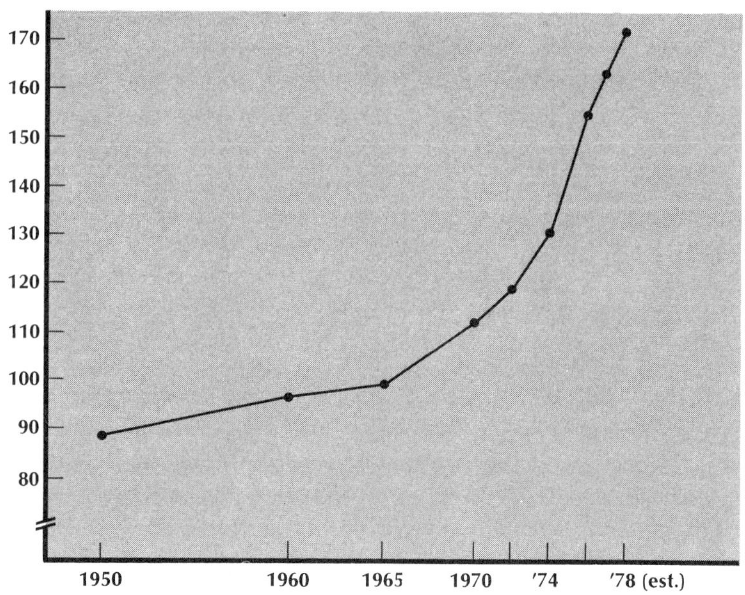

power? To find out, you must convert again to 1967 dollars, your *constant dollar* measuring stick. If you divide:

$$\frac{\$12{,}000}{1.589} = \$7{,}551 \text{ in 1967 dollars,}$$

you will see that you didn't get a raise at all, in real terms. Only your *nominal income* (or money income) went up. You got a raise in name only.

Because of the inflationary pressures in our economy, the CPI has become one of the most prominent indicators of social well-being. The importance of the index has led to a careful government study of its accuracy and ability to capture the effects of price changes for consumers in different occupational and geographic locations. The study gave rise to two additional versions of the CPI shown in Table 2–2. There is now a CPI for all urban consumers, CPI–U, and a CPI-W which relates to urban wage earners and clerical workers. In addition to these national indices, there are measures for major cities and regions. The logic behind all CPIs is the same, however. An effort is made to capture a representative consumption budget and to track changes in the weighted average of the prices of items in that budget.

The relationship between consumer price indices and career choice is that you will want to keep up with, or even better, get ahead of inflation. Thus, when you have taken a job you must produce enough real goods of sufficient value to earn some real purchasing power. You can't expect to keep up with inflation just because it's there. *Productivity* is the key to increased real income. Thus, before rejoicing over a raise in pay, check to see if it really is a raise. In real terms, you must cover the increase in your cost of living before you have received a real increment in your earnings. When looking at salaries in particular occupations, it is not only the current salary that is relevant but growth in the immediate past and projected future growth—in *real* terms, that is, divided by the past and future price indices.

WHO GETS WHAT?

No one wants to become a statistic, but sooner or later we are each counted in many ways. What you earn on the job and other ways will determine just where you are counted in terms of family income. Just to give some perspective on the topic of "Who gets what?" consider Table 2–3. Notice that the figures are for family income in constant 1976 dollars. That is, all inflation effects have been taken into account.

In 1976, almost 50 percent of all families earned more than $15,000 annually. Compare that with 1955 when only 20 percent of the families had earnings in that category. Also notice the change in the percentage which earned less than $10,000. Based on this evidence, you must admit that things have gotten better.

The next table is more complete and gives the distribution of earnings for 1976. While Table 2–4 gives some additional insight into the "Who" ques-

Table 2–3
Families by total income: Selected years
(constant 1976 dollars)

Year	*Median income*	*Percent distribution* Under $3,000	Under $10,000	Under $15,000
1976	$14,958	3.9	30.0	50.2
1970	14,465	4.8	30.0	52.7
1965	12,552	6.8	37.1	63.0
1955	9,393	12.0	54.6	81.3

Source: U.S., Department of Commerce, Consumer Income, Series P–60, no. 107 (September 1977), p. 10.

Table 2–4
Families and unrelated individuals by total money income, 1976
(figures as of March 1977)

Total money income	*Families*	*Unrelated individuals*
	Thousands	
	56,710	21,459
	Percent	
Under $2,000	2.0	12.4
$ 2,000 to $ 2,999	1.9	14.7
3,000 to 3,999	3.1	11.9
4,000 to 4,999	3.4	8.2
5,000 to 5,999	3.9	7.2
6,000 to 6,999	3.9	6.2
7,000 to 7,999	3.9	5.5
8,000 to 8,999	4.1	4.9
9,000 to 9,999	3.8	4.3
10,000 to 10,999	4.2	4.6
11,000 to 11,999	3.9	2.9
12,000 to 12,999	4.1	3.0
13,000 to 13,999	4.1	2.0
14,000 to 14,999	3.9	2.0
15,000 to 15,999	4.4	1.8
16,000 to 16,999	3.8	1.4
17,000 to 17,999	4.0	1.1
18,000 to 18,999	6.9	1.7
20,000 to 24,999	12.9	2.1
25,000 to 49,999	15.9	1.7
50,000 and over	1.9	0.3
Median income	$14,958	$5,375
Mean income	$16,870	$7,236

Source: U.S., Department of Commerce, Current Preparation Reports, Series P–60, no. 107 (September 1977), p. 2.

Table 2–5
Median family income by education for head of household, 1974

Level of education	*Median annual income*
Elementary	$ 8,241
High school	13,941
College	20,124

Source: *Handbook of Labor Statistics, 1977,* p. 349.

tion, notice in Table 2–5 the distribution of earnings is related to education. The average family headed by an individual having 12 years or more of education definitely has a higher income. What you are observing is, of course, history but the inferences are clear. Of course, education does not guarantee a higher income, but additional education does increase the likelihood that you will find a higher paying job and hold it.

WHERE DO PEOPLE WORK?

Your career choice is an important long-run consideration. The job you select can bring you a great amount of satisfaction along with some real income. But the long run is made up by a series of short-run decisions. Do short-run job considerations lead to careers? Does immediate employment lead to a satisfactory lifetime occupation? You have to be the judge of job satisfaction, but many graduating seniors are concerned about the immediate future. "Is there a job, any job?" becomes an important question. So, where are the jobs? This book cannot offer a placement service, but it can give you some clues based on economic facts.

One of the best places to look for information on careers and job opportunities is found in *Occupational Outlook Handbook,* a publication of the U.S. Department of Labor. The volume, published annually, is available in most college and city libraries and offers interesting information on specific careers and jobs. The report also offers some insight into the future prospects offered by certain fields. Some *Outlook* material is drawn upon in this section.

United States industry is often subdivided into firms which produce goods and those which produce services. A further classification breaks the two major categories into specific types of employment.

Table 2–6 and Figure 2–8 show 1976 employment in terms of the various sectors of all employment. Table 2–7 shows projections for those sectors. The service industries are the most rapidly growing, followed closely by mining and petroleum. However, there are different rates of growth expected across

Table 2–6
Employment by sector: 1976
(percent of labor force)

Manufacturing	23
Contract construction	4
Mining and petroleum	1
Agriculture	4
Transportation and utilities	5
Wholesale and retail trade	22
Finance, insurance, real estate	5
Government	18
Other services	18

Source: *Occupational Outlook Handbook, 1978–79,* p. 20.

Figure 2–8
Employment by sector: 1976

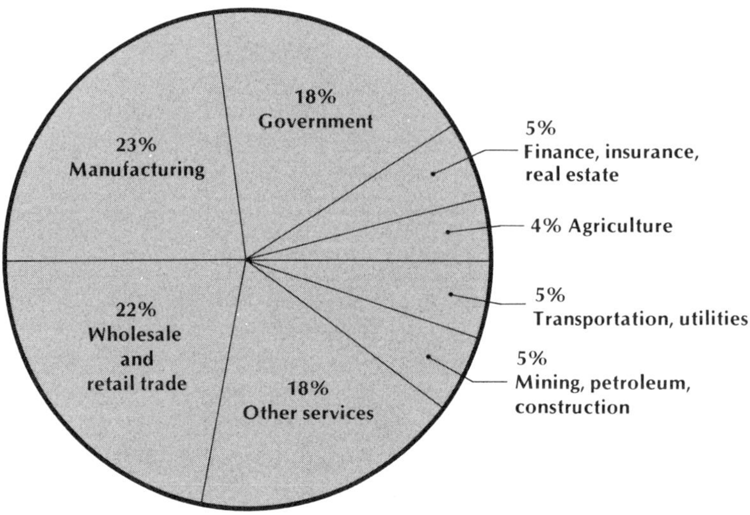

Table 2–7
Projected employment growth by sector: 1976–1985
(percent change)

Services	40
Government	22
Finance, insurance, real estate	30
Contract construction	38
Wholesale and retail trade	20
Mining and petroleum	39
Manufacturing	20
Transportation and utilities	16

Source: *Occupational Outlook Handbook, 1978–79,* pp. 21–22.

the next seven years. Table 2–7 shows the projections. A word of caution is in order here. As the world turns, these projections change. Indeed, the tables can change dramatically in just one year.

Attention should also be directed to government employment. That sector, which includes state, local, and federal, has been the most rapidly growing of all sectors. Most of this growth has taken place at the state and local level. Thus, opportunities in education, health, sanitation, and planning are among the many careers offered by the public sector. As indicated in Table 2–7, government is expected to grow rapidly through the mid–1980s, ranking above all other sectors.

Ten occupation categories are defined broadly within the various industry and government sectors. Table 2–8 and Figure 2–9 show those occupational

Table 2–8
Major employment groups: 1976
(approximate percent of total labor force)

Clerical	15.2
Professional and technical	13.0
Crafts	11.0
Services	10.5
Managers	9.0
Sales	5.0
Nonfarm labor	4.0
Farm workers	3.0

Source: *Occupational Outlook Handbook, 1978–79,* p. 22.

groups and the share of workers in each group. Obviously, the white-collar group accounts for the greatest number of workers, thus the greatest opportunity for jobs. Perhaps we should point out that the "professional and technical worker" category was the third largest group in 1976, but it is expected to grow by only 18 percent before 1985. This group includes teachers, dentists, accountants, clergy, economists, and many other careers requiring significant training. Of course, not every occupation in this broad category will grow at this rate.

As an economy grows it generates job opportunities. There are also replacements needed for workers who retire. So the kinds of growth and the characteristics of various industries interact to determine future needs. Table 2–9 shows a projection for workers in the 1976–85 period. Both growth and replacement needs are identified in the table.

While data can be very valuable in making decisions, each individual must weigh carefully his or her own interests, talents, and preferences in the job search. The fact that projected jobs in agriculture are small, for example, is no indication that there will be a lack of opportunity. Remember, demand

Figure 2–9
Major employment groups: 1976

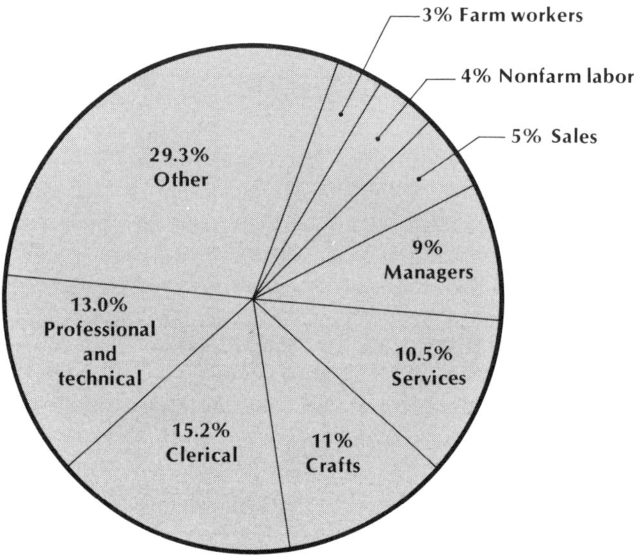

Table 2–9
Projected employment growth by type: 1976–1985
(percent growth)

Clerical	29
Professional and technical	18
Services	23
Managers	21
Crafts	22
Sales	17
Nonfarm labor	11
Farm workers	−34

Source: *Occupational Outlook Handbook, 1978–79,* pp. 23–25.

and supply enter the final determination. Each group of opportunities must be assessed before one writes a particular career off the search list.

THE HUSBAND-WIFE CAREER PROBLEM

Up to this point employment and career choice have been described from the standpoint of one individual. While this approach is certainly valid for singles, there is more to be said for couples. In 1974, the fraction of married women of working age employed in the labor force rose to 43 percent. That is, 43 percent of all married women who could have been employed were working. To give some perspective on this, in 1950 the percentage was 23.8. That is a significant change!

When both husband and wife view themselves as seeking careers the job decision becomes obviously more complex. How will decisions be made when a wife finds an outstanding opportunity in Detroit if her husband sees a growing career in Atlanta? The decision on which way to go is a joint one. And there will likely be some giving and taking.

In some cases, couples examine this problem carefully *before* it occurs. Couples should be prepared to face a decision which could test the bonds of love and marriage. For example, it can be more or less agreed that if the wife is a medical doctor and the husband is an accountant, that the wife's career will dominate the decision. The approach here is to consider which income will be lifted by the greatest amount over a lifetime by making a given move, and which person has the greatest ability to adjust and find a job with ease. The greater the specialization, the smaller the flexibility. There may be opportunities for accountants everywhere, but specialists in tropical medicine may be fairly immobile.

Another approach involves maximizing combined income. Once again, the maximization should relate to expected lifetime earnings. Following this approach, each individual will consider his or her opportunity in the light of the partner's opportunity. In some cases, the husband's position would dominate. In others, the wife's would prevail.

As demand for highly skilled people increases, some employers will become more concerned with employing both husband and wife. Thus, one partner's employment opportunity could lead to a career for the other partner.

In addition to these considerations, it is likely that dual career options will be greatest in metropolitan areas. Thus, the benefits and costs of city living will become an important consideration when examining the options.

Finally, it should be pointed out that happiness is the end purpose of all economic decision making. Moves which might increase income have been emphasized. Increasing one's income can bring happiness in some ways, but it can also lead to misery if a husband or wife is called upon to sacrifice a career.

WHERE TO GET MORE INFORMATION

In addition to *Occupational Outlook,* you get information on jobs from many other places. Other sources are listed below.

Sources of information on jobs

- Family and friends.
- Placement offices.

- Service clubs and fraternities.
- Private and state employment services.
- Trade unions and professional associations.
- Magazines and newspapers.
- Veterans' organizations.
- The firm where you now work.

Finally, be prepared to persist when the search begins. It is easy to listen to those who claim to have tried all sources and turned up nothing. Those who try one more source usually get ahead of those who stop.

SUMMARY

This chapter has been devoted to the world of work. It introduced some basic concepts about labor markets and how wages are determined by competitive forces. Demand and supply of labor were key concepts in that discussion.

A discussion of lifetime income followed the section on labor markets. Short discussion dealt with the concept of discounting future income streams and provided a framework to use in making comparisons between different situations where the timing of income was a significant factor.

The job search discussion came next. This section emphasized the cost of search, real income and how to compute it by using the CPI, differences in real income among various locations, and how family incomes vary. Of course, the job search relates to specific occupations. A discussion of where people work provided information on employment by sector and gave projections of future growth in those occupational categories.

Since many employment decisions involve more than one earner, a discussion of the husband-wife career problem was provided. The emphasis here was on joint decision making and on how to view the problem of maximizing joint income and happiness. Finally, sources for obtaining employment information were provided.

KEY WORDS

Annuity
Constant dollars
Consumer price index
Demand for labor
Discount rate
Equilibrium wage level
Inflation
Marginal product of labor
Nominal income
Opportunity cost
Present value
Productivity
Real income
Search costs
Supply of labor

PROBLEMS

1. At this point in your college career you probably have some tentative career in mind. Look up your intended occupation in *Occupational Outlook* and summarize the relevant information. Discuss the reason for your choice and whether you think you should reconsider.

2. Joe Zephyr is a married graduate student at a large school in the southeast completing an M.A. in accounting. He has three job possibilities. In each case his wife will be looking for a secretarial position. His choices are:

a. Junior accountant in a large firm in Atlanta, starting salary: $18,000; prospects for advancement: good.

b. Chief accountant at a small hospital in a small community in Nebraska, salary: $16,000; prospects for future: uncertain.

c. A Civil service position in Anchorage, Alaska, salary: $20,500; promotion prospects: good.

Considering all factors, what advice will you offer Joe? Why?

3. Using supply and demand concepts, explain why aircraft engineers in Seattle, Washington, had a difficult time when Boeing Corporation lost a major aircraft contract. Also, show how the supply of labor in other markets was affected.

4. Take the following series of money income and convert it to real income.

1950	$20,000
1960	$22,000
1970	$25,000
1976	$30,000

Chapter 3

Keeping records: What, how, why?

Never ask of money spent
Where the spender thinks it went.
Nobody was ever meant
To remember or invent
What he did with every cent!
Robert Frost

There is some truth in this poetry. Trying to account for every cent is the direct route to frustration. But there is greater frustration in keeping no records at all. It is frustrating not to have the necessary records to fill out an income tax form, verify a credit card billing, or figure out for yourself or your irate spouse just where the money went. Somewhere between the two extremes of complete records and no records lies a simple but adequate record-keeping system which is not very time consuming to maintain and does not bury you in an avalanche of irrelevant papers, receipts, and cancelled checks.

Why do you need a record-keeping system? Basically, it serves four purposes:

1. To provide information and verification on income, support, and deductible expenses for income tax purposes.
2. To insure that bills are paid and that bills received are accurate.
3. To keep track of the value of assets and the amount and nature of insurance coverage.
4. To make possible the construction of a personal income statement and balance sheet on which virtually all subsequent decisions are based.

Any financial records not needed for one of these purposes are of questionable value.

This chapter will establish a basic record-keeping system which you can adapt to your own needs. The questions to be examined are:

- What records do I need to keep?
- How do I store them?
- How long do I keep them?
- Why do I need a personal income statement and balance sheet?
- How do I prepare a personal income statement?
- How do I prepare a personal balance sheet?

WHAT RECORDS DO I NEED TO KEEP?

You need to save any cancelled check which might be needed as proof of payment or proof of expenditure for tax purposes. You should not discard paid and/or receipted bills which could be useful for the same reason. You should save charge slips and record charges made on credit cards and charge accounts to verify billings and to keep total charges under control. These three categories will constitute the bulk of the flow of financial statements. In addition, there will be a stock of insurance policies, old tax returns, stock certificates, savings bonds, savings passbooks, titles to cars, boats, and real estate, leases, installment contracts, organizational membership certificates/dues notices, wills (original and copies), a personal property inventory, and miscellaneous finance-related records which need to be saved, sorted, and stored.

While not strictly financial in nature, school records, medical records, military service records, birth certificates, and other documents which need to be safeguarded will probably find a resting place among your financial records. Those which are difficult or impossible to replace belong with the wills, bonds, insurance policies, and so forth in safe and fireproof storage. Less vital or more replaceable nonfinancial records can be put in less secure storage such as a drawer, box, or file cabinet.

Finally, there will be your own creations—income statements, balance sheets, short-term records of various kinds, and after Chapter 4, budgets. Some of these need to be saved for some period for reference in making the next set. The annual income statement and balance sheet should be saved for several years for comparison purposes.

Not all checks need to be saved. Checks written to cash or to the grocer, the hairdresser, or the bowling alley have no discernible future use. The information you can derive from them for income statement purposes can be found more easily and stored more compactly in your check register, which is one of your most useful sources of past spending data.

Likewise, a written record of charges made and payments on charge accounts will simplify the problem of saving a drawer full of charge slips. Once the bill comes in and matches the charge slips they can be discarded unless needed for tax reasons. The monthly charge statement plus your written record then become the longer lasting record from which you can derive tax (especially interest paid) and income statement information.

What about other paid bills such as utility, tax, medical, milk, and dues? Some need to be saved for tax purposes and most need to be saved or recorded on a short-term basis as part of expenditure-tracking. Frequent pruning of the "need-to-saves" from the "can discards" keeps the flow of paper down to manageable levels. Finally, saving a series of pay stubs will provide income and withholding information for income tax estimates and income statements.

In summary then, you should keep bills, receipts, cancelled checks, bank statements, and pay stubs:

- For a short time if you only need them for your income statement and budget. Discard after recording or if your check register is sufficient.
- For a few months if credit purchases are involved and you need to review billing accuracy.
- For a minimum of three years and a maximum of seven to infinity if they contain information needed for taxes. Tax records will be discussed in more detail in Chapter 19.
- Indefinitely, if they will be useful in settling your estate.

In addition, you need to find a way to sort and store all of the other important documents, financial and nonfinancial, which we identified in this chapter.

HOW DO I STORE THEM?

Each kind of record presents different storage problems.

Checks belong in a check file, which you can buy at a stationery, office supply, or discount store. They should be sorted into such categories as housing, automotive, and medical which correspond to your budget categories and income tax deductions. Sort and discard unneeded cancelled checks every month after reconciling your statement. Old check registers, deposit receipts, and bank statements can be filed in the back. At least once a year, weed it out. Anything more than three years old which still needs to be saved should be put in longer term storage (a shoebox in the attic?). Many cancelled checks which were relevant at the time of filing will no longer be needed.

Receipts for credit purchases need a special envelope, box, or drawer where they can be held until you receive the monthly statement and check the billing. If it represents an expenditure you are *tracking* (following the expenditure for a few months to arrive at an estimate), record the expenditure and date. The receipt can then be discarded unless there is tax or other reason for saving. File folders in a small file cabinet, envelopes in shoe boxes, expanding cardboard files, or any other filing system which can bring order to an assortment of bills and receipts in a variety of sizes can be used for storage. Pay stubs, dividend statements, and other income records can also be stored that way. Medical expenses (bills, receipts, cancelled checks) need to be saved for either claims on medical insurance or tax deductions. With major medical (discussed in Chapter 12), records need to be kept on a per person basis. Sometimes the bill from the doctor will itemize on a per person basis. If not, note the person for whom the expense was incurred in the bill or file folder.

Bills due deserve priority storage to insure they are paid. A desk drawer, cigar box, or "in box" reserved for bills, envelopes, and stamps only will facilitate keeping bills handy and ready to pay. You will probably want to save many of the "stubs" or receipted bills as a cross-check on your check register to see which you have paid and for what the money was spent.

Income statements, written tax records, balance sheets, written charge account records, budgets, and other personal financial planning statements belong in a loose-leaf notebook for ready reference, additions, readjustments, and removal to storage.

"Important papers"—wills, bonds, stock certificates, car and real estate titles, personal property inventory, savings passbooks, insurance policies, any other essential financial records, and some of the important nonfinancial records mentioned earlier—require maximum security storage. A safe-deposit box is the first choice for many of these items. However, you should check the laws of your state to see what, if anything, can be retrieved from a safe-deposit box immediately after the death of the sole renter or a co-renter of the box. In many states the safe-deposit box is *not* the place for a will. A good second choice is a home safe or fireproof box, although theft is a risk in this case. Reproducible items—old tax returns, duplicate wills, birth certificates—can be stored in an ordinary file cabinet.

In summary, then, a "storage and retrieval" system requires:

1. A check file.
2. A place to store credit receipts (box, drawer, envelope).
3. A bill drawer or bill box for current unpaid bills, envelopes, and stamps.
4. Storage (file, shoe box, folders) for receipted or paid bills.
5. A loose-leaf notebook for written financial records.
6. A safe-deposit box, home safe, or fireproof box for irreplaceable records.
7. A small file, file drawer, or shelf for file folders for important but replaceable records.

HOW LONG DO I KEEP THEM?

Some records—wills, titles, insurance policies, stock certificates, records of stock purchase and retirement contributions—need to be kept forever, or until they or the asset they represent are sold. Most tax records, including old returns and checks for deductible expenses, need to be kept only three years, the normal federal audit cycle. The Internal Revenue Service can go back even farther, however, if they suspect fraud (but notice will be given within the three-year period). In the case of an asset which might ultimately be sold at a taxable capital gain or deductible loss, such items as records of purchase, improvements, and partial sales should be kept indefinitely.

Income statements, balance sheets, and other "homemade" records can be kept as long as you feel they are useful—two to three years should be sufficient unless you have a sentimental attachment to them. Balance sheets and income statements should be saved at least long enough to use as a starting point in preparing the next one. Checks, receipts bills, and other short-term records can be weeded (mercilessly), filed, or discarded once or twice a year. Discard if they serve no purpose (tax, intrinsic value, proof of asset ownership, needed for income statement or balance sheet, and tracking).

WHY DO I NEED A PERSONAL INCOME STATEMENT AND BALANCE SHEET?

One could easily argue that the bulk of personal records kept in this country are for the benefit of the Internal Revenue Service. Certainly many of the records you will be keeping will be used for this purpose—interest, contributions, taxes paid, employee business expenses. But a well-run household, like a well-run business firm, also uses records for its own internal purposes of planning, management, and control. The basic documents for next year's financial planning for a business, club, church, political party, or household are the most recent income statement and a current balance sheet. The best way to see and decide where you are going is to see where you are, where you have just been, and how you got there.

The *income statement* and *balance sheet* which are developed in this chapter will be used in later chapters to develop a budget, determine credit capacity, decide how much housing you can afford, make decisions about the kinds and amounts of insurance you need and can afford, provide basic tax data, and make investment decisions.

Income statements and balance sheets are not a mere academic exercise. *Business Week* in January 1974, published a special supplement on the executive's personal finances. They insisted that the only logical starting point was a personal income statement and balance sheet. *Money* magazine has a monthly feature entitled "One Family's Finances" in which they discuss the income, expenditure patterns, career choices, long-range goals, and saving and investment plans of a particular real family, ranging from Miss America to a retired part-time bus driver. They develop an income statement and balance sheet as the essential financial profile for their subject family each month. These statements are basic planning tools. The rest of this book will refer to them in almost every chapter.

HOW DO I PREPARE A PERSONAL INCOME STATEMENT?

An income statement is a summary of income and expenditures, usually for a full year. A year is best for personal income statements because it indicates virtually all regular recurring expenses, some of which would not show up over short periods. A typical form is reproduced as Figure 3–1. It is prepared on a cash flow basis, so that only income actually received and outlays actually made (bills paid, cash purchases) are recorded. Bills and income due but not paid/received at the end of the year appear on the balance sheet.

Income includes all cash inflows (except the tax refund accounted for elsewhere) and is usually the easiest to determine from your pay slip, savings bank passbook, dividend statements, and occasional mysterious entries in your check register (special fees, gifts, and so forth). Income tax and social security tax withheld are read directly from the pay stub. Tax refunds or tax due is usually an annual event of sufficient moment to be remembered and/or recorded in the check register.

The difficulty in preparing an income statement lies in the expenditure part, usually in the easy-to-spend, hard-to-track categories of food, clothing, and recreation. Your first try at an income statement will probably carry a disproportionately large entry in "miscellaneous." As you get in the habit of keeping records in your check register and develop a tracking system for variable expenses this category of "miscellaneous" should shrink.

The expense categories are not all-inclusive, but they cover the bulk of most household's expenses. Some of the categories are self-explanatory and information sources are obvious. Others are more difficult to pin down, both what to include and where to get the information.

Housing is the monthly rent or mortgage multiplied by twelve. Insurance and taxes may be included in the monthly payment in an escrow account. Utilities include heat, electric, gas, water, and telephone. These will vary from month to month. Your check register should give you these figures. Repairs and maintenance include not only the new roof but the new rosebush, faucet, or doorbell. Furnishings, including linens, curtains, and kitchen items, may go in "other" or in a separate category. These smaller items are the ones often lost in the shuffle. If you buy them on credit, those credit statements may help track some of these items for you. Otherwise, you will have to estimate.

Food is easy to underestimate but also easy to track. Underestimates arise from forgetting the beef bought for the freezer, lunches or other meals away from home, snacks, milk delivered in between trips to the store. Food is easy to track because most of us are creatures of habit—a month's careful records

Figure 3–1
Income statement

Income:			
Wages and salaries	________		
Interest and dividends	________		
Other income (________)	________		
Total income			________
Less income tax withheld	________		
Plus refund or less additional income tax paid	________		
Less Social Security taxes	________		
= Income for consumption, saving, and investment			________
Consumption expenditures:			
Housing		________	
Rent or mortgage	________		
Utilities	________		
Repairs, maintenance	________		
Insurance, taxes	________		
Other (________)	________		
Food		________	
Clothing		________	
Transportation		________	
Gasoline	________		
Car payments	________		
Repairs	________		
Insurance, taxes	________		
Other (________)	________		
Recreation		________	
Medical expenses		________	
Doctor, dental	________		
Prescriptions, medicine	________		
Insurance	________		
Other (________)	________		
Contributions, gifts		________	
Education, books, etc.		________	
Personal allowances		________	
Life insurance		________	
Employee business expenses		________	
Child care, household help		________	
Installment loan payments		________	
Other		________	
		________	
Miscellaneous		________	
Total expenditures			________
Amount saved/invested			________

(including meat used from the freezer) will give us a representative sample until the next major round of food inflation. Your checkbook may prove a useful source of information but the small purchases are the ones which will throw your estimate off the track. A purist, incidentally, would separate food proper from all the other items we buy at the supermarket—pet food, cleaning supplies, and so forth. That is the record keeper's option.

Clothing is a little easier to track than food. Clothing is often purchased on credit or by check, so your trusty bill/statement/check register information system should be more helpful than in the case of food. If you are having trouble determining clothing costs, try one of the following:

- Charge or pay by check only. Write a C next to checks for clothing. Make a note in the check register of the amount of clothing if the check includes several items. See the example in Figure 3–2.

Figure 3–2
Check book records

BE SURE TO DEDUCT ANY PER CHECK CHARGES OR MAINTENANCE CHARGES THAT MAY APPLY

DATE		CHECK NUMBER	CHECKS ISSUED TO OR DEPOSIT RECEIVED FROM	AMOUNT OF DEPOSIT			AMOUNT OF CHECK		BALANCE	
									450	00
10	9	129	J. C. Penney (C 12.16)				26	19	423	81
10	10	130	Safeway (groceries 33.18)				40	00	383	81
10	10	131	Allstate (car insurance)				102	-	281	81
10	10	132	United Fund T				10	-	271	81
10	11	-	Deposit - salary	600	-				871	81
10	12	133	cash (movie, sitter - $7)				10	-	861	81
10	12	134	Kiddie Nursery T				25	-	836	81
10	12	135	Smalltown Savings & Loan				245	-	591	81
10	12	136	Friendly Finance				83	20	508	61
10	12	137	Dr. Williams (Susie) T				15	-	493	61

- Track clothing expenses by keeping a written record of all clothing purchases in a section of your loose-leaf record-and-budget notebook. List date, item, and amount (you may want to list for whom). This kind of tracking works for any variable category but it is difficult to discipline yourself to track more than two at a time. Tracking clothing may take an extended time because purchases tend to be seasonal and lumpy.

The clothing category generally includes shoes, repairs, alterations, laundry, and dry cleaning.

Transportation lends itself in part to the tracking approach just described. Car payments, taxes, and insurance come directly off the check register, but information on gasoline and repairs requires that you either charge and pay monthly (which may raise your cost per gallon) or pay cash and keep a written record, perhaps in the glove compartment.

Recreation also lends itself to tracking. Part of it will be "lumpy"—dues to the country or sailing club, tennis and camping gear, trips, and vacation. These are easy figures to come by. The rest of recreation is likely to be small and in cash—movies, bowling, concerts, hobbies, plays, and other occasional entertainment. Tracking again is the solution for the many small expenditures in this category.

Medical expenses are usually easy to determine. Insurance premiums are often deducted from your pay. A drugstore charge account will provide prescription and other medical expense records. (Make sure this service is not offset by significantly higher prices. Charge accounts can provide great record-keeping convenience for the family with enough self-discipline to keep them paid in full every month except those of abnormally higher than expected expense.)

Contributions which are tax deductible should be made by check. Gifts are harder to determine, especially small ones. Larger gifts charged or paid for by check can be noted in the check register with a *G*, as with the *C* for clothing. Tracking is a possibility here also.

Education is a broad category including tuition, lessons, books, magazines, newspapers, etc. with possible overlap into recreation. Paperback books and magazines are small purchases most likely to be overlooked.

Personal allowances are funds which each member of the family is given to spend and for which he or she is not required to account. Adults may overlap categories by estimating recreation, food, and education items which come out of personal allowances. This should be a fixed weekly or monthly sum.

Life insurance is a fixed monthly or annual premium. Do not overlook group insurance for which the premium may be withheld from your paycheck.

Employee business expenses may also overlap other categories. Books, association dues, car expenses, subscriptions, and uniforms may fit as well into other categories but should be segregated as a tax-deductible expense. The variety of employee business expenses ranges from protective netting for beekeepers to toys and games for kindergarten teachers.

Child care and household help are usually large enough and regular enough to estimate closely. Weekly expenses need to be multiplied by 52 (annual) or 4⅓ (monthly).

Installment loan payments exclude car and house payments already accounted for. Furniture loans, boat loans, education loans, and so forth are possible entries. Home improvement loans belong under housing.

What is left for *other?* Alimony, child support, purchases of nonhouse fixed assets (bicycles, car trailers, luggage, cameras), gambling—make your own list.

Miscellaneous is computed last. Total the expenses to this point and subtract these expenses from income available. What is left is either saved (or dissaved) or miscellaneous. Compute or estimate your actual year's saving, positive or negative, and subtract from what is left; the balance is miscellaneous.

The check register in Figure 3–2 illustrates how useful a check record can be in tracking income, expenditures, tax deductions, and other expenses. If free, low-cost, or minimum balance free checking is available, paying by check rather than in cash as often as possible will facilitate record keeping. Note the *C* for clothing, *T* for tax deductible (contribution, child care for working mother), and itemized partial expenses in a larger check (checks 129, 130, and 133) for clothing, groceries, and recreation. Although the interest on the mortgage (check 135) and car payment (check 136) is also deductible, you probably will not need the *T* on every monthly installment as a reminder. Susie is listed as the cause of the expenditure for check 137 because major medical insurance may require per person deductibles.

HOW DO I PREPARE A PERSONAL BALANCE SHEET?

A personal balance sheet identifies your *assets, liabilities,* and *net worth* at a point in time. The balance sheet answers the following questions:

1. If tomorrow I died, and my heirs settled the estate, or if today I disposed of all my worldly goods, discharged my liabilities, and took the balance in cash to retreat to a cave, what would it all add up to?
2. What are my financial holdings and personal possessions worth?
3. How much would it take to pay off all my debts immediately?
4. What would be left over?
5. Is the size of the leftover (net worth) growing or shrinking from year to year?

The balance sheet is a useful planning tool. It will grow in net worth as you buy (and pay for) a house, a car, furniture. Any purchases of assets (items lasting more than a year) on your income statement will show up on the balance sheet. Any debts incurred to pay for assets, services, or short-term consumption will also appear on the balance sheet. Net worth should normally grow from year to year. It can shrink and even become negative if current consumption consistently outruns income or if a major financial disaster strikes. A long stretch of consistently negative net worth can lead to bankruptcy. A positive net worth (value of assets exceeds value of liabilities) indicates that you are solvent. *Solvency* means that complete liquidation of assets and liabilities would leave a balance greater than or equal to zero. Insolvency, or negative net worth, is a serious danger signal for a household, a business, or an organization of any kind. Businesses fold, banks close, organizations disperse, and households file for bankruptcy because of insolvency.

"What do you mean we can't go on living beyond our means? We've always lived beyond our means!"

Reprinted by permission The Wall Street Journal

There is a second danger signal which can be read from a balance sheet—illiquidity. *Liquidity* refers to how quickly an asset can be converted to cash or how soon a bill or liability must be paid. Banks which were solvent had to close temporarily in the 1930s because of illiquidity. They could not convert their assets to cash rapidly enough to meet the demands of depositors. Assets and liabilities on any balance sheet are listed in order of decreasing liquidity. Let us look at the balance sheet in Figure 3–3 to identify liquid assets and liabilities, using three months as an arbitrary cutoff point.

On the asset side, any assets down to (but not including) certificates of deposit can be turned into ready cash at no loss within three months. Certificates of deposit and government bonds can be liquidated at only some moderate interest cost. On the liability side, short-term debts and the next three months' payments on installment loans, mortgages, and any sums due in three months on noninstallment loans would constitute liquid debt. If liquid debt exceeds liquid assets, you have a liquidity problem. How serious it is depends on the rest of your income and expenditure flow over the same period.

Balance sheet information is much easier to find than income statement information. You can count your cash, balance your checkbook, and determine from the passbook the current value of passbook savings and certifi-

Figure 3–3
Balance sheet
December 31, 19____

ASSETS

Financial assets:		
Cash	________	
Checking account	________	
Passbook savings	________	
Cash value, life ins.	________	
Money owed to you	________	
Certificates of deposit	________	
Government bonds	________	
Corporate bonds (includes municipals)	________	
Stocks	________	
Annuities, vested pension funds	________	
Other	________	
Total financial assets		________
Tangible and other assets:		
House	________	
Car	________	
Boat	________	
Personal property	________	
Ownership of small business	________	
Other real estate	________	
Other	________	
Total tangible and other assets		________
Total Assets		________

LIABILITIES

Short-term debts:		
Unpaid bills	________	
Taxes due	________	
Current charges (charge accounts)	________	
Total short-term debts		________
Medium-term debts:		
Installment loans	________	
Automobile	________	
Furniture, appliances	________	
Home improvement	________	
Other	________	
Total installment loans	________	
Noninstallment loans		
Discounted notes	________	
Education	________	
Other	________	
Total noninstallment loans	________	
Total medium-term debts		________
Long-term debts:		
Mortgage (balance due)	________	
Others	________	
Total long-term debts		________
Total Liabilities		________

Net Worth
(Assets less liabilities) ________

cates of deposit. Schedules of cash-in values of E bonds are available at a bank or in an income tax workbook. The cash value of life insurance in any given year is given in the policy (table of cash value per thousand dollars face value). Regular statements of the value of annuities and pension funds will be given to you by fund managers. Stocks and bonds can be valued by the last quotation in the newspaper. The house is listed at current market value, a figure you should reappraise regularly for insurance purposes. The car has a market value somewhere between the official (dealer's "bluebook") wholesale and retail prices. A boat's value can be estimated by classified ads or depreciated prices of new boats. Personal property will be inventoried and valued for insurance purposes in Chapter 12. Some unusual assets—stamp collections, heirlooms, furs—may require appraisal. Ownership of small business will be largely judgmental. Later balance sheets will be relatively easy to update by using the first one as a starting point.

On the liability side, your bill box, budget, and charge account records will identify unpaid bills and installment loans. The balance due on an installment loan is a somewhat complex calculation which will be discussed in Chapter 5. It will be less than the sum of the remaining payments because there are partial interest rebates for paying off early.

Your "important papers file" should contain records of other loans. The mortgage lender should supply an annual statement which includes, among other information, the principal balance on the mortgage. This is the amount (plus prepayment penalty, if any) which would be required to discharge the mortgage immediately.

Income statements and balance sheets are basic tools for all areas of personal financial management. Because these tools will be used so often, a filled-in income statement and balance sheet for a hypothetical couple, George and Henrietta Buyers (and son Henry George, age 3), are given in Figures 3–4 and 3–5 for reference in problems at the end of subsequent chapters.

Note that the income statement and balance sheet tell us a lot about George and Henrietta—income, assets, spending patterns, and savings habits. We can deduce a good deal about their lifestyle from these financial statements. Like many young couples, they have incurred some debt to acquire physical assets—car, furniture, appliances (the discounted note). Food, mortgage payments, and car payments take up more than half of their budget. They limit recreation and clothing expenses, make only modest contributions, and managed this year to reduce their debts a little and add to their assets. (Debt reduction is a form of saving, in that it usually consists of payments for assets which add to your balance sheet.)

The Buyers have been fortunate because their medical expenses are low, but they are clearly "just getting by" despite having only one child and an income just under the national average. Their liquidity situation is fairly good—liquid assets total $1,710, short-term debts only $326, and even

Figure 3–4
Income statement
George and Henrietta Buyers

Income:			
Wages and salaries	$12,000		
Interest and dividends	100		
Other income (________)			
Total income			$12,100
Less income tax withheld	−1,547		
Plus refund or less additional income tax paid	+ 200		
Less Social Security taxes	− 702		
= Income for consumption, saving, and investment			$10,051
Consumption expenditures:			
Housing		$3,850	
Rent or mortgage	2,400		
Utilities	900		
Repairs, maintenance	200		
Insurance, taxes	350		
Other (________)			
Food ($40/week)		2,080	
Clothing		700	
Transportation		1,533	
Gasoline	163		
Car payments	720		
Repairs	250		
Insurance, taxes	350		
Other (seat cover)	50		
Recreation		200	
Medical expenses		250	
Doctor, dental	70		
Prescriptions, medicine	30		
Insurance	150		
Other (________)			
Contributions, gifts		200	
Education, books, etc.		100	
Personal allowances		520	
Life insurance		240	
Employee business expenses		40	
Child care, household help		—	
Installment loan payments		—	
Other		—	
Miscellaneous		148	
Total expenditures			$ 9,851
Amount saved/invested			$ 200

short-term plus medium-term debts only $746. They have obviously been careful to save in the past and pay off debts promptly, perhaps in the years before little Henry George was born when Henrietta worked. But miscellaneous, recreation, personal allowances, education, gifts, and contributions—the heavily discretionary elements of the budget—total only $1,168 or about 12 percent of total consumption. It is apparent that only tight

Figure 3–5
Balance sheet
George and Henrietta Buyers
December 31, 19___

ASSETS

Financial assets:		
Cash	$ 40	
Checking account	150	
Passbook savings	1,000	
Cash value, life ins.	200	
Money owed to you	—	
Certificates of deposit	—	
Government bonds	120	
Corporate bonds (includes municipals)	—	
Stocks	—	
Annuities, vested pension funds	200	
Other	—	
Total financial assets		$ 1,710
Tangible and other assets:		
House	$25,000	
Car	1,500	
Boat	—	
Personal property	3,200	
Ownership of small business	—	
Other real estate	—	
Other	—	
Total tangible and other assets		29,700
Total Assets		31,410

LIABILITIES

Short-term debts:		
Unpaid bills	$ 250	
Taxes due	—	
Current charges (charge accounts)	76	
Total short-term debts		$ 326
Medium-term debts:		
Installment loans		
Automobile	$ 420	
Furniture, appliances	—	
Home improvement	—	
Other		
Total installment loans	420	
Noninstallment loans		
Discounted notes	1,000	
Education		
Other		
Total noninstallment loans	1,000	
Total medium-term debts		$ 1,420
Long-term debts:		
Mortgage (balance due)	$20,000	
Others		
Total long-term debts		$20,000
Total Liabilities		$21,746

Net Worth
(Assets less liabilities) $9,664

controls over impulsive spending keep their income statement barely in the black and their balance sheet from being tipped toward illiquidity.

SUMMARY

This chapter established the basic record-keeping system which will be needed in all the financial decisions you will be making throughout this book. Records are kept for tax reasons, insurance reasons, budgeting, and verification of billings and payments. A record "storage and retrieval" system requires a check file, check register, bill drawer, storage for credit receipts, and receipted or paid bills, a notebook for written records, a safe-deposit box or fireproof box, and a file or file drawer to sort, save, and protect various kinds of records. Frequent pruning of the avalanche of financial papers is essential to keep the system from breaking down under an overload.

A personal income statement and balance sheet are the most compact and useful summaries of these records. They are used in all financial decision making.

Information for the income statement is derived mainly from the check register with some assistance from old budgets, department store bills, and a tracking system. Balance sheets are less difficult to prepare because they rely less on memory and more on itemizing readily determinable monetary values of assets and liabilities. The income statement is a profile of current spending and lets you know where your money went and how close to the margin you are operating. The balance sheet identifies both solvency—whether total assets are worth more than total liabilities—and liquidity—whether you could pay off your short-term debts quickly out of short-term assets. The balance sheet also shows the net result of past earning, spending, and saving patterns. Taken together, an income statement and balance sheet provide a "financial biography" of the family who developed the income statement and balance sheet.

KEY WORDS

Asset
Balance sheet
Income statement
Liability
Liquidity
Net worth
Solvency
Tracking

PROBLEMS

1. Fred and Sue want to untangle their financial affairs. They have no idea where their money goes, or what they own or owe. They know they have a house, a cash-value life insurance policy, a car, a mortgage, some personal property, no savings, ten shares of AT&T, some bills (including a never-paid balance on Visa), and a car payment. They only use the checking account for big bills (mortgage, car payment, insurance, Visa). All their cancelled checks are in the dresser drawer. They pay everything else in cash. Advise them on developing a record-keeping system. Figure out how much of the income statement and balance sheet they could prepare right now, and how much will have to wait until they have improved their record-keeping system.

2. Evaluate your own record-keeping system. Prepare a personal income statement and balance sheet.

Chapter 4

Making a budget and making it work

First Handwriting: Order your priorities.
Second Handwriting: Will they be here in time for Christmas?
Anonymous (Graffiti)

In Chapter 3 the first major step toward developing a *budget* was taken. Present spending patterns—the income statement—were identified and the net result of past spending, saving, and borrowing—the balance sheet—was summarized. An income statement, however, differs from a budget in one important respect. An income statement is an ex post account. It shows what you did—good, bad, right, wrong, wise, foolish. A budget is a statement of intentions or plans. Beginning with the income statement as information, the budget process requires that expenditure plans be increased in some categories and decreased in others according to the budgeteer's preferences. New or larger income sources are used to adjust the expenditure plan upward. As goals are achieved or new goals are established, adjustments are made in planned saving which leads to changes up or down in other categories to accommodate the adjustment in saving.

Budgeting may not sound like your image of the way money is or should be handled. Spending should be fun, and budgeting sounds like drudgery—keeping records, making plans, forbidding yourself a spending spree, and counting pennies at the grocery store. But like any other activity—taking a trip, shopping for clothes, building a garage, running a meeting—getting and spending money will run more smoothly, more satisfactorily, and with better results with planning. Budgeting is the floor plan of your lifestyle.

In this chapter we will examine the budgeting process in the following order:

- How other people spend their money?
- What information do I need to set up a budget?
- What are the steps in setting up a budget?

- How do I convert annual outlay into monthly budgets?
- How do I implement a budget?
- How do I budget my time?

HOW OTHER PEOPLE SPEND THEIR MONEY

Each family's spending pattern is unique. This uniqueness is the result of all the things that make families unique—number, ages and sexes of family members, income, region, ancestry, education, occupation, hobbies, tastes, and past decisions. Nevertheless, there are some typical spending patterns we can examine as a starting point.

Table 4–1 and Figure 4–1 show the dollar and percentage allocation for the low, medium, and high income urban families used as a basis for cost-of-living comparisons by the U.S. Department of Labor. These are recommended or suggested spending patterns (saving is not included) based on standards of nutrition and housing. The intermediate budget is just slightly above the median family income.

Table 4–1
U.S. Department of Labor budgets, 1976
(family of four, wife not employed)

	Low	*Intermediate*	*High*
Total income	$10,041	$16,236	$23,759
Less taxes (income and social security)	1,429	3,134	5,476
= Total consumption and other items	$ 8,612	$13,102	$18,283
Food	3,003	3,859	4,856
Housing	1,964	3,843	5,821
Transportation	767	1,403	1,824
Clothing and personal care	1,064	1,496	2,713
Medical care	896	900	939
Other consumption*	468	869	1,434
Gifts, contributions, life insurance, work expenses	452	732	1,233

* Includes reading, recreation, tobacco, alcohol, education, miscellaneous.
Source: *Statistical Abstract of the United States, 1978*, p. 482.

A slightly different approach is to aggregate all consumer purchases. (The definition "purchases" excludes saving, insurance, and a few other items.) This approach does not provide a breakdown by income level.

A summary of these actual overall expenditure patterns in percentage terms is given in Table 4–2. Note that this does not represent the percentage allocation for any particular income level or family size.

Several general patterns emerge. Food, housing, and transportation dominate the budgets at all levels of income. Together these three items account

"Now don't start talking about the bills."

Reprinted by permission The Wall Street Journal

for 50.3 percent of total consumption and 57 percent, 56 percent and 53 percent of the low, intermediate, and high 1976 U.S. Department of Labor budgets, respectively.

Clearly, also, the intermediate and high budgets permit many more dollars of discretionary spending on clothing, personal care, and gifts and contributions.

Figure 4–1
Percentage allocation of consumption: U.S. Department of Labor budgets, 1976

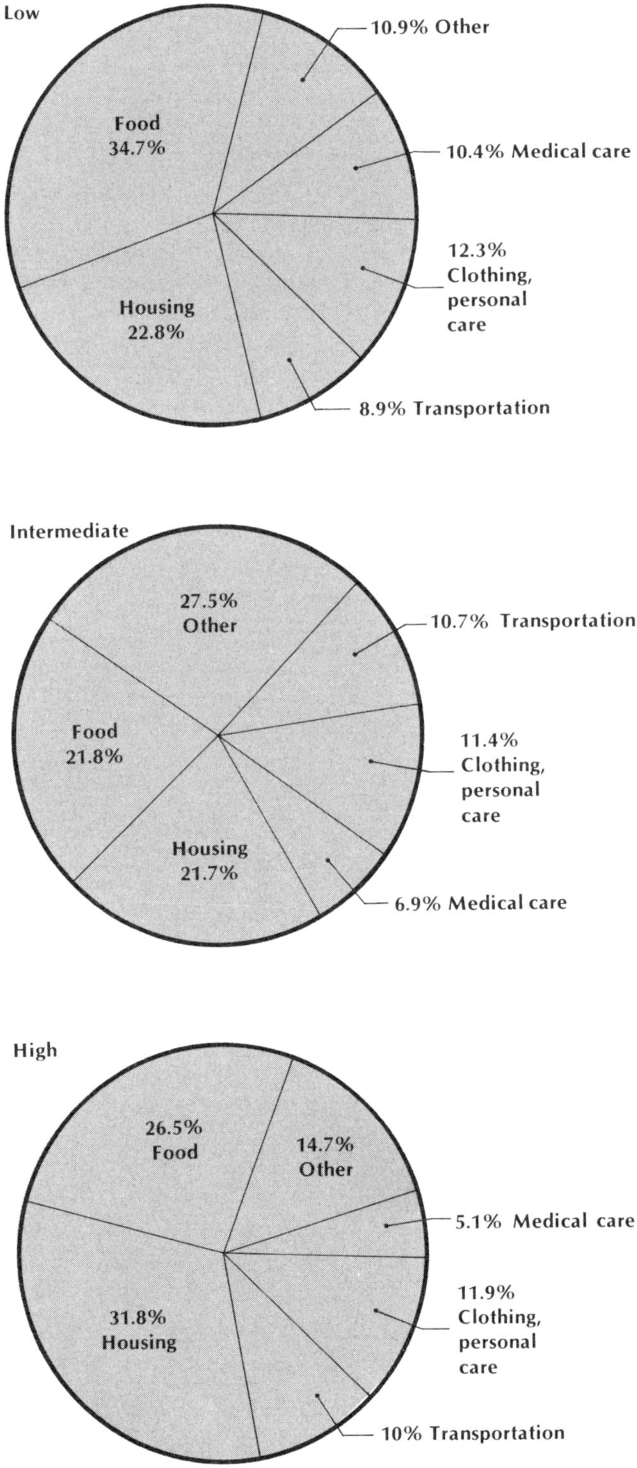

Table 4–2
Average percentage allocation of consumption, 1970–1975

Food, beverages, tobacco	22.9
Clothing, accessories, jewelry	8.8
Personal care	1.6
Housing	15.3
Household operations (utilities, repairs, etc.)	14.4
Medical care	8.4
Personal business	5.1
Transportation	13.3
Recreation	6.7
Other	3.5

Source: Adapted from the *Statistical Abstract of the United States, 1978*, p. 431.

A person who has not yet established his or her own spending patterns might use these percentages as a guide for a first budget. A far better guide is your own income statement, which tells you how you have been spending money in the past. While you may not want to continue spending in the same way, the income statement does tell you in what categories you are spending heavily and what established spending habits will have to be watched most carefully—especially in highly variable areas like food, clothing, and recreation.

WHAT INFORMATION DO I NEED TO SET UP A BUDGET?

While the income statement is a basic tool, and actual or suggested spending patterns of other families may provide a starting point, additional information is needed. Since a budget is monthly or weekly or biweekly you will need a fairly clear idea of the *time distribution of income and expenditures*. Income may vary due to dividend receipts, the "end" of social security payments if your annual income exceeds the ceiling, bonuses, commissions, part-year work, or other reasons. While it is easier to budget a regular income, a roller-coaster income provides even more reason to work at budgeting in order to generate a surplus in the abundant months to provide for the leaner stretches.

Expenditures, too, can be irregular. While payments for food and rent come at depressingly regular intervals, medical expense, car insurance, vacation time, and other large infrequent expenses seem to pop out of nowhere to wreck a carefully—if precariously—balanced budget. Part of your prebudget information is a listing of when and in what amounts these extra income increments and expenditure demands can be expected to occur. None of us has perfect foresight, but it doesn't require much vision to know that Christmas comes in December, vacations come in the summer, and the car insurance falls due in October and March.

A third vital piece of information, in addition to the income statement and the distribution of income and expenses through the year, is the translation of those goals discussed in Chapter 2 into concrete dollar terms. How much progress can be made this year toward a boat, paying off debts, a second home, a down payment on a first home, education for the children, a nest egg, a stereo system? Cast in such tangible and appealing terms a savings goal, annual and monthly, is easier to justify as a vital part of the budget.

The final piece of data needed is a list of planned or anticipated changes in the budget. You may be expecting a salary increase, higher utility bills, or perhaps higher auto insurance costs. You may be planning a conscious effort to hold down food expenses, or miles driven, or clothing outlay.

Figure 4–2 itemizes prebudget information for Brenda and Joe, whose budgeting process we shall follow from start to finish.

The time distribution of income and expenditures is as follows:
Dividends (other income) in July.

Figure 4–2
Income statement

Income:	
Salary (Joe)	$ 7,000
Wages (Brenda)	6,000
Other income	200
Total income	$13,200
Less taxes:	
Federal income taxes (withholding less refund) Joe–$852; Brenda–$710; refund–$300	$ 1,262
Social Security taxes	761
	$ 2,023
Leaves take-home pay	$11,177
Expenditures:	
Housing	
Utilities	$ 960
Mortgage	2,400
Repairs, taxes	400
Insurance	150
Food ($30/week)	1,560
Clothing	960
Transportation (gasoline, repairs, insurance, property taxes)	1,100
Recreation	700
Medical	450
Gifts	400
Contributions	300
Personal allowances	832
Life insurance	300
Miscellaneous	200
Total expenditures	$10,712
Saved this year:	$ 465

Joe's salary is $550 a month with a $200 bonus twice a year in June and December.

Brenda only works during the school year and is paid in ten equal monthly installments, September 1st through June 1st.

Their utility bills average $80 a month but will be $100/month in July and August (air conditioning) and January and February (heating), $80/month in June, December, and March and only $64/month the other five months.

Their spending on gifts is divided evenly between December and May (weddings and birthdays).

Auto insurance ($300) comes twice a year in February and August. They take a vacation every July which is about $300 of their recreation budget. Property taxes are due in October. Homeowner's insurance is paid in November. A large part of their medical expense—$200—is their annual August physical and dental checkup which they pay for in September and October. Sailing club dues of $180 (part of recreation) are paid at the end of each quarter. The rest of their expenses are fairly regular from month to month. (This is a reasonably representative pattern of irregularity in income and expenditures.)

The third kind of information required was their savings goals. Joe and Brenda list the following goals:

1. $ 500 in debts to be paid off in 18 months.
2. $2,000 for a new boat in three years.
3. $ 600 down payment on a new car in one year.
4. $ 300 this year added to a nest egg for an emergency fund, education, and retirement.

These goals would be set with reference to their balance sheet. Saving is directed toward the acquisition of assets, financial or physical, and the reduction of liabilities. Your balance sheet will identify your existing assets and liabilities as a starting point.

Finally, in addition to the above information, Joe and Brenda have set some revised expenditure goals and are anticipating some changes in income and spending. The following are Joe and Brenda's hypothetical adjustments for their first try at budgeting.

	Annual increase or decrease
Food	−$156 ($3/week)
Auto insurance	+ 30
Utilities	+ 180
Clothing	− 120
Income	+ 600 ($300–Joe; $300–Brenda)
Home repairs	+ 100
Withholding taxes	+ 122 (income and social security)

This information should be sufficient for them to draft a trial budget.

WHAT ARE THE STEPS IN SETTING UP A BUDGET?

After assembling the income statement, patterning the time distribution of income and expenditures, establishing savings goals, and anticipating or planning changes in income and expenditures, you are ready to set up a budget.

Step 1. Establish a *budget period.* You can match your budget to your income period (weekly, biweekly, monthly) or to your expenditure patterns (usually a mixture of weekly and monthly). Shorter planning periods of one to two weeks have the advantage of allocating all your income at once if you are paid weekly or biweekly. But the weekly budget can fall into the all-too-common pattern of cash the check, buy the groceries, pay the most pressing bills, and coast downhill to the next payday. Big bill weeks coincide with meatless Monday and no nest egg ever appears for recurring large expenditures like insurance and vacations or for savings goals. All this reduces to two knotty problems with a weekly budget. First, some method must be found to set aside regular sums for monthly bills each week as well as these other items. Second, the planning horizon shrinks to seven days—no place from which to gain a long-run perspective.

The opposite problem arises under a monthly budget, although it stems from the same source. Instead of the "coast to payday" syndrome, there is the familiar cry of "too much month left at the end of money." Once the regular monthly bills—mortgage, utilities, car payment—are paid and the first week's groceries are bought there is a tendency to overlook the later-in-the-month bills, to provide too little for unexpected expenses, and to optimistically expect to be able to eat more cheaply later in the month. The checking account balance begins to look like totally discretionary income and as such melts too quickly.

Monthly budgets, despite this caveat, probably have the most to recommend them. They represent a middle ground between recurring daily to weekly expenses (food, lunches, recreation), the larger number of regular monthly bills, and the less frequent one to four times a year expenditures on insurance, property taxes, association dues, vacations and other infrequent items. Monthly budgets probably allow as long a planning horizon for one "injection" of income as most people are willing to tolerate.

Step 2. Sort out all expenditures into four categories: fixed monthly, variable monthly, fixed infrequent, variable infrequent. (Fixed and variable weekly can be converted to monthly by multiplying, not by 4, but by 4⅓. There are 52 weeks in a 12-month year, not 48.) While nothing is fixed forever—houses can be sold, insurance policies cancelled, and so forth—some items will be fixed in terms of our planning horizon.

Fixed monthly could include mortgage or rent, installment loan payments, some kinds of insurance, child care, pledged contributions, lessons, union dues, personal allowances, and savings.

Variable monthly expenses are items which occur every month but can vary somewhat. Common variable monthly expenses include food, utilities, clothing, recreation, unpledged contributions, gasoline, and medical and dental expenses.

Fixed infrequent refers to predictable items that only come one to four times a year—automobile, homeowner's, and life insurance, annual organization dues, property taxes, tuition, magazine subscriptions, and similar predictable but occasional expenses.

Finally, *variable infrequent* refers to items that occur less often than monthly in varying amounts—Christmas gifts, vacations, car repairs, home repairs, major dental work, and large cash purchases or down payments on consumer durables.

Each of these categories is dealt with differently. The first category, fixed monthly, is the simplest. These can be listed directly on the budget. Variable monthly needs to be estimated from past records and is subject to adjustment. This category is the one with the most "budget-wrecker" potential—especially food, clothing, and recreation. Some method must be devised for segregating these funds to insure that spending will be held within the planned ceiling.

In setting up a "model" monthly budget the annual amounts for fixed infrequent and variable infrequent are divided by 12. This will enable you to compare average budgeted expenditures and savings to average monthly income to determine whether planned expenditures need adjusting.

Step 3. Determine your average monthly income after withholding. Add all income sources including interest, dividends, and 12 monthly or 52 weekly paychecks and divide by 12.

Step 4. Compare expenditures to income in your average or "model" monthly budget and make any necessary adjustments.

Step 5. Provide for infrequent expenditures in one or more of the following ways.

a. Set aside a fixed sum each month—preferably in a separate savings or checking account—to pay for them.

b. Allocate "extra" income—interest, dividends, tax refund, bonus, overtime—in a supplementary budget to cover infrequent expenditures.

c. Distribute them as evenly as possible throughout the year. Vacations in July and Christmas in December, car insurance in October and March, annual physical in February, big clothing purchases in August, January, and April, life insurance in May, club and organizational dues in November, magazine subscriptions in June, and property taxes in September is a feasible pattern. Some items cannot be shifted, but many can be, or can be prepaid if necessary.

d. Admittedly risky—but you can let planned saving be low in high expense months, and high in low expense months.

Step 6. Revise the budget every six months or so (probably more often at first) in response to changes in income, expenses, plans, and goals.

Let us follow this process for Joe and Brenda. A monthly budget seems most appropriate for their income and expenditure pattern. The mortgage, contributions, personal allowances, and life insurance (which Joe pays monthly) are their fixed monthly expenses.

Food, utilities, car repairs and gasoline ($660 of the $1,100 transportation), clothing, and part of recreation ($220—all but vacation and sailing club) are variable monthly expenses.

Saving is computed in the accompanying table (ignoring interest):

Item	***Need***	***Monthly***
Debts	$500 in 18 months (requires $333 this year)	$ 27
Boat	$2,000 in 3 years (requires $667 this year)	54
Car	$600 this year	50
Nest egg	$300	25
Monthly saving required	. . . .	$156

With the adjustments they plan, this part of their budget is shown in the accompanying table:

	Annual	***Monthly***
Mortgage	$2,400	$200.00
Utilities	1,140	95.00
Contributions	300	25.00
Life insurance	300	25.00
Personal allowances	832	69.33
Food	1,404	117.00
Clothing	840	70.00
Car repairs, gasoline	660	55.00
Recreation (regular)	220	18.33
Savings	1,872	156.00
Total	$9,968	$830.66

The infrequent expenditures (after planned adjustments) consist of gifts, car insurance and taxes, home repairs, insurance and taxes, medical expenses, and gifts. Miscellaneous is entered at $200 a year or $17 a month. These additional entries are shown in the accompanying table:

	Annual	Monthly average	When due
Gifts	$ 400	$ 33.33	December, May
Car insurance/taxes	440	36.67	February, August, October
Home repairs, insurance, taxes	650	54.17	October, November and ?
Medical	450	37.50	September, October
Miscellaneous	208	17.33	?
Recreation (vacation, club dues)	480	40.00	?
	$2,628	$219.00	

The totals for the average monthly and infrequent bills are: Annual–$12,596; Monthly average–$1,049.66.

The next step is to compute income. Their old take-home pay of $11,177 has increased by $478 ($600 in raises less $122 in additional withholding) to $11,655 or $971.42 a month. Their new average monthly expenses exceed their new average monthly income by $78.25. This is a normal result for a first "draft" of a budget. They need to go back and consider which items can be cut. Here are some possibilities:

1. *Utilities.* With the aid of cost-cutting tips from their local electric and gas company, they may be able to reduce this by $5 a month.
2. *Repairs—home and car.* Vital repairs should not be put off, but a little do-it-yourself know-how could cut costs, maybe $3 a month.
3. *Gifts.* Homemade gifts cost less and are more appreciated. A little ingenuity might save $7 a month here.
4. *Recreation* (vacation). They are going to try to cut their vacation cost from $300 to $240 with a shorter or less expensive trip. Another $5 a month.
5. *Clothing.* They will try to trim back another $10 a month.
6. *Food and personal allowances* are already cut as low as they are willing to go. Most of the other expenses are fixed and they are still $58.25 over budget. Joe and Brenda reluctantly pare back *saving* to $98 a month. They will have to postpone the boat and car for a little longer than they had planned.

It is important *not* to cut savings first unless those savings goals rank very low on your priority list. Look at the other items before modifying saving plans.

Joe and Brenda now have an average monthly budget which is shown in the accompanying table:

Budget, 1976

	Budgeted monthly average
Housing	
Mortgage	$200.00
Utilities	90.00
Repairs, insurance, taxes	52.00
Food	117.00
Transportation	
Car repairs, gasoline	55.00
Insurance, taxes	36.67
Contributions	25.00
Gifts	25.00
Life insurance	26.33
Clothing	60.00
Personal allowances	69.33
Recreation	53.33
Medical	46.00
Savings	98.00
Miscellaneous	17.33
Monthly average	$971.00

The next step is to deal with those swings in income and expenditures in converting an average monthly budget into twelve monthly budgets, all slightly different. Using the information on page 62 about the timing of their income and expenditures, and using saving as the adjustment mechanism, we obtain the monthly pattern charted in Table 4–3. Since they do not know when the car and house repairs will come, these are budgeted for January and February.

Note that in allocating uneven income and expenses they use a combination of all four methods suggested in Step 5. The tax refund and semiannual bonus help see them through the lean summer months (Step 5*b*). Large expenses are spread so that at least one occurs every month except March and June, the two peak savings months (Step 5*c*). Primarily, however, Joe and Brenda allow fluctuations in savings to accommodate variations in income and expenses without losing track of their yearly saving goal (Step 5*d*). If they find that this approach tends to keep them from reaching a savings goal, then they may need to segregate their savings into two separate accounts. One account would be a long-run, "don't touch" account for goals, and the other a short-term account which builds surpluses in January, March, April, June, September, November, and December to match the deficits in other months (a variation on Step 5*a*).

Table 4–3
Monthly budget pattern

	Jan.	*Feb.*	*Mar.*	*Apr.*	*May*	*June*	*July*	*Aug.*	*Sept.*	*Oct.*	*Nov.*	*Dec.*	*Year total*	*Monthly average*
Income:														
Joe	466	466	466	466	466	661	466	466	466	466	466	661	5,982	498.50
Brenda	518	518	518	518	517	518	—	—	517	517	517	517	5,175	431.25
Other	—	—	300*	—	—	—	200†	—	—	—	—	—	500	41.67
Total income	984	984	1284	984	983	1179	666	466	983	983	983	1178	11,657	971.42
Expenses:														
Housing														
Mortgage	200	200	200	200	200	200	200	200	200	200	200	200	2,400	200.00
Utilities	110	110	90	74	74	90	110	110	74	74	74	90	1,080	90.00
Taxes	—	—	—	—	—	—	—	—	—	300	—	—	300	25.00
Insurance	—	—	—	—	—	—	—	—	—	—	150	—	150	12.50
Repairs	100	74	—	—	—	—	—	—	—	—	—	—	174	14.50
Food	117	117	117	117	117	117	117	117	117	117	117	117	1,404	117.00
Transportation:														
Repairs, gas	78	70	50	50	50	50	50	50	50	50	50	50	648	54.00
Ins., taxes	—	150	—	—	—	—	—	150	—	140	—	—	440	36.67
Contributions	20	20	40	40	40	40	0	0	25	25	25	25	300	25.00
Gifts	—	—	—	—	150	—	—	—	—	—	—	166	316	26.33
Life insurance	25	25	25	25	25	25	25	25	25	25	25	25	300	25.00
Clothing	80	60	60	80	60	60	30	30	80	60	60	60	720	60.00
Personal allowances	70	69	69	70	69	69	70	69	69	70	69	69	832	69.33
Recreation	18	18	64	18	18	64	258	18	64	18	18	64	640	53.33
Medical	25	25	25	25	25	25	25	25	100	100	25	25	450	37.50
Savings	124	29	526	268	138	421	(236)	(345)	161	(213)	153	269	1,295	107.92
Miscellaneous	17	17	18	17	17	18	17	17	18	17	17	18	208	17.33
Total expenses	984	984	1284	984	983	1179	666	466	983	983	983	1178	11,657	971.42

* Tax refund.
† Dividends.

SHOULD I USE A STANDARD BUDGET FORM?

Yes, if you can find one which matches your expenditure pattern reasonably well. A ready-made form will save you the trouble of writing down all the categories every month. No, if your expenditure and/or income pattern is sufficiently different from that normal pattern so that you have to cross out and add many categories. Any good stationery store will have a selection. Loose-leaf pages and pencil allow for corrections, adjustment, and starting over. Standard forms are most likely to fit younger, one-earner, low-to-middle income ($8,000–$25,000) families. A typical form for annual and monthly budget is provided at the end of this chapter. Table 4–4 lists a few of the major differences you are likely to encounter in nonstandard budgets.

What factors besides age and income might make you a *nonstandard family?* Singles, retired persons, divorcées, childless couples, and two-earner

Table 4–4
Budget adjustments for "nonstandard" families

Category	*Different budget entries*	*Higher than average*	*Lower than average*
Singles	No personal allowance	Clothing Income taxes Recreation	Housing Saving Medical (?) Life insurance
Retired persons	No child care No work expenses	Medical expenses Travel	Life insurance Food Clothing Housing (if owned) Income tax Income Saving
Divorcées	Alimony Child support Legal fees	Travel (?)-children Housing (2 households) Work expenses (if both work)	Incomes Taxes (?) (if only one works)
Two-earner families	Definitely personal allowances	Child care Household help Work expenses Income tax Social Security tax Food (convenience, eating out)	Recreation Life insurance
Childless couples	No child care	Income taxes Recreation	Housing Medical Clothing Insurance Savings (?)

families all differ from the typical family of four with a single breadwinner whose expenditure patterns we examined at the beginning of this chapter.

Retired persons of moderate means may be almost beyond budgeting. Their expenses are patterned, life holds fewer surprises, and their saving goals are behind them. Divorced couples need to keep careful records to prove dependency for taxes, to show use of child support funds, and to negotiate adjustments in child support and alimony. Prospective divorcées need to recognize that the largest financial cost of a broken marriage is not the legal fees but the cost of establishing and maintaining a second household. Singles need to give some thought to the future, for few stay single forever. Two-earner couples need to recognize the high cost of earning a second income and also to provide some independent funds for each partner, which can range from personal allowances to two separate budgets which divide the financial responsibilities between them. Some couples have separate checking accounts with a clear division of who pays what. A division of labor does not eliminate budgeting; the budget is first established and then divided. Wives tend to wind up with groceries, babysitters, and other day-to-day expenses while husbands pay the mortgage and utility bills, but with current experiments in alternative lifestyles the most satisfactory division is a purely individual matter. Childless couples can spend on themselves some of the astronomical sums required to rear a middle-class American child. And all but the standard one-earner family with children may well find they can skimp more on life insurance.

The budget is not engraved in store. It changes over time. Unexpected expenses can outrun the margin of safety provided in miscellaneous. Unexpected windfalls occur. These possibilities are reason enough for the loose-leaf-and-pencil, six-month review approach. But once the basic budget is established, tested and adjusted, it is not difficult to redraw the map every year as your income grows, expenditures change, old goals are met and new ones established, and plans are reformulated. While the budget is a never-ending process, the first one is the hardest.

HOW DO I IMPLEMENT A BUDGET?

If you are single, divorced, or a head of a single-parent household, you already have the answer. You have no other adult whose cooperation must be enlisted. Getting a budget accepted and followed is more difficult when there are two or more adults or near-adults in the household.

Involve them all in the budgeting process. Get their ideas on goals, where you are spending too much or too little, how to share the surplus or deficit, and what large ticket items are coming up and how soon.

Let everyone participate in the record keeping bill paying, nitty-gritty of following the budgets. Take turns, or divide the responsibility if that works better. Make sure everyone over the age of five has some personal funds, however modest, for which he or she does not have to account, as well as enough regular funds for predictable personal expenses. Each individual needs to develop a subbudget for lunches, cosmetics, bus fare, organization dues, school expenses, and so forth that can be incorporated into the overall spending plan. Much of this will come under the heading "personal allowances."

Keep it simple. No one, not even you, is going to cooperate indefinitely in a complex financial setup with elaborate bookkeeping requirements. Leave some miscellaneous fund in the budget—just don't let the miscellaneous take over the bulk of the budget.

HOW DO I BUDGET MY TIME?

There is a second scarce resource at our disposal which a person also needs to budget. Time is money in reverse. Time is sold in the marketplace for wages. Interest is paid not only for willingness to risk capital but also for waiting time for the return of capital. Time is bought when money is borrowed or others are hired to work for us. Money is spent on convenience foods, household help, and gadgets to save time. On the other hand, money is saved by spending time to make clothes, grow vegetables, and do our own repairs. And often there are regrets over not having either the leisure time to enjoy our money or the money to enhance our use of leisure time.

Like money, time has some uses over which people have little control. It is physically necessary to sleep and eat. Social custom dictates that time be spent dressing, bathing, exchanging amenities with others. Most people have work that must be done, sometimes a specified amount of work but more often a predetermined number of hours. Are there any uses of time left over which one has any control?

At the turn of the century, the factory work week was 70 hours. Today it is 40. Perhaps those extra hours have been filled with other activities, but those activities still represent discretionary time. There are 168 hours in a week. Even if 56 are spent sleeping and 40 working, there are still 72 hours a week left for other uses—gardening, jogging, eating, drinking, volunteer work, housework, shopping, writing, taking courses, and fixing cars. Unstructured time, like unstructured money, tends to be dissipated and to disappear. You may deliberately choose to spend many of your leisure hours in pursuits less than life's noblest, just as you may choose to spend some of your money on purple nail polish, playing foosball, and cigarettes. The deliberate choice is what matters. Getting the most for your time, like getting the most for your money, requires that you:

a. Find out how you are now spending your weekly ration of 168 hours.
b. Decide what categories you want to increase or decrease.
c. Do some rough schedule planning of your day.

d. Leave a safe margin for miscellaneous.
e. Adjust your "time budget" (schedule) as your obligations, opportunities, and preferences change.

Like an income statement, an analysis of your use of time will help you decide whether and how additional activities can be fitted into your schedule, or when it is time to drop an old one.

Time is not money, but time is scarce, and it can be bought and sold for money. It deserves some of the same careful attention most of us reserve for money.

SUMMARY

This chapter dealt with the core of personal financial resource management, the budget or spending plan. Knowing how other people spend their money does not necessarily imply any "right" or "best" spending pattern. Each individual or family must develop a spending plan of its own based on income, age, family composition, goals, tastes, and habits—in a word, on lifestyle.

The basic information for a budget is an income statement, the time distribution of income and expenditures, goals (short-run and long-run), and anticipated (or planned) changes in income and expenditures from last year's.

In establishing a budget, a budget planning period is chosen; planned expenses are sorted into monthly and infrequent, fixed and variable; average take-home pay is determined; expected income is compared to expected expenses are sorted into monthly and infrequent, fixed and variable; average large infrequent items is selected. This final document is subject to regular review and adjustment.

Standard budget forms are useful for families whose expenditures categories match typical expenditures fairly closely. Nonstandard families—singles, retired, divorced, two-earner—are given special attention since their categories as well as expenditure patterns will differ from the "standard" two-parent, two-child household. The problem implementing a budget with the necessary consent and cooperation of other adults and near adults (adolescent children) called for solutions in prebudget involvement and post-budget participation.

Finally, the related but usually neglected question of budgeting time was discussed in general terms. Time is not money, but it can be a close substitute. Time, like money, is scarce, and anything scarce deserves to be managed so as to maximize the benefit and enjoyment from its use. The process of managing (budgeting) time is remarkably similar to the budgeting process for income and expenses.

KEY WORDS

Budget
Budget period
Fixed expenses
Infrequent expenses
Nonstandard families
Time distribution of income and expenditures
Variable expenses

TYPICAL BUDGET FORMS

Budget for the year 19__

Anticipated income:			
Wages, salaries	________		
Interest, dividends	________		
Other (______)	________		
Total Income			________
Less withholdings:			
Federal income tax	________		
State income tax	________		
Social security tax	________		
Other withholding	________		
Plus tax refund expected or less tax expected due on income	________		
Net income available			________
Planned spending:			
Housing		________	
Rent or mortgage	________		
Utilities	________		
Taxes	________		
Insurance	________		
Repairs, Miscellaneous	________		
Food		________	
Clothing		________	
Transportation		________	
Fuel	________		
Payments on car	________		
Insurance	________		
Property taxes	________		
Repairs, tags, etc.	________		
Other transportation	________		
Other insurance		________	
Life	________		
Disability	________		
Medical	________		
Recreation (vacations, movies, etc.)		________	
Contributions and gifts		________	
Work-related expenses			
Travel	________		
Child care	________		
Dues, uniforms, tools, etc.	________		
Medical expenses (other than insurance)		________	
Doctor	________		
Dentist	________		
Medicines	________		

TYPICAL BUDGET FORM (*continued*)

Personal		______
Personal care (cosmetics, haircuts, etc.)	______	
Personal allowances	______	
Education		______
Lessons	______	
Tuition	______	
Books, magazines, newspapers	______	
Other		______
______________________	______	
______________________	______	
Savings		______
Miscellaneous		______
Total (= net income available)		______

Monthly budget for the month of ______, 19__

Income:		
Wages, salaries	______	
All other income	______	
Less withholding	______	
Net income available this month		______
Fixed monthly expenses:		
Rent/mortgage	______	
Savings‡	______	
Life insurance	______	
Contributions	______	
Installment payments	______	
Other (______)	______	
Variable monthly expenses:		
Food	______	
Clothing	______	
Gasoline, car repairs	______	
Personal allowances	______	
Recreation†	______	
Education	______	
Personal care	______	
Medical expense	______	
Work-related expenses	______	
______	______	
______	______	
Gifts	______	
Utilities	______	
*Variable infrequent expenses**		
Property taxes		
house	______	
car	______	
Other insurance		
health, disability	______	
house	______	
automobile	______	
Recreation†	______	
Repairs—house, cars	______	
Other (______)	______	
Miscellaneous	______	
Total (= net income available this month)		______

PROBLEMS

1. Using your personal income statement and balance sheet, draft a trial budget following the procedure in this chapter.

2. George and Henrietta Buyers from Chapter 3 have decided to draw up a budget. You have their income statement. They give you the following additional information.

   Their wages and salaries are paid in 12 equal installments.

   George expects a $1,000 raise next year, of which $58.50 will go to Social Security taxes and $160 will be withheld in income taxes. They expect a $200 tax refund in April. Their dividends come in August and their interest at the end of each quarter. Henrietta plans to change jobs July 1, and she expects a $200-a-month salary hike at that time (less $11.70 in Social Security taxes and $33 in income tax withholding). Their vacation (recreation) costs $350 in August. The car will be paid for in May. Property taxes are due in October, home insurance in July, tuition in September and January. Half of gifts is in December, and the rest is evenly spread throughout the year. Half of clothing is concentrated in March and September; the rest is divided evenly among the other ten months. Changes planned in expenditures:

Clothing	−$60/yr.
Utilities	+$5/mo.
Gasoline	+$5/mo.
Saving	+$15/mo.
Food	+$22/mo.
Gifts	+$50/yr.
Property taxes	+$40/yr.
Furniture	$200 (October)

   Draw up an annual budget, average monthly budget, and 12 monthly budgets for George and Henrietta. If their income and expenditures do not match, make and explain any needed adjustments.

Notes for Budget Form on page 74:

* Amount budgeted this month. May be 1/12 of annual expense, or may be zero in some months in some categories and larger in other months, depending on your personal budgeting system.

† Recreation will probably have both regular monthly expenses and a few large infrequent expenses.

‡ If you use the method described in this chapter, saving may be variable rather than fixed.

Chapter 5

Major consumer decisions I: Borrowing and using credit

Neither a borrower nor a lender be . . . .
Shakespeare's *Hamlet*

Despite Polonius' sage advice, most individuals will be both borrowers and lenders many times during their lifetimes. Debtor's prison has been replaced by more respectable bankruptcy proceedings, and the embarrassment of a never-paid tab at the corner grocery has turned into the status symbolism of a sheaf of credit cards. However, as the 1970s saw consumers getting ever deeper into debt (about $32.6 billion in new debt in 1974 excluding mortgages), they were also accumulating more liquid financial assets—savings accounts, bonds, mutual funds. These represent debt or ownership claims against others. New financial assets of these kinds came to $129.9 billion in 1974, leaving the household sector as a net lender in that year to the tune of $97.3 billion. Business and government were the net borrowers.

This chapter considers the major questions which arise in the management of personal debt:

- When and why should I borrow?
- How much credit is too much?
- How much does credit cost?
- How much should I pay down?
- What about paying off early? (Rule of 78s)

- How do I allocate the interest for tax purposes? (Rule of 78s)
- Where do I borrow?
- How do I qualify for a loan?
- What about credit cards?
- What kinds of problems can I get into with credit?
- Where do I go for help when I get in over my head?

WHEN AND WHY SHOULD I BORROW?

There are good reasons to borrow money. Borrowing to buy a house, a car, or a washing machine which yields a substantial return on investment in services, satisfaction, and convenience makes good sense. The rate of return on investing in storm windows, for example, has been estimated at 30 percent a year in fuel savings. This rate of return is far greater than the rate of interest you would have to pay on a loan taken out to purchase storm windows, and it is higher than the rate of return that you could earn on investing the money in something else. Borrowing to finance education or training which would increase your future income is another investment use for personal loans. The purchase of assets, including consumer durables, and investment in improving skills are two of the most common and economically justifiable reasons for borrowing. Investments of this type will long outlast the monthly payments.

"I didn't ask you where you got the money so why should you ask me what I'm going to do with it?"

Reprinted by permission The Wall Street Journal

A second good reason to borrow is to match your lifetime income to your lifetime needs and expenditures. Young couples just starting a household have substantial needs—car, appliances, furniture—but frequently have relatively low income. Older couples are more likely to find their incomes reaching a peak just when their children are grown and the mortgage on the house is retired. For them, income exceeds expenses. While they undoubtedly can find uses for the additional income, it could have made life easier and more pleasant had they been able to transfer some of that income backwards to the time when their needs were greater and their incomes smaller. Borrowing makes this transfer from "surplus" to "deficit" years feasible, as illustrated in Figure 5–1.

Figure 5–1
Lifetime income and expenditure pattern

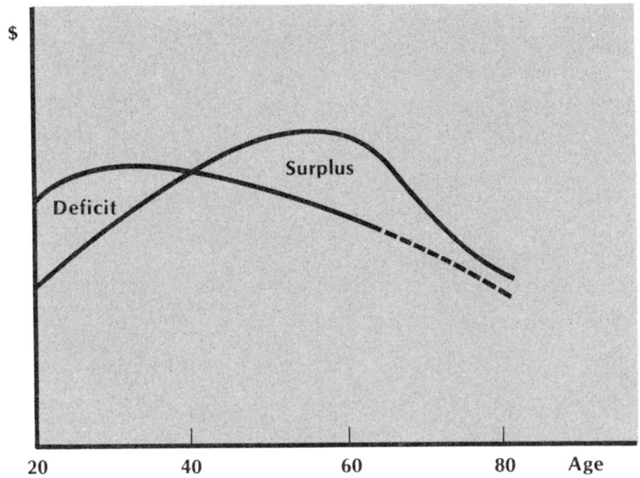

American credit habits are consistent with these suggested reasons for borrowing. Automobile, consumer durable, and home improvement loans collectively constituted 72 percent of installment credit and 59 percent of all consumer credit in 1974. The age distribution pattern verifies the backward shifting of income suggested earlier. Only about one sixth of all families with one or both adults over 65 were in debt, while nearly two thirds of families in the 25–34 range had installment debt. It is clear that borrowing is undertaken primarily by young families for the purchase of assets.

HOW MUCH IS TOO MUCH?

The "preconsumer credit era" rule for spending was disarmingly simple. What you could purchase was limited by the cash in your wallet and the balance in your bank account. Today this simple and inflexible rule has been replaced by numerous guidelines. Generally, the rules of thumb on how much you can afford to owe are expressed in terms of the percentage of after-tax income going to pay off loans and/or the amount of time it will take to pay off debts at the current rate. Assets and expenditure patterns are sometimes taken into account.

Bankers suggest and often use a rule of thumb that no more than 15 percent of your take-home (disposable) income be required to meet payments on all debts and loans other than the home mortgage. A second rule offered is that devoting 10 percent of take-home pay to pay off loans should get the debtor out of debt in no longer than 18 months. Neither of these rules is absolutely binding. They may be inappropriate for some families and situations, but banks consider them to be good guidelines for avoiding financial trouble.

A household's capacity to service (repay) debt depends primarily on the lifestyle, as indicated by income and expenditure patterns. Thus, another popular rule is based on a look at the income statement (Chapter 3). If *discretionary income* is defined as:

Discretionary income = Disposable income less food, shelter, utilities, and insurance,

Figure 5–2
Test for debt capacity

	Score yourself
1. Are your liquid assets equal to	
a. less than one month's take-home pay? 0	
b. one to two months' take-home pay? 1	
c. two to four months' take-home pay? 2	
d. more than four months' take-home pay? 3	_____
2. Are your monthly payments (excluding mortgage)	
a. more than 15 percent of take-home pay? 0	
b. 15–20 percent of take-home pay? 1	
c. under 10 percent of take-home pay? 2	
d. no monthly payments? 3	_____
3. Is your total debt outstanding (excluding mortgage)	
a. more than 20 percent of your annual take-home pay? 0	
b. 15–20 percent of your annual take-home pay? 1	
c. 10–15 percent of annual take-home pay? 2	
d. under 10 percent of annual take-home pay? 3	_____
4. Do your normal monthly expenses for food and shelter	
a. exceed 60 percent of take-home pay? 0	
b. take 50–60 percent of take-home pay? 1	
c. take 40–50 percent of take-home pay? 2	
d. take under 40 percent of take-home pay? 3	_____

A rating of	means
10–12	You can easily afford to borrow.
7–9	You could probably assume more debt.
4–6	Danger signals flashing!
0–3	Time for credit counselling.

then no more than half of your discretionary income should be devoted to debt service. If installment and credit card payments are absorbing more than half of your discretionary income, too little is left for emergencies, unexpected expenses, savings, recreation, and all the other budget-wreckers one is likely to encounter. This rule is more difficult to apply than the "15 percent-a-month" or the "10 percent-a-month-for-18-months" rules, but it is probably a more accurate assessment of a family's *debt capacity.* A large family with a big mortgage payment and substantial expenses for food and utilities will have less discretionary income and debt capacity than a smaller family in more modest housing and the same disposable income.

Finally, to see if you are already too deeply in debt, take the test in Figure 5–2, which is a composite of assets, income, expenditure patterns, and current indebtedness.

Any one of the four guidelines will sound a warning signal indicating that more of existing debt should be paid off before assuming additional repayment obligations. Danger signals did, in fact, flash in 1973–74. In that year consumer credit reached a dangerous 20.5 percent of disposable personal income, the delinquency rate reached an exceptionally high 2.7 percent and personal bankruptcies were being filed in record numbers.

HOW MUCH DOES CREDIT COST?

Under 1971 federal legislation popularly known as *Truth in Lending,* the lender is required to provide the borrower with substantially more information about the terms of the loan than was formerly required. The typical lender's form reproduced in Figure 5–3 indicates the total finance charge, the amount of the down payment, the number and dollar amounts of monthly payments, and the true interest rate (*annual percentage rate,* or APR). The rate which had previously been most commonly quoted for loans other than discounted notes[1] or mortgages was the "add-on" rate. For example, on a $1,000, 12-month loan, an add-on rate of 6.5 percent would mean that 6.5 percent of $1,000, or $65, would be added on to the total debt. The total repayment would be $1,065 in principal and interest, or $88.75 a month. But this understates the true annual interest rate because the borrower does not have the use of the entire $1,000 for the full 12 months. Because the borrower is repaying the principal in regular installments, he or she only has the use, on the average, of about half the sum borrowed or about $500. Thus the true annual rate is nearly twice the add-on rate, or 12 percent in this case.

[1] A *discounted note* does not involve installment payments. Instead the interest is deducted at the beginning and the face value of the note is due at the end. A note for $1,000, repayable in full in 12 months and bearing 10 percent interest, would net the borrower $909.09 at the same time of the loan and will be due as a single repayment of $1,000.

Figure 5-3

PROMISSORY NOTE

$ ______________________ Anytown, USA, January 5, 1979

For value received, I promise to pay to the order of
Friendly Commercial Bank

____ Dollars
in installments derived as follows:

(1) Proceeds .... $__________
(2) Credit Life Insurance Premium .... $__________
(3) Amount Financed [items (1) and (2)] .... $__________
(4) Finance Charge .... $__________
Annual percentage rate .... %
(5) Total of Payments [items (3) and (4)] .... $ __________

Total of payments is $__________ which the undersigned promise(s) to pay in __________ monthly installments of $__________ each, commencing __________, 19______, or, if no date is specified, one month after date hereof, and on the same day of each successive month thereafter until said indebtedness is paid in full.

In the event any installment is not paid upon the date it is due, the holder hereof may at its option declare the entire amount immediately due and payable. Should the holder hereof accept any installment or part payment hereunder after the full amount shall have become immediately due and payable or otherwise grant indulgence to any party hereto this shall not alter or affect the holder's rights hereunder with respect to any subsequent payment or default.

The undersigned agree(s) to pay for all costs of collection hereof including a reasonable attorney's fee of 15% of the amount due if placed in the hands of an attorney for collection.

The undersigned acknowledges receipt of a copy of this note which was completely filled in prior to execution thereof including the disclosure provisions contained herein.

[Maker(s)] Addresses

A simple formula for calculating the approximate APR is

$$\text{APR} = \frac{2 \times \text{Finance charge} \times \text{Number of payments per year}}{\text{Amount of loan} \times (\text{Number of payments} + 1)} \times 100.$$

On the above loan, $\frac{2 \times 65 \times 12 \times 100}{1000 \times 13} = 12\%$.

CORRECTING FOR TAXES AND INFLATION

This is not yet the "true" cost of borrowing, however. There are other complications which affect the decision to borrow and are part of the cost. One is taxes and another is inflation.

The income tax savings for the person who itemizes deductions in excess of the zero balance amount on federal and state income taxes can be substantial. A person in a 25 percent federal tax bracket and a 7 percent state tax bracket (the tax on the last dollar of earned income) will find that every extra $1 of interest paid reduces his taxes by 32 cents. In the above example, the borrower's finance charge would be reduced to $44.20 after taxes and the "after-tax APR" would be only 8.16 percent. Clearly the tax advantages of borrowing are highest to those in the highest tax brackets and least to those in low brackets or those who do not itemize.

Inflation also reduces the cost of borrowing. Borrowing now to buy a car, furniture, and so forth, while the price is lower and repaying the bank while the prices of cars, furniture, and everything else is rising is often a good decision. The borrower gets the benefit of buying at the low price and repaying with dollars which would have bought less. The dollars he or she could otherwise have saved to buy a car would not have stretched to buy as much car in two or three years time as they did just this year. For example, if the interest rate is 12 percent and inflation is 5 percent a year, the prospective car buyer can either buy the $3,000 car now and pay in installments, or save and pay cash in three years. But in three years of 5 percent annual inflation, the car will cost $3,472.88. The total of three years' payments on a $3,000 car at 12 percent interest is $3,573, so the net dollar cost of credit is only about $100 and the inflation-adjusted APR is only 2.2 percent.

Table 5–1 puts these two corrections together at several alternative tax

Table 5–1
Correcting the APR for taxes and inflation

Tax bracket	*Annual inflation*	*Nominal APR*	*Corrected APR*
20%	2%	8%	5.07%
20	2	12	7.6
20	5	8	3.1
20	5	12	4.6
20	10	8	−0.2
20	10	12	−0.3
35%	2%	8%	3.87%
35	2	12	5.8
35	5	8	1.9
35	5	12	2.8
35	10	8	−1.4
35	10	12	−2.1
50	2%	8%	2.7%
50	2	12	4.0
50	5	8	0.7
50	5	12	1.1
50	10	8	−2.6
50	10	12	−3.9

rates and inflation rates. Note that while the tax correction applies to the interest only, the inflation correction applies to the principal repayments as well. While the first principal repayment reflects no inflation, the last one reflects inflation for the entire period, so that in a year of 10 percent inflation the value of a monthly payment has eroded by 5 percent on the average. The APR actually becomes negative for high enough tax brackets coupled with substantial inflation.

SAVINGS INTEREST FORGONE

One further correction is required to get a fully corrected "true" cost of borrowing. The money paid in installment payments could have instead been deposited in your savings account earning interest. The interest forgone, another example of opportunity costs, is a part of the cost of borrowing. For example, a $1,000 loan paid in 24 installments at 12 percent will

Figure 5–4
Computing the true cost of borrowing

1. Dollar cost of credit		$349.00
2. Inflation correction		
First year ½ × 6%* × 12 × 65.25†	$ 23.49	
Second year 1½ × 6% × 12 × 65.25	$ 70.47	
Third year 2½ × 6% × 12 × 65.25	$117.45	
Total		−$211.41
Deflated cost of credit		$137.59
3. Tax savings		
30%‡ × $349 (cost of credit)		−$104.70
4. Interest lost		
First year 6 × $65.25† × 5½%	$ 21.53	
Second year 18 × $65.25 × 5½%	$ 64.60	
Third year 30 × $65.25 × 5½%	$107.66	
		+$193.79
5. Less taxes on interest forgone		
30%‡ × $193.79		−$ 58.14
6. Corrected dollar cost of credit		$168.54
7. The correct APR is		

$$\frac{200 \times \$168.54 \times 12}{2{,}000 \times 37} \times 100 = 5.46\%$$

Note: The combined effect of inflation, taxes and interest forgone has cut the effective cost of credit in half.

* Inflation rate.

† Monthly payment, which can be obtained from an interest amortization table.

‡ Tax bracket; state and federal combined.

§ Interest rate on savings account.

mean about $128 in interest and monthly payments of $47 each. If you were to have banked the $47 a month instead at 5 percent compounded quarterly, at the end of two years you would have had $1,180. Even after income taxes (at a combined state and federal rate of 32 percent) on the interest you would still be able to purchase the $1,000 item and be $122 ahead on the cash price and $250 ahead of the time payment price which includes interest. Weighted against this gain is the question of your willingness to postpone enjoyment of the purchase for two years and whether the price will rise in two years to the point of eliminating the gain.

A procedure for making these approximate corrections to the APR is shown in Figure 5–4, which includes all three considerations—inflation, taxes, and savings interest forgone. The example shown is for a three-year loan of $2,000 at an APR of 11 percent, 6 percent inflation, 30 percent tax bracket and 5½ percent savings interest.

THE DOWN PAYMENT AND THE REPAYMENT PERIOD

There is a natural inclination to minimize the downpayment and also minimize the monthly payments by stretching out the length of the loan for as long as possible. Automobile loans, which until recently were made for two to three years, are now being stretched to four and five years to keep monthly payments within acceptable limits. The interest cost of "5 percent down, forever to pay" can be substantial. Some examples:

1. An extra $1,000 down payment on a 12 percent, ten-year home improvement loan saves $10.81 on the monthly payment and $297 in interest over the life of the loan.
2. An extra $500 down on a 12 percent three-year car loan saves $16.54 on the monthly payment and $95.44 in interest over the life of the loan.
3. Stretching a $8,000, 11 percent home improvement loan seven years to ten cuts the monthly payment by $26.86 but increases the total interest paid by $1,671.
4. Stretching a $4,000, 12 percent car loan from three years to five years cuts the monthly payment from $132.31 to $88.40 but raises total interest paid by $541.

Additional examples can be worked out with the aid of a set of *interest amortization tables,* which are schedules of monthly repayments for various amounts borrowed, interest rates, and numbers of years.

THE RULE OF 78S

There are two good reasons for knowing how much interest is charged to each monthly payment of a loan. One reason relates to income taxes, and the other has to do with the rebate available for the early payoff of a loan.

On a two-year loan of $2,500, at an APR of 12 percent, extending from July 1977 to June 1979, the total interest paid is $316.40. How much of the total interest should be deducted on Schedule A of the federal income tax each year? At first glance it would appear 25 percent in 1977, 50 percent in 1978, 25 percent in 1979—$79.10, $158.20, and $79.10. But because the amount owed is greatest in the early months of the loan and least in the final months, more of the interest is charged to the early period of the loan. In the example above, $136.05 (43 percent) is credited to 1977, $152.20 (50 percent) to 1978, and only $22.15 (7 percent) to 1979. These are the amounts which would be deducted on the tax return in each of those years.

The rule which enables you to determine how much interest to deduct each year on your tax return also determines the amount of interest rebate to which you are entitled for paying the balance early at any given time during the life of the loan. Since the interest is greatest at the beginning of the loan, the amount of rebate will decline rapidly as the loan gets closer to the final repayment.

The *Rule of 78s* is used for these calculations. And the term, Rule of 78s, comes from the computation on a one-year loan. The sum of the digits 1 through 12 is 78. The total interest is apportioned as follows:

$^{12}/_{78}$	*1st month*
$^{11}/_{78}$	*2d month*
.	.
.	.
.	.
$^{11}/_{78}$	*12th month*
$^{78}/_{78} = 1$	

For example, a $1,000 loan at 12 percent would require monthly payments of $88.72, according to the interest amortization tables. $88.72 × 12 = $1,064.64. Total interest is therefore $64.64, the excess of repayments over the original $1,000 borrowed. When the Rule of 78s is applied, you will find the following:

1st month's interest	$^{12}/_{78} \times \$64.64 = \$9.94$
4th month's interest	$^{9}/_{78} \times \$64.64 = \$7.46$
12th month's interest	$^{1}/_{78} \times \$64.64 = \$0.83$.

Let us apply this to the tax and repayment problems. If the loan was taken out in September 1977 and three payments were made in 1977 and the remaining nine in 1978, then the deduction for 1977 would be $(^{12}/_{78} + {}^{11}/_{78} + {}^{10}/_{78}) \times \$64.64 = {}^{33}/_{78} \times \$64.64 = \$27.35$, or 42 percent of the interest. The remaining 58 percent of the interest or $47.29 would be deducted on the 1978 return.

If you went to pay the loan after six months, you would be entitled to an interest rebate. Again, the Rule of 78s tells us the balance due and the interest saved.

The bank is entitled to

$1,000		
47.23	....	Interest $\left(64.24 \times \frac{12 + 11 + 10 + 9 + 8 + 7}{78}\right)$
$1,047.23		
532.32	......	Total of six payments already made
$ 514.91	......	Balance due
$ 532.32	......	Total of remaining six monthly payments
$ 17.41	......	Interest saved by paying early.

The following is a more general expression of the Rule of 78s.

Let A = amount of interest paid (dollar cost of credit); let p = number of payments (for example, 36 on a 3-year monthly installment loan), then the interest in month n is

$$\frac{(p + 1) - n}{\frac{p + 1}{2} \times p} \times A.$$

For example, a 36-month loan, total interest = $438.36: interest in the 12th month =

$$\frac{37 - 12}{\frac{37}{2} \times 36} \times \$438.36 = 0.0375 \times \$438.36 = \$16.45.$$

How do you determine A? It should be given on your original statement, but it can also be estimated closely from an interest amortization table, a page of which is reproduced as Table 5–2. The three-year loan in the example above was for $3,000 at 12 percent, which required 36 monthly payments of $95.91 each, or a total of $3,438.36. Subtracting the $3,000 principal leaves $438.36 as the dollar cost of credit.

WHERE TO OBTAIN LOANS

Where to seek loans depends on such factors as credit rating, the purpose of the loan, the collateral offered, the amount the borrower needs, and the length of time he or she wishes to take to repay. The major sources of consumer loans are commercial banks which account for 39 percent of all such loans; finance or small loan companies, 21 percent; credit unions, 13 percent; life insurance loans, 12 percent; and retail outlets, 11 percent.

Among the lending institutions of a given type, the range of rates will be fairly narrow. Rather than giving a substantially lower interest rate to a more attractive credit risk, lenders compensate in other ways—larger maximum loan, smaller down payment, less collateral, or longer to repay. Because many types of lending institutions are subject to interest ceilings, and because some do not wish to be bothered with the nuisance of repossession and resale, some will send the poorer credit risk to a different type of lender rather than lend to him either at a higher rate or for a shorter term.

Commercial banks

Commercial banks make loans to individuals for automobiles, home improvements, or general purposes. They generally do not lend on stocks or land as collateral, although it may be possible to obtain a personal loan and use them for such purchases. Interest rates range from 9 to 12 percent for three to five years on new cars with higher rates and shorter terms for used cars. Other personal loans generally command 11 to 13 percent interest with terms from one to three years. Banks also are the principal sources for the discounted notes described on page 80 with maturities from 3 to 18 months. Maximum amounts vary from bank to bank and depend on the credit rating, assets or collateral, and ability to repay of the specific borrower. Home improvement loans, also available from savings and loan associations, range up to $10,000 and up to seven years' duration with typical interest rates presently in the 11 to 14 percent range.

Credit unions

A credit union, which one joins at work or through a professional or social organization, is another potential source of loans. Typically the maximum is $2,500 for up to three years at a rate of up to 1 percent per month on the unpaid balance yielding a true interest rate of 12 percent a year. The quality of management, the actual interest rate charged, the maximum available, and the repayment periods permitted vary somewhat from one credit union to another.

Insurance cash value

A popular, low-cost, indefinite repayment loan may be available from a life insurance company to the policy holder on cash value policies—whole life, twenty pay life, endowment, and so forth. It is possible to borrow up to 95 percent (100 percent with some insurers) of the cash value of the policy at a rate of interest stated in the contract. Older policies offer loans at 5 or 6 percent; newer policies written in the 1970s contain an interest rate guarantee of 8 percent, still more attractive than bank rates.

Savings and loan associations and mutual savings banks

Savings and loan associations and mutual savings banks are usually viewed as mortgage lenders, which is indeed their primary lending activity. These institutions also make shorter term loans, however. Passbook loans are available with the savings account as collateral at interest rates just slightly above the passbook rate, and mobile home loans of up to seven years and home improvements loans of up to ten years are also often available from

Table 5–2
Amortization table

Monthly payment required to amortize a loan

TERM AMOUNT	1 YEAR	2 YEARS	3 YEARS	4 YEARS	5 YEARS	6 YEARS	7 YEARS	8 YEARS	9 YEARS	10 YEARS	11 YEARS	12 YEARS	13 YEARS	14 YEARS	15 YEARS
$100	8.88	4.70	3.31	2.62	2.21	1.94	1.75	1.61	1.51	1.42	1.36	1.30	1.26	1.22	1.19
200	17.75	9.39	6.62	5.24	4.42	3.88	3.50	3.22	3.01	2.84	2.71	2.60	2.51	2.43	2.37
300	26.62	14.09	9.93	7.86	6.63	5.82	5.25	4.83	4.51	4.26	4.06	3.89	3.76	3.64	3.55
400	35.49	18.78	13.24	10.48	8.84	7.76	7.00	6.44	6.01	5.68	5.41	5.19	5.01	4.86	4.73
500	44.36	23.47	16.54	13.10	11.05	9.70	8.75	8.05	7.52	7.10	6.76	6.48	6.26	6.07	5.91
600	53.23	28.17	19.85	15.72	13.26	11.64	10.50	9.66	9.02	8.51	8.11	7.78	7.51	7.28	7.09
700	62.10	32.86	23.16	18.34	15.47	13.58	12.25	11.27	10.52	9.93	9.46	9.08	8.76	8.50	8.28
800	70.98	37.56	26.47	20.96	17.68	15.52	14.00	12.88	12.02	11.35	10.81	10.37	10.01	9.71	9.46
900	79.85	42.25	29.77	23.58	19.89	17.46	15.75	14.49	13.52	12.77	12.16	11.67	11.26	10.92	10.64
1000	88.72	46.94	33.08	26.20	22.10	19.40	17.50	16.10	15.03	14.19	13.51	12.96	12.51	12.14	11.82
2000	177.43	93.88	66.16	52.39	44.20	38.80	35.00	32.19	30.05	28.37	27.02	25.92	25.02	24.27	23.64
3000	266.15	140.82	99.23	78.58	66.30	58.20	52.50	48.29	45.07	42.55	40.53	38.88	37.53	36.40	35.45
4000	354.86	187.76	132.31	104.77	88.40	77.60	70.00	64.38	60.09	56.73	54.03	51.84	50.04	48.53	47.27
5000	443.57	234.70	165.39	130.96	110.50	97.00	87.50	80.48	75.11	70.91	67.54	64.80	62.55	60.67	59.09
6000	532.29	281.64	198.46	157.16	132.60	116.40	104.99	96.57	90.13	85.09	81.05	77.76	75.05	72.80	70.90
7000	621.00	328.57	231.54	183.35	154.69	135.80	122.49	112.66	105.16	99.27	94.55	90.72	87.56	84.93	82.72
8000	709.71	375.51	264.61	209.54	176.79	155.20	139.99	128.76	120.18	113.45	108.06	103.68	100.07	97.06	94.53
9000	798.43	422.45	297.69	235.73	198.89	174.60	157.49	144.85	135.20	127.63	121.57	116.64	112.58	109.20	106.35
10000	887.14	469.39	330.77	261.92	220.99	194.00	174.99	160.95	150.22	141.81	135.08	129.60	125.09	121.33	118.17
11000	975.85	516.33	363.84	288.12	243.09	213.40	192.49	177.04	165.24	155.99	148.58	142.56	137.60	133.46	129.98
12000	1064.57	563.27	396.92	314.31	265.19	232.80	209.98	193.14	180.26	170.17	162.09	155.52	150.10	145.59	141.80
13000	1153.28	610.20	430.00	340.50	287.28	252.20	227.48	209.23	195.28	184.35	175.60	168.48	162.61	157.72	153.61
14000	1241.99	657.14	463.07	366.69	309.38	271.60	244.98	225.32	210.31	198.53	189.10	181.44	175.12	169.86	165.43
15000	1330.71	704.08	496.15	392.88	331.48	291.00	262.48	241.42	225.33	212.71	202.61	194.40	187.63	181.99	177.25
16000	1419.42	751.02	529.22	419.08	353.58	310.40	279.98	257.51	240.35	226.89	216.12	207.36	200.14	194.12	189.06
17000	1508.13	797.96	562.30	445.27	375.68	329.80	297.48	273.61	255.37	241.07	229.63	220.32	212.64	206.25	200.88
18000	1596.85	844.90	595.38	471.46	397.78	349.20	314.97	289.70	270.39	255.25	243.13	233.28	225.15	218.39	212.69
19000	1685.56	891.83	628.45	497.65	419.88	368.60	332.47	305.80	285.41	269.43	256.64	246.24	237.66	230.52	224.51
20000	1774.27	938.77	661.53	523.84	441.97	388.00	349.97	321.89	300.43	283.61	270.15	259.20	250.17	242.65	236.33
21000	1862.99	985.71	694.61	550.04	464.07	407.40	367.47	337.98	315.46	297.79	283.65	272.15	262.68	254.78	248.14
22000	1951.70	1032.65	727.68	576.23	486.17	426.80	384.97	354.08	330.48	311.97	297.16	285.11	275.19	266.91	259.96
23000	2040.41	1079.59	760.76	602.42	508.27	446.20	402.47	370.17	345.50	326.15	310.67	298.07	287.69	279.05	271.78
24000	2129.13	1126.53	793.83	628.61	530.37	465.60	419.96	386.27	360.52	340.33	324.17	311.03	300.20	291.18	283.59
25000	2217.84	1173.47	826.91	654.80	552.47	485.00	437.46	402.36	375.54	354.51	337.68	323.99	312.71	303.31	295.41
26000	2306.55	1220.40	859.99	681.00	574.56	504.40	454.96	418.45	390.56	368.69	351.19	336.95	325.22	315.44	307.22
27000	2395.27	1267.34	893.06	707.19	596.66	523.80	472.46	434.55	405.58	382.87	364.70	349.91	337.73	327.58	319.04
28000	2483.98	1314.28	926.14	733.38	618.76	543.20	489.96	450.64	420.61	397.05	378.20	362.87	350.24	339.71	330.86
29000	2572.69	1361.22	959.22	759.57	640.86	562.60	507.46	466.74	435.63	411.23	391.71	375.83	362.74	351.84	342.67
30000	2661.41	1408.16	992.29	785.76	662.96	582.00	524.95	482.83	450.65	425.41	405.22	388.79	375.25	363.97	354.49
35000	3104.98	1642.85	1157.67	916.72	773.45	679.00	612.45	563.30	525.76	496.31	472.75	453.59	437.79	424.63	413.57
40000	3548.54	1877.54	1323.05	1047.68	883.94	776.00	699.94	643.77	600.86	567.22	540.29	518.39	500.33	485.29	472.65
45000	3992.11	2112.23	1488.44	1178.64	994.44	873.00	787.43	724.25	675.97	638.12	607.82	583.18	562.88	545.96	531.73
50000	4435.68	2346.93	1653.82	1309.60	1104.93	970.00	874.92	804.72	751.08	709.02	675.36	647.98	625.42	606.62	590.81

TERM AMOUNT	16 YEARS	17 YEARS	18 YEARS	19 YEARS	20 YEARS	21 YEARS	22 YEARS	23 YEARS	24 YEARS	25 YEARS	26 YEARS	27 YEARS	28 YEARS	30 YEARS	35 YEARS
$100	1.16	1.14	1.12	1.10	1.09	1.07	1.06	1.05	1.04	1.04	1.03	1.02	1.02	1.01	1.00
200	2.31	2.27	2.23	2.20	2.17	2.14	2.12	2.10	2.08	2.07	2.06	2.04	2.03	2.02	1.99
300	3.47	3.40	3.34	3.29	3.25	3.21	3.18	3.15	3.12	3.10	3.08	3.06	3.05	3.02	2.98
400	4.62	4.53	4.45	4.39	4.33	4.28	4.23	4.20	4.16	4.13	4.11	4.08	4.06	4.03	3.98
500	5.78	5.66	5.57	5.48	5.41	5.35	5.29	5.24	5.20	5.16	5.13	5.10	5.08	5.04	4.97
600	6.93	6.80	6.68	6.58	6.49	6.41	6.35	6.29	6.24	6.20	6.16	6.12	6.09	6.04	5.96
700	8.09	7.93	7.79	7.67	7.57	7.48	7.41	7.34	7.28	7.23	7.18	7.14	7.11	7.05	6.95
800	9.24	9.06	8.90	8.77	8.65	8.55	8.46	8.39	8.32	8.26	8.21	8.16	8.12	8.06	7.95
900	10.40	10.19	10.02	9.87	9.73	9.62	9.52	9.43	9.36	9.29	9.23	9.18	9.14	9.06	8.94
1000	11.55	11.32	11.13	10.96	10.81	10.69	10.58	10.48	10.40	10.32	10.26	10.20	10.15	10.07	9.93
2000	23.10	22.64	22.25	21.92	21.62	21.37	21.15	20.96	20.79	20.64	20.51	20.40	20.30	20.13	19.86
3000	34.65	33.96	33.38	32.87	32.43	32.05	31.72	31.44	31.18	30.96	30.77	30.60	30.45	30.20	29.79
4000	46.20	45.28	44.50	43.83	43.24	42.74	42.30	41.91	41.58	41.28	41.02	40.79	40.59	40.26	39.71
5000	57.75	56.60	55.63	54.78	54.05	53.42	52.87	52.39	51.97	51.60	51.28	50.99	50.74	50.32	49.64
6000	69.29	67.92	66.75	65.74	64.86	64.10	63.44	62.87	62.36	61.92	61.53	61.19	60.89	60.39	59.57
7000	80.84	79.24	77.87	76.69	75.67	74.79	74.02	73.34	72.75	72.24	71.78	71.39	71.03	70.45	69.49
8000	92.39	90.56	89.00	87.65	86.48	85.47	84.59	83.82	83.15	82.56	82.04	81.58	81.18	80.52	79.42
9000	103.94	101.88	100.12	98.61	97.29	96.15	95.16	94.30	93.54	92.88	92.29	91.78	91.33	90.58	89.35
10000	115.49	113.20	111.25	109.56	108.10	106.84	105.74	104.77	103.93	103.19	102.55	101.98	101.48	100.64	99.27
11000	127.04	124.52	122.37	120.52	118.91	117.52	116.31	115.25	114.33	113.51	112.80	112.18	111.62	110.71	109.20
12000	138.58	135.84	133.50	131.47	129.72	128.20	126.88	125.73	124.72	123.83	123.06	122.37	121.77	120.77	119.13
13000	150.13	147.16	144.62	142.43	140.53	138.89	137.45	136.20	135.11	134.15	133.31	132.57	131.92	130.84	129.05
14000	161.68	158.48	155.74	153.38	151.34	149.57	148.03	146.68	145.50	144.47	143.56	142.77	142.06	140.90	138.98
15000	173.23	169.80	166.87	164.34	162.15	160.25	158.60	157.16	155.90	154.79	153.82	152.96	152.21	150.96	148.91
16000	184.78	181.12	177.99	175.29	172.96	170.94	169.17	167.63	166.29	165.11	164.07	163.16	162.36	161.03	158.83
17000	196.33	192.44	189.12	186.25	183.77	181.62	179.75	178.11	176.68	175.43	174.33	173.36	172.51	171.09	168.76
18000	207.87	203.76	200.24	197.21	194.58	192.30	190.32	188.59	187.07	185.75	184.58	183.56	182.65	181.15	178.69
19000	219.42	215.08	211.36	208.16	205.39	202.99	200.89	199.07	197.47	196.07	194.84	193.75	192.80	191.22	188.61
20000	230.97	226.40	222.49	219.12	216.20	213.67	211.47	209.54	207.86	206.38	205.09	203.95	202.95	201.28	198.54
21000	242.52	237.72	233.61	230.07	227.01	224.35	222.04	220.02	218.25	216.70	215.34	214.15	213.09	211.35	208.47
22000	254.07	249.04	244.74	241.03	237.82	235.04	232.61	230.50	228.65	227.02	225.60	224.35	223.24	221.41	218.40
23000	265.62	260.36	255.86	251.98	248.63	245.72	243.18	240.97	239.04	237.34	235.85	234.54	233.39	231.47	228.32
24000	277.16	271.68	266.99	262.94	259.44	256.40	253.76	251.45	249.43	247.66	246.11	244.74	243.54	241.54	238.25
25000	288.71	283.00	278.11	273.89	270.25	267.08	264.33	261.93	259.82	257.98	256.36	254.94	253.68	251.60	248.18
26000	300.26	294.32	289.23	284.85	281.06	277.77	274.90	272.40	270.22	268.30	266.62	265.13	263.83	261.67	258.10
27000	311.81	305.64	300.36	295.81	291.87	288.45	285.48	282.88	280.61	278.62	276.87	275.33	273.98	271.73	268.03
28000	323.36	316.96	311.48	306.76	302.68	299.13	296.05	293.36	291.00	288.94	287.12	285.53	284.12	281.79	277.96
29000	334.91	328.28	322.61	317.72	313.49	309.82	306.62	303.83	301.39	299.26	297.38	295.73	294.27	291.86	287.88
30000	346.45	339.60	333.73	328.67	324.30	320.50	317.20	314.31	311.79	309.57	307.63	305.92	304.42	301.92	297.81
35000	404.20	396.20	389.35	383.45	378.35	373.92	370.06	366.69	363.75	361.17	358.90	356.91	355.15	352.24	347.44
40000	461.94	452.80	444.97	438.23	432.39	427.33	422.93	419.08	415.71	412.76	410.17	407.90	405.89	402.56	397.08
45000	519.68	509.40	500.59	493.01	486.44	480.75	475.79	471.46	467.68	464.36	461.45	458.88	456.63	452.88	446.71
50000	577.42	566.00	556.21	547.78	540.49	534.16	528.66	523.85	519.64	515.95	512.72	509.87	507.36	503.20	496.35

Source: Jack C. Estes, *Interest Amortization Tables* (New York: McGraw-Hill, © 1974), pp. 58–59.

this source. Rates for loans other than passbook are generally in the same range as commercial bank rates, but it pays to shop for the most favorable rate.

Manufacturer's credit agency

New automobiles may be financed directly through the manufacturer's own credit agency, at rates usually slightly higher than commercial bank rates. They accept lower risks since the loan is secured by the car.

Finance companies

Finance companies are a higher cost credit source which generally deal with higher risk borrowers for fairly short terms. Rates range from 24 percent to 42 percent a year, depending on state interest ceilings. Finance companies will lend for new and used cars, vacations, Christmas, debt consolidations, home improvements, and a variety of other purposes. They accept lower credit risks and lower income borrowers than commercial banks and as a result are more often involved in repossession and bankruptcy proceedings. They are often willing to make loans available in smaller amounts than other lenders.

Retail outlets

Still another source of installment credit is the seller or retail outlet—of furniture, appliances, mobile homes, stereo equipment, and other durables. The share of these lenders in total credit has declined with the growth of bank cards, but such credit is still available. Most furniture and appliances are still financed on credit, at least in part. While some dealers maintain their own credit, and a majority allow 60–90 days to pay without finance charges, many retailers sell their installment debt to a credit company such as General Electric Credit Corporation, one of the nation's largest. Interest rates are about the same as those payable on bank cards and charge accounts which run one to 1.5 percent a month, or 12 to 18 percent a year. Bank cards and charge accounts are taken up in a later section of this chapter. The credit company legally becomes a holder in due course of the note and has the right to collect the balance due with interest, to repossess the goods with interest on default, and to sue for a deficiency judgment if necessary. Under recent credit legislation, information on the payment schedule, down payment, finance charge, and so forth, must be supplied to the borrower by the original seller at the time of purchase. This information is part of the sales contract and is therefore binding on subsequent holders of the installment obligation.

QUALIFYING FOR A LOAN

Naturally, if you need a loan you want to borrow from the cheapest source. If an insurance loan, a passbook loan, or a credit union loan is not feasible, the choice narrows to a bank or a finance company in most instances—a bank for a good credit risk, a finance company for a poorer risk. If the loan is for furniture or other durables the retail outlet is also a possibility. For some kinds of loans, creditworthiness may make the difference between getting a loan and not getting a loan. For a mortgage, your credit rating may mean the difference of 0.25 percent in the interest rate, or between a required 10 percent or 20 percent down, or between staying put and buying a dream house.

How does the lender assess the amount of risk undertaken in lending to a particular borrower? The assessment is a composite of several factors—the applicant's assets, income, job stability, present indebtedness, and past credit record being the most important. Forms similar to that in Figure 5–5 are in common use among banks. (The alert reader will notice how much of it resembles a balance sheet.) Loans are not given out like lollipops, however. Bankers are, by the nature of their business, quite conservative in dispensing money. If too many loans become bad debts, the bank experiences a decline in the value of assets, most of which are IOUs or promises to repay, relative to the bank's liabilities plus net worth. The banker is answerable for the soundness of the bank's assets to his depositors, his stockholders, the Federal Reserve Bank of his district, and the Comptroller of the Currency in Washington. Recent bank problems stemming from real estate loans to developers who have gone bankrupt have forced bankers to become even more careful about the quality of their loans, both personal and commercial.

Finance companies, too, scrutinize the applicant, but they customarily have a larger cushion for bad debts because of the higher interest rates charged, and have of necessity become more adept at using collection techniques such as threats to repossess, garnishment (withholding of amounts due from wages, not legal in all states), and collecting through small claims court. Thus, they will accept applicants not rated as satisfactory for bank loan purposes. Finance companies provide a useful and necessary service by making credit available to marginal borrowers.

SOURCES OF CREDIT

Although the distinction between credit and loans is somewhat blurred, there are two different types of credit available. One is the loan of a certain sum to be repaid at specified intervals in predetermined amounts which we discussed earlier in this chapter. The other, known as open-ended credit, allows you to buy now and pay later in varying amounts over a variable

Figure 5–5
Loan application

70506

Office ______ Acct. No. ______ Officer Code ______

Date ______ Amt. Req. $ ______ No. Pmts. Requested ______ Type Loan Requested ☐Secured ☐Unsecured

Name of Maker ______ First Middle Last Social Sec. No. ______

M Maker
S Spouse as comaker or endorser
C Co-Maker other than spouse
B Business

SHOW CODE HERE ☐

Name of Co-maker ______ First Middle Last

Makers Street Address ______ How Long This Add. ______ Yrs. ______ Mos. No. of Dep. ______

City, State and Zip ______ Phone ______

Endorser's Name ______ Co-maker or Endorser's Phone ______

Employer's Name ______ How Long Employed ______ Yrs. ______ Mos.

Income $ ______ ☐Wk ☐Mo Job Title or Profession ______ Employer's Phone ______

Alimony, child support or separate maintenance income need not be revealed if you do not wish to have it considered as a basis for repaying this obligation. If you choose to reveal such income check here ☐, state the amount and source in this section and complete section A below.

Amount of Other Income $ ______ ☐Wk ☐Mo Source of Other Income ______

	Dollars	Cents
Old Balance		
New Adv		
Total Adv		
DEALER Auto Ins.		
DEALER Life Ins.		
DEALER A & H Ins.		
Dealer Total		
BANK Auto Ins.		
BANK Life Ins.		
BANK A & H Ins.		
Total Proceeds		
Discount		
Misc.		
Reg. Reserve		
Spec. Reserve		
Total Note		

Date of Note ______
Date First Pmt. ______
Date Final Pmt. ______
Number Pmts. ______
Reg. Pmt. Amt. ______
Irr. Pmt. Amount ______ Irr. Pmt. No. ______
Mos to Maturity ______

Bank Credit Life Code: 0 Do not create a credit life policy record; 1 Create a credit life policy record ☐

If this is a secured credit or if spouse is contractually liable complete this section.

Show Code Here ☐
M Married
U Unmarried
S Separated

SECTION A This section should be completed if the spouse is contractually liable or the applicant is relying on income from alimony, child support or separate maintenance from another person.

Name ______
Address ______
Employer ______ Emp. Phone ______
How Long Employed ______ Yrs ______ Mos Income $ ______ ☐Wk ☐Mo Job Title ______

Collateral ______ Year ______ Model ______

Charge Account Code
0 Do Not Charge Checking Acct
1 Charge Checking Account

SHOW CODE HERE ☐

Checking Acct. Name ______
Checking Acct. Number ______

Age ______ Date of Birth ______ Mo. Day Year

Dealer Life Code ☐ Branch Code ☐ Bank Life Insurance Code Must be shown →

Purpose Of Loan ______

Maker's Previous Employer ______ Years Emp. ______

Maker's Previous Address ______ Years This Add. ______

Property Owned ______ In What Name ______ Value $ ______

Mortgaged To Whom ______ Amt. of Pmts. $ ______ Mortg. Bal. $ ______

Nearest Relative (Name & Address) ______

Last Car Financed ______ Cust. of Which Banks ______ ☐ Loan ☐ Check ☐ Saving ______ ☐ Loan ☐ Check ☐ Saving ______ ☐ Loan ☐ Check ☐ Saving

List All Obligations and Credit References

Reference ______ Reference ______
Reference ______ Reference ______
Reference ______ Reference ______

Auto Ins. Agent ______ Name of Employee Contacted ______
Name of Ins. Co. ______ Policy No. ______
Amount of Deductible ______ Date Verified ______
Date Mailed IST-411 ______ Date Lien Sent To Be Recorded ______

The undersigned applicant(s) (including each person signing) warrants that the above information is true, accurate and complete and affirms that it is given with the intention that it be relied upon by the First National Bank of South Carolina in extending credit to the undersigned. The applicant has not knowingly withheld any information which might affect his credit, and agrees to notify the bank in writing of any material change therein. The applicant hereby authorizes the bank to obtain from his employer or any other source such information as may be desired in connection with this application and authorizes such source to provide the same.

______
Signature of Applicant

______
(If spouse is to be contractually liable for this credit, sign here.)

Form IST 198 Rev. 11-1-77 · IST Source Document

Figure 5–5 (*continued*)

Applicant's Name ______________________ Officer's Name ______________________

Collateral:

Year	Make	Series	No. Cyl.	Body Style	Mileage	Dealer Cost (New)	Black Book Loan Value (Used)	Amt. Financed

High Performance Engine ☐ Yes ☐ No 4 In The Floor ☐ Yes ☐ No

Work Space

Employment Verification:

Name of Employer		Employer's Phone No.
How Long Employed ____ Yrs. ____ Mos.	Salary $ ☐ Wk. ☐ Mo. ☐ Yr.	Job Title or Position
Date Verified	Name of Contact	Name of Investigator

FIRST NATIONAL BANK INFORMATION — Other Account Relationships

DDA Acct. No.	Date Opened	Balance
Savings Acct. No.	Date Opened	Balance

Other Accounts With Bank:

Account Number	Date Opened	Collateral	High Credit	Terms	Balance	Credit Rating

Direct Investigation:

Name of Creditor	Date Opened	Collateral	High Credit	Terms	Balance	Credit Rating

Credit Bureau:

Date Originally Filed ____ Mo. Day Year Last Credit File Update ____ Mo. Day Year

Name of Creditor	Date Opened	Collateral	High Credit	Terms	Balance	Credit Rating

If rejected, list specific reason(s) for adverse action:

____

____

____

Lending Officer Signature

Courtesy of First National Bank of South Carolina

period, with no charge until the credit is actually used. Installment loans from retail outlets for purchase of durables tend to fall into both categories. In other words, you can either buy a refrigerator on the basis of a loan with specified payments or charge the purchase to your account and make periodic payments. In either case, of course, your method of payment would be cleared by the credit manager of the store.

Credit cards and charge accounts, multipurpose or limited use, are the second form of credit available to consumers. The original big three of the *multipurpose credit cards* were American Express, Carte Blanche, and Diners' Club. These cards are available for an annual membership fee to those whose credit ratings and income are satisfactory. They are honored by a multitude of restaurants, hotels, motels, car rental agencies, airlines, theaters, the telephone company, and numerous other kinds of establishments. In addition to the holders' membership charge, the participating businesses pay a fee from 2 to 8 percent to the credit card agencies.

Gasoline credit cards, the most popular plastic status symbol, are honored by either a single brand or a group of cooperating brands and can also be used for hotels, motels, and car rentals in some cases. There is no fee charged to obtain one.

The newest and fastest growing form of credit card is the *bank card.* Developed in California, the two giants in the field—Master Charge and Visa, formerly Bankamericard—quickly spread across the nation with the aid of interbank clearing arrangements. At present some 4,000 banks issue Visa and more than 6,000 issue Master Charge. These cards are accepted at a great variety of establishments—hotels, motels, restaurants, department stores, specialty shops, gasoline stations. Merchants pay fees of 3 to 6 percent of billings and generally make up much of their cost by reducing losses from bad debt through lower billing and bookkeeping expenses and by faster receipt of payments. Large department stores and department store chains are rapidly switching to the convenience and universal appeal of bank cards. The bank card share of credit rose from 1.2 percent in 1968 to 5.6 percent of credit outstanding and 10.2 percent of *new* credit in 1975, a truly phenomenal rate of growth.

The advantage of bank cards, gasoline cards, and other multipurpose cards is convenience in purchase and payment. Less cash is needed by the consumer. In fact it is often easier to charge on a bank card than to cash a personal check, especially when traveling. The disadvantages are obvious; annual interest of 12 to 18 percent on most cards and a possible loss of budget control. Convenience apparently outweighs the negative considerations for many, since some 65 million bank cards are presently fattening American wallets.

How does the would-be card holder start his collection? If you want a bank card, the process of obtaining one is not as easy as it was when these cards were first issued. Poor credit experience has led banks to tighten their issuing requirements. The issuing bank will ask you to fill out a form very similar to the loan application shown earlier in Figure 5–5. Included on the form is your requested credit limit. Based on that application and a routine credit check, the bank may issue a card with a specified expiration date, reject the application, or issue a card with a lower credit limit than requested. Renewals may be for longer periods and/or higher credit limits if the cardholder establishes a satisfactory repayment record.

Finally, there is the familiar single-store or single-chain card. Most familiar are the cards of three of the nation's top five retailers—Sears, Penneys, and Montgomery Ward. These permit purchases in any of their stores across the nation. Like the bank cards, they feature monthly billing, 12 to 18 percent annual interest and extended periods of repayment. It is highly likely that most, if not all, of these one-chain credit cards will ultimately be displaced by bank cards in the next ten years.

METHODS OF BILLING ON CREDIT CARDS AND CHARGE ACCOUNTS

The variety of billing methods on credit cards is diminishing under the dominance of the bank card method of *average daily balance* where interest is charged on the average amount owed during the month. There are several other methods still in limited use. Higher interest results from the *previous balance* method, with interest charged on the balance before credits and before new charges. Lowest interest usually results from the *adjusted balance* method, with interest charged on the previous balance less credit for payments made during the month and without adding in new purchases. The most common method, average daily balance, has two submethods. One

Figure 5–6
Sample statement

Bargain Basement Department Stores
1 Main Street
Anytown, U.S.A.

John and Jane Sellers
2 North Street
Anytown, U.S.A.

Statement for period 1–5–77 to 2–3–77

Date			
1–5	Previous balance	$226.34	
1–9	Purchase	23.25	
1–12	Purchase	18.75	
1–20	Payment—thank you		$50.00
2–3	Finance charge	?	
2–3	New balance	?	

method only subtracts credits. A newer variant also adds new purchases to the average daily balance as they come in. Many Master Charge issuers, among others, used this method. The borrower loses the traditional privilege of thirty days free credit on such purchases since they now accrue interest before he or she is billed. Most credit card plans charge no interest in any month in which your balance is paid in full. Some Visa issuers charge no interest when 90 percent of the balance due is paid.

The statement for John and Jane Sellers shown in Figure 5–6 can be used to illustrate the computations by each of the four methods.

1. Under simple average daily balance, the Sellers owed $226.34 for 15 days and $176.34 for 15 days.

   Average daily balance = $201.34
   Finance charge at 1.5 percent per month = $3.02

2. Under average daily balance including new purchases they owe $226.34 × 4/30 + $249.61 × 3/30 + $268.36 × 9/30 + $218.36 × 14/30 =

   Average daily balance = $237.55
   Finance charge of 1.5 percent per month = $3.56

3. Under the previous balance method, they owed $226.34 at the beginning of the period.

   Finance charge at 1.5 percent per month = $3.40

4. Under the adjusted balance method, interest is charged on previous balance less credits, or

   $226.34 − $50 = $176.34
   Finance charge at 1.5 percent per month = $2.65

As a general rule, adjusted balance results in the least interest being paid, while either method 2 or 3 will be highest depending on whether the customer makes net additions to or net substractions from the balance due.

PROBLEMS WITH CREDIT

The number one problem with credit, of course, is assuming more debt than can be managed. There are some other, less obvious problems with credit. First, credit requires a more thorough record-keeping system. Second, errors in billing and recording payments by either the creditor or the credit user can give an undeserved poor credit rating. And finally, there are some unscrupulous people in the lending business. Agents seeking to bring a delinquent person to court have been known to discard legal papers and claim they were served; the borrower's day in court may come and go without any awareness on his or her part until someone comes to repossess the television set. Purchasers may buy and finance misrepresented merchandise and still have to pay in full including finance charges or be dragged through court at the risk of their reputation and credit standing. *Truth in Lending* and the Fair Credit Reporting Act, which will be discussed in Chapter 7, have eliminated most of the worst abuses. Nevertheless, some or all of the following provisions frequently appear in contracts and entail some obvious risks to the borrower.

1. *The balloon clause*—a large final payment which will probably have to be refinanced, keeping the borrower perpetually in debt.
2. *The add-on clause*—new purchases are added on to the contract; a default on any payment entitles the seller to repossess all of the merchandise back to the first purchase.
3. *The acceleration clause*—if one payment is missed, all remaining payments are immediately due and payable.

WHERE TO GO WHEN CREDIT GETS OUT OF HAND

Suppose our hapless friends, the Borrowers, are barely making their monthly payments, living from paycheck to paycheck, and the wife becomes pregnant and has to quit her job, the roof develops a leak, and the dog needs surgery for ulcers. Where do the Borrowers go?

There are several options short of jumping off the leaky roof. One option is to work things out with creditors. Some of them are willing to stretch out a loan or postpone a payment or two in this situation. Bankers generally recommend avoiding a debt consolidation loan, which lumps all the little payments into one medium size payment plus additional finance charges and sometimes other fees for the service of collecting and disbursing. Instead, the next stop could be a *credit counselling service.* Credit unions sometimes provide this service as do other organizations in metropolitan areas. These agencies can frequently arrange extended repayment at lower monthly payments and handle the transfer of funds from debtor to creditors. They will also help the debtor put his or her financial house in order, by reassessing spending patterns and trying to keep such a crisis from recurring.

If it is not possible to work out such an arrangement, the next choice is a lawyer to arrange for a Chapter 13 proceeding—the *"wage-earner plan"* of the Federal Bankruptcy Act. First, any items used to secure loans, such as an automobile or furniture, will be repossessed. A court-appointed referee will arrange a three-year repayment of as much of the remaining outstanding loans as possible. Furthermore, all future interest charges will be forgiven. The court will then collect from the debtor and disburse the money to creditors. Most of the debtor's assets other than those which are security for loans—his home; his car, if not subject to lien; his personal property, and a limited amount of financial assets—are left untouched.

The final alternative is *bankruptcy* proceedings. Virtually all the bankrupt's assets except for some limited personal property established by the state will be liquidated and the proceeds distributed to creditors. This is a last resort; bankruptcy haunts the debtor's footsteps for years afterwards and should never be undertaken lightly.

SUMMARY

Dealing with credit is one of the most difficult areas of personal financial management. The sources of loanable funds are numerous and tempting. There are many times and purposes for which it is appropriate to borrow, subject to limits set by several guidelines suggested in this chapter. Once "credit capacity" has been determined, a credit source should be shopped for with the same care devoted to shopping for cars, furniture, and clothing. Credit is costly, the exact cost depending on the source of funds and the purpose of the loan. The standardized annual percentage rate—APR—now makes it possible to make direct comparisons between rates offered by different lenders. Taxes and inflation reduce the cost of borrowing; so do larger down payments and shorter repayment periods. And interest can be allocated for purposes of income taxes and early repayment according to the Rule of 78s, with more of the interest charged to the early months of the loan when the balance owed is greatest.

Loans are available from a variety of sources, most commonly commercial banks, finance companies, savings and loans, credit unions, life insurance companies, and retail outlets. The loan source chosen depends on the purpose, size and duration of the loan, and the credit rating of the borrower. Credit rating in turn depends on income, assets, employment, and past credit history.

Credit is also available on limited or multipurpose credit cards at interest rates usually in the 12 to 18 percent range.

Credit counselling services, wage earner plan, and voluntary bankruptcy are the options available to the heavily overextended credit user.

KEY WORDS

Acceleration clause
Add-on clause
Adjusted balance
Annual percentage rate (APR)
Average daily balance
Balloon clause
Bank card
Bankruptcy
Credit counselling
Debt capacity
Discounted note
Discretionary income
Interest amortization table
Multipurpose credit card
Previous balance
Rule of 78s
Truth in Lending
Wage-earner plan

PROBLEMS

1. Norma E. owes six more monthly payments of $65.70 each on a three-year loan. The original amount borrowed was $2,000 to be repaid in 36 equal installments.

a. What is the APR on her loan?

b. If she pays if off six months ahead of schedule, to how much of an interest rebate is she entitled?

c. The loan was taken out in February with the first payment in March. How much interest can she deduct on her first year's income taxes?

2. Fred J. is considering borrowing $3,000 for three years at 12 percent from a commercial bank to add on to his home. Building costs are going up at a rate of 5 percent a year. He is in a 25 percent state-federal tax bracket. Interest on his savings would earn 6 percent a year.

a. Approximately how much is the corrected APR or the "true" cost of borrowing for Fred?

b. What alternative loan sources should he investigate?

c. Using the table on page 88, what would his monthly payments be?

d. How much more in total interest would he pay if he borrowed $3,000 for five years instead of three?

3. Peter and Ellen Smith are considering borrowing $5,000 to buy a lot. They list the following information.

Monthly take-home pay	$700
Food, clothing, shelter, insurance	350
Current monthly installment payments	110
Total debt outstanding	900
Liquid assets (savings)	200

Applying the four tests given in this chapter to Peter and Ellen's situation, determine if and how soon they can afford additional debt and approximately how much additional debt they can afford.

Chapter 6

Major consumer decisions II: Housing

. . . I am not hungry for berries; I am not hungry for bread. But hungry, hungry for a house . . . .

Gwendolyn Brooks

Whether an apartment, a brick house, a tent, or a condominium, housing is a significant factor in your lifestyle. The variety of people's habitats is endless. So, it seems, are the costs associated with keeping those habitats.

The cost of housing represents one of the largest items in most household budgets, ranking close to the cost of food. Unlike food, however, housing tends to generate a fixed, less controllable stream of costs. Decisions are made less frequently. Thus housing is a major consumer decision.

Data for four-member family budgets shown in Table 6–1 reflect the cost of housing in several selected cities. While there is some variation, something mentioned in Chapter 2 when considering job opportunities, one is impressed by two things—size and uniformity. Around the national average of 19.3 percent of the budget devoted to shelter, the range is 15 to 25 percent for the cities listed.

Since so much money will be spent for shelter over a lifetime, the possible gain associated with managing the housing decision can be large. This major decision can be approached by dealing with the following questions:

- How much housing can I afford?
- Should I rent or buy?
- Is housing a good investment?
- What about the purchase process?
- How does housing fit into my lifestyle?

Table 6–1
Annual costs of an intermediate budget for a four-person family, Autumn 1975
(dollars)

Area	*Total budget*	*Food*	*Housing*	*Transportation*	*Clothing*	*Personal care*	*Medical care*
Northeast							
Boston, Mass.	$18,090	$4,128	$4,865	$1,330	$1,150	$332	$ 791
Lancaster, Pa.	14,939	3,989	3,186	1,251	1,139	322	681
Portland, Me.	15,684	4,171	3,674	1,312	1,155	310	749
Nonmetro areas	15,221	3,911	2,900	1,290	1,030	294	722
North Central							
Cedar Rapids, Iowa	15,265	3,477	3,544	1,314	1,249	356	728
Chicago, Ill.	15,712	3,838	3,788	1,319	1,106	343	877
Milwaukee, Wisc.	16,293	3,549	3,943	1,273	1,237	348	773
Nonmetro areas	14,022	3,515	3,196	1,247	1,098	313	674
South							
Atlanta, Ga.	14,166	3,748	2,928	1,240	1,075	341	795
Dallas, Texas	13,924	3,513	3,035	1,334	1,019	343	924
Orlando, Fla.	13,680	3,410	3,154	1,279	992	305	850
Nonmetro areas	13,253	3,574	2,802	1,263	1,004	304	701
West							
Denver, Colo.	14,724	3,623	3,120	1,275	1,316	312	774
Los Angeles, Calif.	15,186	3,656	3,441	1,336	1,110	326	1,001
Honolulu, Hawaii	18,694	4,603	4,415	1,438	1,096	385	864
Nonmetro areas	13,801	3,423	3,027	1,234	1,118	319	740
Anchorage, Alaska	21,229	4,581	5,838	1,523	1,330	463	1,286

Source: *Handbook of Labor Statistics, 1977*, pp. 272–73.

RENT OR BUY?

Almost any form of housing can be purchased or rented. Some people who could easily purchase a house choose to rent. The decision is more than a simple question of dollars and cents. As with all decisions, there are questions of security, preferences for certain styles of living, pride in ownership versus freedom to relocate, and other personal considerations. Some of the major advantages and disadvantages are listed in Table 6–2 for three housing options—apartment, house, and mobile home, each of which may be rented or purchased.

Table 6–2
Modes of housing—plus and minus

Apartment	+	Free to move on short notice, if renting
	+	Group recreational and social facilities
	+	Low maintenance expenses
	+	Small deposit needed, if renting
	–	You must get along with landlord
	–	Problems for large families or pets
	–	No investment gain, if renting
House	+	Pride of ownership, if purchasing
	+	Wide choice of styles and construction
	+	Privacy
	+	Investment gain after several years, if purchasing
	–	Reduces mobility relative to apartment
	–	Maintenance costs are higher
	–	Utility bills higher, because of larger size
	–	Cash on hand necessary if buying
Mobile home	+	Convenient, for small families
	+	Mobile home parks provide recreational facilities
	+	Low maintenance
	+	Low cost of ownership or rental
	+	Lower property taxes than conventional house
	–	Restricted locations, zoning laws
	–	Close contact with neighbors in park
	–	Limited gain on investment, if buying

WHAT ABOUT THE COST?

People who rent apartments and houses to others are in business for a profit. Obviously, if they are to survive, they have to make a return on their management effort and be compensated for their risk. Otherwise they might choose to invest in some other type of asset. The main element of risk or cost is the prospect of vacant units. When everything else is equal, these two costs—*management fee* and *occupancy risk*—add up to a basic difference in the cost of owning your own home or renting one. When you are the owner and manager these two costs are internalized. Offsetting this saving from ownership—assuming occupancy risk and management responsibility—are other considerations. How long do you expect to be in a particular location? What are your investment alternatives? What is the value of your time? What effects do tax deductions and inflation have on your decision?

Of all these considerations, the tax effect is most significant in dollar terms. Remember, mortgage interest expenses are tax deductible. And the interest portion of a mortgage payment is heavy, particularly during the early years of a mortgage.

Business Week magazine reported a rent-buy comparison for different housing alternatives which takes some of these questions into account.[1] Their study is based on a family of four, paying average income taxes. It was assumed that a purchased house would appreciate in value at 7.5 percent per year, a fairly realistic assumption for our inflation-biased economy. The terms of the mortgage in their study were 20 percent down payment, 9.25 percent interest, and 25 years to pay. To draw an accurate comparison, they assumed that the renter placed his or her down payment fund into an investment which yielded 10 percent annually.

Each of their families was faced with a decision to buy or to rent. If they buy, they invest money in a house which appreciates in value. Notice the *leverage* which they gain. With a down payment of 20 percent they obtain a large asset which increases in value. The 20 percent serves as a lever for the 80 percent borrowed. Furthermore, interest cost of the investment becomes a tax deduction for the owner. If the family rents, they have only their down payment to invest, and no interest to deduct on their tax return. In fact, interest earned on their savings becomes taxable income.

Charts A–D, taken from the *Business Week* study, show the result. Note the significant differences: federal taxes are always higher for the renter, but combined taxes and living expenses may be lower. Of course, there is no equity build-up for the renter. Recall that in the comparison the renter has a one-time cash investment which provides income.

One caution should be observed in considering the advantage of owning. There is a heavy one-time cost associated with buying. *Closing costs,* the cost of initiating a mortgage, obtaining legal title, and paying certain transactions taxes, run two to three percent of the mortgage value. This cost is paid at the time the loan is made. Thus, you don't want to rush in and buy a house unless you expect to be in it for several years because of the large transactions cost. Of course, if you just love owning your own home, you may be willing to pay that high one-time price for just short periods of ownership. In any case, closing costs are a significant consideration.

---

[1] Reprinted from the January 12, 1976, issue of *Business Week* by special permission.

Chart A
Buy or rent?
(income: $25,000/home: $40,000)

	House	Condominium	Co-op	Rent
Your tax deductions:				
Exemptions and miscellaneous	$ 5,200	$5,200	$ 5,200	$5,200
Mortgage interest	2,946	2,946	3,186	0
Real estate tax	1,200	1,200	1,200	0
Total	9,346	9,346	9,586	5,200
Your federal tax bill	3,025	3,025	2,964	4,352
Your living costs:				
Homeowner insurance	175	175	175	75
Real estate taxes	1,200	1,200	1,200	0
Maintenance	420	210	210	0
Utilities	840	600	600	840
Heating	1,200	800	800	0
Maintenance charge	0	480	1,600	0
Rent or mortgage payments	3,288	3,288	3,489	4,200
Total living costs	7,123	6,753	8,074	5,115
Total costs (taxes and living expenses)	$10,148	$9,778	$11,038	$9,467
How your equity increases:		End 1 year	+ $ 1,960	0
		End 5 years	+ $ 9,300	0
		End 10 years	+ $17,500	0
		End 15 years	+ $23,800	0

Chart B
Buy or rent?
(income: $35,000/home: $50,000)

	House	Condominium	Co-op	Rent
Your tax deductions:				
Exemptions and miscellaneous	$ 6,000	$ 6,000	$ 6,000	$ 6,000
Mortgage interest	3,682	3,682	3,983	0
Real estate tax	1,500	1,500	1,500	0
Total	11,182	11,182	11,483	6,000
Your federal tax bill	4,995	4,995	4,899	6,900
Your living costs:				
Homeowner insurance	200	200	200	90
Real estate taxes	1,500	1,500	1,500	0
Maintenance	420	210	210	0
Utilities	840	700	700	840
Heating	1,200	800	800	0
Maintenance charge	0	600	2,400	0
Rent or mortgage payments	4,111	4,111	4,362	5,400
Total living costs	8,271	8,121	10,172	6,330
Total costs (taxes and living expenses)	$13,266	13,116	$15,071	$13,230
How your equity increases:		End 1 year	+ $ 2,700	0
		End 5 years	+ $15,400	0
		End 10 years	+ $30,000	0
		End 15 years	+ $43,000	0

Chart C
Buy or rent?
(income: $50,000/home: $70,000)

	House	***Condominium***	***Co-op***	***Rent***
Your tax deductions:				
Exemptions and miscellaneous	$ 6,625	$ 6,625	$ 6,625	$ 6,625
Mortgage interest	5,154	5,154	5,576	0
Real estate tax	2,100	2,100	2,100	0
Total	13,879	13,879	14,301	6,625
Your federal tax bill	9,214	9,214	9,038	12,704
Your living costs:				
Homeowner insurance	220	220	220	100
Real estate taxes	2,100	2,100	2,100	0
Maintenance	600	300	300	0
Utilities	900	750	750	840
Heating	1,680	1,120	1,120	0
Maintenance charge	0	840	3,080	0
Rent or mortgage payments	5,754	5,754	6,106	6,600
Total living costs	11,254	11,084	13,676	7,540
Total costs (taxes and living expenses)	$20,468	$20,298	$22,714	$20,244

How your equity increases:	End 1 year + $ 4,420	0
	End 5 years + $25,000	0
	End 10 years + $49,400	0
	End 15 years + $72,000	0

Chart D
Buy or rent?
(income: $70,000/home: $100,000)

	House	***Codominium***	***Co-op***	***Rent***
Your tax deductions:				
Exemptions and miscellaneous	$14,000	$14,000	$14,000	$14,000
Mortgage interest	7,364	7,364	7,966	0
Real estate tax	3,000	3,000	3,000	0
Total	24,364	24,364	24,966	14,000
Your federal tax bill	12,989	12,989	12,700	18,565
Your living costs:				
Homeowner insurance	275	275	275	150
Real estate taxes	3,000	3,000	3,000	0
Maintenance	720	350	350	0
Utilities	960	800	800	960
Heating	1,680	1,120	1,120	0
Maintenance charge	0	1,200	6,080	0
Rent or mortgage payments	8,221	8,221	8,724	9,000
Total living costs	14,856	14,966	20,349	10,110
Total costs (taxes and living expenses)	$27,845	$27,955	$33,049	$28,675

How your equity increases:	End 1 year + $ 7,450	0
	End 5 years + $ 41,900	0
	End 10 years + $ 84,400	0
	End 15 years + $126,000	0

IS HOUSING A GOOD INVESTMENT?

Buying a house is much like investing in stocks and bonds. It is possible to make money or lose money on the investment itself. Of course, unlike stocks and bonds, a house can be lived in and enjoyed. Some miserly souls may feel the same attachment to their stock certificates!

How has housing performed as an investment asset? One way of answering that question is found in a series maintained by the U.S. Department of Commerce. A standard house has been defined and the sales price of this hypothetical house has been tracked through time. The figures in Tables 6–3 and 6–4 summarize its performance as an asset, based on two alternative measures. Table 6–3 is a housing price index for the United States for four different regions with 1972 equal to 100 percent. You can calculate the percentage change from year to year and see how housing values have increased. For example, take the West in 1974 and compare the price index with 1975. The percentage change from 126.3 to 141.7 is 12.1 percent. Note the dramatic differences in the index between regions for the identical house.

Table 6–3
U.S. housing price index
(1972 = 100)

Year	*United States*	*Northeast*	*North Central*	*South*	*West*
1973	108.9	108.4	107.7	106.9	112.7
1974	119.1	118.3	115.8	115.2	126.3
1975	131.0	128.3	126.8	125.7	141.7
1976	142.0	133.5	138.1	134.6	157.3

Source: *U.S. Department of Commerce News* (November 11, 1977).

Table 6–4
Average sales prices for new one-family houses in United States

Year	*Price*	*Year-to-year increase (percent)*
1971	$30,700	
1972	32,700	+6.5%
1973	35,600	+8.8
1974	38,900	+9.2
1975	42,800	+10.0
1976	46,400	+8.4
1977*	52,400	+12.9

* Preliminary.
Source: *U.S. Department of Commerce News* (November 11, 1977).

Table 6–4 gives the average sales price for the standard house. Here you see that the same house which sold for $30,700 in 1971 cost $52,400 in 1977. The year-to-year increase is also shown. Based on the figures in Table 6–4, the standard house appreciated in value at an average rate of approximately nine percent per year from 1971 to 1977. This is slightly better than the increase in the cost of living as measured by the consumer price index (CPI) across the same period. Thus, the average person who owned housing during this period had a hedge against inflation, a pretty good investment.

For many people housing is the best investment they make in a lifetime. Some refer to purchased housing as a "forced" saving because house payments have to be made, and the equity in the house increases from year to year. You might consider this investment somewhat like an ordinary life insurance policy—there is an element of cost, an element of saving, and a return to the savings element in the form of increased value.

DOWN PAYMENTS, INTEREST RATES, AND MORTGAGE LENGTH

When borrowing money for housing you may select from several lenders. But no matter where you go to borrow, there are some common variables to consider and the same decisions to be made. "Will I make a large down payment and go for a short mortgage or will I put a small amount down?" "Should I wait for lower interest rates, if they appear likely in the near future?" Each of these is a judgmental decision, but some of the financial dimensions of the problem can be identified.

Chapter 5 indicated the interest cost of smaller *down payments* and longer repayment periods. These considerations are even more important in a long-term large transaction such as buying a house as indicated in Table 6–5. Table 6–5 shows the effect of various down payments on the size of the monthly payments and the total interest paid.

Table 6–5
Effect of size of loan
($44,000 house, 8.75% interest, 25 years)

Down payment	*Amount of loan*	*Monthly payment*	*Total interest*
$4,000	$40,000	$332.53	$59,760
6,000	38,000	315.90	54,772
8,000	36,000	299.28	53,784

The length of time you take to repay a loan also has a bearing on the amount of interest you will pay. There is the external trade-off to consider: the longer the time, the smaller the payment. However, interest costs increase dramatically as time increases, as indicated in Table 6–6.

Table 6–6
Effect of repayment period
($40,000 loans, 8.75% interest)

Payment period (years)	*Monthly payment*	*Total interest*
20	$358.70	$46,088
25	332.53	59,760
30	317.30	74,228

Finally, you must consider the interest rate on the mortgage. A borrower has little, if any, control over the interest rate. National financial markets determine the going rates. But rates do change significantly through time, and the rate you pay when you take on a mortgage may be with you for many years. In addition to national economic forces, some 15 states have *usury laws* which set upper limits for mortgage interest rates. Such constraints may seem wonderful to the borrower who gets a loan at rates below the national average, but artificial controls reduce the amount of money available to lenders in the limiting states. It is likely that down payments will

"Whatever you do, don't invite the Cosworth's. I'm sick and tired of hearing about their 5½% mortgage."

Reprinted by permission The Wall Street Journal

be higher and credit checks much more severe. Savers like to put their funds in those places where the return is highest.

It may be possible to postpone borrowing if rates are unusually high in hopes that they will soon fall. At any given time and interest rate level, the precise rate you pay will depend on the risk involved in your individual loan. Lenders prefer that you have a substantial financial commitment to the house. They know that you will take better care of the property and be more punctual in making your monthly payment if you have a "piece of the action." For example, in 1976 savings and loan associations in South Carolina were charging 9 percent for 90 percent loans; 8.5 percent for 75 percent loans. The effect of interest rates on monthly payments and total interest is shown in Table 6–7. All these factors—interest, amount borrowed, and time—are combined in Table 6–8.

Table 6–7
Effect of interest rate
($40,000 loan, 8.75% interest, 25 years)

Interest rate	*Monthly payment*	*Total interest*
8%	$312	$53,680
8.5	325	57,720
8.75	332	59,760
9	339	61,810
9.5	353	65,960

Table 6–8
Monthly mortgage payments per $1,000 for typical interest rates and time periods*

	Interest rate						
Years	*8.00*	*8.25*	*8.50*	*8.75*	*9.00*	*9.25*	*9.50*
20	8.36	8.52	8.68	8.84	9.00	9.16	9.32
25	7.72	7.88	8.05	8.22	8.39	8.56	8.74
30	7.34	7.51	7.69	7.87	8.05	8.23	8.41
33	7.18	7.36	7.54	7.73	7.91	8.10	8.28
35	7.10	7.29	7.47	7.65	7.84	8.03	8.22

Note: To use this table you must know the interest rate and the number of years and amount you want to borrow. For example, you can borrow $18,000 for 20 years at 8.75 percent interest. The approximate monthly payment would be calculated as follows:

$$18 \times \$8.84 = \$159.12.$$

* Based on principal of $1,000.
Source: Prepared by John B. Gatch.

HOW MUCH HOUSING CAN I AFFORD?

If you do make that decision to buy a house or condominium, the next issue is how much you can afford. There are some rules of thumb to help in answering the question. These rules are based on the experience of many, many households; thus, they are worth considering.

To get started you must develop a new household budget on the assumption that you have bought that dream house or condominium. You might use the same list when considering a new apartment. There are always some new expenses associated with a new lifestyle. You may be surprised when your "necessities" begin to include homeowners insurance, garden tools, lawnmower, new furniture, drapes, carpets, property taxes, and higher utility bills. This begins a list which can be as short or as long as your self-control and imagination make it. So put the figures down carefully. You might use Table 6–9 as a guide.

Table 6–9
New home living costs

Expenses	***Amount***
Utilities:	
Electricity	________
Gas, fuel oil	________
Telephone	________
Water	________
Garbage	________
Sewage fee	________
Day-to-day household operations:	
Cleaning equipment	________
Garden and lawn tools	________
Lines, dishes, etc.	________
Fixed cost fund:	
Insurance (fire, liability, life, etc.)	________
Taxes	________
Repair and improvements:	
Repair and improvements (furnishings, appliances, redecoration)	________
Total housing expenses (excluding mortgage payment):	________

With your total "new home" expenses estimated, you must find the money to cover your monthly payment. Substitute these housing expenses for your present housing expenses in the budget developed in Chapter 3 to see whether the new house leaves you in deficit, in bare minimum balance, or with a little margin for error, extravagance, or surprises.

With the figures from your budget in mind, you can apply some rules of thumb as a simpler approach. One rule is that the total loan you secure should not exceed 2.75 times your annual take-home income. A second rule is that one week's take-home pay should cover your monthly mortgage payment. If your income is on a monthly basis, multiply your take-home pay by 0.23 to get the maximum monthly house payment. These should come out to about the same figure. Remember, your bank will eye your plans to borrow with these rules in mind.

After making these estimates, you may find that something has to give. You can lower your sights on the house if necessary, or pull in your belt on the expenses. But be realistic. Nothing is worse than owning a house or condominium and not being able to enjoy it because of empty rooms, bare walls, or an air-conditioner which you can't afford to use.

THE PURCHASE PROCESS

Buying a house, condominium, or mobile home is somewhat like buying a car. You have to shop and "dicker" with the seller. Shopping begins usually with the newspaper. Very quickly location decisions have to be made. And there are many important considerations in the choice of a house which is right for you. As someone has said, the decision to buy a house includes three major factors—location, location, and location.

Specifically, consider where the house is in relation to your place of work, recreation, worship, family locations, schools, and other points to which you might be oriented. Transportation is a major issue. The house you live in becomes a focal point in your transportation system.

When you consider specific houses in particular neighborhoods you will want to keep in mind the adage of the real estate salesman—"Don't overbuy the neighborhood." In other words don't buy the only $50,000 house in a subdivision of $35,000 homes. The appreciation of real property values is caused in part by the interaction of adjacent properties. The higher priced homes tend to be reduced in value by the less expensive ones, whereas the reverse works in favor of the lower priced homes.

Contracts with builders, realtors, and owners develop quickly in the search process. A realtor will usually earn a 6 percent commission for his or her services, but the fee may well be worth the cost. (Although the commission is paid by the seller, not the buyer, some or all of it will be reflected in the price of the house.)

Using a realtor may well be a question of time. Your time may be more valuable to your earning a living than searching for houses and dickering with sellers. The realtor specializes; you may wish to also.

Once the final selection has been made you will begin the bargaining process. A formal offer must be made. Usually the offer will be a contract to buy, subject to loan approval, which you will sign and give to the seller or agent. Don't be bashful when making the offer. You may want to offer less than the listed price, although in doing so you run the risk that your offer may be turned down and another accepted before you can get back with a higher offer. On the other hand, you may save a few thousand dollars by "dickering." The price of a house is not really determined until it is actually sold. Until that point is reached, all you have are bid and asked prices.

The formal offer should specify the conditions of the property to be purchased, as well as a legal description. Changes which you desire such as landscaping, painting, electrical work, or plumbing should be stated. If the house or apartment is presently occupied you should list the items which you expect to go with the house—special lighting fixtures, drapes, blinds, carpet, window air-conditioners, shrubs, or any other item you may have discussed with the seller.

A *binder check* will normally accompany your offer. This earnest money may be $500 or $1,000 and will apply to the purchase price if your offer is accepted. However, if the offer is accepted and you back out, kiss the money goodbye.

If the offer is accepted, the next step is to find a lender. Most likely you will have already investigated lenders before making your offer. Lenders and types of loans come in a surprising variety.

Home loans are available in the following types and sources.

Type	***Source***
Conventional	Savings and loan associations Mutual savings banks Insurance companies Mortgage bankers
Federal Housing Administration (insured)	Mortgage bankers Insurance companies Savings and loans
Veterans Administration (guaranteed)	All of the above
Farmers Home Administration	Farmers Home Administration district offices
Federal Land Bank	Federal Land Bank or Production Credit Association district offices

"Conventional" loans are no more conventional than the others listed; however, they have that label because they originated with the older lenders. They are loans between private parties—for example, savings and loan associations and individual borrowers. There is no major element of government subsidy, insurance, or control in the transaction. You would generally expect to pay at least 10 percent down on a loan of this type, with the expectation that the lender might well require mortgage guaranty insurance which would pay off the loan if you defaulted. When mortgage insurance is required, you will have an additional fee added to your monthly payment.

Twenty percent down is more typical. A lower interest rate loan is likely with a larger down payment from any lender because the lender views your down payment as your stake in the property. You will show greater concern for the property if you have more of your hard-earned cash in it.

Federal Housing Administration (FHA) insured mortgages are "conventional" in the sense that they are loans between private parties. They are special because an agency of the federal government provides insurance that the loan will be paid off. FHA performs the role of a *cosigner*. You have someone backing your credit. Of course you will pay a price for this in the amount of 0.5 percent of the mortgage balance owed.

The attraction of the FHA-insured mortgage is twofold. First, people who might not qualify for loans otherwise can borrow because of the insurance feature. In addition, it is possible to borrow with a lower down payment. There are also disadvantages. One is the limit; FHA will insure loans up to $45,000. The insurance does not replace your down payment. FHA loans require at least 3 percent down on the first $25,000, 10 percent on the next $10,000, and 20 percent on the excess over $35,000.

Because of the role of FHA as an insurer, the government sets the maximum interest rate which can be charged on the mortgage. In 1978 it was 9.5 percent, a rate which corresponded to the market rate. When the FHA rate is lower than the market rate the borrower must somehow compensate the lender for the interest which he forgoes in making FHA loans instead of conventional ones. This is done by the payment of *"points."* One point is equal to one percent of the amount of the loan. On a loan of $30,000, one point would equal $300. There is generally a charge of eight points for each percent difference between the going rate on conventional mortgages and the FHA ceiling rate. This payment is made at the time of the loan.

In addition to this charge, FHA loans generally cost more for the lender to handle. The government requires special inspections of the property. Every step of the closing process is involved because of the role played by FHA as an insurer of your loan. To see if FHA is more advantageous than a conventional loan, you must compare costs. Some of the features serve to reduce your costs, others increase them.

If you are a veteran, you should check to see if you qualify for a *VA-guaranteed loan*. Once again, an agency of the federal government offers the possibility of putting its credit on the line with yours. There are a number of details to be worked out in getting your *certificate of eligibility* from the Veterans Administration (VA) and the details change. Thus, you should check with your local VA office and follow its advice.

To a certain extent the VA-guaranteed loan is similar to FHA-insured loans. The lending process is more expensive because closing costs are higher and because interest rate ceilings on loans may require that you pay points, as on an FHA loan. There is no cash down payment required on VA loans so long as the appraised value of the property is no greater than the amount of the loan. The lender will be one of the sources listed in the chart.

They will work with the Veterans Administration in handling the guarantee based upon your Certificate of Eligibility. You must realize that the loan is still voluntary from the standpoint of the lender. Eligibility makes it possible for you to qualify for the VA process but it does not insure that a loan will be forthcoming.

If you live in a rural area, you may be able to borrow from the *Farmers Home Administration* or the *Federal Land Bank*. Farmers Home makes loans in towns of less than 10,000 population or in rural unincorporated areas, generally to families who cannot borrow from other sources. The interest charge may be quite low. However, there are income limits on these loans which are quite restrictive. If your family income is much above $10,000, you might as well forget this possibility. Check with Farmers Home to see what the standards are in your area.

Still another possibility is the Federal Land Bank which is a private lender, not a branch of the federal government. In effect, this bank sells bonds and then lends money to people in rural areas having a population of 2,500 or less. Their mortgage loans have a maximum length of 30 years for amounts up to $33,000. Generally all Federal Land Bank loans are for 80 percent of the appraised value of the property. The loans have one unique feature, however. The interest rate charged is variable: it goes up and down with the market rate. Thus, you might borrow and be paying at the rate of 8.75 percent. At a later date, the bank finds it is able to obtain money at a lower rate. As a result, your interest charge goes down. Rates can also go up in response to market interest rates.

It is worth your time to check each of the sources mentioned here. A few

Table 6–10
Steps in financing a home

				Survey and title search	***Closing the loan you could pay***
Loan application →	Credit check →	Appraisal →	Loan approval →	Mortgage and note Terms and clauses →	Origination fee (Association fee) Attorney's fee Appraisal fee Credit report fee Title insurance Survey Recording fees Revenue stamps Deed preparation Deed stamp and recording tax
Get legal assistance to represent you in all paper work					

telephone calls may turn up a better deal. But be careful. Ask about membership fees, closing costs, points, down payment, and maximum length. You want to be sure that the full cost is considered.

STEPS IN FINANCING A HOME

Once you have selected a lender you will begin a rather complex process. Much of this process has been mentioned in our earlier discussion. In general, the process will take the steps described in Table 6–10.

THINGS TO CONSIDER IN CHOOSING A MORTGAGE LENDER

In addition to the important considerations already discussed, you will want to have firm answers to the following questions:

- Is there a penalty for *early payoff*?
- Can the mortgage be assumed by another person?
- Can I renegotiate the interest rate, if rates go down?
- Will the lender collect funds from me and pay my property taxes and insurance?
- Can I add to the loan if I wish to enlarge my house or acquire other property?

The first question can be significant. Suppose you come into some cash and wish to pay off your mortgage. Or, perhaps you find a lower interest rate elsewhere and you want to pay off one loan and borrow from another lender. If there is a penalty, you may be limited in either of these strategies. Many mortgages allow payoff without penalty.

The mortgage is usually the property of the lender. Any transfer to another borrower must be made with the lender's approval. How difficult is it? If you have an attractive mortgage, one with a low interest rate, you may have a plus when you try to sell your house if the lender will be willing to transfer it.

With Federal Land Bank loans the interest moves up and down, but with most other lenders there is a fixed rate of interest. Again, there are questions you will need answered. What if you have a 9.75 percent loan and the rate falls to 7 percent? Can you refinance? How easy is it? What are the penalties?

When you borrow for a house you will be required to buy an insurance policy. You may choose to have comprehensive homeowner's coverage or the minimum the lender requires. (See Chapter 12.) In addition, you will be paying property taxes. Many lenders set up an *escrow account* into which you pay a monthly amount and from which they pay your loan-associated expenses, specifically taxes and insurance. In some cases, you will receive interest on the escrow account while the funds are accumulating. The whole matter is generally one of convenience. (When you sell your house, if you have an escrow account, remember to settle its disposition with the buyer.)

Finally, you may wish to improve your house or condominium. Will it be necessary for you to get a new loan, renegotiate your old one, or can you just add to the existing mortgage? Ask about this when you talk with the lending firms.

THE CLOSING PROCESS

Once all these questions have been settled and you have made the deal, the day will come when you, the seller, and the lender meet together around a mahogany table and clinch the deal. It's called the *closing*. For you, it is the beginning.

In this process many things are happening. Generally your attorney and the attorney for the lender will be present. Legal rights will be transferred. All costs associated with closing and the down payment will be made. You will assume a loan and receive a legal deed and a payment book. The latter will be with you for some time.

There are many peculiarities in the various states which will affect your particular closing. Table 6–11 is a statement of loan costs from a savings and

Table 6–11
Statement of loan costs from a savings and loan association in South Carolina

	Plan 1	*Plan 2*	*Plan 3*
Cost/value of property	$40,000.00	$40,000.00	$40,000.00
Down payment	8,000.00	4,000.00	2,000.00
Amount of loan	32,000.00	36,000.00	38,000.00
Basic loan costs:			
Association charge (1%)	320.00	360.00	380.00
Attorney's fee ($100 + 0.25%)	180.00	190.00	195.00
Recording fee	7.50	7.50	7.50
S.C. documentary stamps (0.4%)	12.80	14.40	15.20
Loan insurance premium	–0–	200.00	400.00
Credit report	10.00	10.00	10.00
Total loan costs	530.30	781.90	1,007.70
Other costs:			
1st year property insurance	240.00	240.00	240.00
Interest (any part of month remaining to 1st)	?	?	?
Stamps on deed	44.00	44.00	44.00
Total other costs	284.00+	284.00+	284.00+
Cash requirements:			
Down payment	8,000.00	4,000.00	2,000.00
Basic loan costs	530.30	781.90	1,007.70
Other costs	284.00+	284.00+	284.00+
Total cash requirements	8,814.30+	5,065.90+	3,291.70+
Monthly payments 25 years at	8.75%	9%	9%
Principal and interest	$263.36	$302.40	$319.20
1/12 annual insurance	20.00	20.00	20.00
1/12 annual property taxes	27.00	27.00	27.00
1/12 annual loan insurance premium	–0–	7.50	7.92
Total monthly payment	310.36	356.90	374.12

loan association in South Carolina. Most of these costs will be found in other states. There are three plans shown based on differing amounts of down payment. Note that the interest rate varies with the down payment. You can check through the line items and get some idea of the total process involved when a house is purchased.

HOW DOES HOUSING FIT INTO MY LIFESTYLE?

Since everyone has to live somewhere, this chapter has described the major financial choices which will be available to you. Along the way there has been some discussion of your lifestyle and how your choice of housing affects your general happiness. Emphasis was also placed on the role of housing as an investment since for most people, it is the largest single purchase for both consumption and investment.

Since we have compared purchasing housing to buying a life insurance policy or other methods of "forced" savings you may want to know how you might use these savings as your housing needs change. First, if you purchase a house in your early adult life, you will have accumulated some cash value in it by the time your children are college age. At that point, you might want to refinance your house, obtain money for college expenses, and resume the payments on the mortgage. If you don't have educational expenses to worry about, you may want to start a business or take a once-in-a-lifetime vacation using the same strategy.

If you reach retirement years with a house in which you have lived for a long time, it is likely that your house no longer fits your lifestyle. Consider selling it and using the funds to acquire a more suitable home, or renting the house and using the money to cover retirement. There is a tax consideration here which may encourage you to sell at retirement. Usually, you have to pay income taxes on gains from investments, including the gains from selling your housing investment. However, you may have a tax-free gain available to you once in your life, when you sell your house at or after age 65. Check the latest income tax rules, Uncle Sam may have made it a little easier for you to get your money and yourself out of your house and into another lifestyle.

SUMMARY

The purchase of housing is one of the biggest financial decisions most people will ever undertake. Often renting is a better short-term solution, depending on mobility, income, tax bracket, and other considerations. In addition to its function as a major consumer good, housing has also proved an attractive investment in recent years.

The down payment and repayment period will be important in determining the size of the monthly payment and the repayment period. The total amount of housing you can afford to buy is a function of your income and nonhousing expenditure patterns, subject to some rules of thumb which lenders apply.

The purchase process begins with the search, bearing in mind location, neighborhood, and your family's needs and preferences. This is followed by an offer, a financing arrangement with one of a number of possible lending sources, and finally a closing. The choice of a mortgage lender should be given considerable thought because of differences in closing costs, interest rates, prepayment penalties, escrow accounts, and other factors which may affect your total costs and/or your ability to sell the house in the future.

The investment in the house can be tapped for education, retirement, and other needs either by refinancing or (particularly at retirement) by selling.

KEY WORDS

Binder check
Certificate of eligibility
Closing
Closing costs
Conventional loan
Cosigner
Down payment
Early payoff
Escrow account
Farmers Home Administration
Federal Housing Administration
Federal Land Bank
Leverage
Management fee
Occupancy risk
Points
Usury laws
VA-guaranteed loans

PROBLEMS

1. Richard Small has an annual take-home salary of $30,000. At present he estimates his marginal income tax rate to be 25 percent. (The marginal rate is the percent he pays on the last dollars of his income or the amount of tax he avoids when his taxable income is reduced by some amount.) Richard is considering the purchase of a $50,000 home. He has $10,000 saved for the down payment. He can obtain a 9.25 percent loan for 25 years. In talking with the lender, Richard learns that about 90 percent of the mortgage payments made in the first four years will be interest. That is, only 10 percent of his payments will go toward the reduction of the loan itself. What advice will you give Small regarding his plans?

2. You have been assigned a temporary position with your firm which will require you to live for four years in the Washington, D.C. area. At present you are renting an apartment but had made plans to buy a home. Your income is $35,000 per year. Consider the rent-or-buy problem from the standpoint of your four-year assignment. What are the pros and cons of buying versus renting?

Chapter 7

Consumer power in our market economy

Some see private enterprise as a predatory target to be shot, others as a cow to be milked, but few are those who see it as a sturdy horse pulling the wagon.

Winston Churchill

INTRODUCTION

A market economy is recognized by the extent to which consumers and producers enter into voluntary transactions. As active participants in the system it is sometimes difficult to really understand the role of the individual consumer in the overall economy and to recognize his power in determining what will be produced. It's more than not being able to see the trees for the forest; we *are* trees in the forest. And each one of us has some degree of power over the size and shape of the forest.

Sometimes the simplest of actions reveals the most powerful of all concepts. For example, consider this: A consumer walks into a supermarket. Note that this is done voluntarily. He walks through the store, examining items and their prices as he walks. The consumer makes a decision. He voluntarily takes a particular brand of peanut butter off the shelf and puts it in his basket. For some reason, he chooses one brand at the expense of the others. Going on through the store, the consumer selects other items, buying beef, *not pork chops,* a bottle of wine, *not beer,* a loaf of wheat bread, *not plain bread.* All the while, he may be tallying the total cost of his selections trying to see if he will have enough money left to buy some gas for the trip home. Realizing that he has gone over his budget, the consumer *voluntarily* decides to put the peanut butter back on the shelf. He has traded off some peanut butter for gasoline!

Now the big moment comes. The consumer goes through the check-out. The clerk voluntarily gives up the items in the basket to the consumer in exchange for his money. What can we conclude?

Why would the store prefer money to food? And why would the consumer prefer food to money? Apparently both parties think that they will be better off having made the exchange. And since they entered into the transaction voluntarily, who can say otherwise? But the beef may be old; the wine may be sour; and the bread may be moldy; and the money may be counterfeit! While these things may and do happen, their occurrence is the exception, not the rule. Why?

This chapter will provide an answer to the questions just posed and elaborate on the point made in this simple example. Looking at the consumer and his role in our market economy, the following questions will be addressed:

- How do consumers influence economic activity?
- Do buyers have power? How can they better use it?
- Do citizens have power as consumer?
- What role has government taken in consumer affairs?

HOW DO CONSUMERS INFLUENCE ECONOMIC ACTIVITY?

From our introduction, it is apparent that consumer choices influence the prices and composition of goods and services available in the market. Because of consumer preferences, many products never see the light of day. That is, firms develop products which they think might sell and then test-market them. If consumers leave the goods on the shelf, the firm goes back to the drawing board. However, if the shelves empty quickly, the firm expands output. In other cases, firms develop new and better products through chemistry, test them, build plants to produce them, cover the market with advertising, ship the goods to stores, and then see the goods returned unsold. Shoes made of Corfam are an example. The consumer decided that leather, or canvas, or going barefoot was better! Obviously, the goods we see being sold through time are those which have passed the market test. While we might wonder why certain things are not produced, we can generally be assured that those things produced must satisfy enough people to keep the goods on the market. The fact that our favorite flavor of ice cream or most-preferred color of paint is not available in the market generally indicates that there is insufficient demand to bring the goods forward. At a price, however, someone would probably provide even the strangest product.

The examples just given may seem trivial, but they illustrate a basic point. There must be sufficient consumer demand for particular products in order for them to compete for the consumer dollar. And so long as consumers purchase those things on the market, it is likely that they will continue to be supplied. But it may be difficult to match precise specifications to available products. What about cars which give 50 miles to the gallon or food which has no additives? The goods desired are usually available in some form, but not in every form. That is, one can buy a Honda and get high mileage, but one cannot buy a Cadillac and expect the same fuel economy. Natural foods are available also, at a price. But all foods are not produced with the same recipe. The *heterogeneity of products* in the market reflects the variety of tastes and incomes present in the population.

Competition between firms brings variety to the consumer. Where only one firm or agent provides a good, it is quite possible that the producer will be less sensitive to the changing demands of the consumer. For example, one can look at a shopping center parking lot and observe the large variety of cars driven by consumers. Sometimes it is difficult to find any two cars which are identical. The same is true with clothing and prepared food. The interesting and varied tastes of consumers are reflected by the purchases. However, where monopolies have been granted by government or where the market will only support one firm, uniformity tends to prevail. The hours for all post offices are the same and the variety of services they offer are identical. Of course, it is illegal for anyone to compete with the post office by offering to carry scheduled mail. Along the same lines, telephone service, which comes with a monopoly license from government, tends to be uniform across fairly large geographical areas. You can consider local monopolies in the same way to see if the idea holds. Many communities can only support one bank or one shoe store. Depending on the distance to the next competing place of business, service can be less consumer oriented and more related to the convenience of the employees of the bank or store.

All the products in the marketplace are substitutes for each other. Some are close substitutes—one brand of peanut butter for another. Others are more remote—peanut butter for gasoline. For this reason, competition still exists even when there is only one supplier of a particular good or service. Put differently, consumers still determine the extent to which a seller will set the price or change the quality of his product. That is, *consumer sovereignty* still exists.

It is tempting to belittle consumer sovereignty by saying: "Yes, but people have to have gasoline, peanut butter, telephones, mail service, food, and clothing. So, we are all at the mercy of the sellers?" However, we can observe the behavior of consumers and realize that people do not behave as if they have to have any of these things. That is, when the price goes up, some buyers go away; they substitute.

Economists often summarize the discussion we have given by saying that consumers influence the market by voting. They vote with dollars. And unlike the political mechanism, where one person has one vote which cannot be subdivided among candidates or issues, in the market people can subdivide their votes. They can vote all their income on one product or they can make very fine divisions of their income among thousands of goods. This enables the consumer to register intensity of desire, not just choice. And the message comes through loud and clear. Producers have every reason to respond to their customers. After all, the producers want as many votes as possible. There are many producers, many consumers, and many votes. And the consumer starts with all the votes.

DO BUYERS HAVE POWER? HOW CAN THEY USE IT?

Perhaps you are now convinced that consumers do have power. But do they use it as effectively as they might? Consider this: A consumer has her greatest impact on the market when she considers alternatives for purchases, gathers information before making decisions, and carefully allocates her dollars between competing goods. Indeed, a major purpose of this book and of a course in consumer economics is to have some impact on the process of your individual decision making, in particular to make those choices more deliberate and informed. Better decisions will lead to greater impact in the market. But there is a limiting factor here, an economic consideration. Just as there is an optimal amount of peanut butter or economy cars, there is an optimal amount of effort to be devoted to making choices.

The gains from shopping

A buyer can afford to spend a certain amount of time shopping. What are the gains from shopping? What are the costs? If a person can earn $200 per day at work, it is certainly not worthwhile to take a day off to shop for paint, if the total cost of the paint is less than $200. It would be impossible to save enough by shopping to offset the loss of earnings. In other words, the shopper would have to find a seller who would give him the paint and throw in some brushes in order to come out ahead. The job of shopping (and it is a job) should be assigned to a person whose opportunity cost matches the possible gain from shopping. The market recognizes this. Stores and shopping centers stay open late in the evening and on weekends in those areas where salaries are high. In addition, catalog shopping, telephoning, reading advertising and consumer information magazines, and other efficient methods of search can be employed to make comparisons.

No matter how you shop, eventually decisions have to be made. And informed decisions will have impact. Those decisions will help the seller in his search for the right product to satisfy the consumer. In a market system, both the seller and the buyer are engaged in a search process. Information is transmitted when transactions occur.

The gains from complaining

Information and impact continue to occur after a purchase has been made. In the introduction, it was pointed out that a buyer may pay good money for food which turns out to be garbage. There are occasions when what you get is not exactly what you see. And there are various ways to redress the problem, depending on the nature and extent of the problem. A first and most effective step is taken when the consumer confronts the seller with the problem. Recall that the seller needs information in order to function efficiently. There must be feedback as well as feed-forward in any efficient market.

To have impact when disappointed with a purchase, take a first step by registering a complaint. The sooner, the better. A consumer who pays the posted price is paying for a certain expected amount of satisfaction. When that increment of happiness is not delivered, the seller should be informed. Acting quickly and logically (not emotionally) serves both the buyer and the seller.

In general, dissatisfaction should be registered with someone who can do something about the problem. Generally, however, an unhappy customer holds forth with a salesclerk, waitress, or secretary. A visit to the manager of a store, a telephone call, and preferably a letter to the president of a firm can be time well spent. In each case, the problem should be described carefully, giving all the details—the date of the transaction, who, when, where, what—should be presented. And rather than using heat, at first, to bring results, a little market psychology might help. Let the seller know that you understand the market. In other words, tell the seller that you realize that dissatisfied customers can't help a business and that you want to be helpful. It's been known to work wonders. In fact, recognition of the market's ability to redress consumer problems has led firms to take a number of constructive steps.

It is now the general rule, rather than the exception, for larger firms to have an office of consumer affairs. Generally speaking, such an office has the responsibility to keep the firm aware of consumer interests and to keep consumers aware of the firm's policies and actions. Specialists in consumer economics, consumer law, and other related fields round out the staffs in such organizations. In some cases, panels of consumers from various parts of the country or sectors will be organized to act as a sounding board for managers who may be planning a new product or sales operation. The evidence of these operations is seen in the form of better product labeling, improved packaging, more convenient hours of operation, more carefully written operating instructions for major appliances; that is, better consumer information.

While considering the problems which consumers have and how to make sellers more aware of them, you should also look on the brighter side. There are occasions when clerks in stores, officers in banks, and other managers perform at an exceptional level. If those actions have market value, consumers will respond favorably. Consumers will vote with their dollars! For example, a tire salesclerk may do an unusually good job in following his customers' experience with the firm's product. The clerk may keep them informed of alternative products which they should consider, check on the performance of tires already sold, tell when sales are underway, and keep a running record of cost and mileage for each customer. The customers might respond by giving their business to the salesclerk and by telling their friends. But there is another step which might be taken. Tell the clerk's boss.

Once again, information is most effective when it flows to decision makers. That is, if the manager or owner of the tire firm is told of the outstanding work of the salesclerk, the clerk may be rewarded more quickly. This will encourage the other employees to adopt the successful strategy. In this way, the consumer impact on the market can be increased.

People are generally quick to complain about poor service, but much less efficient in complimenting good service. This behavior is only natural. There is a short-run loss when a product fails prematurely or when service is less than satisfactory. There is no loss when things turn out better than expected. Economic logic tells you that you will not be so diligent in exercising your power for good as when you are damaged. Still, however, long-run considerations suggest that there is a gain to be had in both cases. That is, there is an opportunity cost which you accept when you fail to pass on good news or to compliment the good seller. But there is one result for which you should be prepared. Most managers would faint if they received as many letters complimenting unusually good service as they do complaints for unusually bad service.

A recent experience with household movers is a case in point.[1] Federal regulations require interstate movers to record the estimates they give when contracting to move furniture and other household goods between states. The ultimate rate or cost of moving a certain amount of goods is also regulated. So the bill for moving will be the same, no matter who moves the goods. But initial estimates of the cost may vary from one mover to another.

In examining the estimates, it was found that approximately 50 percent of all estimates fell within plus or minus 10 percent of the final charge. When estimates were lower than the final bill consumers complained. But when estimates were higher than the final charge, no one recorded their surprise. It is only natural. Still, the fact that complaints came in caused the Interstate Commerce Commission (ICC) to propose further regulations for the moving industry.

Doing business with "long-run" firms

Firms of a highly temporary nature may lack the incentive to provide outstanding service. They may not be building for the long run. Indeed, they may not even be building for tomorrow. The door-to-door seller comes to

[1] See 41 *Federal Register* 37350, September 3, 1976.

mind. But we must not castigate all door-to-door salespersons. The Avon representative, for example, is in business for the long run. At least the employer is. Look further. Are there sellers who clearly have no local tie, no apparent investment, no cost associated with leaving a consumer in the lurch? If you can answer yes to these questions when considering a business deal, it might be wise to look elsewhere. You should at least consider the benefits and costs of doing business on such a basis.

Because of the so-called *fly-by-night operator,* people have formed organizations which help in identifying firms. Two of the best known such organizations are the local *Better Business Bureau* and *Chamber of Commerce,* which may provide certification to any seller who requests it and can prove his or her ability to provide satisfaction. Government action also comes to play in this area. Regulations are on the books of some states, and in certain cases, at the *Federal Trade Commission* (FTC), which require a "cooling-off period" during which time a consumer can decide if he really wants to go through with a contract.

In all of this, the best protection comes when an individual decides to look out for himself. After all, no one has any greater incentive than the individual.

LAW AND THE CONSUMER

All things considered, consumers do have impact, even in a market that is not perfect. Consumers will suffer economic losses, and sometimes they will be large. Furthermore, there will be times when a telephone call or letter just won't get a response. There may be questions about what the seller implied when she offered her goods for sale in the market. Questions may also surface about the consumer's effort to carry out the instructions which came with the product. In a large category of cases, consumers may turn to a legal remedy to recover their losses. Their effort will likely be subject to the *Uniform Commercial Code*.

The Uniform Commercial Code (UCC) is a significant law which makes the assumption that the consumer ". . . is entitled to rely on receiving an acceptable level of quality from suppliers and merchants."[2] That is, the UCC presumes that goods sold in commerce will be usable for the purpose stated or as generally expected by a consumer. In a sense, there is an implied warranty associated with merchandise offered for sale to the general public. Of course, a seller may limit his responsibility by use of a disclaimer on any implied warranty. That is, he may state in writing that there is no warranty implied, that the merchandise is offered for sale "as is." In that case, the old rule of *caveat emptor,* "let the buyer beware" applies. There are other limits

[2] William L. Trombetta, "Product Liability and the Uniform Commercial Code," *Atlanta Economic Review* (May–June 1977), p. 22.

to a seller's responsibility which may come to play in a given situation. To some degree these limits turn on reasonable behavior on the part of the seller. Perhaps a seller could not reasonably be expected to foresee the use to which a product might be applied. For example, if a food mixer is used to make concrete, it is highly unlikely that the producer would be made to replace a failed electric motor or the entire mixer. A court might rule that the consumer was responsible for his own damages.

The UCC does provide the legal means for a consumer to recover damages when he or she suffers economic loss as a result of faulty merchandise. The effect of such legal remedies on sellers and buyers is interesting. For both buyer and seller, the cost of carelessness is increased, so both parties to a contract have an incentive to be responsible.

In addition to individual suits which a consumer might file against seller, recent development in the law offers the vehicle of the *class action suit*. The class action suit changes the economic costs of bringing action. For example, if a person finds that her new car has defective brakes, she may grin and bear it and pay the cost of altering the brakes. The cost may be $100, not enough to justify bringing a legal action. But if the unhappy owner finds that a thousand other people have the same problem, she may bring suit in behalf of that class of auto owners. This raises considerably the magnitude of the damages and the importance of the case in the eyes of an attorney and the court.

Class action suits have been supported by state attorneys' general offices as well as by various consumer organizations and trade associations. A case involving the example of faulty wheels will illustrate the process of a class action suit.[3] Two light truck owners found that they had a common problem with 200,000 other owners of General Motors (GM) trucks. The two owners had tried to get their trucks fixed by the dealer, but had not been successful. Thus, they brought a class action suit asking for approximately $430 million in damages. Facing such a suit, GM attempted to settle out of court. GM had a side to the story also. They pointed out that many of the "faulty" wheels had shown up when camper bodies were placed on the trucks. Nonetheless, the attorneys for the plaintiffs continued to pursue court action. Meanwhile GM was voluntarily replacing a large number of faulty wheels.

In 1977, a similar situation developed when the purchaser of a new Oldsmobile learned that his car had a Chevrolet engine in it. (The Chevrolet engine was for all practical purposes identical to the Oldsmobile engine, but there were minor differences.) It seems that GM had engine shortages at the Oldsmobile division and so it substituted the similar Chevrolet engine. Still, the buyer felt that he had been misled by GM advertising and the dealer

---

[3] See Ronald G. Shafer, "Consumer in Court," in *Consumerism*, ed. Barbara M. Murry (Pacific Palisades, Calif.: Goodyear Publishing Co., 1973), pp. 373–77.

which sold the car. A suit was filed in behalf of all similar car owners. Other suits were filed by state attorneys in behalf of citizens who might similarly be damaged. In this case, GM offered either to extend the warranty of the Chevy–Olds engines or to accept the used vehicles in on trade, charging a nominal fee per mile driven up to the time of trade. GM has also become more careful when writing advertising copy.

TESTING SERVICES

A competitive market responds to costs no matter what the source. As a result of consumer impact registered by dollar votes and legal costs which might result when products are less than represented, old firms leave the market and new ones enter. In addition to the entry and exit of producers, other more specialized firms emerge. Independent laboratories, for example, earn their keep by offering to test and certify the quality of products. Underwriters Laboratory (UL) is an example. A firm might contract with UL to give an impartial inspection of its electrical products and to certify them if they pass an established safety standard. The producing firm pays for the service and adds the cost to the product price. If the consumer places a value on such certification, he will be willing to pay more for the product. Thus, independent laboratories can survive.

There are other examples of private organizations which provide certification, official seals of approval, and published recommendations for products. Consumers' Union, publisher of *Consumer Reports,* is one of the best known. In each case, the firm has an incentive to act so as to maintain confidence in its certification. If inspection becomes less than impartial, either the seal or the certification may become meaningless. Thus, the discipline of the market serves to reduce the risk associated with faulty products and to minimize the unhappiness which might result for consumers.

While the competitive marketplace brings forth some things which consumers might not like, it also generates an effort to redress problems. As with most activities there are some benefits and costs. Let's first consider trade associations and the development of industry standards in their most favorable light.

TRADE ASSOCIATIONS

When individual sellers or manufacturers recognize that they face a problem common to their profession or industry, it is likely that they will attempt to organize an effort to solve the problem. This is especially so if sellers or manufacturers perceive gains to be had by finding solutions. *Trade associations* form for the purpose of finding such solutions, and there are literally thousands of such groups. In fact, there are so many trade associations that there is even an association of trade association secretaries! What do they do for the consumers?

The problem of the fly-by-night operator discussed earlier is one which might give rise to a trade association. An industry can be damaged severely if only a few firms make a practice of bilking the public. If a vacuum cleaner producer chooses to sell his product by making false claims on a "get the order and leave town" basis, then the public may become suspicious of all vacuum cleaner companies. The same idea applies to life insurance companies, producers of nonprescription drugs, used-car dealers, and a host of other sellers. Recognizing this *externality* (a cost imposed on a group of people who have no voice in the transaction), the legitimate firms in the industry may organize a trade association. To differentiate themselves from the underhanded seller, the trade association may promote a standard of quality and behavior to which its members will adhere. They may also attempt to educate the public by providing consumer information on their products. Thus, industry self-regulation has become a standard part of the market economy.

Trade associations engage in many other activities on behalf of their members. But membership is voluntary. Thus, the firm which chooses not to be a member may still operate in the market. Consumers still have the opportunity to make a full range of choices. Obviously, not every firm which joins a trade association will meet the ideals set by the association. By the same token, not every nonmember will fall below the standards of the association. Still, trade associations have an important function in the market. They are a response to the power of the consumer in some cases.

We have described some of the good points associated with industry organizations. What about the bad? A famous quote by Adam Smith, the recognized father of economics, suggested that managers of firms seldom come together for social purposes but that conversation turned to ways to collude and thereby improve the lot of the businessmen, at the expense of consumers. There is a tendency for business organizations to try to improve things for consumers and for themselves. The consumer benefits when competition is encouraged. Firms tend to benefit when monopoly is encouraged. Thus, trade associations can become the vehicle for attempts to restrict the entry of new sellers into markets or to restrict output and raise price. There are federal laws which can be used to attack such anticompetitive practices, but the tendency for reduced competition is inherent in the process of collectively improving things for the consumer. A frequent result of trade associations and other industry groups is persuading government to regulate "improvements" or enforce "standards." It is clearly possible that what is best for some consumers may not be best for others. And once government regulates the quality of products, generally the choice is in favor of the higher priced, "higher quality" product. Some consumers and firms win, others lose; but all get the same quality, if they can afford it.

GOVERNMENT AND THE CONSUMER: CAN GOVERNMENT HELP?

Every action by the federal government has impact on consumers. In some cases the effect is very indirect. For example, mismanagement of the nation's monetary system can contribute to inflation which reduces the consumer's real purchasing power. Taxes can and do have the same impact. Highway construction; housing programs; defense spending; the construction of dams, recreational areas, hospitals, schools, office buildings; and a thousand other activities bring both benefits and costs to the consumer. The focus here is specifically on some of the actions by government which are aimed directly toward the consumer.

The federal government seeks to please consumers through legislation and regulation. Congress passes laws which establish requirements to be met by regulatory actions. We have already mentioned a far-reaching agency of government which certainly affects the consumer—the Interstate Commerce Commission. The ICC was formed in 1887 by the Act to Regulate Commerce. At the time of its passage, the act was geared to regulate railroads with respect to their pricing of services and the level of service rendered to the public. Eventually all surface transportation entered the ICCs regulatory process so that today all interstate *common carriers* must satisfy certain requirements when offering their services to the public. For example, bus fares and routes are regulated. When you step on a Greyhound Bus, you are entering a regulated common carrier. The fare you pay, the number of seats, and other accommodations on the bus are regulated as are the services offered at the terminal. Trucklines and movers of household goods are regulated. In each case, regulations have been promulgated partly on the basis of consumer interests. While the decisions in Washington D.C., may be far removed from the market, there is an attempt made to listen to consumers and to meet their needs.

Since the regulators are removed from the market, they have a problem in determining what consumers really want. Obviously, low fares and excellent service sound appealing. But can bus companies and movers provide that attractive combination? In some cases, low fares and excellent service are an impossible dream. Thus, the regulated firms attempt to obtain assistance from government in meeting the challenge, and quite often that assistance comes in the form of subsidies. Consumer tax dollars are siphoned off indirectly to assist firms so that the firms can have low prices and good service. Indirectly the consumer pays. Indeed, the consumer always pays. Who else is there?

This example serves to illustrate the basic regulatory problem. When market forces—demand and supply—are interrupted, the consumer voice has to be redirected. Instead of voting with dollars and buying what satisfies him, the individual consumer is forced to join ranks with other consumers and vote with his vote. The political market is less sensitive to individual tastes and demands than is the economic market. Sometimes the uniformity of service turns out to be bad. This problem is reinforced by the fact that competition is reduced by regulation. If firms are told what to produce and how much to charge, it becomes difficult to innovate, to expand, to contract, and even to go out of business. Thus, some consumers begin to subsidize others. For example, if a particular bus route attracts so few customers that it can not cover cost, other routes will have to generate a surplus. The bus company may not be allowed to reduce its service on the low demand route because it would not be good for those consumers. But what about the other consumers? Regulation raises serious questions about government's ability to assist the consumer. But there are other things to consider.

More specific consumer legislation came on the scene in the early 1900s.[4] The Food, Drug, and Cosmetics Act of 1906, for example, spoke to the problem of adulteration in foods products and the misbranding of packages. The *Food and Drug Administration* later developed from this legislation. Later, the 1962 drug amendments of the Food, Drug, and Cosmetics Act of 1938 were passed. This action set up a review process for all new drugs and established a requirement that all drugs currently sold be evaluated for safety and efficacy. Once again, the legislation and regulation which came about had benefits and costs. On the benefit side, consumers were given greater assurance that food, drugs, and cosmetics would be safe. On the cost side of the equation, it became very difficult to introduce new drugs, to enter the food processing business, or to market "wonder" cosmetics, all of which caused potential losses to consumers. It must be recognized that safety standards can be set so high that consumers might suffer. The higher the standard, the greater the cost. And when prices go up, some consumers will be rationed out of the market. It has been said, for example, that aspirin would have never passed the new hurdles which have been established by the Food and Drug Administration. Others have called aspirin the greatest wonder drug of modern times.

There are other actions which will be mentioned to illustrate the extent of the federal government's effort to bring better things to the consumer. The Meat Inspection Act of 1907 ushered in a series of actions to reduce the likelihood of low quality meat entering the market. The Federal Trade Commission Act of 1914 established the Commission and gave it far-reaching powers to prohibit unfair competition. Later amendments gave the FTC the power to regulate advertising and practically all activities which might mislead consumers.

Other legislation includes the Automobile Information Disclosure Act of 1958, the National Traffic and Motor Vehicle Act of 1966, the Fair Packaging and Labeling Act of 1966, the Consumer Credit Protection Act of 1968,

[4] See Barbara B. Murry, "Major Federal Consumer Protection Laws, 1906–1970," in *Consumerism,* ed. Barbara B. Murry. (Pacific Palisades, Calif.: Goodyear Publishing Co., 1973), pp. 78–85. Much of this discussion is drawn from her article.

Interstate Land-Sales Full Disclosure Act, and the Fair Credit Reporting Act of 1970.

Out of this legislation and a host of others, *regulatory commissions* have developed which produce thousands of regulations aimed toward the consumer. Once again there is controversy about the net result. Consider some recent actions with respect to automobile safety. Seat belts, buzzers, heavy bumpers, padded dash boards, fuel efficient engines, price and gasoline economy labeling, air emission controls, and tire standards have each been mandated for automobiles. At present passive restraints—air bags or more complex belts—are being prescribed for the auto industry. Each of these actions offers some added benefit, and each generates a cost. As a result of the costs, some consumers will be forced to drive old cars much longer or not drive at all. Others who drive safer cars may feel more secure and become slightly more careless. People who need large cars for a large family may no longer have the choice—they may have to buy two or three small cars. Each regulation presents a complex economic problem.

Action by the Food and Drug Administration is equally complex. Should a food additive be banned if evidence arises showing the additive to be associated with cancer? Cyclamates were banned because of such evidence. Consumers who preferred diet drinks were forced to find a substitute. Then, after later evidence came in, it was learned that cyclamates were safe. Saccharine took the place of cyclamates in the meantime. And now that additive is under fire. Should a person on a medically prescribed diet be allowed to take one risk in order to reduce another? Would information be better than a ban? The regulatory puzzle is indeed complex. Simple solutions for complex problems spring from it. Some consumers gain, others lose, and it is not clear that the benefits are greater than the cost.

The regulatory process brings new information into the market even when regulations are being considered. For example, in 1976 the Food and Drug Administration proposed a new labeling requirement for baby food.[5] Under the proposed regulation which had come as a result of a consumer groups petition, baby food producers would be required to list the percentage of each ingredient placed in each jar. A range of values could be stated but the totals would have to reflect the final content. Included in the requirements were additives such as sugar or salt. Particular concern was shown for the amount of sugar being added to baby food.

The regulation of baby food as proposed would have been quite costly for producers to meet. The ingredients of most food are measured by a recipe; that is, the input is measured, not the output. Many changes occur in the processing of food, which might be difficult to control precisely.

During the regulatory proceedings, new information about consumer demand began to surface. And perhaps because of the findings, a new

[5] See 41 *Federal Register* 37593 and 37595, 7 September, 1977.

"It's from the Consumer Protection Agency, demanding that we submit proof that the gates *are* made of pearl."

Reprinted by permission The Wall Street Journal

product was born. Beech-Nut Products introduced a line of sugar-free baby food! This happened without a regulation. There must be many cases where firms change their products because of what they learn from regulatory agencies. While the changes can be beneficial and the resulting products successful, one still must consider the cost of getting the information from which these improvements flow. Taxpayers pay part of the cost of operating regulatory commissions. Firms and their stockholders bear the cost of preparing testimony and submitting evidence. In total, the cost could exceed the benefits.

In addition to these highly specialized examples which may offer assistance to consumers, there are some broader initiatives taken by government. One set of actions goes back to the earliest discussion of the role of the consumer in the competitive market. Since it is generally agreed that more goods come from competition than monopoly, promoting competitive practices is an important role of government for consumers.

At the same time that the regulatory role of government was expanding in the United States, steps were also being taken to legislate competition. The evidence of this is found in the so-called *antitrust laws.*[6] These include the *Sherman Antitrust Act* of 1890, the *Clayton* and *Federal Trade Commission Acts* of 1914, and the *Robinson–Patman Act* of 1936. With the exception of the Robinson–Patman Act, the antitrust legislation generally supported competitive pricing, the absence of collusion and price fixing on the part of sellers, and the merits of many sellers in a market as opposed to one or a few sellers. The Robinson–Patman Act, on the other hand, was geared to protect small firms from the competition of larger ones. Thus, in that case, higher consumer prices may have been supported in order to keep the corner grocery store from going under when chain stores with low prices came to town.

Under the antitrust laws, cases can be brought against firms by the federal government or by individuals. In some cases, large firms have been broken up into smaller ones. Standard Oil is the classic case. In other cases, firms are instructed as to how they shall price their products. In still other instances, firms have been fined for colluding to raise price and restrict output. To the extent that such action brings greater competition at a lower cost, the consumer benefits. This kind of action is highly consistent with the role of the consumer in a market economy.

Consumers have recognized the power of government in the marketplace and the power that pressure groups have in influencing legislation, regulation, and the executive branch of government. Just as firms in many industries and members of most professions have done, consumers have formed trade associations. Consumers Union is a prominent and highly effective example of a consumer trade association. This voluntary association engages in many activities. In addition to lobbying before regulatory commissions and in Congress, and thereby raising consumer oriented issues, the consumer groups support extensive research organizations and laboratories which test products and report findings. They also publish magazines and newsletters and attempt to provide more and better information to their members. As would be expected, consumers are often split on a particular issue. But when a consensus is found, lobbying organizations can be effective. Still, there are

[6] For a good discussion of these see William G. Shepherd and Clair Wilcox, *Public Policies toward Business,* 5th ed. (Homewood: Richard D. Irwin, Inc., 1979), chap. 4.

benefits and costs. Efforts to bring specific regulations or actions may appear on the surface to be helpful. The final result may turn out otherwise. Cyclamate provides an example. Against such experiences, one must weigh the importance and value of information and net beneficial actions which have been supported by consumer organizations. Given the nature of the political process it is almost necessary that consumer interest groups have a voice in Washington. Decisions are being made which affect everyone. Other groups are highly organized and working to influence action in their favor. A balancing of forces can be helpful.

Some interest groups have become part of government itself. The Department of Agriculture, for example, looks after the interests of farmers. The Department of Labor supports the welfare of workers, and the Department of Transportation oversees the interest of the transportation sector. Proposals as early as 1929 for the establishment of a federal consumer agency were entertained.[7] At that time, the organization was referred to as a "consumer counsel." Having no success in that effort, the consumer movement sought support and was successful in 1941, when the Congress created the Office of Bituminous Coal Consumers' Counsel, a consumer organization in the executive branch. Later efforts pushed for a cabinet level Consumer Department and finally President Lyndon Johnson created the President's Committee on Consumer Interest in 1964. Esther Peterson became the first person to fill the post of special assistant to the President for consumer affairs. Later, in 1967, Betty Furness assumed the role. In both cases, consumer issues became more highly focused in the executive branch.

In 1971, President Nixon enlarged the consumer counsel's role and created the White House Consumer Advisor Office, naming Virginia Knauer to head that office. All along efforts were being generated to create a new agency, an Agency for Consumer Advocacy. These efforts continued through the Ford administration and have now reached a new momentum under the Carter administration. Whatever the outcome of the new administration's effort, one can be certain that consumer interests will still have a strong role to play on the Washington scene.

SUMMARY

This chapter has been devoted to a discussion of the consumer's role in our market economy. To focus on the consumer, the concept of voluntary voice and informed decision making were emphasized. Those are the two factors which combine to give the consumer power. After describing a typical buyer-seller situation, this chapter discussed ways by which consumers might increase their impact on the market and how the market tends to

[7] See *Consumer Protection Legislation* (Washington, D.C.: American Enterprise Institute, 1977).

respond to such efforts. Trade associations, legal remedies, independent laboratories, government regulation, and consumer organizations also play major roles in providing information and standards and affecting the composition of output in our market system.

The individual consumer has the greatest opportunity and incentive to affect the quantity, quality, and variety of goods and services in the market. The name of the game is choice, and dollar votes determine the winners.

The appendix to this chapter suggests sources of information and assistance to consumers.

KEY WORDS

Antitrust laws
Better Business Bureau
Caveat emptor
Chamber of Commerce
Class action suit
Clayton Antitrust Act
Common carrier
Consumer sovereignty
Externality
Federal Trade Commission Act
Fly-by-night operator
Food and Drug Administration
Heterogeneity of products
Regulatory commission
Robinson–Patman Act
Sherman Antitrust Act
Trade association
Uniform Commercial Code

PROBLEMS

1. Discuss the consumer's role in a market economy. Explain how competition between five supermarkets or banks leads to better service for the consumer.
2. Identify some of the benefits and costs related to governments' efforts to improve things for the consumer.
3. How would you go about registering a complaint with a shoe repair company if the newly replaced soles on your shoes fell off the first day? What if the problem was more serious? For example, how would you approach an automobile manufacturer if the engine in your new car began to use excessive amounts of oil?

APPENDIX: SOURCES OF CONSUMER INFORMATION AND ASSISTANCE

The consumer movement in the United States has led to significant actions by private firms and by government. This chapter has introduced some of the issues to you. It is suggested that you do further reading on the subject and that you be aware of the many sources of information and assistance which have been made available for consumers. To meet the needs of the last item—sources of information and assistance—consider:

Wasserman, Paul, and Morgan, and Jean. *Consumer Sourcebook*. Detroit: Gale Research Corporation, 1974.

This 531-page book is filled with names, addresses, and summaries of information sources which relate specifically to consumer problems.

For other background information we suggest these books:

Aaker, David A., and Day, George S. *Consumerism: Search for Consumer Interest*. 2d ed. New York: The Free Press, 1974.

Murry, Barbara M., ed. *Consumerism*. Pacific Palisades, Calif.: Goodyear Publishing Co., 1973.

Driscoll, James G. *Survival Tactics*. Princeton, N.J.: dow Jones Books, 1973.

Faber, Doris. *Enough: The Revolt of the American Consumer*. New York: Farrar, Straus & Giroux, 1972.

Fetterman, Elsie, and Schiller, Margery K. *Let the Buyer Be Aware!* New York: Fairchild Publications, Inc., 1976.

Nadel, Mark V. *The Politics of Consumer Protection*. Indianapolis: The Bobbs-Merrill Co., Inc., 1971.

National Academy of Engineering. *Product Quality, Performance, and Cost*. Washington: National Academy of Engineering, 1972.

Peterson, Mary Bennett. *The Regulated Consumer*. Ottawa, Ill.: Green Hill Publishers, Inc., 1971.

For reading on a periodical basis, consider *Consumer Reports* and *Money Magazine*.

In addition to background reading and source material, you should find the address for your local Better Business Bureau, Chamber of Commerce, and your state's office of consumer affairs. You might also check with the major public utilities—electric company and telephone company—to see if they offer consumer advice. Finally, you might check the land-grant university in your state. Each land-grant university has extension specialists who provide information for consumers.

PART II

These five chapters are concerned with the hazards which may keep you from attaining and maintaining your intended lifestyle and how to minimize those risks through insurance. An introductory chapter discusses the nature of insurance, followed by specific chapters on life insurance, health and disability insurance, and property and liability insurance. Chapter 11 discusses the types of insurance benefits provided by your employer, including Social Security and other fringe benefits.

PROTECTING YOUR LIFESTYLE

Chapter 8

Introduction to insurance

The misfortunes hardest to bear are those which never come.
James Russell Lowell

Misfortunes which never come—or do come—can have the financial anguish softened by a risk-sharing device. As old as the Old Testament, as American as barn raising, as complex as constructing a mortality table, and almost as basic as bread and butter, *insurance* is as commonplace as television in the United States. American lives are insured to the incredible tune of over two trillion dollars. If all Americans were to collect on their life insurance at once, the sums would more than exhaust the Gross National Product. Annual premiums for all major lines of insurance in 1976 came to over 80 billion dollars. (See Figure 8–1.)

Insurance comes in a dazzling variety of sizes, coverages, companies, agents, packages and combinations. Life, disability, health, auto, property, malpractice, personal liability—what could they all possibly have in common? This chapter will try to identify the common threads which unite all these diverse insurance and risk management decisions. Specifically, the chapter will address the questions

- What is insurance?
- What risks can and should be insured?
- How do I determine my personal insurance needs?
- Where (or from whom) do I buy insurance?
- What do I do after I buy it?

WHAT IS INSURANCE?

Insurance is a method of reducing individual risk by pooling those risks with others subject to the same risk. By insuring, you trade a small chance of

Figure 8–1
Insurance premiums paid

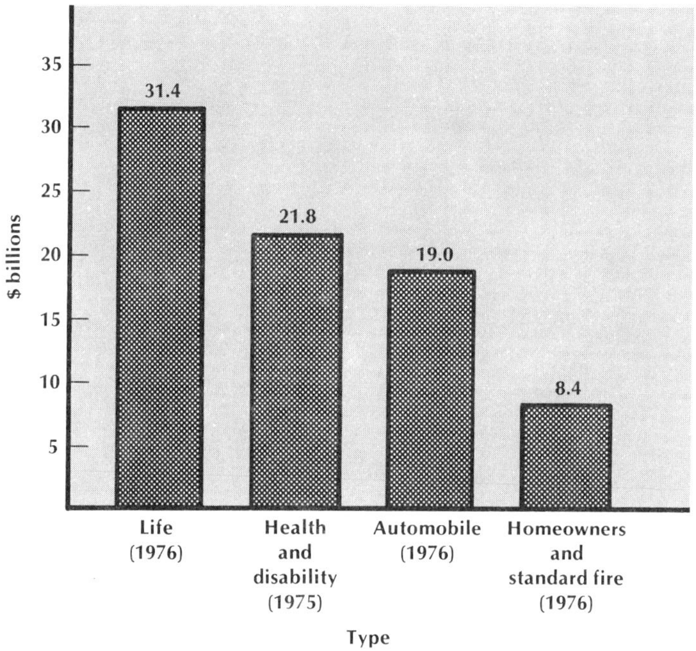

a large loss for the absolute certainty of a small loss—the *premium*. The premium is almost certain to exceed the expected value of your loss. For example, if in any given year one house in 500 is totally destroyed by fire, lightning, or other calamity, and you own a $40,000 house, your expected loss is 1/500 × $40,000 = $80. (This ignores the possibility of partial loss or damage.) You could contribute $80 to a fund with the 500 other homeowners, giving a total fund of $40,000 to replace the one house in that group which can be expected to be destroyed by fire in that year. This would be a simplified case of risk pooling, or insurance.

In reality there are some complications. First, there are costs in administering the fund such as keeping records, collecting premiums, safeguarding funds, and verifying losses. Second, one house in five thousand might be the *average* expected loss, but even in a much larger group some year-to-year variations above and below that average can be expected. A *reserve* must be established in order to provide for higher-than-average loss years. When the covered group is smaller, the potential percentage variation is greater, which means high start-up costs for newly organized insurance companies.

Insurers account for these complications in the *load factor,* which is the difference between the *pure premium*—enough to reimburse average annual losses—and the actual cost, the gross premium charged clients. These additional costs include some return to stockholders, an allowance for accounting, sales, collections, claims, adjusting, and other overhead costs, and some funds to build up a loss reserve. The load factor is 30 to 60 percent of the total premium. Thus, for our hypothetical case, the person subject to a possible fire loss can choose between the loss of about $160 certain (the premium), or a 499 : 500 chance of losing nothing, and a 1 : 500 chance of losing $40,000. He may choose to take a chance and retain that risk. If he chooses to transfer the risk to an insurance company or other pool, he is insuring the risk. It is also possible to transfer part of the risk and retain the rest through deductibles and other devices, as we shall see later.

The lower the probability of loss, the greater will be the incentive to insure. This is the case because the premium is low relative to the *size* of the potential loss, even if it is not low in relation to *expected value* of loss. The greater the probability of loss, the larger the premium will be in relation to the value of the insured asset, and the less attractive insurance becomes to the potential buyer. This explains why it is easy to buy fire insurance anywhere but difficult to insure against catastrophies like floods and earthquakes. The probability of some fire (most of which will do limited amounts of damage) in any house in a given year is only 3.5 percent. The probability of loss from earthquakes in California and Alaska, or floods along the Mississippi is noticeably greater, although the size of the potential loss (the value of a house) is about the same.

Insurance, then, is a way of transferring risk through pooling with others subject to similar risks. In a frontier settlement, insurance almost came with the community. Anyone whose barn burned, whose crops were destroyed, or who suffered a long and disabling illness or death of the breadwinner could count on community assistance in making good their economic loss. Today, in a more complex and impersonal world, we choose instead to guarantee reimbursement of loss through insurance. The principle is the same.

WHAT RISKS CAN BE INSURED?

Insurers have a variety of ways of classifying risks. One such classification is into pure versus speculative risks. Pure risks involve only two possibilities, loss or nonloss, while speculative risks can lead to loss, gain, or no change. The latter category includes gambling, buying land and stocks, and business ventures, which are uninsurable risks. Risks with only loss versus no loss possible outcomes are more likely to be *insurable*. These would include most kinds of destruction of or damage to persons, property, and income.

Within this category of pure risks there are further qualities of risks that make an insurance solution more or less feasible, available, or financially attractive. These factors are:

1. *Moral hazard.* This is the temptation to create a loss to collect the insurance. Usually this is minimized by careful restraints on the *amount* of insurance written, so that the insured will just recoup actual losses and make no net gain. Arson, suicide, and overuse of medical insurance for trivial complaints are all examples of moral hazard. It has even been argued that mandatory auto insurance creates a moral hazard of sorts by making drivers less careful than they might otherwise be. Some writers distinguish between moral hazard—the temptation to create a loss in the hope of actual gain—and morale hazard—the tendency to be less careful in preventing or avoiding loss because one is insured. Both these factors drive up rates and lead to various protective devices by insurers, such as ceilings on amounts of insurance, deductibles, coinsurance, independent appraisals of value before insuring, suicide clauses, and the requirement of insurable interest.

2. *Catastrophic potential.* Certain lines of insurance are subject to almost an either/or situation; either no losses, or huge losses in an entire area. Commonest examples are flood (especially along the Mississippi and in coastal areas), earthquake (especially along the West Coast), and crime (in inner cities). Nuclear disaster is one of the newer categories, especially with the proliferation of nuclear power plants. Some kinds of product liability, especially involving chemicals, are rapidly developing a catastrophe potential. Much of the insurance in these lines is subsidized by government. The main difficulty in writing insurance against catastrophes lies in concentration of hazards. People in the immediately affected area want to buy, but it is hard to sell in outlying areas because the premium reflects both low- and high-risk groups. A premium which covers both groups will be too high to attract peripheral, low-risk area individuals and too low to cover losses if only high-risk area residents are included. The most feasible way to compel risk sharing by low- as well as high-risk areas is through the taxing power of government.

3. *High probability losses.* Either losses which are extremely likely or insurance coverages which generate frequent claims, make insurance a less satisfactory solution to risk. Why? The premium can be expressed as

$$PR = P_L \cdot V_L (1 + L.F.)$$

where PR = premium, P_L = probability of loss, V_L = value of loss, and $L.F.$ = load factor.

This can also be written

$$\frac{PR}{V_L} = P_L (1 + L.F.).$$

The probability, P_L, is always between zero and one. As P_L becomes larger, the premium PR becomes a larger percentage of the potential value of the loss, V_L, making insurance less financially attractive. A famous (probability apocryphal) story from the early days of flight relates that the insurance premium for transatlantic flight was 105 percent of the face value. Loss was considered certain, and the 5 percent covered the overhead. Insurance is best suited to low probability losses; once the probability of loss exceeds 20 percent the premium becomes so large relative to the value of the insured asset or income that a more sensible solution would be to use the premium to establish your own reserve against expected losses—in other words, to retain the risk.

4. *Small losses.* The cost of servicing a policy or claim differs a little with size. A $1,000 life insurance policy requires about the same overhead as a $100,000 policy, and a $10 claim costs about the same to process as a $500 claim. Insurers can cut costs per dollar of coverage considerably by minimizing small claims, while at the same time individuals can easily afford to bear small losses themselves. If there is one consistent rule of thumb in all lines of insurance, it is the *large loss principle*—cover the small dollar risks yourself and use insurance for the risks which could (financially speaking) "wipe you out." Insurers encourage following this principle by offering large discounts for deductibles in property and health insurance, and by offering a substantially reduced cost per $1,000 on larger liability and life insurance policies.

Based on these considerations, which risks should you insure (transfer) and which should you *retain*? Those events for which the probability is low and the potential loss large are the best candidates for insurance. Basically, when you insure, you are protecting your income against unexpected demands beyond your control and your assets from loss, damage, or destruction. The larger your liquid assets or emergency fund, the more retention you can afford. As your assets grow, therefore, you can increase the share of the risk you assume for smaller losses and thereby cut your insurance premium outlay.

HOW DO I DETERMINE MY INSURANCE NEEDS?

Your income statement and balance sheet will identify the assets and income you need to protect. Major assets subject to insurable risk fall into two groups. The first group includes the house, car, and personal property. The second group consists of financial assets which might have to be liquidated to meet liability claims or to meet expenditure demands in excess of your income due to liability, death of a breadwinner, disability, or major medical expenditures. These same disasters can be a drain on your income, which can also be insured.

In the process of identifying *what* you can lose, you have also begun to identify the kinds of perils to which your assets can be exposed. Insurable risks fall into the following categories:

1. Damage to physical property from fire, flood, hail, lightning, earthquake, vandalism, negligence of others, and a host of other perils, natural and of human origin (a more complete list is given in Chapter 10).
2. Liability for your own negligence or misjudgment which results in payments to others out of your income and/or assets. Major sources of individual liability claims are automobile liability, professional liability (mainly malpractice), and personal liability (generally injury to others on your property or damage to other people's property by you, your children, your dogs, and so forth). Personal, professional, and automobile liability are considered in Chapter 12 in connection with the package homeowner's insurance and automobile insurance policies.
3. Loss of income or depletion of financial assets resulting from death or disability of the income earner. Life insurance and disability income insurance are the main insurance lines in this category. Disability insurance is discussed in Chapter 10 and life insurance in Chapter 9. Social Security, which covers both these hazards, is discussed in Chapter 11.
4. Excessive demands on income or depletion of financial assets due to accident, injury, prolonged illness, or major legal or dental expenses. Accident and health insurance are the major lines here, although legal expense and dental expense insurance are becoming increasingly popular. These lines are discussed in Chapter 10.
5. *Outliving your assets.* An estate is accumulated during the income producing years and depleted during the retirement years. You will probably want some protection against the "hazard" of living too long, which could leave you unable to support yourself in later years. Social security, pension plans, and retirement annuities all guard against this hazard. These are discussed in Chapter 11 and also in Chapter 20.

Each of these lines of insurance has a different procedure for determining needs, but they all refer back to the income statement and balance sheet for several purposes:

1. To identify assets and income to be protected.
2. To determine the extent to which you can retain losses (based on liquid assets).
3. To determine how income and expenditure patterns could or would be adjusted in case of financial disaster.
4. To identify the coverages you already have, so as not to duplicate or over insure.
5. To determine how much you can afford to pay in insurance premiums.

These assets and income have already been identified in general terms. Let us do it specifically for our friends George and Henrietta in Chapter 3.

Figure 8–2
Expenditure reductions due to death or disability, George and Henrietta Buyers

Death		*Disability*	
Saving	−$ 200	Saving	−$200
Clothing	− 200	Clothing	− 100
Car payments*	− 720	Recreation	− 100
Recreation	− 100	Personal allowance	− 100
Personal allowance	− 260	Employee business expense	− 40
Employee business expense	− 40		
Life insurance	− 240	Life insurance	− 240
Food	− 200	Other	− 150
Other	− 200		
	−$2,160		−$930

* Assumes credit life insurance on car, waiver of premium benefit on life insurance.

They have an after-tax income of $10,051. In case of death or disability, they could reduce expenditures somewhat, perhaps as indicated in Figure 8–2.

They might be able to identify some categories in which expenses could be reduced in case of other financial disasters, but most of these reductions are based on the assumption that George will not be there to eat, wear clothes, and spend other money (death) or that his outside activities will be sharply curtailed (disability).

The income statement also provides some useful information about potentially insurable expenses. Information on past medical expenses, auto repairs, and house repairs should be helpful in deciding whether to insure at all and how large a deductible to take. Finally, the income statement, when converted to a budget, identifies what is already being spent on insurance and helps in deciding how much one can afford in additional premiums.

The balance sheet for George and Henrietta in Chapter 3 indicates financial assets of $1,710 less short-to-medium-term debt of $1,420. This means a net $290 in assets which could be tapped for short-term (less than six months) emergency, or which could be tapped by others in case of a liability judgment against them. Their insurable assets consist of a house, a car, and $3,200 in personal property. Their relatively poor liquidity position suggests that

a. George and Henrietta cannot afford very large *deductibles* on collision, comprehensive, and homeowner's, or very long waiting period on disability.

b. At present their liability, life insurance, and major medical needs are governed more by the income they could be forced to forgo than by assets they might lose.

WHERE DO I BUY INSURANCE?

Life insurance is not bought, it is sold, according to those who sell it. But you can be one jump ahead of the life insurance salesman. Don't wait for a salesperson to knock on your door. Do a little research yourself; some possible information sources are suggested in Chapter 9. At least part of your insurance will probably come in an employee fringe benefit package, which may include life, disability, health and sometimes even legal and dental expense insurance. Here your purchase options may be somewhat limited. Auto insurance is something you will have to buy, seeking out an agent when you acquire a car. Property insurance for renters is something you will have to shop for; for a homeowner, the pressure to insure promptly usually comes from the mortgage lender. Nonfringe benefit health and disability can be purchased from a variety of companies.

As a general rule, the agent is a major consideration in automobile, homeowner's and renter's insurance. Rates are regulated and policy terms are fairly standardized, although enough differences exist to make it worth the effort to get several quotations. But these policies are likely to require frequent service, for which an established and reputable agent is of great value. If several are available, you have a choice between an *exclusive agent*—reprsenting a single national company, such as Nationwide, State Farm, and Allstate—or an *independent agent,* who places policies with a number of different companies. If you move or travel a great deal, the big national companies with exclusive agents are most likely to have a local agent to provide service on your policy wherever you are. However, many large national companies which sell through independent agents also have broad geographic representation. On the other hand, if you have special needs—unusual coverages, higher limits than usual, and so forth—independent agents are more likely to be able to tailor a policy with one of their "stable" of insurers to meet your needs. More and more of both groups of agents have also branched out into the other personal lines of insurance—disability, health, and life. One-stop shopping is now feasible, but the gain in convenience *may* be offset by either higher total cost or less satisfactory coverage.

In life insurance, the opposite is true; the company is more important than the agent. The chances of your outliving the agent's career in life insurance are extremely good, since the average life insurance salesperson switches to another career long before your life expectancy expires. Furthermore, there is much greater disparity in rates among life insurers, so you need to shop around in order to get the most coverage at the lowest price. Because of the long-term nature of most life insurance contracts, you need to examine the financial soundness of your company. (A. M. Best Co. publishes annual rating guides for all types of insurance companies.) Finally, you will need to make a decision between a *stock* (investor-owned) and a *mutual* (policyholder-owned) *life insurance company*. In property and liability lines most insurers are stockholder owned, because a large reserve against year-to-year variations in losses is required, which can most easily be built initially with stockholder capital. In life insurance, year-to-year variations are smaller, and the reserve build-up can be charged in the premium and refunded as "dividends" if reserve build-up becomes excessive. Consequently life insurance is dominated by large mutual companies, although there are a great many smaller stock companies. Since you, the policyholder, are assuming a moderate amount of risk in a mutual company, you should expect your net premium (actual premium less dividends) to be lower with a mutual than with a stock company. This is commonly but not universally true. Remember, stock company premiums are guaranteed; dividends from mutuals are not. In any case, in shopping for premiums both stock and mutual companies should be considered in all lines.

Finally, health and disability coverage are available from several sources. If you are old or poor (or in military service), you have insurance with the federal government. The nonprofit Blue Cross and Blue Shield corporations are major marketers of fairly standardized policies. Commercial insurers of both life and property/liability also sell health and disability insurance. Again, it pays to shop for rates.

In life, health, and disability, *group insurance* is frequently available. The group might be employees of a single employer, or it could be members of a professional association, lodge, civic group, fraternity, alumni association, religious denomination, and so forth. Rates are generally lower for group policies than for individual policies, primarily because of lower selling costs and administrative costs. (Some of these are born by the employer or association; other costs are reduced per participant because of large volume at one sale.) Less common are group medical, legal, and dental insurance plans. One disadvantage in many group policies is the lack of ready local service. Investigate possible sources of group insurance in your insurance shopping. Group insurance is most suited to the life and disability lines, where service demands are least frequent.

WHAT DO I DO AFTER I BUY INSURANCE?

First, read the policy. Make sure you received what you intended to buy in coverage, limits, exclusion, face value, benefits, and beneficiaries. Find out who the agent is and how he can be reached. Store the policy—especially homeowner's!—in a safe, fireproof place. Write down the policy number and keep it somewhere handy, especially the automobile policy number which may be needed to purchase license plates or in case of accident.

Second, keep your insurance portfolio current. Review your decisions and coverages every year in the light of changed income, assets, liabilities, hazards, dependents, and feelings about risk. Make any necessary adjustments in coverage including limits, deductibles, and beneficiaries. Particularly in need of annual review are the following items:

1. The value of your house for homeowner's insurance in the light of rising replacement costs.
2. The value of personal property in response to both rising replacement cost and acquisition of new property. Special note should be made of acquisitions requiring separate coverage—boats, coins, stamps, furs, jewelry, works of art. Keep your inventory current. (See Chapter 12.)
3. The limits of liability on both automobile and personal policies, in response to increases in assets and income (representing both what you can lose and what you can afford to pay in premiums) and also larger judgments awarded in court tests.
4. The face value of life insurance. The need increases with greater income, more dependents, and more liabilities, and decreases as dependents approach the age of independence as assets accumulate. Face value should be adjusted accordingly. Death, divorce, or other changes may also necessitate changing the beneficiary.
5. Limits on major medical insurance in response to rising costs of medical care.
6. Deductibles should be adjusted upward as your liquid assets (or emergency funds) accumulate. This form of self-insurance has tremendous potential for keeping rates down.

Third, make sure that someone—family, cousin, friend, banker—knows where the policies are kept in case someone has to file a claim on your behalf. Keep a list of policies, coverages, account numbers, and agents in an accessible location. If you are dead, injured, hospitalized, disabled, or in jail, someone else is going to have to pursue your insurance claim for you.

SUMMARY

Insurance is essential to protect the lifestyle you have established in earlier chapters. It protects your income and assets from large, unexpected demands or losses through risk pooling. Risks especially suited to insurance are those where the size of the potential loss is larger but the probability of loss is low. Insurance is available only when the risk is a matter of loss versus nonloss. Speculative risks with the possibility of gain are not insurable. Other factors determining availability and cost of insurance are moral hazard and the prospect of catastrophic losses. Retention is possible for either small losses or for partial coverage of large losses through deductibles. The amount of risk you choose to retain depends on your attitude toward risk and on your liquid assets.

The income statement and balance sheet are useful sources of insurance information. They identify the income and assets which can be lost or damaged, the amount you can afford to pay for insurance, by what amount expenditures could be reduced in case of death or disability, what average annual insurable expenses (medical, dental, legal) you are presently self-insuring, and how large a deductible you can afford.

Major categories of insurance are damage to property, liability (personal, automobile, professional), life, disability, health, and retirement income.

Insurance can be purchased from either a stock or a mutual company, individually or on a group basis, and (in many lines) from an exclusive agent or an independent agent. Premium shopping is important in all lines but especially in life insurance. The agent is more important in automobile and in renter's and homeowner's insurance because of service. The company—its premium and its financial soundness—is more important in life insurance.

After buying insurance, the policy should be read, safely stored in an appropriate place where someone else can find it easily, and updated regularly on the basis of changed economic circumstances.

KEY WORDS

Deductible
Exclusive agent
Expected value
Group insurance
Independent agent
Insurable risk
Insurance
Large loss principle
Load factor
Moral hazard
Mutual company
Premium
Pure premium
Reserve
Retaining risk
Stock company

PROBLEM

Helen and John have been married two years. He is an accountant, and she is a nurse. Together they make $23,000 a year. They have one child, rent an apartment, own two cars and a boat, and have $9,000 in personal property. They have $3,000 in liquid assets. Identify their risk exposures and make some general suggestions about how they should set up an insurance program (particularly self-insurance, deductibles, and choosing companies and/or agents).

Chapter 9

Life insurance

I don't want to achieve immortality through my work,
I want to achieve it through not dying.

Woody Allen

Life insurance is perhaps the most widely owned and least understood form of insurance. The primary purpose of life insurance is to protect surviving dependents from the loss of income if the breadwinner dies. In insuring a house, a car, or a boat, there is no difficulty answering the question "What is it worth?" But it is far more difficult to deal with the question "What am *I* worth?" Like jury awards for pain and suffering in liability cases, our estimate may be astronomical. Unlike juries, however, individual purchasers are forced to reduce their estimates of their own monetary value to a level commensurate with their ability to pay insurance premiums.

In addition to the amount, there are many other questions to be asked in selecting a life insurance policy to meet your particular needs. The questions addressed in this chapter are:

- Who needs insurance?
- How much insurance do I need?
- How long do I need it?
- What kind of insurance should I buy?
- How much will it cost?
- How do I choose a company?
- What happens if I decide to cancel my policy?
- How can my beneficiary collect the proceeds?
- What about group life insurance?
- How do I protect myself against living too long?

WHO NEEDS INSURANCE?

Anyone whose death would create a financial hardship for another person needs insurance. An income earner with dependent spouse, children, and/or parents in the most obvious case in point. But a mother engaged in full-time care of small children may also need insurance to cover the cost of replacing her services.

Insurance may also be used to provide cash to settle estate taxes, to avoid having to sell assets at a loss—especially stocks and real estate, for which market conditions are highly unpredictable. Insurance can provide funds to cover estate taxes, thereby leaving other assets untouched.

In addition to these uses of insurance, business owners may use insurance to provide for the continuation of a firm after one major owner dies. Each owner takes out enough insurance on the other to enable him to buy the other's share from his estate and thus continue the business.

Finally, there are some arguments for insuring children. However, insurance is generally used to protect income and assets. Children, on the other hand, generate no income, and delightful as their company may be, the cold, calculating accountant's view of children is that they are liabilities, not assets. They generate expenses, not income. If the child dies, you will undoubtedly suffer much anguish, but no financial loss. The cost of the burial is a consideration, but that cost may be far less than the cost of support.

Life insurance, then, has four major uses: to protect surviving dependents from loss of income when the breadwinner dies, to replace the domestic services of a mother of small children, to provide ready cash for final expenses and estate taxes, and to guarantee continuation of a business firm.

HOW MUCH INSURANCE DO I NEED?

Suppose you are 25, and earn an after-tax income of $10,000 a year. You can expect to work for 40 more years giving you a total expected income of $400,000 if you get no raises. On that basis and using a 6 percent interest rate, the *discounted present value* of your expected future earning is $150,463. (See the appendix on the Mathematics of Finance.) If increases in pay are projected at 4 percent a year, your total earnings will increase to $950,225. When discounting is applied to that amount, the discounted present value of the earnings will be $273,555. By estimating your expected lifetime income, you can make a rough approximation of what you are worth for insurance purposes. The discounting technique is essentially the same method used to determine the value of an item of capital equipment—a machine, a house, or a manufacturing plant.

In making these calculations, there were no provisions made for retirement or Social Security benefits. Those refinements and others would have to enter in, of course, when arriving at a specific insurance objective.

Just as with a machine or a house, however, you will have to subtract some operating costs. Houses, machines, and people require maintenance. If you are no longer around, you will not have to be fed, clothed, or entertained; you will no longer have your teeth filled, your hair cut, your Social Security taxes paid. These items will probably account for 25 to 30 percent of your income. Adjusting the second estimate downward by 25 percent, you can be replaced—financially speaking—by a lump sum of $205,166. This is an estimate of the amount of insurance you need to keep your dependents going without you. This looks like an astronomical sum, and it is, especially when compared to the national average of about $30,000 in insurance per family in 1976.

There are several factors which could reduce this sum to a more reasonable figure. Recall the discussion of lifetime patterns of income and expenditure in earlier chapters. At some point the children are grown, the mortgage is paid, and the amount needed to sustain a particular standard of living declines. If you presently have an unemployed spouse, your death could bring changes; he or she may remarry, train for a new career, go back to work. Furthermore, Social Security survivors' benefits will take up a large share of the slack. You may have some savings or other assets which can be used to provide income to your survivors. Finally your survivors may be able to adjust their standard of living downward if necessary.

This leads to a different approach to life insurance which might be called the *needs approach*. Different periods of life require different sums of money to supplement survivors' earnings and Social Security benefits. Particularly heavy demands are likely to occur when the children are young, for college education, and for that interim period between Social Security survivors' benefits, which end when the youngest child is 18, and the onset of retirement benefits which begin when the surviving spouse reaches age 62.

The following example develops a needs approach for a hypothetical person, married, age 25, spouse not employed, with two children aged 3 and 1. Peter West has worked for four years at $10,000 a year but expects his income to increase at 4 percent a year in the future. His wife, Susan, plans to work part time when the younger child is 6 and expects to earn $5,000 a year. They have $2,000 in liquid assets. To indicate their standard of living and identify what the family needs, Peter and Susan have developed an income statement which is reproduced in Figure 9–1.

The income statement identifies the standard of living which insurance is expected to sustain and the expenditure pattern which must have space for insurance premiums.

Peter and Susan identify the following categories of insurance needs:

1. Final expenses. Burial, paying off short-term debts, medical and legal expenses, estate settlement.
2. An emergency or contingency fund.

Figure 9–1
Income statement
Peter and Susan West
January 1–December 1, 1977

Income:	
Peter's salary	$10,000
Interest	100
	10,100
Less income taxes	667
Less Social Security taxes	59
Income available for consumption and investment	$ 9,374
Expenses:	
Rent	2,400
Utilities	720
Food	3,120
Clothing	600
Medical care	300
Transportation	900
Recreation	400
Gifts, household furnishings	350
Peter's work expenses	160
Miscellaneous	224
Savings	200
	$ 9,374

3. Education for the children.
4. Family income.

Final expenses can vary widely. For example, a funeral currently costs about $1,200 to $1,800. In addition, the Wests consult their balance sheet and find that they have about $900 in bills. They assume that $900 would be a typical amount of unpaid bills. Since their estate is currently too small to incur any taxes, they allow about $500 for legal and other expenses.

It is their intention to discuss the matter of estate taxes and other final expenses with their attorney when their estate becomes a little larger and they revise their wills. (See Chapter 21.)

An *emergency or contingency fund* should consist of two to three month's net income. Since the Wests already have $2,000 in liquid assets, this is approximately correct (net income is $781 a month).

College education for the children is a difficult matter to forecast. The costs of education have been rising sharply, but there is no certainty that they will continue to rise at the same rate in the future. A reasonable expectation might be that college education costs will rise at the same rate as the general price level. At present, $3,500 a year will send a resident student to a state university for a year in most states. With two children and plans for four-year programs of study, the Wests will need $28,000 for educational expenses. Note that this sum should *not* be discounted to account for interest earnings which would accrue between the time of insurance settlement and the date when college expenses begin. That growth in interest can be used to compensate for increases in cost caused by inflation. The amount needed for education, along with all other figures, should be reviewed at least every five years. At the time of review, consideration is given to the ages of the children, the accumulation of other assets toward their college expenses, and the rise in actual college costs. If a parent dies, the children would be entitled to some Social Security survivor benefits while they are full-time students between the ages of 18 and 22. These funds can be subtracted from the education funds required. (See Chapter 11 for a more detailed explanation of Social Security benefits.)

Family income needs can be very large, modest, or even negative, depending on the individual situation. A young family may be entitled to substantial Social Security benefits. A working wife/husband or one not presently employed but equipped with marketable skills and a willingness to work can substantially reduce family income needs. These needs should be calculated by developing a modified income statement based on the surviving three-person family.

A summary of needs for insurance for the West family is presented in Figure 9–2. Notice that the need for final expenses, contingency fund, and children's education should be considered independently of family income needs. The first two are immediate needs which need to be met regardless of any anticipated surplus which may come later.

The family income needs are neither inflated to account for a rising cost of living nor discounted to account for anticipated interest to be earned on the lump sum insurance settlement over the years before it is all used. Since one cannot perfectly anticipate either the rate of inflation or the interest rate, the most reasonable—and simplest—assumption to make is that the two will be offsetting. While there have been a few years for which this was not true, on the average the interest rate for most savers just offsets the cost of inflation. The 5 to 6 percent rate of inflation anticipated through 1985 is approximately the yield on safe, conservative, short-term investments.

The family income needs for the West family are divided into five periods based on the ages of the children, Social Security benefits, and a conservative estimate of the wife's earning capacity. The first period reflects their current standard of living adjusted downward by 25 percent to reflect the reduced family size. When the second child is six the mother intends to return to work, which reduces Social Security benefits. At this point, the children continue to receive survivor benefits but the widow is no longer entitled to benefits since she is earning. (See Chapter 11 for a further explanation of the earnings test for surviving widows/widowers with dependent children.) Income needs are then adjusted upward because childhood and adolescence are more expensive in terms of food, clothing, recreation, and other needs.

Figure 9–2
Life insurance needs
Peter West

Immediate needs:		
Final expenses	$ 2,900	
Contingency fund	0	
College education (2 children)	28,000	
	$30,900	
Family income needs:		
Period 1:		
Annual needs	7,030	($9,374 × 0.75)
Less Social Security benefits	9,948	
Less other income	200	(interest)
Multiplied by number of years *5*	–0–	
Period 2:		
Annual needs	10,000	
Less Social Security benefits	8,532	
Less other income	5,000	
Multiplied by number of years *10*	–0–	
Period 3:		
Annual needs	8,500	
Less Social Security benefits	4,056	
Less other income	5,000	
Multiplied by number of years *2*	–0–	
Period 4:		
Annual needs	7,000	
Less Social Security benefits	0	
Less other income	8,000	(Susan works full time)
Multiplied by number of years *20*	–0–	
Period 5:		
Annual needs	6,000	
Less Social Security benefits	4,464	(based on Susan's earnings)
Less other income	–0–	
Multiplied by number of years *18*	27,648	
Total family income needs: $27,648		
Total insurance needs: $58,548		

The brief third period reflects the reduction in Social Security benefits and household expenses when the first child leaves for college (or work) at age 18 and the household is reduced to two members. In period four, the widow is alone and self-supporting with no Social Security benefits. Death of a breadwinner during this period could be devastating to a widow who has withdrawn from the labor market for an extensive period to run the household and raise the children. At this point in their lives, the Wests are assuming that Susan will be employed or at least employable. Certainly the plight of homemakers widowed in their 50s after many years out of the labor market emphasizes the need to reassess life insurance needs regularly as work expectations, income, assets, and expenditures change.

The final period is that of the widow's retirement. Social Security benefits and perhaps her own retirement provisions may cover this need. The conservative assumptions about Susan's savings and pension require some additional income to meet her limited needs during retirement years. In fact, the assumptions for this case make the final period the only one which generates a positive family income need. Note that in any period where needs are estimated as negative, a zero is entered. Human nature indicates that expenditures will expand to fill the income available. It is not realistic to expect that surpluses during periods of anticipated "negative needs" will actually materialize and be carried forward to cover deficit years.

While on the subject, the Wests should develop a life insurance needs profile for Susan for two reasons. First, it would be costly for Peter to provide the necessary child care and household services for the children without Susan. While he would no longer have to feed, clothe, and entertain Susan, it will be more expensive to provide needed domestic services through the marketplace. Second, the family is probably relying on Susan's anticipated future income to enhance the family's standard of living, provide for the higher expenses of late childhood and adolescence, and generate some surplus to be set aside for the children's education. In Susan's absence, Peter may not be able to meet these needs on his own income. A worksheet similar to Peter's should be developed for Susan. While Susan is not currently generating a money income, the value of her current services and her anticipated future income indicates that she, like Peter, is a valuable financial asset in need of insurance protection.

It is crucial that individuals build their own assumptions into the insurance worksheet depicted in Figure 9–2. A higher standard of living, anticipated greater college expenses, and less sanguine assumptions about Susan's employability would have greatly increased the West's life insurance needs. For example, the expectation that Susan would be able to provide for her own retirement would have cut insurance needs to little more than half of the amount indicated. Either additional children or an assumption that Susan would remarry would have further altered the picture. Along these lines, it might be advisable to work out insurance needs on two alternative "best case" and "worst case" sets of assumptions. The important assumptions consist of:

1. Additional children.
2. Spouse's work pattern, earnings, and retirement provisions.
3. Anticipated standard of living.
4. Expectations of inflation and yield on investments.[1]
5. Anticipated changes in Social Security benefits.

The assumptions you choose to make will reflect your unique lifestyle.

[1] If these are assumed to be other than offsetting, the reader will require the use of discounted present value techniques described in the appendix to this book.

HOW LONG DO I NEED IT?

Insurance agents tend to stress the permanent need for life insurance. Certainly there are some needs—especially final expenses which never disappear. But many life insurance needs are temporary in nature. As noted earlier, children get older; the period of their dependency lessens and finally ends. Assets can begin to accumulate. The mortgage is paid off. It may become necessary to insure against outliving your assets. However, as needs decline and assets accumulate, it is possible that the day may arrive when you no longer need life insurance.

Insurance coverage needs to be reviewed at regular intervals—at least every five years. Additional review will be needed when you marry, divorce, have children, see children leave home, experience a sharp rise in income, receive an inheritance, or encounter any of the other ups and downs of life which significantly change your income, expenses, and responsibilities.

WHAT KIND OF INSURANCE SHOULD I BUY?

Basically there are only two kinds of life insurance. One is *term,* which is temporary insurance. Like property insurance, liability insurance, and health insurance, term insurance expires at the end of the contract period—which may be anywhere from a year to "until age 65." If you do not incur a claim, you get nothing back. Term insurance is pure protection, with no guaranteed payment unless you die during the contract period.

The second type of insurance is permanent or *cash value insurance.* The policy for this insurance guarantees that the face value of the policy will be paid off in full at some point as long as the policy is kept in force. For example, if you have a $10,000 whole life policy, as long as you continue to meet the premiums, either you or your beneficiary will eventually receive $10,000. In the case of whole life, your beneficiary receives $10,000 when you die or you receive it at age 100. With a $10,000 20-year *endowment* policy, you are guaranteed $10,000 at the end of 20 years or when you die, whichever comes first. Your "savings goal" of $10,000 will be met whether you live to the end of the contract period or not. The compulsion to save is one of the attractions in whole life insurance, especially for those who find it difficult to save on their own.

Cash value policies are all variations on the idea of endowment, or a policy guaranteeing the payment of face value within a specified period of time. A true *endowment policy* is the most expensive form of insurance (and one of the least popular). It is not difficult to see why. If you buy a $5,000, ten-year term policy, the insurance company is in essence "betting" on the small probability of your death in that ten-year period. If the chance of your dying in that period were one percent, their expected loss on the average ten-year term policyholder is one percent of $5,000, or $50—plus, of course, a margin of safety and operating expenses, as explained in Chapter 8. But with a ten-year, $5,000 endowment policy, they must be prepared to pay out $5,000. While the chance of paying out the proceeds before ten years is small, the insurer is certain to pay $5,000 at the end of ten years. Obviously the premium for an endowment policy will have to be much higher than for a term policy of the same face value.

Characteristics of term insurance have been combined with those of endowment policies to yield several other standard forms of life insurance. These include:

1. Term-to-65 or term-to-expectancy (your expected year of death based on your present age), which builds up modest cash values in the early years of the policy. These cash values drop off and disappear toward the end of the policy period.
2. *Renewable (level) term,* sold most commonly for five to ten years and renewable at the policyholder's option regardless of the state of his or her health at the time of renewal. The premium rises with each renewal, reflecting increased age and greater probability of death during the policy period. The face amount remains the same; the policy may allow increases or decreases in face value.
3. *Decreasing term,* in which the premium stays constant but the face amount of the policy declines each year until it expires. A popular policy for covering the balance due on a mortgage, this type of policy is also useful for covering predictably decreasing insurance needs, for example, covering the period of dependency of minor children.
4. *Whole life* (also called ordinary life), which is endowment at age 100. Premiums for whole life are higher than term, but lower than endowment. This is the most popular policy.
5. *Twenty-pay,* 30-pay, or single premium *whole life;* or life paid up at 65, one of the most popular policies. These policies are again whole life (or endowment at age 100) but are not paid for over the entire period to age 100. Rather, the premium is paid as a single lump sum, or in 20 or 30 annual installments, or until age 65. The annual premiums will be high in the latter two cases compared to the annual premiums for whole life in the same face amount. But the total premium outlay will be smaller; the insurance company will have the use of more money earlier in the policy and can earn more interest, a saving passed on in lower total premiums.
6. Combination policies, most commonly whole life combined with level or decreasing term, to meet a combination of temporary or short-term insurance needs and long-term to permanent needs.

Figure 9–3 illustrates the percent distribution of life insurance in force by type.

Figure 9–3
Percent distribution of life insurance in force by type, 1976

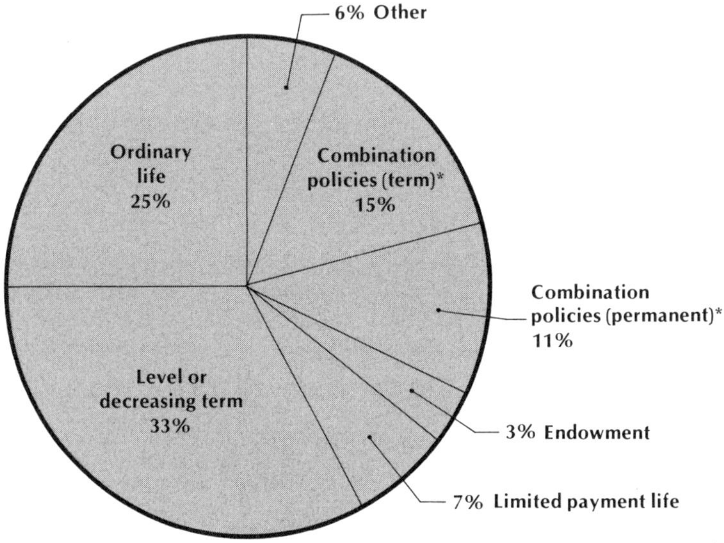

* The permanent and term components, respectively, of permanent-term combination policies and multiperson coverage policies.

Source: *Life Insurance Factbook 1977* (New York: American Council of Life Insurance) p. 14.

HOW MUCH DOES IT COST?

Prices in life insurance are quoted as so many dollars per year per thousand dollars of face value. Table 9–1 gives the prices of various types of policies from a company whose prices are about the middle of the range. The company quoted is a nonparticipating insurer. That is, the firm does not pay out cash dividends to its policy holders as do participating companies. The payment of dividends, of course, reduces the full cost of insurance. When considered on a final cost basis, the cost of insurance by participating and nonparticipating companies is about the same. Other factors can cause significant differences in cost, however.

The differences in the costs of the various policies shown in Table 9–1 is substantial, indicating that the decision about which type of life insurance to buy can be as important as how much face value to purchase. In addition to the expected large differences by type of policy, there are also substantial differences in premium for the same type of policy from different companies. You will be paying those life insurance premiums for a long time. A little time spent understanding your options and getting price quotations from several companies could generate significant savings.

In addition to your age, the company, and the type of policy, there are four other factors bearing on the cost of your life insurance policy. One is

Table 9–1
Cost per $1,000 for different kinds of life insurance policies*

	Male age 25	*Male age 45*
Annual renewable	2.40	5.31
20-year decreasing term	3.45	9.13
10-year renewable term	5.02	11.16
5-year renewable term	5.33	10.37
Term-to-65	8.32	16.31
Whole life	13.21	27.53
Whole life paid up at 65	14.98	35.07
Endowment at 65	18.06	44.47
20-pay life	21.32	35.07

* All quotes from a single nonparticipating company. Rates will vary from company to company but the *relative* costs of different types of policies will be similar. Rates for females are usually lower because of their longer life expectancies. Ages refer to age at time of issue.

whether or not you are classed as a *standard risk* or "rated up." The second is how frequently you pay premiums—annually, semiannually, quarterly, monthly, or weekly. The third is the size of your policy. The fourth is whether or not your policy receives dividends. Some insurance companies are owned by their policyholders. These are the mutual companies which pay dividends to their policyholder-owners. Other insurers are stock companies. These firms generally offer no dividend to policyholders.

The majority of applicants—92 percent—are accepted as standard risks and insured at standard rates. Another 3 percent are rejected for insurance, and the remaining 5 percent are insured at substandard (higher) rates. Overweight, underweight, chronic medical problems, family history, occupation, and risky hobbies or avocations (skindiving, mountain climbing) are reasons for charging a higher rate. The surcharge in the premium ranges from 15 percent to 45 percent or more depending on the nature, number, and extent of the problems identified.

Paying less frequently will reduce your premium for two reasons. First, the company will save the costs of additional billings or collections. Second, the company will have the use of your money for the entire period, since the premium is collected at the beginning of the period. A sum of $120 on January 1 will earn them more interest than $120 paid in 12 $10 monthly installments. These savings are passed on to the policyholder in the form of reduced premiums. A form of insurance which was once very popular, called industrial insurance, involved weekly or monthly door-to-door collections of small premiums for insurance policies with a face value of $1,000 or less. Industrial insurance was very expensive in terms of cost per thousand because of the small size and high collection costs.

In addition, there are economies of scale in insurance. The cost of selling and servicing a $100,000 policy is no greater than for a $10,000 policy. This saving is reflected in a lower cost per thousand. One company quotes a premium of $12.48 per $1,000 for nonparticipating whole life policies (age 25, male) or under $25,000, while it is $9.90 per $1,000 for policies of $100,000 or more. The difference of $2.58 per $1,000 represents a substantial saving over the life of the policy.

Finally, there is the question of dividends. Nonparticipating policies are those which pay no dividends. *Participating policies* do, but the amount of the *dividend* is not guaranteed. The quoted premium is usually higher in a participating policy, but the net premium (gross premium less dividends) is likely to be lower after dividends. This fact makes it difficult to compare participating and nonparticipating policy prices. For example, a company which offers both types quotes a premium per $1,000 (whole life, age 25) of $13.37 on nonparticipating, $17.44 on participating. But their dividend scale indicates a dividend of $1.85 in the second year (per $1,000 face value) increasing to $8.95 after 20 years. In ten years, the average annual premium after dividends would be $14.66 (if dividends held at that level), bringing the net premiums closer together. In 20 years, the average annual premium would have fallen to $12.83 on the participating policy.

HOW DO I CHOOSE A COMPANY?

Best's Flitcraft Compend, the standard reference work for life insurance agents, provides information on the 450 companies which do 99 percent of the life insurance business in the United States. There is a staggering variety from which to choose. Although they all offer basically the same set of products, there are differences in the kinds and combinations of policies offered, the size and safety of the company, the local agents, the prices of comparable policies, the ownership of the company, and the availability of dividends. These last two items refer partly to stock versus mutual companies; but many stock companies issue both participating and nonparticipating policies.

Information on a particular company can be found in Best's Life and Health Insurance Reports, an annual volume which examines assets, insurance in force, and measures of size and safety. This volume will help you identify some fairly large companies which offer a broad selection of policies.

The local agent is an important consideration since you will have to depend on his honesty, reliability, and willingness to discuss the entire range of policy options available to you. However, there is always a good chance that the agent you see in 5, 10, or 15 years to review and adjust your coverage, or the agent with whom your beneficiary deals when you die, will be someone else. Agent turnover is high. So is the frequency with which

Americans move from one area of the country to another. The company, therefore, is more important over the long-term period of the contract than is the particular agent.

The choice between a stock company and a mutual company rests on two considerations; stockholder dividends and policyholders dividends. The majority of life insurance companies are stockholder-owned, but the bulk of individual policies are written by the mutual companies. The mutual companies are owned by the policyholders, who elect the board of directors. The only assets of mutual companies are those purchased with the inflow of premium income. Mutual companies normally issue only *participating* policies, that is, policies entitled to dividends. Stock companies are owned by the stockholders, who put up the initial capital and secure dividends on the stock based on the company's net earnings, which depend on less experience, operating costs, and income on invested assets. Stock companies issue both participating and nonparticipating policies. Nonparticipating policies have premiums which cover the cost of insurance and some profit to stockholders to compensate them for the risks they incur—risks of higher than expected loss experience and operating costs or lower than expected earnings on the insurance company's invested assets. Participating policies will have a higher basic premium to provide a cushion against those risks. But if the company's overall performance is good, they can expect that dividends will reduce their overall cost over the life of the policy to less than the cost of an equivalent nonparticipating policy. Insurance dividends are regarded by the government as a refund of the overcharge in premiums and are not considered income for tax purposes.

It is difficult to compare the cost of participating and nonparticipating policies because the dividend scale is not guaranteed. Interest must also be taken into account; when offsetting expected future dividends against present higher premiums, the dividends must be discounted because dollars in the future are worth less than dollars in the present.

WHAT HAPPENS IF I DECIDE TO CANCEL MY POLICY?

If you have a cash value (whole life or endowment) policy which you have held for two years or more, you usually are entitled to some kind of settlement when you discontinue the policy. This settlement can be taken in one of three forms, called *nonforfeiture options,* which are spelled out in the policy. All of these options are based on the cash value at the last anniversary of the date of issue. You can take the cash value as a lump sum, convert the policy to extended term insurance at the same face value, or convert it to paid-up life insurance at a reduced value. For example, you might have bought $10,000 whole life insurance at age 35. You decide to discontinue at age 45. The cash values will vary from company to company, but a representative figure at age 45 is $141 per thousand, or $1,410.

You can take the $1,410 in cash, or you can convert the policy to extended term, using the cash value as a single premium. This amount would buy $10,000 level term for a period of 14 years and 91 days. The alternative is to convert the policy to paid-up life with a face value of $2,724. The term policy in this example will expire at approximately age 59. The paid-up life will continue in force until age 100. There will be no additional premiums in either case.

Insurance cash value has another use if you continue to pay premiums. You can borrow this sum from the insurance company at a rate of interest given in the policy. Rates of 5 and 6 percent are available in older policies, while 8 percent is common in more recently issued policies. You may pay the annual interest only, repay in installments or in a lump sum, or use dividends on a participating policy to pay interest, principal, or both. Any loan outstanding at the time of death will be subtracted from the face value of the policy. The interest on an insurance loan can be used as an itemized deduction on your income tax.

The cash value can also be used to convert the policy to an annuity after age 55, an option discussed later in this chapter.

HOW CAN MY BENEFICIARY COLLECT THE PROCEEDS?

The *beneficiary* is the person designated in the policy to receive the proceeds of your policy when you die. The person who buys the policy designates the beneficiary—perhaps spouse, child or children, parents, the company for which you work, or your partner. The money can be paid out in several ways, of which the most common are:

1. Lump sum.
2. Interest only, principal at a designated later date, (A minimum interest rate will be specified in the policy.)
3. Income of a specified amount per year (including principal and interest) until the funds are exhausted.
4. Income for a specified number of years (or life) at whatever amount principal and interest can provide.

For example, a $10,000 policy can be paid out as $10,000 cash, or annual interest of $400 (at 4 percent) with the $10,000 principal to be paid out in 5, 10, or 20 years. Or it can be paid out in monthly installments (at 3 percent interest) of $97.20 for 10 years (or $1,161.80 per year for 10 years). Or it can be paid in installments of $1,000 per year for as long as the funds last, which at 3 percent interest would be about 12 years. And, finally, the beneficiary can accept a paid-in-full life insurance policy with the type, face value, and time period determined by the value of the proceeds.

Which option should be selected depends on several considerations. The beneficiary may or may not be someone who can invest, manage, and spread out the income over the time period required, in which case one of the last three options might be better, especially if dependent children are involved. If, on the other hand, most of the needs are immediate—final expenses, debts, perhaps education and training for a dependent spouse—then a lump sum settlement might be the solution.

WHAT ABOUT GROUP LIFE INSURANCE?

Group life insurance is often an inexpensive way to obtain at least part of your life insurance coverage. It is sold to a group whose existence is not for the purpose of buying life insurance. A group of employees of a common employer, a professional association, labor union, and creditor-debtor groups (credit life insurance) can all serve as a basis of a group life policy. Most frequently it is sold to the employer as a fringe benefit for employees. There is a single master contract. Selling costs are low; group insurance is essentially "wholesale" insurance. The insurance sold is almost always term, and the premiums are about 50 to 70 percent of comparable individual term policies for the average group member. Of course if you are not "average," it is possible that your cost of insurance could be lower on a private plan basis. Any group life insurance which you have should be counted toward meeting the total insurance needs calculated earlier in this chapter. However, you should always compare rates before buying.

HOW DO I PROTECT MYSELF AGAINST LIVING TOO LONG?

This may seem like a strange question in a chapter devoted to the problem of dying too early. But the two hazards, dying too young and living too long, are closely interrelated. Both are concerned with the lifetime distribution of income and expenditures under conditions of uncertainty about the age of death. If you die young, you will not have the opportunity to earn the income and accumulate the assets needed to provide for the expenses of dependents during their period of dependency. If you live well beyond your life expectancy, the income from (and principal of) assets accumulated before retirement may be exhausted before your need for income ends. The solution to this second problem is a form of insurance in reverse called an *annuity*. Annuities are also available in the form of retirement income policies.

An annuity is a payment to you or a designated beneficiary of a regular monthly/yearly sum of money for a period of time. The sum can be fixed or variable, the beneficiaries individual or multiple, the time period 10 years, 20 years, or until the beneficiary dies, and the starting date immediate or some designated time far in the future. Annuities come in all styles, sizes, and varieties to suit the varied needs and preferences of individual buyers. They need not be used only for retirement; they can also provide income for dependent children, beloved nieces, and aged parents.

An annuity can be purchased for a lump sum or in installments prior to the date at which you begin recovering payments (most commonly age 65). You can purchase an annuity of $100 a month at age 65 (male) from a typical company for a single (lump sum) premium of $11,940. A female would pay $13,090, because of her greater life expectancy. If you wish to guarantee payments to you or your heirs for a specific period (for example, 10 years), the premium goes up to $12,280 (male) or $13,310 (female). The payments consist partly of interest, partly of return of principal, and partly of insurance benefits. The surplus funds from those who die before exhausting their principal go as insurance benefits to the continued support of those who live beyond their life expectancy and more than exhaust their annuity's principal and interest. A more detailed explanation of annuities is given in the appendix on the Mathematics of Finance.

Single premium annuities can be purchased with the accumulated cash value of your life insurance policy at age 65, an option which is spelled out in your policy. As you may have realized, some of the settlement options available on your life insurance policy are in the form of annuities.

Deferred annuities can be purchased by lump sum or in regular installments with payments to you at a specified future date. Deferred annuities specifically intended for retirement have substantial tax advantages. Tax-deferred annuities are discussed in Chapter 20.

STANDARD LIFE INSURANCE ENDORSEMENTS

In addition to the types and features of life insurance described in this chapter, in practically every case, a life insurance policy will offer add-on features or *endorsements*. These features add small charges to your premium, and they may be worth considering.

First, *double indemnity* may be added. This feature doubles the payment of the policy in the event of accidental death. In other words, the face amount of the policy is increased twofold. Triple indemnity may be purchased also. Since accidental death has a low probability and double or triple indemnity offers a significant payoff, this feature might be viewed as bargain basement insurance.

The second endorsement—*waiver of premium*—enables your insurance to remain in force in the event of a disability. In other words, if you should suffer an accident which causes you to be unable to work, the insurance company pays your premium for you. This benefit would continue while you are without income.

Finally, you can purchase a *guarantee of insurability*. This endorsement makes it possible for you to purchase future insurance without being subject to a physical examination. In other words, you are assured of the purchase of additional insurance at set future dates. This feature is of particular interest to younger people who might have concern about their future health.

SUMMARY

Life insurance is a complex purchase decision. Its main use is providing for replacement of your income in case of death for your surviving dependents. Life insurance needs can be computed either as discounted present value of expected future income or on a needs approach.

Needs include final expenses, contingency funds, children's education, and family income by periods. Social Security benefits, changing family expenses, and other sources of income determine family income needs. The income statement and balance sheet provide information about assets and debts, income and expenses from which an insurance needs profile can be developed. Changes in the family situation—ages, work situations, assets, debts, expenses—will call for a review and adjustment of insurance needs. Insurance needs should be determined for both spouses since a wife's death can generate reduced income and increased outlays for child care and household help.

There are basically two kinds of insurance—term, or pure protection, and cash value, which includes a savings account in the form of benefits certain. A variety of intermediate forms—whole life, 20-pay life, decreasing term, combination policies—can also be purchased.

Prices are quoted in dollars per thousand, with annual renewable term the cheapest and 20-pay life the most expensive for a 25 year old. Premiums vary greatly from company to company as well as from one kind of policy to another. Age is the single most important determinant of the premium for a particular type of policy. Other factors keeping cost per thousand down are being a standard risk, paying less often, buying a larger policy, and receiving dividends on participating policies.

Companies should be chosen by their size, the quality of their assets, the kinds of policies available, and (last) the local agent. Stock companies may offer both participating and nonparticipating policies. Mutual companies, which sell the bulk of life insurance policies in the United States, offer only participating (dividend-paying) policies.

If you cancel a cash value policy after two or more years, you will secure either a cash settlement or a choice between extended term insurance and paid-up life insurance at a reduced face value. The cash value can also be borrowed at relatively low rates of interest, or used to purchase an annuity after age 55.

The beneficiary can collect the proceeds as a lump sum; interest only, principal later; or in the form of a regular income until the principal plus interest earnings are exhausted.

Group life is a low-cost form of term insurance, usually purchased for employees of a common employer.

The hazard of living too long can be insured against with an annuity, which is a payment of regular income to you. An annuity may be purchased in a lump sum at retirement, in advance, or in installments. Some retirement annuities have distinct tax advantages.

Endorsements which can be added to the policy include double indemnity, waiver of premium benefit, and guaranteed insurability.

KEY WORDS

Annuity
Beneficiary
Cash value
Decreasing term
Discounted present value
Dividends
Double indemnity
Emergency fund
Endorsements
Endowment
Family income needs
Final expenses
Group life insurance
Guaranteed insurability
Life insurance
Needs approach
Nonforfeiture option
Participating policy
Renewable term
Standard risk
Term insurance
Twenty-pay life
Waiver of premium
Whole life (ordinary life)

PROBLEMS

1. Compute life insurance needs for George, whose income statement and balance sheet are given in Chapter 3. Using his balance sheet and income statement and the life insurance needs form in this chapter as a guide, what kind of policy would you recommend? Does Henrietta also need insurance? What could happen to change their insurance needs? Assume that Henrietta is 25 years old and plans to go to work part time when Henry George is six and full time when he is 12, with a take-home pay of $3,000 a year part time and $7,300 full time. Make appropriate assumptions about income required for time periods after the first.

2. One of the continuing debates in life insurance is that of whole life versus "buy term and invest the difference." Using the rates given in this chapter for whole life and term to 65, and investing the difference at 8 percent, how much would you accumulate by age 45? Use Table 4–2 in the appendix on the Mathematics of Finance to determine the accumulated amount. The whole life policy would have a face value of $1,000 and a cash value of $255 at age 45. Considering taxes at 25 percent on your interest return, which is the better choice? Why?

Chapter 10

Health and disability insurance

Financial ruin from medical bills is almost exclusively an American disease.

Roul Turley

Health and disability insurance protect you from the costs of a wide range of hazards. A broken toe, a fall out of a tree, an appendectomy, the birth of a baby, a loss of income due to sickness or accident, an extended period of hospitalization following a stroke, a new crown for a tooth, a big bill for prescription drugs—all of these can be covered, partly or completely, by policies belonging to the broad category of health and disability insurance. Frequently, health and disability insurance is provided by your employer as part of a fringe benefit package, discussed in Chapter 11.

Protection from the burden of medical expenditures may seem like transferring some routine expenditures to a third party—in effect, budgeting your medical expenses by paying regular premiums. This is to some extent true for the "average" family. But because health costs are one of the most unpredictable and most uncontrollable components of the budget, medical disasters have every bit as much potential for wrecking your budget and wiping out your carefully accumulated assets as premature death, automobile accidents, or having your house burn to the ground. And injuries or prolonged illnesses which leave you unable to work can create an insurable risk that is potentially larger (in dollars) than the life insurance risk. If the earner dies, at least there is one less person to feed, clothe, house, and entertain. But a disabled adult continues to incur all the normal expenses of living, plus the added costs of medical care, while suffering the same loss of income used as the basis for buying life insurance.

Health care expenses averaged $552 per capita in 1976, which would be $2,208 for a family of four. Direct payments by households plus private insurance benefits (which must be funded by your premiums) accounted for about 60 percent of the total, with the remaining 40 percent funded by the government. With an average family income just over $15,000, the cost of health care—direct payments plus premiums—is about 9 percent of the after-tax budget. These averages conceal a great deal of variation from the healthy to the sickly, the safe to the accident-prone, the prime years of 10 to 30, to the very old and very young. As in other insurance, it is not the average loss that needs to be covered by insurance but the very small possibility of an extremely large loss—a stroke or heart attack with a long recuperation, an extended terminal illness, or a major disabling accident.

This chapter will examine the family of health and disability insurance policies, focusing on:

- Kinds of policies.
- What determines the premium.
- Kinds of companies.
- How much you need.
- Special contract provisions.
- Prepayment plans.
- Prospects for national health insurance.

Figure 10–1 illustrates health insurance coverage by type in force in 1975.

KINDS OF POLICIES

Health insurance is available to meet two needs. The first is outlays for hospital, medical, surgical, dental, and nursing care, and prescription drugs. The second is loss of income because of accident or illness. The first group includes hospital expense insurance, medical/surgical expense insurance, dental insurance, major medical insurance and comprehensive (a combination policy). The second type consists of replacement of income policies, also known as accident insurance, disability income protection, income protection plans, and other names. Some policies combine expense insurance with income protection insurance in a single "umbrella" policy.

Hospital and medical insurance

Hospital expense insurance can be purchased separately or as part of a package with related coverages. Hospital expense insurance is usually written in terms of so many dollars per day, with the patient paying any excess; or the "usual and customary charges" for a defined level of care, typically a semiprivate room. Hospital expense policies can be purchased separately or in combination with other policies.

The daily amount paid by hospital expense insurance covers room,

Figure 10–1
Health insurance coverage by type, 1975

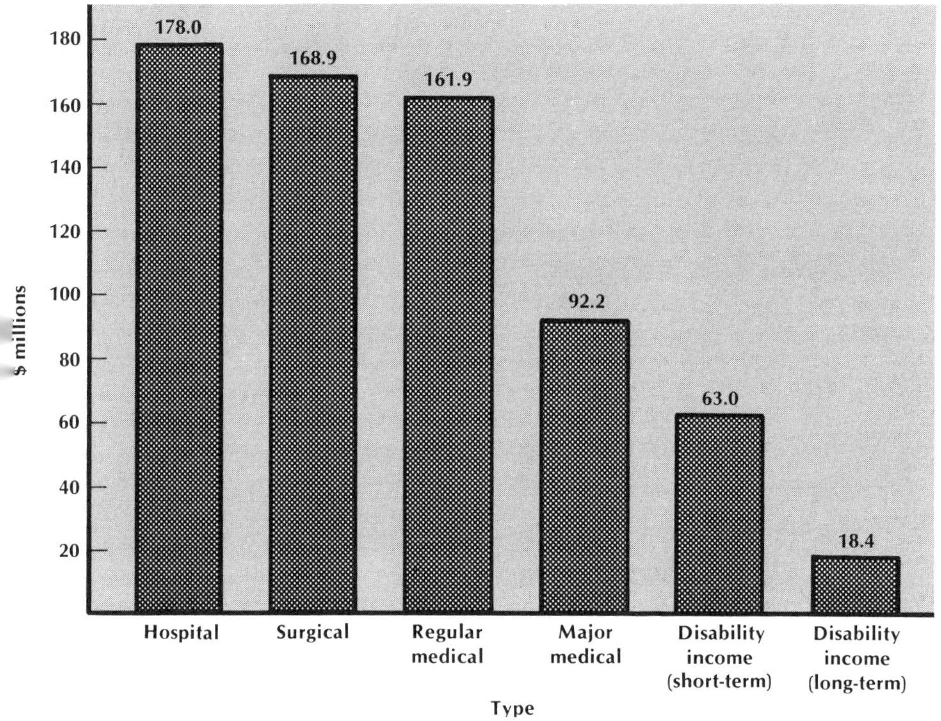

Source: *Source Book of Health Insurance Data: 1977* (New York: Health Insurance Institute, 1977).

board, nursing care, and other services for which the hospital makes a per diem charge. These charges vary greatly from one section of the country to another and within hospitals from the least costly ward to the most costly private, intensive care type of service. Hospital expense insurance also covers miscellaneous hospital services—anesthesia, ambulance, operating room, X rays, medicines, surgical dressing and supplies. Some policies offer a dollar maximum, others apply a deductible and/or coinsurance provisions, discussed later in this chapter. Hospital expenses are the fastest rising component of total health care costs, rising an average of 12 percent a year since 1965, and also the largest single component—nearly 40 percent of total health care. Almost 80 percent of the U.S. population has some form of hospitalization insurance.

Medical surgical expense insurance covers payments to physicians, the second largest component of health care cost, some 13 percent of the total. Surgery is covered on a basis of a specific rate of payment for a specific operation; for example, $150 for an appendectomy. The amounts provided vary greatly from contract to contract. Physicians frequently charge more than the contract amount, with the extra cost being borne by the patient. Medical expense coverage is often limited to hospitalized illnesses where surgery is not required—pneumonia, stroke, heart attack, and similar major illnesses. Most policies also cover office calls subject to a dollar limit and/or a specific number of calls. Policies which do not cover routine office visits may cover outpatient treatment for accidents and injuries. Major medical insurance, discussed below, will pay part of the cost for outpatient treatment not covered by a surgical/medical expense policy. In 1975, 39 percent of physicians' fees were paid by private insurance carriers; 75 percent of the population had insurance for physicians' services.

Nursing care may be included in a package policy, sometimes for hospital only, sometimes for home care as well, subject to limits on the amount per day and the total number of days. Only about one third of the population is insured for out-of-hospital nursing care; most of that coverage is under Medicare.

Dental care insurance is not widely available on an individual basis, but is sold to a limited extent on a group basis, usually as a fringe benefit. Only 16 percent of the U.S. population has any dental insurance. Because claims are frequent and small, dental care is not as amenable to insurance. As was pointed out in Chapter 8, large infrequent losses are best suited to insurance.

Major medical insurance is a type of policy which is most similar to other lines—life, property, and liability. Major medical developed to complement basic hospital/surgical/medical expense insurance, although it can be purchased separately. While other policies offer limits per day or on the number of days, major medical has a total dollar limit—for example, $10,000 per person. Once the $10,000 is exhausted, if you keep the insurance in force, some fraction of the benefits will be "restored" each year, subject to a lifetime maximum. Major medical uses a deductible plus coinsurance, sometimes also known as cost-sharing. The deductible is a flat dollar amount—$50, $100, $500 for each person covered. You pay any expenses up to this amount before insurance starts to pay for expenses. In addition, the coinsurance or cost-sharing provision requires that you bear some fixed percentage of expenses over and above the deductible and any expenses over and above the maximum limits of the policy. Usually you pay 20 percent and the insurer pays 80 percent. A simple example will illustrate *restoration, deductibles,* and *coinsurance*.

John Smith has major medical with a limit of $5,000, $100 deductible, 80/20 percent coinsurance, and 20 percent per year restoration subject to a $50,000 lifetime ceiling. He has an extended stay in the hospital which costs $6,500.

John has exhausted his benefits, but at the beginning of the next year he will have $1,000 (20 percent of $5,000) restored. The same amount minus any new claims will be restored each year until his benefits are again at the

John's bill		Insurer's bill	
Deductible	$ 100	Coinsurance 80% of ($5,000–$100)	$3,980
Coinsurance 20% of ($5,000–$100)	980		
Excess over ceiling ($6,500–$5,000)	1,500		
Total	$2,580	Total	$3,980

$5,000 maximum. The insurance on the rest of his family is not affected by his claim.

Major medical insurance is based on the large loss principle, and it is suitable for people with adequate income and reserves to handle small claims and coinsurance out of their own resources. There are two related reasons for the use of deductibles and coinsurance. First, the deductible eliminates many small claims which are costly to process. This results in substantial cost savings which are passed on to the policyholder. The larger the deductible you select, the smaller your premium will be. This premium saving can be used to purchase higher limits on the policy itself.

The second reason for deductibles and coinsurance is to reduce overuse, or moral hazard. Moral hazard is present to some extent in all lines of insurance. There is temptation to engage in arson, have or fake an auto accident, or create an injury to generate an insurance claim. Moral hazard is particularly a problem in health insurance. If all or most of your expenses are covered by insurance, you may be tempted to seek care for minor illnesses, problems, or accidents which you would otherwise leave untreated or treat yourself. This is particularly true of elective surgery, routine short-run illnesses, plastic surgery, and psychiatric care. The requirement that you pay a portion of the cost through deductibles and coinsurance reduces the temptation to overuse covered health services.

Major medical covers the biggest risk—a medical "wipe out" of income and assets rather than just an above-average bill to be worked into the budget. Major medical insurance would seem to have the highest priority among the types of insurance discussed, but it is in fact not as widely held as hospital/medical/surgical insurance. Less than half of the U.S. population has major medical insurance.

Comprehensive health insurance combines hospital/medical/surgical insurance with major medical into a single policy. After the benefits of the former are exhausted, or more likely, when claims arise in excess of the amount hospital/medical/surgical insurance will cover, major medical takes over. For example, you may be hospitalized at a per day rate in excess of what basic hospitalization will provide, or have surgery which costs more than the surgical schedule will pay, or more X rays for an accident than

"Orthodox medicine has no known cure for your condition. I could recommend a good quack."

Reprinted by permission The Wall Street Journal

medical insurance will cover, or numerous visits to the doctor's office which are not covered because you have a nonhospitalized illness. Once these unreimbursed costs reach the deductible on the major medical portion of your policy, major medical will pay its coinsurance share of the amount over the deductible. Let us follow John Smith through a second illness.

John is hospitalized for surgery. The hospital bill comes to $700, which is $200 more than the hospital expense insurance will pay. The surgeon charges $400, but the surgical portion of his policy only pays $250 for this surgery. Once he is home, he continues to visit the doctor and take medicine at a total cost of $400, not covered by the basic hospital/surgical/medical portion of his policy. From his total cost of $1,500, hospital/surgical coverage pays the hospital $500 and pays surgical $250 for a total of $750. John then pays the $100 deductible on the major medical portion, leaving $650, which is split 80/20—between the insurance company and John—$520 to the insurer, $130 to John. John pays $230, and his comprehensive policy pays $1,270. If he had only major medical, 80/20 coinsurance with a $100 deductible, John would have paid $380 ($100 deductible plus 80 percent of $1,400) and the insurer $1,120.

It is also possible to buy limited policies for specific illnesses, some of which are called *"dread disease"* policies. Polio insurance was common prior to the development of the Salk vaccine. Currently one of the most widespread policies is cancer insurance, because of the frequency of cancer—one person in four—and high costs of surgery and chemotherapy. Like major medical, these policies have a total dollar limit plus limits on the various types of coverage, for example, hospital and medical/surgical. To illustrate the cost of dread disease insurance, a group policy offered by one major insurer covering cancer plus ten other diseases with total lifetime benefits of $41,900 costs $33.60 a year for a family whose oldest member is under 40.

Disability income insurance

The second group of policies are the income protection plans or *disability income policies*. Some disability protection is provided by Social Security. While this is an important starting point for disability insurance, the Social Security coverage has two shortcomings. First, it restores only a fraction of lost earnings. Then, there is a six-month waiting period before benefits are collected.

Disability income policies provide a flat number of dollars per week or month with a *waiting period* before you start to collect benefits. Thirty days is a common waiting period. However, you can agree to a longer one. The dollar amount, for example, $300 per month, must be reasonable in relation to your income. The lower the dollar limits and the longer the waiting period, the lower your premiums will be. The waiting period serves the function of a deductible, reducing small claims for short-term disabilities. Privately issued policies, unlike Social Security, offer a fixed duration of benefits, for periods of six months to life.

Disability income policies are available on an individual or group basis. In group insurance, they are often combined with hospital/medical/surgical expense policies. Some disability policies cover only the loss of income due to accidents.

In addition to Social Security, a few states have publicly financed programs to protect against income losses due to temporary, nonwork-related disability. Workers' Compensation, described in Chapter 11, also provides disability income protection as well as medical expense benefits.

Whatever the coverage, the definition of disability presents a difficult problem. Policies distinguish between total and partial disability, temporary and permanent disability. Temporary and permanent disability are self-explanatory. Total disability is traditionally defined as inability to work at *any* occupation for wage or profit. In practice this is usually qualified to mean any job for which the insured is reasonably suited by education, training, or experience. A surgeon, for example, would not be expected to work as a dishwasher. Most commonly, policies will apply the broader definition to a specified period, such as five years, after which they revert to the more stringent "any occupation" definition.

Partial disability is the inability to perform one or more of the duties of your occupation. In this case, you are entitled to reduced benefits.

In individual disability policies, you select the dollar limits, subject to company regulations on the amount you can buy in relation to your income. Group policies usually provide payment as a fixed percentage of salary, most commonly one half to two thirds.

Disability insurers are concerned about the problem of moral hazard—the temptation to simulate or stretch out a disability so as to collect benefits. They set limits on the amount of coverage you can buy, and they base the limits on your income and expected Social Security disability benefits. The waiting period, which serves as a deductible, also helps to reduce moral hazard.

In 1975, about 63 million people had short-term disability protection policies; about 18 million had long-term coverage. Of these, only 15 million and 7 million, respectively, were individual policies; most disability coverage is bought and sold on a group basis.

WHAT DETERMINES THE PREMIUM?

The cost of health care insurance has risen rapidly in recent years because of sharp increases in hospital care costs and medical/surgical fees. Both of these categories of medical costs have been rising more rapidly than the consumer price index (CPI). Of course, insurers have to recover their costs. So, rates are adjusted on the basis of the cost of service and the claims experience of the group covered by the insurer. If you happen to be covered under a group plan at your place of employment or through an organization, the rate you pay will reflect the claims paid to the group. For example, if your group has smaller claims than another group, your rates will rise more slowly. Group health insurance rates are ultimately based on current costs of hospital/medical/surgical care and on the deductibles, per day benefits, extent of coverage, and overall policy limits selected for the group.

As an alternative to coverage under a group plan, you may choose to purchase your own individual policy. Health insurance premiums for individual policies are also adjusted on the basis of recent loss experience. Your particular rate is based on your selection of deductibles, coinsurance, benefit level, and your geographic location, income, age, and sex. Hospital costs and medical/surgical fees vary greatly from one section of the country to another. Higher income people incur larger medical claims than those with lower incomes. As to the effects of age and gender, persons 65 and over have substantially higher medical expenses than 25 year olds, and female claims run slightly higher than those for males.[1]

Short-term disability insurance is usually written for six-month periods and is often available on a group-plan basis. The cost of this coverage is quoted as prices per ten dollars of weekly or monthly benefits. Overall, group disability premiums depend on the occupation, the ages covered in the group, the percent female, and the treatment of maternity disability.

Rates for individual disability insurance policies depend on sex, age, and occupation. In general, disability risk increases up to age 60 and is greater for females than for males at all ages up to age 60. Occupations are classed into several broad groupings based on disability risks. When these factors are considered, your rate will be based on the waiting period before benefits begin to be paid, the monthly income you will be paid, and the total time limits stated by the policy.

KINDS OF COMPANIES

Blue Cross–Blue Shield (BC–BS), a nonprofit organization which specializes in group policies, is the largest seller of health insurance. That one firm writes approximately 40 percent of all private health insurance policies. BC–BS, having pioneered in health insurance in the 1930s, offers hospitalization under the name Blue Cross and sells its medical/surgical coverage as Blue Shield insurance.

Commercial insurers, such as Travellers and Connecticut General, issue all types of health insurance for groups and individuals. Furthermore, life insurers often have a complementary health-disability line. Commercial insurers are more selective in underwriting than the nonprofit Blue Cross–Blue Shield, however. Because of their selectivity, it is possible for commercial insurers to have lower rates. Thus, if you are young and healthy, it could pay you to shop for rates.

A third source of health expense coverage, the *health maintenance organization,* is discussed later in this chapter.

The federal government is the most recent and fastest growing competitor in the health insurance field. Disability insurance was added to Social Security in 1950 and is a major source of actual and potential disability income benefits. In 1965 the government entered the hospital insurance field when it

[1] *Source Book of Health Insurance Data: 1976–77* (New York: Health Insurance Institute, 1978), p. 66.

provided basic hospital coverage through Medicare for people over 65 and through Medicaid for low-income families. Medicare, Part A, is financed by payroll taxes, and Medicaid is paid for out of general tax revenues. Both federal programs cover hospital and posthospital services on a share-the-cost basis. Under Part B of Medicare, supplementary medical insurance may be purchased to cover medical and surgical care for those over 65. Even Part A of Medicare has a deductible clause which places a charge on the patient after the 61st day of confinement. Supplemental coverage under Part B has an annual deductible and carries 80/20 coinsurance.

HOW MUCH YOU NEED

To determine your needs for health and disability insurance you must first inventory what you have. The chances are good that some coverage is provided through your job-related fringe benefits. Certainly Social Security is a major component of disability benefits. And you are eligible for those if you have paid into Social Security for at least 18 months. On reviewing what you have, you may find that your health and disability insurance needs are adequately met by the combined resources of your cash reserves, budget medical expenses, fringe benefit health and disability coverage, and Social Security benefits. Nonetheless, to arrive at that conclusion you will need to make a careful assessment of your own situation.

Estimating needs for hospital expenses and medical insurance

On the basis of the large loss principle, major medical deserves first priority in assessing health insurance needs. There are two decisions to be made here: the size of the deductible, and the overall policy limits. The choice of a deductible, in turn, should be based on your average insurable expenses. This carries you back to the income statement and balance sheet.

Your income statement will identify your average health care expenditures. If these are consistently low, you might want to risk a larger deductible, which will reduce your premium. For example, if your medical expenses for two people averaged $150 per person per year, and you are considering a $100 versus a $500 deductible per person, which should you choose? If the saving in premium for a $500 deductible was $100 or more, your outlay for premiums plus average medical expenses would be less than with the $100 deductible. With the $100 deductible, your medical expense outlay would be $200, the deductibles for two people, plus a premium of perhaps $300 a year, for a total of $500. With a $500 deductible, you would pay the entire $300 average expense plus the premium, because the two of you would not exhaust the deductible. If the premium were less than $200, the total cost would be less.

Before you jump into a policy with a large deductible, however, there are three cautions. First, your emergency reserve plus budgeted medical expenses must be enough to cover the deductible (in this case, $200 on the low deductible and $1,000 on the high deductible policy). These resources must also be sufficient to cover any coinsurance or cost-sharing obligation on your part. Second, medical expenses are highly variable and unpredictable. Your past average expenses may be an inadequate guide to what to expect in the next few years. Finally, your decision about a deductible will reflect your personal attitude toward risk. If you prefer to minimize uncertainty, you may want to turn the bulk of the "budgeting" of volatile medical expenses over to the insurer at the cost of a higher but predictable premium.

Estimating needs for disability income

Disability income protection needs have some similarities to life insurance needs. In both cases, you are establishing a way to provide for lost income. However, in the case of disability insurance you will be estimating your need for a monthly income payment, whereas life insurance needs are usually estimated on the basis of one lump sum payment—the face value of the policy.

Figure 10–2 has been developed to assist you in calculating your monthly disability income needs. By referring to the figure, you will notice that the first item relates to your present monthly after-tax living expenses. If you become disabled, you will not be working. Therefore, you will not have to deal with payroll taxes. With a disability, you may have lower living expenses since the usual cost of traveling to work, dressing for the job, and other expenses may be reduced. In any event, your expense reductions should be based on a realistic expectation of any adjustments in monthly work expenses, taxes, insurance premiums, recreation, and other costs. You can refer to your income statement to assess these reductions.

The next item on the form in Figure 10–2 requires you to consider your

Figure 10–2
Monthly disability income need

1.	Present monthly living expenses (after taxes)			________
2.	Less any anticipated expense reductions*			________
3.	Less other monthly income:			
	Social Security benefits	________		
	Spouse's income	________		
	Investment income	________		
				________
4.	Equals net monthly disability income needs			________
5.	Number of years needed	________		
6.	Inflation factor	________	(× line 4)	________
7.	Equals monthly disability income need			________

* Disability insurance premiums, working expenses, recreation, investments, and so forth.

other sources of income, those which will either not be affected by your disability or those which might be triggered by the disability. Your monthly Social Security disability benefits fall into the latter category. The amount for these can be found in Chapter 11. To the Social Security benefits you will add the income of other family members plus any investment income which you might have. The total of these three items gives the total other monthly income. Your monthly living expenses minus your total monthly income gives your net monthly disability income needs.

Now, another decision has to be made. How long will you expect to need disability income? Of course that is definitely a lifestyle question. You might want to cover a transition period of five years, a much longer period if you have small dependent children, or even until retirement age. Of course, you can consider several periods of time and estimate alternative costs. The number of years chosen will obviously have a dramatic effect on the purchase price of disability income coverage.

Unlike life insurance, disability income is provided on a monthly basis across a specified period. If you become disabled, you do not receive a lump sum payment which can be placed in an interest-earning savings account or invested while you draw out the funds. Since disability income payments are fixed and since inflation is not, you will have to make an adjustment. In other words, you will have to increase the monthly income listed on line four of Figure 10–2 in order to end up with real income during the time for which the income is needed. This adjustment can be made with the help of the data in Table 10–1.

Notice in Table 10–1 the inflation factor for 6 percent and ten years. The factor is 1.318. In a sense, the factor means that 13.18 years of 6 percent

Table 10–1
Inflation factors

Number of years	*Rates of inflation*			
	2%	*4%*	*6%*	*8%*
2	1.030	1.062	1.091	1.123
10	1.095	1.201	1.318	1.449
20	1.154	1.942	1.839	2.288
30	1.312	2.172	2.635	3.776
40	1.480	2.701	3.641	6.476

Note: Inflation factor for n years at a rate of inflation r is

$$I.F. = \frac{\sum_{i=1}^{n} (1 + r)^i}{n}$$

The currently needed monthly benefit, multiplied by this will determine an "average" monthly benefit over the time period indicated which will compensate for inflation.

inflation is equal to ten years without inflation. By selecting the number of years you need for disability income and then choosing an inflation rate, you will have the correct factor. When your net monthly disability income need shown on line 4 of Table 10–1 is multiplied by the inflation factor, you then have your final answer—monthly disability income need.

Having estimated your monthly disability income need, you will want to check thoroughly on any disability income sources for which you might qualify. Workers' compensation insurance, the continued payment of salary, fringe benefit insurance are three additional sources of income which might reduce your final need for disability income. In fact, it is possible that with two working adults in the household, the combination of Social Security benefits and other sources of income could leave you with no final insurance needs at all. Alternatively, you may need only temporary insurance coverage.

These last points are illustrated in Figure 10–3 where disability insurance needs have been calculated for Peter West. The items required for the calculations are taken from West's income statement in Chapter 9 and from the Social Security tables in Chapter 11. For Social Security purposes, we will assume that Peter West's average yearly earnings are $10,000. Checking Table 11–7 you will note that Peter is eligible for $502 and his wife receives benefits of $376.60, which is just above the maximum family payment of $878.50. We use $878 in Figure 10–3.

Figure 10–3
Monthly disability income need
Peter West

1. Present monthly living expenses*		$765
2. Less anticipated expense reductions†		50
3. Less other monthly income:		
Social Security benefits	$878	
Interest	8	$886
4. Equals net monthly disability income needs		–0–

Note: Peter's Social Security benefits are sufficient for his present needs, but he needs a larger emergency fund or short-term disability insurance to tide him over the six-month waiting period.

* Eliminates $200 in savings from annual income statement.

† Transportation	$200/yr
Peter's work expenses	160/yr
Recreation, gifts	240/yr
Total	$600/yr or $50/month

As you can see from Figure 10–3, Peter West has more than enough disability income from Social Security to handle his estimated needs. However, as indicated in the figure, there is a six-month period which one must wait before receiving the first Social Security disability payment. An emergency fund for that period would have to be considered.

To illustrate the problem of disability income when things are not as bright as in the case of Peter West, consider this: what if West had been single, but with the same expenses as used previously. In that case, his disability check from Social Security would be $502. That with his interest income equals $510, leaving net disability income needs of $255 per month. Now suppose Peter wants to cover himself for a two-year disability. Assume that inflation is estimated to be 6 percent per year. In Table 10–1 you will find the inflation factor to be 1.091. That factor multiplied times the $255 per month yields $278.20. This would be the monthly disability income needed based on two years and an inflation rate of 6 percent.

SPECIAL CONTRACT PROVISIONS

In addition to the provisions already discussed, there are several other features to examine. These are preexisting conditions, maternity benefits, and family coverage. Preexisting conditions provisions in health insurance policies often call for exclusion of payments for a known condition, an accident or illness, which exists at the time the policy is taken out. This feature applies in particular to maternity coverage.

Maternity benefits are often optional, since maternity is not, strictly speaking, an illness. There will be an additional premium if maternity coverage is elected. Part of the attending physician's fee and most of the hospital expense will be covered by the usual hospital/medical/surgical expense policy with maternity.

The family can be covered in various combinations. It is possible to buy an individual policy (covering only one person), a family policy, or a policy on one parent and children. This last policy is useful if both adults work and have group protection through the employer. A family policy will cover all members of the family including dependent children to age 19 and sometimes to age 23 if they remain dependent on the parents for support. Newborns may not be covered for an initial period which ranges from 15 days to one year. Coverage of a spouse will terminate if there is a legal separation, divorce, or annulment.

Disability income protection policies usually include provisions for avoiding overinsurance and exclusions. If the insured fails to notify the insurer of other disability policies prior to his or her disability, the benefits will be prorated among the various insurers in proportion to the monthly benefits on each policy. This is intended to reduce moral hazard.

Certain disabilities are excluded. The most common are war-related injuries, self-inflicted injuries, and injuries while piloting an aircraft.

PREPAYMENT PLANS

Pioneered as the Kaiser Plan in California, the prepaid group practice is considered the "wave of the future" in health care. A flat monthly fee covers all types of medical/surgical care from a group of physicians, who are commonly salaried rather than paid a fee for service. Prepayment plans, or health maintenance organizations, have been an integral part of several of the proposals for a system of national health insurance. However, there are many difficulties in expanding the concept out of urban areas and to families other than middle-class wage earners.

NATIONAL HEALTH INSURANCE

The United States is the last major industrial nation without some form of national health insurance. In 1965 the first steps were taken to provide limited federal health insurance for the two highest risk groups in the population. The aged were provided coverage with Medicare, and the poor received Medicaid. Since that time a variety of proposals have been developed for a more inclusive national health insurance plan. Approximately 15 plans are currently under consideration. There are three broad types of plans—comprehensive, catastrophic, and coinsurance. Comprehensive plans involve totally federally financed health care with no deductible and no coinsurance. These plans would be financed by general revenues and a payroll tax. Comprehensive plans generate the most concern over cost and overuse because of the lack of deductibles and coinsurance. There have been suggestions to remedy this problem by federal subsidies to expand the supply of medical personnel and facilities.

Catastrophic plans contain extremely large deductibles which range from $5,000 to $50,000 and would function as a supplement to major medical insurance. This is the least costly and least inclusive approach.

The coinsurance approach is essentially federally financed major medical insurance with a $100 deductible and 80/20 coinsurance. Various financing proposals have been advanced including general revenues, payroll taxes, and employer/employee shared costs, with supplementary financing for those not employed.

Opposition from the medical profession and concern over costs have been the major roadblocks to the passage of some form of national health insurance.

SUMMARY

Health and disability insurance comes in several forms; hospital/medical/surgical expense insurance, major medical, disability income protection, and combination forms. Hospital expense insurance includes medical/surgical espense, nursing care, and dental care. Major medical and hospital/medical/surgical are often purchased as a package policy called comprehensive. Disability income and hospital/medical/surgical expense policies are available in combinations under various names, such as accident and sickness policies. Workers' compensation pays for hospital/

medical/surgical expenses and disability income for job-related accidents and illnesses. Social Security provides disability benefits as well as Medicare for those over 65.

Hospital/medical/surgical expense insurance offers flat rates for various services—so much per hospital day, so many days, a flat fee for a particular type of surgery. There is a low deductible, sometimes none at all. Major medical, on the other hand, uses deductibles and coinsurance to hold down costs and discourage overuse. Major medical offers a choice of deductibles and limits of liability to suit your needs and ability to pay. Dread disease policies offer high limits of liability for a specific illness (such as cancer) or group of illnesses.

Disability income policies provide monthly benefits to replace lost income while you are disabled and cannot work. The dollar limits must be reasonable in relation to your income. The longer the waiting period you select, the lower your premium will be.

Costs of health and disability insurance are based on age, sex, and occupation. Geographic area also affects health insurance costs. Group health policies are experience rated; that is, this year's rates are based on the last few years' claims experience for your group.

The largest underwriter in the health field is the nonprofit Blue Cross–Blue Shield. Commercial insurers and health maintenance organizations are the other private competitors in this field. The federal government also pays for some health care and disability, chiefly Medicare, Medicaid, and Social Security disability benefits.

Major medical is most important in health insurance needs. The deductible should be based on your past medical expenses and your emergency fund. Higher limits of liability are not unduly expensive and are usually well worth the additional premium.

Hospital/medical/surgical expense insurance often comes as a fringe benefit. It covers smaller expenses, which can still amount to fairly large sums for a family of several persons.

Special contract features to consider in health insurance are noncoverage of preexisting conditions, optional maternity benefits, and the age limits within which dependent children are covered on a family policy.

Disability income needs depend on present living expenses, anticipated expense reductions, other income sources, the number of years needed, and the expected rate of inflation.

Disability insurance may exclude coverage for certain sources of disability. Provision for prorating to discourage overuse is a common practice in these policies.

Alternatives to private health insurance include prepayment plans, or health maintenance organizations and the possibility of some kind of national health insurance in the future.

KEY WORDS

Blue Cross–Blue Shield
Coinsurance
Comprehensive health insurance
Deductible
Dental insurance
Disability insurance
Dread disease policy
Health maintenance organization
Hospital expense insurance
Major medical insurance
Medical/surgical expense insurance
Nursing care insurance
Restoration
Waiting period

PROBLEMS

1. Using the form in this chapter, estimate disability insurance needs for George and Henrietta based on the information given about their financial situation in Chapters 3.

2. The Jones family of four is contemplating buying health insurance. They are considering four options, as follows:

a. Basic hospital/medical/surgical expense only (30-day limit, $20 deductible) costs $120/year.

b. Major medical only, limit $50,000; $100 deductible/person costs $90/year.

c. Major medical only, limit $50,000; $250 deductible/person costs $60/year.

d. Comprehensive, combining *a* and *b* costs $200/year.

They have an emergency fund of $900. Their average insurable medical expenses are $800 a year, divided approximately evenly among the four family members. Which policy would you recommend? Why?

Chapter 11

Employer-provided insurance and other fringe benefits

Give me just a little salary with a fringe on the top . . .
Anonymous

INTRODUCTION

Employment usually means a salary. A job can also mean a parking space, low-cost loans, use of a personal credit card, travel to extraordinary resorts, a discount on purchases, use of the company golf course, a large bundle of insurance benefits, a pension, and even more. Of course, not everyone gets all of these benefits. Indeed, some people feel lucky to get a salary! But almost everyone will receive some very important insurance *fringe benefits*.

As you have learned, insurance can be obtained in many ways. You can analyze your own needs, consider the many plans available in the market, listen to the advice and counsel of specialists from the various fields of insurance, and then buy the coverage which best suits your needs. You have great flexibility in developing a risk management program to meet your insurance goals. But, the cost of insurance and other things could be lower if provided in fringe benefits.

When you purchase your own insurance and rent a parking space you are spending after-tax dollars. That is, your purchases are just another item in your budget. Life, health, accident, and retirement insurance can add up to be a major budgeted item, one worthy of careful review and management. On the other hand, if you could obtain a major part of your insurance with tax-free income you could either buy more protection for the same total expenditure or purchase the same amount as a lower cost. The taxes avoided would amount to a discount on the purchase price. Think what you might do with your budget if you could save 25 to 35 percent on your insurance bills! An illustration might help you think about it.

If you are in the 30 percent tax bracket, you must earn $1.42 to have a dollar to spend. The marginal tax rate makes the difference and as you will see in Chapter 19, your marginal tax rate depends on the amount of your taxable income. Thus, the higher your marginal tax rate, the more you can gain by having insurance and other benefits provided for you with pretax dollars. Employee fringe benefits provide that advantage. The facts are that employers purchased almost one billion dollars worth of benefits for their employees in 1976. And these purchases amounted to almost 10 percent of the total wages paid in the economy. For some employees, the value of fringe benefits exceeded 50 percent of the value of their salary! But whether 10 or 50 percent, the subject is worth studying.

This chapter examines the fringe package and other employer-provided insurance and how you might take advantage of these benefits. The discussion will emphasize:

- The advantages and disadvantages of employer provided benefits.
- Employer provided health and life insurance.
- The Social Security package.
- Worker's compensation insurance.
- Unemployment insurance.
- Other items in the fringe benefits.

ADVANTAGES AND DISADVANTAGES OF EMPLOYER-PROVIDED BENEFITS

The most obvious saving involved in fringe benefits is that before-tax dollars are used to purchase benefits. Think about the advantage this way—an employer can afford to spend some maximum amount in hiring an employee. From Chapter 2 you will recall that his or her maximum relates to how much the employee actually contributes to the firm's revenue. For example, suppose you are a sales representative working on straight commission. (Your salary is based on the net profit you produce for the firm.) One month you sell $30,000 in merchandise and when all costs other than employment costs are considered your employer has $3,000 left which could go directly to you. Suppose you get the whole thing. If you are in a 30-percent marginal tax bracket (recall, that is the tax rate applied to the last increment of your income), the tax collector would receive $900 and you would get $2,100. It is your after-tax income which is the important consideration.

If you have an insurance program with either monthly premiums or a monthly budgeted reserve for premiums, you would take the budgeted portion of your after-tax income and pay the bills. Let's say that your insurance bills run $150 a month. This would leave $1,950 for the remaining items in your budget. Now, what if your employer could use part of the $3,000 you earned to pay the insurance bill for you. The insurance cost might still be the same, but your tax bill would be different. The employer would take the $3,000 you earned, subtract $150 for the insurance, and pay you $2,850 in salary. If you were still in the 30-percent tax bracket (that could be reduced since your gross salary is lower), you would pay $855 in taxes. Your net after-tax income would then be $2,850 minus $855 or $1,995. But you already have paid your insurance bill. You would have gained $45 by having insurance as a fringe benefit! Table 11–1 shows the comparison.

Table 11–1
Benefits of employer-provided insurance

	You provide insurance	*Employer provides insurance*
Total earnings produced	$3,000	$3,000
Fringe benefits	-0-	150
Taxes	900	855
After-tax income	2,100	1,995
Insurance cost	150	-0-
Money remaining	1,950	1,995
Net gain		45

While the tax angle provides clear possibilities for gain, there are other advantages to consider. If your employer provides insurance for you, it is likely that the same benefits might be provided to all the firm's employees. Firms generally have a group plan which may be joined by all their employees, and group plans reduce the cost of selling insurance and handling paper work. There might be 1 insurance bill instead of 500. Collections tend to be simpler, and there are economies of management which lower costs.

There is another potential benefit. You don't have to worry about paying the bills and meeting with insurance representatives when your employer provides coverage for you. This may make your budget and your financial planning a little simpler. In fact, some people might never buy insurance for themselves. Their employers do their thinking for them. While all of this may sound great, there are some disadvantages to consider. There are always costs which come with benefits.

A first disadvantage might result if the insurance your employer provides is not exactly what you would buy for yourself. If you are included in a group insurance plan, it is likely that the plan will have standard benefits which fit the needs of the majority of the employees, but not each employee. In a health plan, there may be maternity benefits included as a standard benefit, for example, but if you are single, you might prefer additional coverage in some other area. In other words, employer-provided benefits are not usually custom designed to fit your exact needs. Still, there could be a financial gain because of the tax advantages described earlier.

A second disadvantage relates to the possible inflexibility of employer-provided benefits. Your insurance needs change as your assets and liabilities change. Thus, there are times when you might want more life insurance and less health insurance. The employer package may not allow for these short-term alterations. Of course, you can always use your fringe package as a base from which to start your personal financial planning. By taking that approach, you can still keep some flexibility.

Insurance has been used to illustrate some of the advantages and disadvantages of employer-provided fringe benefits. The same principles apply to any of the nonmonetary benefits provided for employees by firms. Fringe benefits are an important and growing component of compensation packages. For this reason, the tax treatment of fringe benefits might change. Quite possibly, individuals could be required to report the value of certain fringe benefits and pay taxes on them. But until that day, the advantages of getting insurance, a company car, tuition for special courses, and many other benefits will likely continue to offset the disadvantages which may come when someone else picks your program for you.

EMPLOYER-PROVIDED HEALTH AND LIFE INSURANCE

Health insurance

It is a rare occurrence when an individual takes all of the steps to select health insurance, decide upon a plan, and to purchase his or her own coverage. In fact, individually purchased health plans account for only 17.5 percent of all health insurance premiums.[1] Thus, almost 80 percent of all health and hospital insurance is paid for through some employment-related group insurance plan.

Employers not only provide the opportunity for group coverage, they pick up the tab for 67 percent of the average premium paid in group programs. In other words, the typical employee pays one third of the cost of his health insurance. The rest is a fringe benefit. This is an average fringe benefit. The employer's share can vary considerably. In some cases, the employer pays either all of the cost or even provides a clinic or *health maintenance organization* for employers. In other cases, commercial insurance is used, and a major portion of the cost is paid by the employer. In still other cases, Blue Cross–Blue Shield insurance is the vehicle.

---

[1] Council on Wage and Price Stability, *The Complex Puzzle of Rising Health Care Costs: Can the Private Sector Fit it Together?* (December 1976), pp. 83–85.

When health insurance is provided as a fringe benefit, the choice of programs and benefits may be important. Large firms, however, tend to offer more choice. You can get an idea of the major details of coverage from Table 11–2 which reports the results of a 1973 survey of 51,600 group health

Table 11–2
Group health insurance characteristics, 1973

	Percentage of total	
	Plans	**Workers**
Type of financing:		
Employer	47	63
Employer-employee share	33	25
Employee	3	1
Unknown	18	1
Type of insurance:		
Commercial insurance	67	64
Blue Cross–Blue Shield	32	30
Self-insured	1	6

Source: Council on Wage and Price Stability, *The Complex Puzzle of Rising Health Care Costs* (December 1976), p. 102.

insurance plans that covered some 28 million workers in private industry. Variety comes with large groups of employees. A firm hiring 5,000 employees actually has a large enough market to support a number of insurance programs. The 55 health benefit programs made available to federal government employees illustrate the possibilities. These programs include Blue Cross–Blue Shield, various commercial insurance plans, membership in health maintenance organizations, and comprehensive medical plans associated with major hospitals.[2] In each case, the government (the employer) contributes an average of 65 percent of the cost. For example, in 1976, this biweekly contribution ranged from $18.93 to $23.13 for each family enrolled.[3]

Of course, there are few private employers which can match the sprawling expanse of the federal government's operations. Thus, you would not expect to find 55 choices offered by a private employer. However, no matter what the choice there are some basic points to consider when health insurance is offered as a fringe benefit:

1. On interviewing for a job, get the full details on the health benefit program—its costs, family benefits, enrollment procedures, and the procedures for processing claims.

[2] U.S. Civil Service Commission, "The Federal Employees Health Benefits Program," Standard Form no. 2809A (January 1975), 4–5.

[3] U.S. Civil Service, "Federal Employees Health Benefits Programs 1976 Biweekly Health Benefits Rates" (January 1976), p. 1.

2. Compare the benefit packages offered with your needs and the cost of covering your needs on a private basis. You can overinsure and overspend even when your employer is sharing the cost. Caution: be certain to consider the tax treatment of your earnings.
3. If you take a health insurance fringe, be sure to consider your family. They may be included at a small cost. If you don't sign them up, they may not be covered.
4. Keep your personnel manager informed of changes in your family situation which might affect your coverage and cost.
5. Keep your insurance records and identification cards in a safe and convenient place. The copy of your insurance policy should be kept with other insurance records. The identification cards need to be kept in your pocketbook or billfold.
6. Records of your cost of health insurance coverage should be kept for income tax purposes. Also, records of medical bills need to be maintained if they are reimbursable on an annual or quarterly basis.
7. If you change jobs or become unemployed, check to see if you can extend your health insurance coverage on a temporary or even permanent basis. You may have to pay the full insurance cost, but that might be a bargain when compared with privately purchased coverage.

Life insurance

From our earlier discussion of life insurance in Chapter 9, you will recall that there can be a savings component along with the insurance component in life insurance policies. For example, whole life, 20-year pay, and annuity insurance becomes an asset as you make payments. Those policies include various amounts of planned savings. On the other hand, term insurance is just insurance. Your insurance needs determine which policies to buy.

A fringe benefit package could include any combination of the various life insurance vehicles. However, term insurance is the most common life insurance fringe benefit. Some employers provide each employee with a specific sum in term coverage while the individual is with the firm. In fact, term coverage is often a standard component of the health-life fringe. Of course, term insurance offers death benefits only. But, death benefits are an important part of your insurance needs. When the policy is a fringe benefit, the cost is hard to beat. Check the price anyway.

Life insurance with cash value can be a part of a firm's retirement program. For example, an annuity policy is a common vehicle for use in retirement planning. In general, the purchaser contributes to the policy during his or her working years, and the policy contributes to him or her later. All along, there are death benefits available.

If a firm chooses to build a retirement program around insurance, the firm may pay into the program in your name and do so with before-tax dollars.

That is, the firm acts just as if it is buying your insurance. You get the tax saving at the same time of purchase. Furthermore, the firm has the advantage of deducting the cost of the insurance from its tax liability. Once the retirement package is purchased, the insurance generally becomes your asset. When the proceeds are paid out to you, you then pay taxes on them as if they were income. Perhaps your tax rate will be lower then.

Employees of government agencies—schoolteachers and other public employees—can enjoy an insurance fringe benefit of their own making. The Internal Revenue Service allows them to purchase tax-sheltered annuities with before-tax dollars. The tax shelter aspect of the annuity is the fringe benefit. That is, the employee defers taxes on the income which goes to purchase the annuity. As with the retirement insurance described above, however, the individual pays taxes on the income which comes later when the annuity proceeds are paid.

SOCIAL SECURITY: BENEFITS AND COSTS

The *Social Security* program is one which will follow you from your very first job, through retirement, to the grave, and then perhaps to your survivors. While you will pay into the program, so will your employer. Thus, Social Security is a shared-cost fringe benefit. Over a lifetime of work it is possible that you and your employer will pay for more benefits than you will receive. On the other hand, you may pay little and receive much. Social Security is the principal form of social insurance in the United States. The Social Security program is complex and subject to constant revision. Even so, there are some fundamental principles which should be understood.

The Social Security package includes three distinct benefit components:

1. Old age and survivors' insurance.
2. Disability insurance.
3. Medicare.

The first component is the oldest and best known having been started in 1935. The disability element was added in 1954, and Medicare came into the package in 1965.

Today nine out of ten workers are matching the contributions of their employer under Social Security. Nearly one out of seven persons receives a monthly Social Security check, and almost all people over age 65 have some health insurance coverage under Medicare. None of the Social Security benefits are subject to income tax.

Building credit in the system

How do you become eligible for the benefits? In order to obtain benefits you must build up a certain amount of credit in the system. The Social

Security Administration has a lifetime earnings record which it maintains in Baltimore, Maryland, and each year reports of your covered earnings are recorded in your record. You will pay into the system for as long as you are employed, even when you are receiving Social Security benefits.

If you were employed in 1978, you and your employer would each pay 6.05 percent of the first $17,700 of your annual wage. In other words, the *most* you would pay in 1979 is $1,404. There are future rate increases already scheduled. These are shown in Table 11–3.

Table 11–3
Schedule of Social Security contribution rates and taxable pay (1978–1981)

Year	*Rate paid by employee* (percent)*	*Maximum taxable pay*	*Maximum contribution*
1978	6.05	$17,700	$1,071
1979	6.13	22,900	1,404
1980	6.13	25,900	1,588
1981	6.65	29,700	1,975

* Employer pays an equal amount.
Source: *Changing Times,* April 1978, p. 38.

Credit toward benefits is obtained in the system for each calendar quarter that you are paid $250 or more of reported earnings. This amount is indexed each year for inflation. Thus, if you earned as little as $84 per month for a year and had this reported for the Social Security Administration, you would have earned four quarters of credit and that credit would be a permanent

Table 11–4
Work credit required for full retirement and death benefits

When you reach age 62	*Years of credit needed to receive benefits*
1977	6½
1978	6¾
1979	7
1980	7¼
1981	7½
1983	8
1987	9
1991 or later	10

Source: HEW Publication no. (SSA) 78–10047 (February 1978), p. 3.

Table 11–5
Work credit required for survivor's benefits

Born after 1929, die at age	*Born before 1930, die before age 62*	*Years of credit needed to receive benefits*
28 or younger		1½
30		2
32		2½
34		3
36		3½
38		4
40		4½
42		5
44		5½
46	1975	6
47	1976	6¼
48	1977	6½
50	1979	7
52	1981	7½
54	1983	8
56	1985	8½
58	1987	9
60	1989	9½
62	1991 or later	10

Source: HEW Publication no. (SSA) 78–10035 (February 1978), p. 13.

part of your record. You can have your employment interrupted and still maintain your original credit toward benefits. Thus, when your earnings resume your credits begin to accumulate again. However, there is a minimum amount of credit which must be built into the system before you are eligible for any benefits. Sufficient credit or time in covered employment gives assurance that you will receive benefits. The amount of your benefits is another matter. But, consider the work credit requirement first. Tables 11–4, 11–5, and 11–6 describe the requirements for retirement, survivors, and

Table 11–6
Work credit required for disability benefits

If you become disabled before age 24 you need 1½ years of work in the 3 years before you become disabled.

If you are between age 24 and 31, you must have credit for half the time between your 21st birthday and the time you become disabled.

If you become disabled at 31 or later, you need as much credit as you would if you reached retirement age in the year you are disabled. (See Table 11–4). And five years of your work must be in the ten-year period just before you become disabled.

Source: HEW Publication no. (SSA) 78–10035 (February 1978), p. 12.

disability benefits. There are some special exceptions to the information shown in the tables which you will want to check on when either retirement or any other Social Security benefit might be questioned, but, in general, the tables reflect the most current information.

Calculating your benefits

Once you have sufficient credit in the Social Security system you may then calculate the amount of benefits which you can receive upon becoming eligible. The value of the benefits is based on a formula for determining a worker's *Primary Insurance Amount* (PIA) which is based on a worker's indexed earnings. That is, your Social Security benefits are adjusted for the cost of living. A worker's earnings are adjusted for inflation (indexed) to the period immediately before the worker reaches age 62, becomes disabled, or dies. This indexing process will reflect increases in average wages that have occurred since the earnings were paid to the worker in question.

An example will illustrate the computation of average indexed monthly earnings.[4] Suppose an individual had the following record of covered earnings:

Work period	*Annual covered wages*
1951–60	$2,769
1961–70	4,148
1971–78	6,288

The wages in the first period would be divided into the annual covered wage of the last period to obtain the index factor. For the first period, the factor would be 3.532. The second period would be 2.358 and the third, 1.000. These factors would be multiplied by the *total* earnings for each year to obtain the wage indexed earnings. In this example, the total indexed earnings would be $245,915. Now subtract the five years having the lowest earnings. That would be for the years 1951–55 and a total amount of $48,901 ($2,769 × 3.532 × 5). A total of $197,014 would be left.

To obtain the average indexed monthly earnings, divide $197,014 by 276 (23 years × 12 months) to give $174 which is the average indexed monthly earnings. After the wages have been indexed, they will be averaged for the years after 1950 up to the time when benefits are due. The five lowest

[4] This discussion is based on: "Social Security Amendments of 1977: Legislative History and Summary of Provisions," *Social Security Bulletin* (March 1978), pp. 3–20.

years of earnings are excluded when calculating the average indexed monthly earnings (AIME). Under the benefit formula, the worker receives 90 percent of the first $180 of his or her AIME, plus 32 percent of AIME over $180 and through $1,085, plus 15 percent of AIME over $1,085. In the case described, the worker would receive monthly benefits of $333.

A new benefit formula is published each year by the Social Security Administration so as to adjust for changes in inflation and payments into the system. The description here, based on the 1978 formula, gives you an explanation of the calculation of primary income and perhaps clearly indicates the importance of contacting your Social Security office when estimating benefits.

Table 11–7 can be used for estimating monthly Social Security payments. The information in the table is dated since earnings cannot be indexed until after they are earned. The benefits described in Table 11–7 are still useful for approximation purposes. If average earnings are $10,000 you would be eligible to receive a check for $401.60. Your husband or wife would also be able to receive benefits on the basis of your work credits and earnings. In this

Table 11–7
Examples of monthly Social Security payments
(effective June 1977)

	Average yearly earnings after 1950 covered by Social Security						
Benefits can be paid to a:	***$923 or less***	***$3,000***	***$4,000***	***$5,000***	***$6,000***	***$8,000****	***$10,000****
Retired worker at 65	114.30	236.40	278.10	322.50	364.50	453.10	502.00
Worker under 65 and disabled	114.30	236.40	278.10	322.50	364.50	453.10	502.00
Retired worker at 62	91.50	189.20	222.50	258.00	291.60	362.50	401.60
Wife or husband at 65	57.20	118.20	139.10	161.30	182.30	226.60	251.00
Wife or husband at 62	42.90	88.70	104.40	121.00	136.80	170.00	188.30
Wife under 65 with one child in her care	57.20	125.00	197.20	272.60	304.20	339.80	376.60
Widow or widower at 65 if worker never received reduced benefits	114.30	236.40	278.10	322.50	364.50	453.10	502.00
Widow or widower at 60 if sole survivor	81.80	169.10	198.90	230.60	260.70	324.00	359.00
Widow or widower at 50 and disabled if sole survivor	57.30	118.30	139.20	161.30	182.40	226.60	251.10
Widow or widower with one child in care	171.50	354.60	417.20	483.80	546.80	679.80	753.00
Maximum family payment	171.50	361.40	475.30	595.10	668.60	792.90	878.50

* Maximum earnings covered by social security were lower in past years and must be included in figuring your average earnings. This average determines your payment amount. Because of this, amounts shown in the last two columns generally won't be payable until future years. The maximum retirement benefit generally payable to a worker who is 65 in 1977 is $437.10.

Source: HEW Publication no. (SSA) 77–10324.

particular case, the husband or wife would receive $188.34 per month, if they were 62 and dependent on you for their support. Going further in Table 11–7 you will notice that a wife under age 65 with a child (under age 18) could receive $367.60 in benefits beyond those received by her husband in the $10,000 average earnings case.

Survivors' benefits for young workers could be based on an average earnings level above $10,000, since the maximum income subject to Social Security taxes has been over $10,000 for the past six years. For a more complete schedule of benefits, check with the Social Security office in your area.

The discussion here should enable you to see the basic structure of social security retirement and disability benefits. There are also Medicare and death benefits to consider.

Medicare

Your Social Security fringe benefit has an important health insurance component which is designed primarily for workers and their husbands or wives who are 65 or older. Medicare hospital insurance is purchased when Social Security deductions from your salary are matched by your employer. Since you generally pay into the program many years before being eligible for the hospital benefit, Medicare is a form of prepaid health care. The hospital insurance provided under Medicare is for all people 65 or over who otherwise qualify for a Social Security retirement check. That is, if you are 65 and a retired worker, dependent, or survivor of a covered worker, you are automatically eligible for the medical insurance part of Medicare. The insurance can also be purchased if you are 65 or older and have not earned enough work credit to have the benefits. Table 11–8 gives the current requirements for work credit to be eligible for Medicare hospital insurance. As you see in Table 11–8, if you were born after 1929 and have 10 years of covered employment, you have earned the hospital insurance benefits.

The detailed coverage of Medicare insurance should be studied carefully. Information on it and other Social Security benefits can be obtained from the

Table 11–8
Quarters of coverage required for Medicare hospital insurance

Year of birth	*Year you become 65*	*Quarters needed for hospital insurance*
1917	28	28
1921	32	32
1925	36	36
1929 or later	40	40

Source: HEW Publication no. (SSA) 76–10072 (April 1976), p. 4.

nearest Social Security Administration Office. (There is one in every major city.) But, in general, Medicare hospital insurance helps pay the cost of hospital care, inpatient care in a skilled nursing facility, or for care in your home by a home health agency. It also provides benefits for insured workers and their dependents who need dialysis treatment or a kidney transplant because of kidney failure.

In addition to Medicare hospital insurance, those eligible can also purchase Medicare medical insurance. The premium for the medical insurance was $7.70 per month in July 1977. This coverage helps to pay the cost of doctor's services, outpatient hospital care, and many other health services and supplies not covered by Medicare hospital insurance. Once again, individuals concerned with this coverage should obtain and study the latest materials which describe the program, its benefits and costs. While you may not be 65, someone related to you is likely to be in that age group. Indeed, you may be able to reduce your financial responsibilities by obtaining information on Medicare for someone in your family.

Death benefits

Death benefits under Social Security are both simple and complex. The simple part relates to the covered worker. If a person has earned credit under Social Security for 1½ years of work within three years before death a lump sum death benefit of $255 will be paid. Death benefits to survivors are more complex. However, by referring to our earlier discussion of credits and benefits and Tables 11–5 and 11–7, you will see some examples of benefits for widows, widowers, and dependent children.

Disability benefits

Disability benefits under Social Security are important to people of all ages. If you become disabled before age 31 and have 1½ years of covered employment in the three years before your disability, you will be eligible for the disability benefits shown in Table 11–7. People over 32 must generally have at least 5 years of covered employment out of the immediate 10 years before the disability. Once again your average earnings determine the level of benefits. The amount of work credit changes as you grow older. For example, if you become disabled after age 31, you will need as much credit for full benefits as you would if you had reached retirement age in that same year. Furthermore, five years of your work must be in the ten-year period prior to your becoming disabled. To illustrate, suppose you are 32 years old, it is 1980, and you have become disabled. In Table 11–4 you see that 7¼ years of credit are needed to be eligible for retirement benefits. The same credit requirement applies in this case. Now, suppose that your earnings in the last 7¼ years are your highest, and they average $10,000. In Table 11–7 you find the disability benefits for a worker under 65 and disabled. You would receive $502 per month for as long as you were unable to work. Table 11–7 also lists benefits for your wife and other family members during the time you are disabled.

Other features of Social Security

In addition to the general features of Social Security described, you will find a number of special situations to which your Social Security fringe benefits may be applied. There are, in fact, many special cases and for that reason you are urged to review the material available at any Social Security Administration Office. However, consider some particular benefits. There are special benefits and treatment of earnings for:

1. Workers who are disabled by blindness.
2. Children and their surviving parent if a worker-parent dies with fewer credits than shown in the standard table.
3. Individuals who work in someone's home—doing housecleaning, gardening, and/or babysitting.
4. Individuals who are self-employed or employed by a state or local government.
5. Workers who are employed outside the United States.
6. Widows who are 60 or older who remarry.
7. Unmarried, surviving children who are under age 22 and are full-time students.

In each of these situations you should check with the Social Security Office to determine just where you stand. There are over 1,300 offices throughout the country. And remember, you cannot receive any of these benefits unless you apply for them.

By now you probably feel that the Social Security fringe benefit is important but very complex. If you have reached that conclusion, you are correct on both counts. Since the potential benefits are important you should check with your employer to make certain that he has full information on your particular situation. If Social Security is optional, you will want to consider the cost of obtaining the benefits you desire from some alternative source *before* deciding to purchase Social Security.

If your income is high you will be paying the maximum into the system. And if you live to age 65 and earn a higher-than-average salary, you will likely pay much more for Social Security benefits than the same benefits would cost from some alternative source. On the other hand, if you must be included in Social Security you will certainly want to obtain the benefits which it offers.

WORKER'S COMPENSATION INSURANCE

In a typical year, some 2 million workers miss one or more days of work because of injuries and illness which relate to their work. Another 10 million employees suffer injuries which either require medical treatment or alter the worker's normal job assignment. Working can be hazardous to your health! But not working may be even more devastating. A person is twice as likely to sustain an injury at home than at work.

If you are injured at work you will most likely be eligible to receive benefits from *worker's compensation insurance,* a benefit which must be provided by your employer. Each of the 50 states has a worker's compensation act and each act is different. However, the acts generally require employers to participate in a state-managed insurance program or to assure the state that insurance is provided for each employee. As a result of these laws, coverage is provided for about 85 percent of all workers.

Worker's compensation insurance provides cash benefits, reimbursement of medical expenses, and rehabilitation for employees who sustain a work-related injury or illness. Each employer pays a premium based on the number of workers employed and the firm's experience in terms of claims paid to its employees. Thus, the insurance principle is applied here. Risk and the amount of risk exposure determine a firm's payments into the state program.

To illustrate worker's compensation in benefits, assume that you are working in a paper mill and in the course of carrying out your duties you walk behind a blower which has just been started. Dust and trash blow behind your safety glasses, and you later discover that a small piece of steel has become lodged in your eye. You report to the company clinic and they advise you to check with an outside ophthalmologist. Things work out well. The steel particle is removed easily, but you are told to rest your eyes for three days. That means missing work, and you have already used your sick leave. You also get a bill from the doctor for $150.

Most state programs provide medical service to cover a work-sustained injury. Thus, the $150 bill would be paid. In addition, you would most likely receive two thirds of your regular pay while resting your eyes. Generally speaking, worker's compensation programs have a maximum amount of benefits which can be paid for various claims. For example, the two thirds of current pay mentioned is a typical benefit for a temporary disability or illness. If you were permanently disabled and not able to work at all, the maximum weekly benefits might run $63 if you were employed in Louisiana and up to $342 if you had been employed in the District of Columbia.[5] The aggregate maximum or total amount which could be paid is also limited. In Arkansas, for example, the maximum is $39,375.[6]

[5] Amy S. Hribal and Gerri Minor, "Worker's Compensation Laws: Major Amendments in 1976," *Monthly Labor Review* (February 1977), pp. 39–45.

[6] Ibid.

Worker's compensation also provides death benefits which relate to the amount of weekly benefits paid. Your survivors could receive a settlement equal to 500 weeks' benefits, that is 500 times two thirds of your weekly salary.[7] Once again an aggregate dollar maximum could be assigned to the final settlement.

You should recognize that worker's compensation insurance is not intended to replace completely the full economic loss associated with work-related accidents or illness. It does provide some basic coverage. Furthermore, the coverage offered will vary from state to state. Thus, the principles described here are general and are intended to give you a basis for understanding the benefits which could be provided.

To summarize, worker's compensation insurance offers elements of health, disability, and life insurance. Each element needs to be identified when determining the value of your fringe benefit package and used when reviewing your complete insurance needs.

UNEMPLOYMENT INSURANCE

Approximately 97 percent of the work force in the United States is covered by some form of unemployment compensation, another benefit paid by employers. The program is required by federal law but administered by state agencies under specific state legislation. Thus, like worker's compensation, the benefits vary from state to state. If after having worked for a sufficient period, you become unemployed, are willing and able to work, and are making an effort to find employment, you may be eligible for unemployment compensation. Generally speaking, you will have to wait one week before applying to your state unemployment office for benefits, which range from 55 to 60 percent of the average weekly wage in your state. As an example, the state of Indiana pays a maximum of $115 to $160 per week for a claimant with dependents and a minimum of $35 per week.[8] These benefits can be obtained for up to 26 weeks. When unemployment is severe, the maximum period can be extended.

The benefits of unemployment compensation are intended to provide a bottom floor to earnings so that an unemployed person might be able to search for a job and weather the cyclical periods when their employer is forced to make temporary cutbacks. Once again, this is a benefit paid by your employer. You should investigate the regulations for eligibility in the state where you work so that you can be aware of the benefits and how they might apply to you.

---

[7] Mark R. Greene, *Risk and Insurance* (Cincinnati: South-Western Publishing Co., 1968), p. 690.

[8] Joseph A. Hickey, "State Unemployment Insurance: Legislative Change in 1976," *Monthly Labor Review* (April 1977), pp. 46–51.

THE GROWING BUNDLE OF FRINGE BENEFITS

In the 1950s, an employee would have considered an employer to be unusually good if the company provided health and life insurance, as well as the usual Social Security, worker's compensation, and unemployment insurance. Since that time the bundle of fringe benefits has expanded to the point that some firms are considering a *"cafeteria plan"* so that employees might

Table 11–9
Examples of fringe benefits

Accidental death, dismemberment insurance
Birthdays (vacation)
Bonus eligibility
Business and professional memberships
Cash profit sharing
Club memberships
Commissions
Company medical assistance
Company-provided automobile
Company-provided housing
Company-provided or subsidized travel
Day care centers
Deferred bonus
Deferred compensation plan
Deferred profit sharing
Dental and eye care insurance
Discount on company products
Education costs
Educational activities (time off)
Employment contract
Executive dining room
Free checking account
Free or subsidized lunches
Group automobile insurance
Group homeowners insurance
Group life insurance
Health maintenance organization fees
Holidays (extra)
Home health care
Hospital-surgical-medical insurance
Incentive growth fund
Interest-free loans
Layoff pay
Legal, estate-planning, and other professional assistance
Loans of company equipment
Long-term disability benefit
Matching education donations
Nurseries
Nursing home care
Opportunity for travel
Paid attendance at business, professional, and other outside meetings
Outside medical services
Parking facilities
Pension
Personal accident insurance
Personal counseling
Personal credit cards
Personal expense accounts
Physical examinations
Political activities (time off)
Price discount plan
Private office
Professional activities
Psychiatric services
Recreation facilities
Resort facilities
Retirement gratuity
Sabbatical leaves
Salary
Salary continuation
Savings plan
Scholarships for dependents
Severance pay
Shorter or flexible work week
Sickness and accident insurance
Social Security
Social service sabbaticals
Split-dollar life insurance
State disability plans
Stock appreciation rights
Stock bonus plan
Stock options plans (qualified, nonqualified, tandem)
Stock purchase plan
Survivors benefits
Tax assistance
Title
Training programs
Vacations
Wages
Weekly indemnity insurance

Source: David J. Thomsen, *Personnel Journal* (March 1977), p. 125.

develop the benefit mix which best suits their needs. Fringe possibilities seem endless. Table 11–9 illustrates how varied the cafeteria menu might be.

Fringe benefits become increasingly important as you move up in an organization. For example, you can't expect to be offered the key to the executive dining room if you have just been hired as a management trainee. But as you take on greater responsibilities and in doing so begin to represent the firm in significant meetings, you will be given more and more fringe compensation.

Money magazine estimated the value of the best fringes currently available as exceeding 50 percent of salary.[9] The *Money* study was based on a 35-year-old man with wife and two children and a salary of $25,000. Table 11–10 shows what the employer paid for the benefits provided and what the same benefits would have cost the employee.

Table 11–10
Comparison of typical fringe package costs: Employer versus employee

Benefit	*Employer cost*	*Employee cost if purchased privately*
Tuition toward M.B.A. degree	$ 4,500	$ 4,500
10-percent profit sharing	2,500	2,500
Four-week vacation	1,923	1,923
Pension plan	1,770	2,525
Health insurance	645	943
Dental insurance	240	n.a.
Disability insurance	132	432
Group legal services	111	n.a.
$125,000 term life insurance	212	400
Total	$12,033	$13,223

Note: n.a. = not available.
Source: Suzanne Seixas, "Fringe Benefits: Yours versus the Best," *Money* (July 1977), p. 37.

There are several points to make about Table 11–10. First, the total value of the fringe benefits exceeds 50 percent of the individual's salary. This exceeds the average for large firms, but is still realistic. Second, the cost of the same benefits if purchased by the individual would exceed the firm's cost. (In some cases, individuals just cannot buy some of the benefits.) The difference in cost demonstrates the advantage of group plans and economies in centralizing a large number of transactions by having the firm do the buying. Third, Table 11–10 *does not* show the tax savings which accrue to the individual when the firm buys the benefits. On his or her own, the individual would have to spend $13,223 in *after-tax income* to buy the benefits. If the

[9] Suzanne Seixas, "Fringe Benefits: Yours versus the Best," *Money* (July 1977), pp. 35–38.

person were in the 30-percent marginal tax bracket, he or she would have to earn $18,890 in salary to get $13,220 after taxes! The difference in having fringe benefits provided is even greater than shown in Table 11–10!

There is one final point to make about the growing fringe package and your financial planning. When you review your financial picture each year you should check your fringe benefits very carefully. This check should include:

1. An identification of each item of fringe benefits.
2. Some estimate of the value of major items if you purchased them.
3. A review of changes in the fringe offerings and how those changes affect you.
4. A review of your financial needs, any changes in needs, and how these changes affect the fringe package.
5. An investigation of fringe options if you have fringe benefits which are no longer of value to you.

As we have shown, every item in your financial plan can be affected by your fringe package. Thus that package can become crucial to your present and future lifestyle. And, of course, the fringe package is tied to a particular employer. The greater the benefits of the fringe, the larger could be the costs of changing jobs.

SUMMARY

This chapter covered the span of invisible earnings which you may obtain in the course of taking a job and getting on the payroll. As you can see, the subject of fringe benefits is complex and exceedingly important. There is much more to a job than the hours and salary. While the Social Security program was considered in detail, only the surface was skimmed on other fringe benefits. In each case where it was important, suggestions were given about information you ought to request from your employer, and sources of information you might consult when your situation requires you to apply for your fringe benefits. In closing you are reminded once more that the world of fringe benefits changes rapidly. Legislation at both the federal and state levels can bring sudden and significant changes which might affect you and your real earnings. Thus, you are urged to review your fringe package on an annual basis and, where possible, make adjustments to your current needs and future plans.

KEY WORDS

Cafeteria plan
Fringe benefits
Health maintenance organization
Medicare
Old age, survivors', and disability insurance
Primary Insurance Amount (PIA)
Social Security
Unemployment insurance
Worker's compensation insurance

PROBLEMS

1. Discuss the pros and cons of employer-provided insurance. Assume that you would purchase insurance for yourself in any event and elaborate on your approach to comparing the advantages of private versus employer-provided coverage.
2. Bill Davis was born in 1935 and went to work when he was 16. He was employed with Social Security coverage from 1954 to 1975 when he was killed in a tragic auto accident. In 1965, his annual salary was $10,000. He received a $1,000 increase each year thereafter. After his death, Bill's childless widow wondered what her monthly benefits would be. Bill's widow was 42 years old at the time of his death. What are her monthly benefits under Bill's Social Security program?
3. George Harvey worked with an insurance company for 35 years and retired from that job at age 65. During the last ten years of his employment his average earnings were $25,000 annually. What would be his maximum retirement benefits?
4. Why do you suppose fringe benefits have become an increasingly larger share of total compensation during the last decade?

Chapter 12

Property and liability insurance

The only thing wealth does for some people is to make them worry about losing it.

Comte de Rivarol

INTRODUCTION

Property and liability insurance is big business. Americans pay almost $50 billion a year for property/liability insurance. Of this almost 20 percent is paid by individuals, two thirds of that for automobile insurance. The risks covered run the gamut from broken windows and stolen watches to death, disfigurement, and permanent injury. All but a few of the risks covered in this chapter, however, fit into two broad categories. One category is the loss of use of property, damage to, or complete loss of property—your house, car, boat, furniture, clothing, or other personal possessions. The other category is your legal liability for damage to either the person or the property of others as a result of your carelessness or negligence. While these two types of insurance are very different, they are treated together in this chapter because they are usually bought together in package policies.

Liability and property damage resulting from the use of an automobile are packaged together in automobile insurance. Comprehensive personal liability and property damage to your home and contents are the principal components of *homeowner's insurance*. Liability and property damage arising from use of a boat are covered by inland marine insurance, which can be added to a homeowner's policy. The only other commonly purchased policies for individuals involving property and/or liability insurance is professional liability insurance which is covered later in this chapter.

This chapter examines:

- What is property insurance?
- How do I evaluate and inventory my property for insurance purposes?

- How large a deductible can I afford?
- What is liability insurance?
- How much liability insurance do I need?
- What kinds of homeowner's/renter's insurance can I buy?
- What is included in automobile insurance?
- What is no-fault insurance?
- What determines my auto insurance rate?
- What is inland marine insurance?
- Do I need professional liability insurance?
- Why have property/liability insurance premiums risen so rapidly?

WHAT IS PROPERTY INSURANCE?

Property insurance will reimburse you for the loss of or damage to your physical assets—your house, furniture, car, clothing, musical instruments, jewelry, or anything else you might own. The policy will spell out the perils against which your property is protected and the items of property which the policy covers. Special items—silver, jewelry, furs, stamp collections, and art objects—may require a rider or floater attached to your policy along with an appraisal of value and an additional premium. Generally, special coverage is required for these items if the value of a single item—one painting, stamp collection, piece of jewelry, or musical instrument—is greater than some specified limit, depending on the type of property covered. Most of your usual possessions, such as furniture and clothing, are covered in a homeowner's or renter's policy under the heading of "unscheduled personal property."

The perils against which your personal property is protected are spelled out in the policy. This type of coverage is called *named perils.* The broader the range of perils, the higher is the premium. A list of perils against which houses and personal property are commonly protected on a named-peril basis is given in Table 12–1. However, even more costly policies are written on an *all-risks* instead of a named-perils basis. These blanket policies cover property against all risks except for a few very unusual ones, commonly flood, earthquake, war, and nuclear catastrophe. In addition to reimbursement for the loss or damage to the property itself, related expenses can be insured against. The most common related expense is additional living expense while your house is being repaired or rebuilt.

The automobile, that most common of all assets, can be protected against property damage by several coverages. Collision insurance covers damage to your car from an accident in which you were at fault. If the other party is at fault, that person's liability insurance will pay for damage to your car. But cars are subject to other hazards as well. They can be stolen, vandalized, hit

Table 12–1
Common peril coverage

Basic policies cover:

1. Fire.
2. Lightning.
3. Windstorm.
4. Hail.
5. Explosion.
6. Damage by aircraft and unowned vehicles.
7. Smoke damage.
8. Theft.
9. Malicious mischief.
10. Window breakage.
11. Damage to property removed because of fire damage.

Broader coverage adds:

12. Falling objects.
13. Collapse of building.
14. Damage from weight of ice, snow, or sleet.
15. Damage to/by steam or hot water heating system or hot water heaters.
16. Water damage from plumbing, heating, air conditioning.
17. Freezing of plumbing, heating, air-conditioning, and appliances.
18. Damage to electrical appliances, fixtures, and wiring from electrical malfunction.

by falling rocks and trees, flooded, dented by hailstones, and carried away by tornados, just to name a few common perils. Damage to your car from anything except a collision is covered by comprehensive insurance. The major sources of comprehensive claims are theft, vandalism, and damage from hail, tornados, and windstorms. Premiums in different regions of the country reflect the difference in risks from these sources. A list of risks covered by comprehensive insurance is given in Table 12–2.

Table 12–2
Major risks covered by comprehensive automobile insurance

1. Breakage of glass
2. Theft or larceny of car and/or contents (if owned by insured)
3. Damage due to:
   Missiles.
   Falling objects.
   Fire.
   Explosion.
   Earthquake.
   Windstorm.
   Hail.
   Water.
   Flood.
   Malicious mischief or vandalism.
   Riot or civil commotion.
   Collision with bird or animal.

HOW DO I EVALUATE AND INVENTORY MY PROPERTY FOR INSURANCE PURPOSES?

The automobile is probably the easiest property to assess for insurance coverage. The *collision* and *comprehensive* portions of a standard policy specify that the insurer will reimburse the *actual cash value* of the loss, less any specified deductible. The approximate value of a car is the "blue book" value in the National Association of Automobile Dealers' regular report on the wholesale and retail value for used cars. If your car is a total loss, the blue book value is a starting point for determining the amount of your reimbursement. Mileage, condition, and area resale prices will also enter into the final determination of value. When your car reaches the age of five years or more, you might seriously consider dropping collision, comprehensive or both, if your emergency fund is adequate. Cars depreciate rapidly and the cost of repairing property damage on an older car becomes a larger fraction of the total value of the car itself. Indeed, the cost of repair can exceed the book value of the car.

Unlike some other kinds of insurance, property damage insurance involves a fixed and easily determinable dollar maximum—the value of the property itself. Claims are most often for less than the full market value, since partial damage is more common than total loss. Property damage is therefore a good candidate for retaining some risk by the use of deductibles and by dropping coverage on items you can afford to replace.

Houses are also fairly easy to assess, unless they are old, unusual, or unique. The average American house is sold every seven years, so it is not difficult to get a reading on the prices of houses similar to yours in age, location, size and quality from newspaper real estate advertisements. This is one approach. An alternative approach is to compute the replacement cost based on the current cost per square foot in your area, a figure most realtors can easily supply. To illustrate, a 2,000-square foot house at $25 per square foot would cost $50,000 to replace. Decks, garages, and other extras usually run less per square foot. In any case, do not include the value of the lot in your computation. Short of earthquake or nuclear catastrophe, there is little that can cause permanent damage to a piece of bare real estate. While on the subject of the out-of-doors, damage to trees and shrubs can be covered separately in a homeowner's package policy.

Insurance coverage on your house needs to be kept at a minimum of 80 percent of replacement value in order to recover full reimbursement on partial losses. This provision is called the *coinsurance* clause or the replacement cost provision in homeowner's policies. If your house is insured for less than 80 percent of replacement value, the reimbursement for partial losses will be that fraction of the loss which equals

$$\frac{\text{Actual insurance coverage}}{\text{Required minimum coverage}}$$

where required minimum coverage equals 80 percent of replacement cost of house. For example, minimum required coverage on a $40,000 house would be $32,000. If you carried only $20,000 and incurred a $4,000 loss, your reimbursement would be

$$\frac{\$20{,}000}{\$32{,}000} \times \$4{,}000 = \$2{,}500.$$

Personal property is the most difficult to assess and inventory, because of the number and variety of items covered. Your homeowner's insurance will include an allowance for *unscheduled personal property* which is usually one half the value of the house itself. There are, nevertheless, good reasons for inventorying your personal property. Suppose you experience a partial loss. Perhaps only the kitchen or living room suffered substantial damage. An inventory will give you a list of the number and value of items in those rooms. Further benefits can emerge when making up the list. The inventory process itself will uncover some forgotten items which may require supplementary coverage. This coverage is known as a personal property *floater.*

The inventory should be done on a room-by-room basis. Major items should be listed with year of purchase and original price. Minor items can be grouped and estimated, for example, 100 8-track tapes, average cost $7. Photographs of each room from two different angles may help in identifying and verifying unusual items. These photographs should be kept with the inventory itself in a safe-deposit box or in a fireproof box at home.

Valuation of personal property is more complex than inventorying, since replacement cost is usually rising while the value of the property itself is depreciating from age, wear and tear, and obsolescence. *Depreciation* varies greatly from item to item and is based on the article's estimated useful lifetime. Household appliances last anywhere from 7 to 20 years. Upholstered furniture depreciates more rapidly than wooden furniture because of stains, fabric wear, and periodic need for reupholstery and recovering. Clothing has a very short useful lifetime because of wear and tear and changing styles. An average annual rate of depreciation for major items is about 10 percent; 20 to 50 percent might be more appropriate for clothing, costume jewelry, and kitchen items such as dinnerware, flatware, pots and pans, and small appliances. Thus, a four-year-old wooden table with an original cost of $200 and a replacement cost of $300 would be worth about $180. These approximate figures can be used in estimating the value of personal property for purposes of determining insurance coverage needed and to arrive at a dollar figure for personal property on your balance sheet.

Personal property inventory forms can be obtained from your insurance agent, a county home extension agent, and savings banks. These forms can simplify the inventorying task considerably. To maintain accurate values, you will need to make an annual update of the personal property inventory.

HOW LARGE A DEDUCTIBLE CAN I AFFORD?

Deductibles are one of the best ways to hold down the cost of insurance. You probably cannot afford to assume the total risk of loss of your house, personal property, and automobile. But you can usually afford to cover part of the loss yourself. And by avoiding the processing of many small claims, the insurance company saves considerable sums of money, a savings passed on to the insurance buyer in the form of a lower premium. Some of the potential savings in deductibles are given in Table 12–3.

Table 12–3
Sample premium savings from using deductibles

Homeowner's insurance*

Compared to a $50 deductible on the property damage section,

a $100 deductible reduces premiums by 10 percent (up to $25)
a $200 deductible reduces premiums by 20 percent (up to $50)
a $500 deductible reduces premiums by 25 percent (up to $60)

Collision insurance

Compared to a $100 deductible, a $250 deductible for collisions reduces the premium by 24 percent.

* Quotes are from a large national insurance company.

These savings can be used to make total coverage more adequate by increasing the limits on the house, on personal liability, and on automobile liability, or may simply be used to reduce total insurance costs.

The size of the deductible you can afford is determined by your emergency fund, those liquid assets which can be converted to cash within three months at little or no loss minus those debt obligations now due or due within the next few months. Your balance sheet should give you a quick estimate of the size of your emergency fund.

The house and personal property can be insured with deductibles from zero up. Your insurance agent will provide a schedule of premiums for the same house/personal property coverages with different deductibles. On auto insurance, deductibles can be taken on both collision and comprehensive. Your past average insurable loss experience may provide some guidance to the amount of loss you might expect to incur, but the year-to-year variation is highly unpredictable. If you have a history of frequent, small accidents or comprehensive claims such as vandalism, theft, weather damage, you might choose to take a small deductible. If, on the other hand, you rarely have any claims and have an adequate emergency fund, larger deductibles would be appropriate and can generate substantial savings in premiums.

WHAT IS LIABILITY INSURANCE?

Liability is your legal obligation to make restitution for damages done to the person or property of others through your negligence. *Negligence* can result from a positive action, for example, carelessly running your car into someone's picket fence. Or it may be negative—failing to fill a hole in your lawn, which causes the mail carrier to trip and break his or her wrist. Negligence can be your own fault or the fault of your spouse, child, dog, servant, or employee. Unfortunately, the potential extent of liability claims is virtually limitless, since negligence can lead to loss of life, medical expenses, disability, pain and suffering, and damage to property. Claims in the millions of dollars are not rare.

Reprinted by permission The Wall Street Journal

Liability insurance is the only kind of insurance which does not reimburse the insured person but rather an injured third party. While business and service activities lead to liability claims, especially in the areas of *product liability* and *professional malpractice liability,* the two types of liability policies most relevant to the average individual are automobile liability and *comprehensive personal liability*. The latter is usually purchased as part of the homeowner's policy. Comprehensive personal liability covers nonautomobile bodily injury and property damage. Medical payments coverage is most commonly written as $500 per incident and covers medical expenses to persons other than the insured and family who are injured on the premises of the insured or elsewhere by the insured, other member of the family, employees, or animals. The comprehensive personal liability clause of homeowner's policies covers bodily injury and property damage liability claims arising out of negligence. Coverage under the homeowner's policy excludes claims arising from use of ownership of automobiles, aircraft, or watercraft, or from business or professional activities. All of these can be covered in other types of policies. Thus comprehensive personal liability covers a "catch-all" or residual category of liability not covered by specific other policies. The most common limits of liability in the homeowner's policy are $25,000 per occurrence for bodily injury and $250 for "no-fault" damage to the property of others. Major sources of claims are damage done by children and dogs, *attractive nuisances* (such as a swimming pool), and failure to keep property in good repair and free of hazards (weak stairs, broken railings, or toys left in the yard).

HOW MUCH LIABILITY INSURANCE DO I NEED?

As in any economic decision, only you can weigh the cost—the premium—against the benefits—the risk of loss averted—and arrive at an appropriate level of liability coverage. While your financial assets are a starting point, all of them could be lost in a successful lawsuit. State laws vary on the right to attach and/or claim real and personal property in the event of a lawsuit. In addition, in many states it is possible to garnish a portion of a worker's wages and have an employer send payment directly to a court-appointed collector. A few states do not permit garnishment at all.

Even when you insure there are risks which you retain. Put simply, you retain any liability in excess of the limits of liability of your policy. If you have $50,000 in liability insurance, you are fully covered for any damages up to $50,000; but judgments of $75,000, $200,000, or even $1 million could conceivably occur, leaving you liable for the excess. The higher the amount of the judgment, however, the lower the probability that you will ever incur that large a legal liability. Limits in excess of $200,000 are covering very remote contingencies, although a $1 million personal umbrella liability policy is becoming increasingly popular.

Your assets may be more relevant to determining limits of liability insurance if they are negligible; if you have limited assets, you have little to lose and can probably get by with the legal minimum of liability insurance. Few people, however, stay at that end of the balance sheet for long.

Liability insurance limits are thus highly subjective. The greatest risk of a liability judgment for most people arises from owning an automobile in which case higher limits are probably most important.

The state will set a minimum required level of coverage for *bodily injury* and *property damage liability* on automobile insurance. One of the most common minimum limits of liability is 15/30/5. The first figure, $15,000, is bodily injury per person, and the second, $30,000, limits the total liability per occurrence. The third, $5,000, is the limit for property damage liability. Regardless of your state's legal minimum, however, you can be sued for more and lose most, if not all, of your accumulated assets in the process.

Because automobile accidents are the major source of claims, adequate limits of liability are especially important here. A figure of $5,000 for property damage, for example, is substantially less than the average selling price of a new car. Substantially more than $5,000 in property damage can occur in a single accident. A commonly recommended figure is 100/300/25. The cost of increasing liability insurance limits over the legal minimum is less than you might expect. The vast majority of claims are small. The large-loss principle is relevant here as in other lines of insurance. Some comparative figures on comprehensive personal liability and automobile bodily injury liability are given below.

Homeowner's CPL*

Raising limits from $25,000 to $100,000 costs an additional $4 per year.

A $1 million *umbrella policy* costs $200 a year.

Automobile bodily injury/property damage†

15/30/5	costs	$ 85.00	a year
25/50/25	costs	$ 93.20	a year
100/300/25	costs	$105.00	a year

* Quotes for both homeowner's and automobile from a large national insurance company.

† The basic rate will vary greatly by area and classification, but the relative increase is about the same.

WHAT KINDS OF HOMEOWNER'S/RENTER'S INSURANCE CAN I BUY?

There are six kinds of package policies you can purchase, numbered HO-1 through HO-6. HO-4 is specifically for renters, HO-6 for condominium owners. HO-1, HO-2, HO-3 and HO-5 are designed for homeowners. All six are package policies. The property part of the policy covers the dwelling, unattached private structures such as a garage, your personal property, and additional living expenses if you have to find temporary quarters while the house is being repaired. The liability section of the policy includes comprehensive personal liability, medical payments to nonfamily members, and physical damage to the property of others. *Renter's insurance* includes all of the liability coverages, but the property coverages are limited to personal property plus any improvements done and paid for by the tenant. Condominium insurance, just developed in 1974, covers your dwelling plus your prorated share of common property.

The difference between HO-1, HO-2, HO-3 and HO-5 lies not in the components of the package but rather in the perils against which they insure. The perils are listed in Table 12–1. HO-1 insures against the first 12 perils. HO-2 insures against all 18 perils listed. HO-3 is all risks (usual exceptions: war, flood, earthquake, and nuclear attack) on the house and garage, while personal property is covered for the listed perils. HO-5 is all risks on both dwelling and contents. HO-5 is substantially more costly than the others. HO-2 (broad form) is the most popular policy.

Homeowner's policies are highly standardized in wording and content, and their rates are regulated but not identical. The rate on a particular house is mainly a function of construction (wood or brick, one story or two), geographic area, exposure (how closely it is surrounded by other buildings), and the quality of the fire department by which you are served, all of which affect the insurer's loss expectations. Your choices will consist of deductibles, limits of liabilities, and additional "floater" endorsements for special coverages on items such as jewelry and furs which were described earlier. The value estimated for unscheduled personal property, those personal possessions not covered on separate endorsements, is usually one half the value of the house. Additional living expense is 20 percent of the value of the house. Thus, a policy on a $50,000 house would include up to $10,000 in additional living expenses and $25,000 coverage on unscheduled personal property.

WHAT IS INCLUDED IN AUTOMOBILE INSURANCE?

The automobile policy is also a package policy. The major coverages are liability and property damage. Either liability insurance coverage or proof of financial responsibility is required by law in most states. In some states evidence of liability coverage has been displaced by no-fault or first party coverage. If your state insurance law provides for liability (third party) coverage, your policy will include both bodily injury liability with limits expressed as thousands of dollars per person covered and per occurrence and property damage liability. Property damage coverages consist of collision and comprehensive, neither of which is required by law. A car which is collateral for an auto loan may need these coverages to satisfy requirements of the lender, however. Other components include:

1. *Uninsured motorist coverage*—in non-no-fault states, to protect you when you suffer injury or damage by a hit-and-run driver or an uninsured motorist. You would collect as if your insurer was the driver at fault, carrying the state's legal minimum of liability coverage. There is usually a deductible. This coverage may not be available everywhere.
2. *Accidental death*—essentially life insurance, which is valid only if a member of the insured household is killed in an automobile accident.

3. *Towing and labor*—an optional coverage for expenses incurred in a highway breakdown.
4. *Medical expense coverage*—for either passengers in your car or members of your family injured by automobiles as pedestrians—$500 to $5,000 per person.

No-fault insurance

Your state may also require some amount of no-fault coverage which replaces bodily injury liability insurance either partially or completely. *No-fault insurance* replaces the adversary system under which you and your insurance company are pitted against the other driver and his or her insurance company. Instead there is a direct reimbursement from your insurance company to you, regardless of which party is at fault. This makes automobile insurance more similar to other lines of insurance, where fault-finding is not generally an issue. While suicide and arson are grounds for nonrecovery in life and fire insurance, generally the insurance company does not inquire as to whether you were at fault when you died, became ill, fell off the roof, or had an electrical fire in your basement! The process of determining or assigning fault often winds up in the courts and a large part of the cost of automobile liability insurance is the expense of legal and court fees. Presumably if this expense were eliminated, automobile liability insurance rates would be reduced. Along these lines, legal expenses account for about one third of total automobile liability claims expenses. In addition, claims might be settled more quickly. States which have experimented with no-fault have found that insurance premiums either fell or at least rose more slowly than elsewhere, although the savings have been less than was originally hoped.

There are some difficulties with no-fault. By eliminating the legal adversary system, you are placed in an adversary situation with respect to your insurance company. Under a traditional liability system, if you had several accidents which were not your fault, there would be no claims against your policy. Under no-fault, safe and careful drivers, through no fault of their own, may incur several claims and have their rates raised or their insurance cancelled. The insurance "reward" of lower premiums for safe and cautious driving would be much less certain.

A second difficulty arises from the fact that insurance is regulated by the states. A person from a liability-insurance state could collide with a person from a no-fault state. If the first party were at fault, the second party would have double coverage—his or her own no-fault and the other person's liability. (The guilty first party could collect on his or her own collision.) But if the second party, with no-fault, was the "guilty" party, the first person would have no coverage, since the other person has no liability insurance. Uninsured motorist coverage or supplementary liability coverage can usually fill this need. No-fault states are cognizant of this difficulty and try to deal with it in specifying coverages required and allowed, but the overlap of interstate drivers regulated by 50 competing jurisdictions has led to proposals for nationwide no-fault.

Some states have finessed the no-fault issue by having it apply only to a limited amount of injury and/or property damage, such as claims of $1,000 or less. This eliminates the bother of processing smaller claims through the legal system, while reserving the liability principle for larger damages.

WHAT DETERMINES MY AUTOMOBILE INSURANCE PREMIUM?

Rate classification systems vary greatly from state to state, but most, if not all, of the following factors are considered.

1. Age, sex, marital status of drivers. Unmarried male drivers under age 25 are the most accident-prone group and pay substantially higher rates than any other group.
2. Driving history. Accidents, speeding convictions, driving under the influence of alcohol and drugs, and just about any other violation except a parking ticket will raise your rates for liability and collision. Comprehensive rates are generally insensitive to your personal claims history, since they depend on the experience with theft, vandalism, and weather damage in your area.
3. Type of car. Collision and comprehensive premiums will drop as your car gets older, since the potential loss to the company will also fall. Liability rates offer compact car discounts and "hot car" surcharges (sports cars and high horsepower cars), based on past claims experience with these categories of ownership.
4. Discounts are sometimes offered for good students (usually a "B" average or better) and for people who have taken drivers' education. These vary from state to state.

Given the above factors, along with the general level of rates in your area (which depends not only on the state but the claims record in the part of the state in which you live), how can you keep your premium down? Eliminating marginal items of coverage such as for accidental death and collision on older cars and taking as large a deductible as your emergency fund will permit are two actions which you can take. Reducing liability coverage to the legal minimum is probably the poorest way to economize, since the amount at risk is large and the savings from reducing liability coverage are modest. Paying less often—once rather than twice a year—may generate some modest savings.

WHAT ABOUT THE BOAT?

Your boat is listed among the exclusions on your homeowner's policy, but separate coverage can be provided by attaching an *inland marine policy* to the homeowner's policy. If you desire, you can obtain the same coverage with a separate policy. These policies written for individuals cover pleasure craft against property losses (fire, theft, sinking, weather damage, and so forth) and liability for injury to others or property damage arising from the ownership or use of yachts, motorboats, and sailboats. Property damage covers the actual cash value of the craft (and usually the contents as well). Liability could include injury to passengers in your boat or someone else's, injury to water-skiers and swimmers, or damage to docks, trees, boathouses, or other property. Limits of liability are usually lower than automobile and comprehensive personal liability, and premiums are usually low since the probability of having a claim is not as great as on automobile and homeowner's insurance.

DO I NEED PROFESSIONAL LIABILITY INSURANCE?

Professional liability insurance was at one time limited mainly to physicians' malpractice insurance. In recent years, the number of professions in which professional liability insurance is considered advisable has been increasing rapidly. Architects, lawyers, nurses, accountants, investment advisors, teachers, and college professors are among the many service-oriented professionals who have been successfully sued for bad advice, errors in judgment, embarrassment and humiliation, and failure to adequately fulfill their obligation to clients, patients, and students. Outside of the medical profession, professional liability insurance is still relatively inexpensive and is often available on a group basis through an employer or professional association. If you are planning to enter any profession in which your professional activities might render you vulnerable to a lawsuit, check with a professional association about the need for, cost, and availability of professional liability insurance.

Firms which produce products usually carry product liability insurance to protect them against liability for defective, misrepresented, and hazardous products. The scope of product liability has been greatly broadened by recent court decisions. If you plan to go into business for yourself, check into the possibility of product and/or professional service liability insurance. Product liability is potentially a greater risk than any other form of liability.

WHY HAVE PROPERTY/LIABILITY INSURANCE PREMIUMS BEEN RISING SO RAPIDLY?

Although the consumer price index has been rising rapidly, not all of the components have gone up at an equal rate. Among the faster rising components are new cars, car repairs and parts, construction of houses (including repairs), and health care services. Between 1967 and 1976, the overall cost of living rose 70.5 percent. The cost of reshingling a roof rose 133 percent, residing 101 percent, and house maintenance and repairs 92 percent. Hospital service charges rose 169 percent, medical care costs 85 percent, and auto repairs and maintenance 90 percent. These represent most of the major cost items in homeowner's and automobile insurance claims.

In professional liability, both the number of cases and the average jury award have risen sharply—the latter from $62,000 to $350,000 in eight years. Premiums for malpractice have gone up by 200 to 300 percent. Insurers in property/liability lines have been and are still running substantial underwriting losses because premiums have failed to keep pace with claims. Since health care costs, automobile prices and repairs, and housing costs are projected to continue to rise more rapidly than the overall price level well into the 1980s, there is little relief in sight on insurance premiums.

SUMMARY

Property and liability insurance are treated together in this chapter because they are usually purchased together in a package policy. Property insurance covers either loss of or damage to personal possessions—house, car, furniture, clothing, jewelry, and so forth—resulting from a variety of risks. Some items of considerable value, such as jewelry and furs, require special coverage. The perils may be listed in the policy (named perils) or the policy may cover the property on an all-risks basis, with a few listed exclusions.

Indirect expenses arising from either loss of or damage to property are also insurable. These include additional living expense on homeowner's insurance and towing and labor on automobile insurance.

The value of a car for insurance purposes can be estimated from resale prices in the "blue book" and newspaper ads. Property damage insurance (collision and comprehensive) can be dropped on older cars if your emergency fund is adequate.

The value of the house can be determined by market prices of similar houses in your area or by replacement cost on a square footage basis. The lot should not be included. A minimum of 80 percent of market value should be carried for coinsurance purposes.

Personal property should be inventoried on a room-by-room basis, listing date of purchase and original price. The homeowner's policy will allow one half the value of the house for unscheduled personal property, but an inventory will identify unusual items and also provide verification of partial losses.

Deductibles can be taken on property damage insurance on your house, personal property, and car. Deductibles are a good way to keep premiums down. The size of deductibles you can afford depends on your net liquid assets on your balance sheet.

Liability insurance covers your legal obligation to make restitution for injury or damage to the person or property of others. The major sources of liability claims against individuals arise from the ownership of property, carelessness of your children or pets toward the property of others, and automobile accidents. Automobile insurance covers the last of these; the others are covered by comprehensive personal liability, usually purchased as part of the homeowner's package policy. Liability claims arising from the use of aircraft, watercraft, from business, or from professional activities require separate coverage.

The appropriate level of liability insurance coverage is difficult to determine. The state sets minimum required limits for automobile liability insurance but it is usually advisable to carry more than the legal minimum. The greater your assets, the more you can lose in a lawsuit. Customary limits of liability on the homeowners' policy are $25,000/person (bodily injury) and $250 (property damage).

The package homeowner's policy comes in six forms. Forms HO-1, HO-2, HO-3 and HO-5 are for homeowners. They include property damage coverage on the dwelling, unattached structures, unscheduled personal property, additional living expenses, comprehensive personal liability, medical payments (outside the household), and damage to the property of others. HO-4 is for renters and includes all of the above except the dwelling and attached structures. HO-6 is for condominium owners and also includes coverage for a prorated share of common property. HO-3 and HO-5 insure against more perils than HO-1 and HO-2. Rates depend on construction, exposure, geographic area, and the quality of fire protection, all of which influence the insurer's loss experience.

Automobile insurance includes bodily injury and property damage liability, comprehensive, collision, uninsured motorist coverage, medical expense, accidental death, and towing and labor. No-fault is a part of automobile insurance in some states. No-fault replaces part or all of liability coverage with first party coverage. If you suffer injury or damage in an automobile collision, under no-fault you would be reimbursed by your own insurance company, regardless of who was at fault.

Automobile insurance premiums for various classes are based on age, sex, marital status, driving history, and type of car.

Inland marine insurance floaters offer property/liability coverage on boats. Professional liability insurance is carried by most self-employed professionals and some who are employed by others.

Property and liability insurance premiums have skyrocketed in recent years. The two major insured forms of property, houses and cars, have risen in price more rapidly than the price index. Sharp increases in repair costs and larger jury awards in liability cases have also contributed to the increase.

KEY WORDS

Actual cash value
All risks
Attractive nuisance
Bodily injury
Coinsurance
Collision
Comprehensive
Comprehensive personal liability
Deductible
Depreciation
Floater
Homeowner's insurance
Inland marine insurance
Liability insurance
Named perils
Negligence
No-fault insurance
Product liability
Professional liability insurance
Property damage
Umbrella policy
Uninsured motorist coverage
Unscheduled personal property

PROBLEM

Sandra and Edward Evans list the following items needing insurance:

1. One car, three years old, worth $2,600.
2. One house, replacement cost $30,000.
3. Assorted personal property, $12,000.
4. One motorboat, $4,000.
5. Family heirloom silver, $1,200.

They have $1,600 in net liquid assets, a net worth of $16,000, annual income of $20,000. They have had no automobile accidents in five years. The area in which they live has frequent hailstorms and tornados. Their two children play a lot of outdoor games. They have a dog. Minor claims on homeowner's insurance average $80 a year.

A $250 deductible on any homeowner's policy will save them $30 over a $100 deductible, $60 over a zero deductible. On collision and comprehensive, the premium savings over zero deductible are

	Deductible		
	$250	***$100***	***$50***
Collision saving	$70	$35	$15
Comprehensive saving	$12	$ 7	$ 3

Outline a property/liability insurance program for the Evans. Explain your recommendations.

PART III

One way to improve your standard of living is to enlarge your income stream through a program of saving and investment. These six chapters explore the process of saving and the various alternatives in investment from which you can construct a portfolio. Chapter 13 discusses the savings process and the various qualities of investment media which should be considered in choosing investments. Chapter 14 considers savings accounts, Series E and H bonds, and other bank services. Chapters 15 and 16 explore stocks and bonds, while Chapter 17 discusses investing in mutual funds. A final chapter on other investments—commodity futures, collectibles, and miscellany—completes the section.

ENHANCING YOUR LIFESTYLE

Chapter 13

Adding to your assets: The how and why of saving and investing

Never invest your money in anything that eats or needs repairing.

Hobart Brown

INTRODUCTION

Now that you have established a lifestyle and taken the necessary steps to protect it from various insurable perils, the next step is to improve your lifestyle over time. One way to improve your lifestyle is to increase your real income from year to year. An upwardly mobile career path may provide this opportunity, as was discussed in Chapter 2. A second form of enhancement is the acquisition and development of consumption skills—hobbies, sports, reading, conversation, musical and artistic skills. In fact, some consumption skills can also become income producers, although most consumption skills are acquired for their intrinsic satisfactions. The third way of enhancing your lifestyle is to postpone some present consumption to enhance future consumption, both by making future consumption more certain (acquiring financial assets as a fallback) and by enlarging the future income stream with interest, dividends, rent, and capital gains on your investments. This third form of lifestyle enhancement is the subject of the next six chapters.

The remaining chapters in this section of the book deal with the various types of investment media. Chapter 14 concentrates on low-denomination, safe, relatively liquid investments—savings accounts, certificates of deposit, and Series E and H bonds. Stocks and bonds are introduced in Chapter 15 which provides an overview of the variety of securities which you might consider for your portfolio. After having learned about the securities themselves, a discussion of the process of buying and selling stocks and bonds is provided in Chapter 16. Here you will learn about the actual mechanics of investing.

Many people prefer to have someone else invest for them. So, investment companies and mutual funds are covered in Chapter 17. Since anything which increases in value can be thought of as an investment opportunity, a broad array of items is discussed in Chapter 18 which introduces commodity investments such as gold, silver, and antique cars. To complete the sequence, reference should be made to Chapter 6 where housing was discussed. After all, housing represents the major investment for most families.

The chapter at hand is a survey of the savings and investment process, focussed on the following points:

- Why save?
- How do I save?
- Characteristics of investment media.
  - Yield.
  - Risk.
  - Liquidity/Maturity.
  - Size.
  - Growth/Inflation hedge.
  - Tax status.
- Putting an investment portfolio together.
- The investment life cycle.
- Computing the yield.
- Kinds of yield.
- Recent asset performance.
- Expectations, investor information, and beating the market.

WHY SAVE?

This question would be regarded as heresy by anyone old enough to remember the Great Depression. But today the great majority of the American people are too young to have any firsthand knowledge of economic disaster. Those who have grown up in a world of Social Security, unemployment compensation, health insurance, welfare, bank overdraft privileges, and easy credit have a hard time imagining a rainy day for which there is no guaranteed umbrella. Why save?

Saving has long been regarded chiefly to provide an *emergency fund,* and certainly a fund for unexpected expenses is a primary goal. As explained in earlier chapters, an emergency fund will cover the deductibles on your

"Here's a bit of nostalgia for you. I'm saving exactly the same amount per week *now* as I did when I was in grade school."

Reprinted by permission The Wall Street Journal

insurance (and let you save money by taking larger deductibles). An emergency fund also covers uninsured surprises which can occur even in our security-wrapped world—a big income tax bill, a major car repair, an unscheduled trip, a crown for a tooth, legal expenses, a big jump in car insurance, a broken-down furnace or a new roof. While budgeting suggests that these should be anticipated, no one has perfect foresight. An emergency fund of one to three months' take-home pay in fairly liquid form (credit union, passbook savings) should be the first aim of saving.

A second reason for saving is to make possible major financial goals which cannot be paid for out of week-to-week income. Intermediate goals (in time and amount) might be a down payment on a house, car, furniture, boat, major home improvements, a motorcycle, stereo, and a trip to Europe. Goals like these make saving (sacrificing present consumption) less painful.

Longer range, higher priced goals might include education for the children, retirement funds, and building an estate.

Some people save for all of these reasons. Some people save because a nest egg gives them a sense of security. Some people save in order to have capital to invest so that they can become wealthier. A surprisingly large number of people do not save at all. Only 6 to 8 percent of disposable income is saved in any given year.

Goals are an indispensible first step in saving—the why. The second step is *how*. Saving comes more easily to some people than to others. Goals may provide motivation, but you may need to find a way to make saving painless and automatic. If you have difficulty saving, try any of the following techniques:

1. Budget your savings. Make savings a bill that is paid each month along with the electric company, the car payment, and the mortgage. (See the budgeting chapter.)
2. Automate savings. Arrange for a payroll deduction to buy a bond, to deposit in a credit union, or a monthly transfer from checking to savings.
3. Save change. Throw coins in a jar at the end of the day and bank them once a month.
4. Make savings inaccessible. Put some of your savings in certificates of deposit (the interest penalty will deter you from withdrawing), E bonds (a minimum two-months' holding period), or other forms of savings which are inconvenient to cash and spend.
5. Buy whole life insurance. While the rate of return is less than exciting, the regular premium will compel you to save on penalty of losing your insurance.
6. Remind yourself of the joys of compound interest. Five dollars a week at 6 percent compounded quarterly day of deposit to day of withdrawal amounts to $268.41 in a year, $1,526 in five years. Watching your money grow is like watching your weight drop on a diet; it provides the incentive to continue.
7. Set a dollar or percentage goal. Bankers suggest 5 to 10 percent of take-home pay. Six to 8 percent is about average.

CHARACTERISTICS OF INVESTMENT MEDIA

Once you have convinced yourself *why* you should save and found a way *how* to make yourself save, what do you do with your pile of money? Bury your money in the mattress? Stick it in a savings account? The possibilities are endless. Stocks, bonds, mutual funds, real estate, coins, certificates of deposit, options, and commodities are just a few of the many investment possibilities. Choosing an investment *portfolio* is much like acquiring a wardrobe. Starting with safe, basic, all-purpose clothes or investments, you can then expand on the basis of your budget, tastes, and needs. Investments, like clothes, have special characteristics which mean that your ideal investment may be something your neighbor would never give a second glance. Among these characteristics are yield, risk, liquidity/maturity, size, transaction costs, growth/inflation hedge, and tax status.

Yield is the percentage return on investment. Low yielding investments include passbook savings (4½ to 5½ percent), Series E bonds (6 percent), and life insurance (3 to 6 percent). Higher yields are generally available on treasury bonds (7 to 9 percent), corporate bonds (7 to 9 percent), some preferred stocks. Higher yield is generally associated with larger size, greater risk and/or less liquidity. Some investments offer no direct income yield, only the hope of capital gains (coins, stamps, unimproved land). Methods of computing yield are discussed later in this chapter.

Risk refers to the possibility that the yield may decline and/or the value of the investment itself may fall (loss of principal). Sometimes the two are related; a decline in dividends or rental income will also lead to a decrease in the market value of stocks and real estate. Higher yields are offered on lower grade bonds and other securities where the capacity of the borrower to repay is doubtful. The risk is higher—in this case, that is, the risk of loss of principal.

If all investments had equal risk, differences in yield would be much smaller than they actually are. The amount of risk you are willing to assume depends on how much you can afford to lose and especially on your willingness to assume risk. Some people find speculating exciting; others find it nerve-racking. Low-risk investments include government bonds, blue-chip stocks, and certificates of deposit. High-risk investments include gold, real estate, commodities, options, and speculative stocks.

Liquidity refers to how quickly an asset can be converted to cash. *Maturity* is the reverse; it is the length of time before an asset can be redeemed at face value. Liquidity—or illiquidity—is a characteristic of all investments. Maturity refers only to certain fixed dollar assets with a stated face value and a specified repayment date—bonds, certificates of deposit, endowment insurance policies, and some annuities. Highly liquid assets are those which can be freely converted to cash without risk of loss, such as passbook savings and treasury bills (short maturity). Less liquid investments would include real estate and common stocks.

Size can be a vital consideration. Most investments have no maximum, but many have a minimum. Most mutual funds have minimums of $500 to $5,000, certificates of deposit from $100 to $10,000, depending on maturity and yield. Bonds come in $1,000 denominations. Stocks are much less costly to buy in large units (round lots of one hundred shares); thus a minimum size is important in keeping down commissions. Commodities investors are expected to open accounts of a minimum of $10,000. Land and real estates require substantial down payments. In contrast, passbook accounts can be opened with as little as $10, and Series E bonds are available from $18.75 for a $25 bond to $375 for a $500 bond.

Transactions costs range from none on E bonds and savings accounts to 6 percent on real estate, 10 percent on land. Transactions costs consist mainly of sales commissions, but can also include assaying (gold), title transfer fees (land), appraisal fees (antiques), and retail markup (coins and stamps). Management time might also be classed as a transactions cost, ranging from low (savings accounts, mutual funds) to moderate (stocks, bonds) to high (commodities, rental property). In some cases, however, the management costs become a consumption activity or hobby, especially for stock market watchers and commodity investors.

Growth refers to increase in value apart from interest, dividends or other yield. Growth means that the asset can be sold for more than you paid for it. Fixed-dollar assets such as life insurance, Series E and H bonds, savings accounts, and certificates of deposit do not grow. Common stocks, coins and stamps, land and real estate, and commodities rank high in growth potential. Growth is highly variable and difficult to predict. Assets with growth potential can be useful as an *inflation hedge.* As the general price level rises, generally the prices of physical assets (land, buildings, coins, stamps) or direct claims on physical assets (common stock, commodity futures) rise also. But some prices rise more rapidly than others during inflation, and some prices even fall. There is always a risk that the growth star to which your investment wagon is hitched may prove to be a falling star, or at least not one headed for the zenith. There is no guaranteed inflation hedge, as the poor performance of growth stocks during the inflation of the early 1970s can attest.

Tax status refers to the income tax treatment of the returns on your investment. Some kinds of returns are tax exempt, some partially tax exempt, others tax deferred, and many fully taxable.

The yield on investments consists of rental income, interest, and dividends. Rental income can offer substantial tax advantages. Although it is fully taxable, certain costs can be subtracted—interest on money borrowed to finance the real estate purchase, property taxes, depreciation and maintenance costs. These deductions, especially depreciation, mean that your cash flow from rental property is substantially greater than *taxable* rental income in the early years. Interest is generally taxable when earned, but can be deferred until redemption on Series E bonds, and is not subject to federal income tax at all on state and local government bonds (municipals). There is, however, a minimum tax; large incomes from tax-exempt bonds will pay some tax, but at a substantially lower rate. The first $100 of dividends on stock ($200 on a joint return for stocks owned jointly) can be excluded from income for tax purposes, an attraction for small investors.

Capital gains are taxed at a more favorable rate if the asset has been held 12 months or more. There are two methods of computation. Generally if your tax bracket is 50 percent or less, you will choose to include half your gains in gross income for tax purposes. Thus the effective tax rate is half your marginal tax rate. Capital gains can be offset by capital losses. Only the net gain is taxed. Capital gains are only taxed when actually realized by sale or exchange of the asset, so they can in some cases be deferred until a year when income from other sources is low or deductions are high. Capital gains on an owner-occupied house may be deferred if you buy another house within a year or build one within 18 months.

All of these characteristics sound desirable. The ideal investment would offer high yield, low risk, low minimum size, no transactions cost, good growth potential, high liquidity, minimal management time, and favorable tax status. Unfortunately, no investment meets all these criteria at once. For example, rental property has good growth potential, favorable tax status, and often offers an attractive yield, but transactions costs and minimum size can be high, there is a fair degree of risk, and liquidity may be poor. And certificates of deposit offer a moderately attractive yield with no transactions cost, virtually no risk, and are fairly liquid (at an interest penalty); but the higher yield certificates require larger minimum size and longer maturity, there is no growth potential and the returns are fully taxable in the year earned. Other investment media have different mixes of strengths and weaknesses.

PUTTING AN INVESTMENT PORTFOLIO TOGETHER

Most investors would choose to diversify to gain some of the advantages of each type of asset. Your *emergency fund* should be liquid, low risk, and require a low minimum so that you can build it up gradually. Beyond that, your *portfolio* (your personal collection of investments) should match your asset acquisitions to your goals and preferences. In order to "rough out" a portfolio, you need to assess your goals and preferences.

Table 13–1
Attitudes toward risk

		Points
1.	How would you describe your attitude toward risk?	
	Gives me nightmares.	1
	Makes me moderately uneasy.	2
	Some risk acceptable.	3
	Risk makes life exciting.	4
2.	What is your income/tax bracket?	
	Under $10,000/year—19 percent.	1
	10 to 25,000/year—19 to 25 percent.	2
	20 to 35,000/year—25 to 36 percent.	3
	35 to 50,000/year—32 to 42 percent.	4
	Over 50,000/year—39+ percent.	5
3.	How do you like your assets?	
	Easy to liquidate if you need them.	1
	Mixed liquidity.	2
	Hard to liquidate to avoid temptation.	3

If your score is	***Your investment profile is:***
3 to 5	High safety and liquidity, low in tax advantages and amount to invest.
6 to 8	Intermediate.
9 to 12	High risk, low liquidity, tax advantage important.

If you do not have an emergency fund of two to three months' income (take-home pay) in a liquid, low-risk form, you are not ready to invest. Once you reach that stage, you need to begin the investment process with a list of savings goals. List at least four with approximate dollar amounts and when needed. For example:

Boat	3 years	$ 2,500
Repay note	2 years	1,500
Build a cottage on the lake (down payment)	6 years	3,000
Education for child	15 years	15,000
Retirement nest egg	37 years	50,000

The next step is to assess your investment preferences, using the test in Table 13–1.

In the 3 to 5 range, risk aversion, low income, and liquidity preference combine to suggest a pattern of "safe," low-yield low transactions cost assets. Savings accounts, government bonds, and low-risk mutual funds fit your profile. A rating in excess of nine indicates that land, commodities, common stocks, and municipal bonds suit your needs and preferences best. Intermediate ratings might direct you toward a mixed portfolio with stress on corporate bonds, tax-deferred annuities, growth funds, and blue-chip stocks.

Table 13–2
Investment worksheet

Goal	*Amount needed*	*When needed (yrs.)*	*Desirable characteristics*	*Investment medium*	*Yield (%)*	*Investment needed/year*
oat	$ 2,500	3	Liquid Low minimum Risk acceptable High yield	Growth stock	9 (est.)	$700
epay note	$ 1,500	2	Low risk Fairly liquid Low minimum	90-day savings account	5¾	$703 (176/quarter)
ottage	$ 3,000	6	Intermediate maturity Medium risk Higher yield	Mutual fund	9 (est.)	$366
lucation	$15,000	15	Low risk Moderate size Tax benefits	Series E bonds	6	$608
tirement	$50,000	37	Moderate risk Inflation hedge Tax deferral Not liquid	Real estate	8	$228
tal saving per year (5 goals):						$2,605

Note: The compound interest computations are explained later in the chapter.

Most investors will *not* concentrate their assets in a single investment medium but will hold a broad range of assets. This approach is called *diversification*. Ideally, each investment asset will be matched to a suitable goal. If, for example, you are saving for your child's education, you would like low-risk, high-yield, tax deferral if possible, with liquidity unimportant and perhaps even undesirable. Among the assets which might meet these criteria are long-term corporate bonds, certain mutual funds, and some forms of real estate. A boat, on the other hand, is certainly a less pressing savings goal. If it is deferred, it will not be a matter of serious consequence. Higher risk is therefore tolerable, tax aspects less essential, but liquidity more important. Common stocks, a growth-oriented mutual fund, and lower grade corporate and municipal bonds might be suitable media.

Putting all these considerations together should give you a final investment worksheet like Table 13–2 on page 231.

INVESTMENT LIFE CYCLE

Just as your consumption patterns change over your lifetime, your investments can also be expected to change over the course of a lifetime. The portfolio which is appropriate at age 20 will have to be different at 35, 50, and 65. Some of the factors which will change your portfolio are:

Income. As your base income from wage and salary rises, you will probably be less concerned about short-run investment income, more interested in tax sheltering income (as the tax bite rises), and deferring income until retirement. Investments may shift from higher yield money market instruments, income-oriented mutual funds and preferred stocks to rental property, commodities and stocks with appreciation potential, and tax-deferred annuities. After retirement your interests will shift back to income again to provide retirement income to supplement pensions and Social Security benefits.

Dependents. Having dependents to feed, clothe, and educate tends to make most of us more risk averse and more concerned with enhancing present and near-future income. As dependents strike out on their own, your capacity for tolerating risk and therefore your potential for attaining higher returns will tend to increase.

Assets. The larger your stock of investment assets, the more diversified your portfolio can become. Those who put their meager savings into safe, liquid assets and owner-occupied housing in their 20s can test the waters in other types of investment without throwing away their emergency fund "security blanket" in their 30s, 40s, and 50s.

Time. While Linder points out in *The Harried Leisure Class* that most individuals in professional and managerial classes feel subject to a great deal of time pressure, the scarcity of time is probably greatest in the 25-to-50 age bracket when you are getting established both professionally and personally.

The average family sends the last child off to college when the parents are between 45 and 50. The last 15 to 20 years before retirement should generate more free time and investing can become a challenging and rewarding hobby as well as a way to accumulate retirement funds. Rental property, stocks, coins, stamps, antiques, and commodities are good possibilities at this stage of life which might have been bypassed previously as too time consuming.

Marital status. Those who are (or become) single, divorced, or widowed will probably have to restructure their portfolio from joint to individual. Perhaps the other partner was the main investment manager, creating high learning costs for the remaining person. Tastes, risk preference, time preference, and goals will change. Tax status will probably loom larger as a consideration. Singles are more likely to invest as a hobby or in a hobby. Divorced persons may have to scale down their investments because maintaining two households requires more of current income, leaving less.

The combined effects of income, dependents, assets and time available might generate a portfolio lifecycle for a typical family such as that described in Figure 13–1 on page 234.

Computing the yield

The yield is obviously a major consideration in making an investment decision, and therefore deserves further elaboration. Some investments advertise their yields. Government bonds yield 6 percent, savings accounts 5 to 8 percent. Corporate bonds have current yield listed in the bond transactions of the *Wall Street Journal,* stocks list their current dividends, and mutual funds advertise their past performance.

Yield is annual income as a percentage of dollars invested. If an asset sells for $1,000 and pays $75 a year in interest, the yield is 75/1000 = 7.5%. If the asset's price falls to $950, the yield to someone investing at that price becomes 75/950 = 7.9%. If the price rises to $1,030, the fixed dollar yield of $75 becomes 75/1030 = 7.3% of the price to a potential new investor. Prices of outstanding fixed dollar assets bearing fixed returns fall when market interest rates rise, bringing their yield into line with yields on newly issued bonds. Conversely, falling interest rates will drive their prices up. If, for example, the average market yield rose to 8.2 percent, our 7.5 percent asset might fall in price to $914.63, which would bring its yield into line with current market rates.

Yield is also affected by frequency of compounding. Interest or dividends paid quarterly represent a larger yield than the same amount paid on an annual basis because each quarter's interest can be reinvested and also earn interest. Compound interest is used on savings accounts, certificates of deposit, and Series E bonds, among others.

Compound interest can be determined from compound interest tables or

Figure 13–1
A portfolio lifecycle

Age	Family situation	Major considerations	Some appropriate investments
21–35	Newlywed to family starts to adolescent children	Income low but rising Time scarce Assets modest House, furnishings an urgent priority	Savings account (emergency fund) Owner-occupied housing Mutual funds High-grade corporate bonds Life insurance
36–50	Children adolescent through college Wife probably working Start thinking about re-tirement	Income still rising Tax considerations may be important Liquidity ranks high for college funds House will be paid for, may trade up Time is still scarcer Assets continue to grow	*Keep* the above, but additional assets may go into: Education trusts Tax-deferred annuities for retirement Municipal bonds Money market funds Some common stocks, more corporate bonds and growth-oriented mutual funds
50–65	Children gone House paid for Planning for retirement	Income at peak Substantial assets Liquidity ranks low Time is more available Tax considerations rank high	Real estate as a tax shelter with income and capital gains potential Commodities (for capital gains) Hobby-type investment (coins, stamps, antiques) Growth stocks/growth mutual funds Corporate bonds Retirement annuities (tax-deferred)
65–?	Retired	Need supplemental income Drawing on assets Tax less important Ample time to manage investments	Income mutual funds Corporate bonds Blue-chip stocks Income-producing real estate (rental or commercial property)

with the aid of a calculator. Both methods are explained in greater detail in the appendix on Mathematics of Finance. Computation of compound interest is based on the fact that if the interest rate per period is r, at the end of an interest period your investment A is worth $A + rA$ or $A(1 + r)$. The $A \cdot (1 + r)$ is then reinvested and becomes the principal amount so that at the end of the second period you have $A \cdot (1 + r) \cdot (1 + r) = A(1 + r)^2$. At the end of n periods, you have $A(1 + r)^n$. Be sure to use the interest rate per period, not per year. An annual interest rate of 6 percent is 3 percent semiannually, or 1½ percent per quarter. Quarterly compounding will raise your annual yield of 6 percent to an effective yield of:

$$(1 + 0.015)^4 = 1.0614.$$

Compound interest calculations can answer four kinds of questions:

1. If I need $5,000 in three years at 6 percent compounded semiannually, how much do I need to invest right now? There are six interest periods at 3 percent per period in three years, so

$$X(1.03)^6 = \$5{,}000$$
$$X = \frac{5{,}000}{1.194} = \$4{,}187.$$

2. If I have $2,000 to invest at 8 percent compounded quarterly, how long will it take to grow to $4,000? This one is a little trickier because the number of periods is unknown. We can calculate the annual yield:

$$(1.02)^4 = 1.0824$$
$$\$2{,}000(1.0824)^x = \$4{,}000$$
$$(1.0824)^x = 2$$
$$x \ln 1.0824 = \ln 2$$
$$x = \frac{\ln 2}{\ln 1.0824} = 8.75 \text{ years}$$

(where ln denotes the natural logarithm).

Students who are not adept with calculators can solve this type of problem using a compound interest table such as the one given at the end of this chapter.

3. If I have $3,000 to invest now at 5 percent compounded monthly, how much will I have at the end of seven years?

$$\$3{,}000\left(1 + \frac{0.05}{12}\right)^{12(7)} = X$$
$$\$3{,}000(1.00417)^{84} = X$$
$$\$3{,}000(1.418) = \$4{,}254.$$

This problem is complicated only by the use of monthly compounding, which gives a very large exponent. The same problem with annual compounding would reduce to

$$\$3{,}000(1.03)^7 = X$$
$$X = \$4{,}221.$$

4. I have $2,000 to invest. I need $3,000 in three years. What yield do I need?
Compounding annually,

$$\begin{aligned} \$2{,}000(1 + x)^3 &= 3{,}000 \\ (1 + x)^3 &= 1.5 \\ 1 + x &= \sqrt[3]{1.5} = 1.1447 \\ x &= 14.47\%, \text{ an ambitious rate.} \end{aligned}$$

Compounding quarterly,

$$\begin{aligned} \$2{,}000\left(1 + \frac{x}{4}\right)^{12} &= 3{,}000 \\ \left(1 + \frac{x}{4}\right)^{12} &= 1.5 \\ 1 + \frac{x}{4} &= 1.5^{12} = 1.03437 \\ \frac{x}{4} &= 0.03437 \\ x &= 4(0.03437) = 13.75\%. \end{aligned}$$

All of these calculations are based on a single lump sum investment. A further difficulty is introduced when we consider regular annual investments of a fixed sum. Interest compounds not only on the original amount and previous interest but also on additions to principal. The technique for this type of problem is explained in the appendix on the Mathematics of Finance.

Kinds of yields

Yields can be either fixed (in dollars or percent) or variable. *Fixed yields* (rates of return that do not change) are available on all kinds of bonds, savings accounts, certificates of deposit, preferred stock (which pays a fixed dividend), and annuities. *Variable yields* are payments which can fluctuate or disappear and are encountered on common stocks (some pay no dividends at all), mutual funds, rental property, municipal investment trusts, and money-market funds.

No income yield other than the possibility of growth or capital gains is to be expected on unimproved land, commodity futures, gold, coins, stamps, and antiques.

An asset which has a fixed dollar yield and a face value of $1,000 may be bought at a *discount* (less than $1,000) or at a premium (more than $1,000). This discount or premium will affect yield in two ways. For example, you could buy shares of a municipal investment trust yielding 6 percent, at a discount, selling for 900 and maturing in 5 years. If you hold the shares to maturity you will earn not only $60 per share per year in interest but also $100 a share in capital gains in five years. The current yield, as explained earlier, is 0.06(1,000)/900 = 60/900 = 0.0667 or 6.67 percent.

The combined return of interest plus capital gain is called *yield to maturity*. There are several methods for computing yield to maturity. The least complex is as follows. Assuming the interest is paid annually, we see that

$$\text{Yield to maturity} = \frac{\text{Average income per year}}{\text{Average value per year}}.$$

The income consists of total interest plus the capital gain (or loss) if held to maturity. The average book value is the average of the purchase price and the redemption value. In the example above, average income is $80

$$\left(\frac{\$60 \times 5 \text{ yrs.} + \$100 \text{ capital gains}}{5}\right) = \frac{\$400}{5} = \$80$$

and the average book value is (1,000 + 900)/2 = 950. Thus the yield to maturity is 80/950 = 8.42 percent, considerably greater than the annual yield of 6 percent.

RECENT ASSET PERFORMANCE

Capital gains in real estate probably hold the best performance record in the 1970s. Capital gains on well-located land have been running from 10 percent a year up, and rental property yields a steady 10 percent in areas not yet overbuilt. Growth-oriented mutual funds have a good long-term track record; the best performer 1967–76 turned in a 442 percent gain in net asset value over the ten-year period. They do take a buffeting when the stock market turns down, however. Commodities are too volatile to generalize, although gold has appreciated substantially from its regulated price of $35 an ounce in 1968 to a price of $228 in late 1978. Fossil fuels and metals have also appreciated substantially. Growth stocks have fared poorly in the 1970s, but lesser-known stocks have turned in some surprisingly good performances. Hobby-commodity assets (stamps, coins, antiques) have done extremely well during recent periods of inflation. Comic books from the 1930s now sell for as much as $60 each.

Income-producing assets are extremely sensitive to interest rates, which tend to rise during periods of inflation. Rising interest rates force companies to raise stock dividends in order to attract investors. Higher interest rates force down the prices of outstanding fixed dollar assets (bonds, notes, treasury bills) which creates a capital gain potential. At the same time, higher interest rates raise the yield on money-market funds, newly issued bonds, and sometimes cause rate increases for savings accounts and certificates of deposit (which are somewhat less responsive because of rate regulation). Interest rates rose sharply in the early 1970s before leveling off and falling slightly, although they are still far from the "good old days" of the early 1960s of 5 to 6 percent mortgage rates and 3 to 4 percent interest on passbook savings. Money-market funds, which first appeared in the mid 1970s, yield 5 to 7 percent with low minimums and immediate liquidity, and their yields are highly sensitive to market interest rates, unlike passbook savings.

EXPECTATIONS, INVESTOR INFORMATION, AND BEATING THE MARKET

If you want portfolio performance that is better than average ("beating the market"), you need to make the right choice at the right time. People who bought farm land in the right place twenty years ago, who invested in coffee futures before the great 1976 coffee blitz, who invested in IBM and Texas Instruments before computer and calculator became household words (and household necessities), who saved their Dick Tracy comic books and bought U.N. stamps and Indianhead pennies in the 1950s, may have been smarter than the rest of us, or they may have just been luckier. How can you create your own good luck, by anticipating a boom in East Tennessee farmland, penny stocks, 1943 steel pennies, or wheat futures?

There is no sure guide to investment supersuccess, although not for lack of trying. Any bookstore can sell you a dozen investment guidebooks, and magazines and Sunday supplements are filled with advertisements which offer the magic "get-rich-quick formula" for only $5.95. Hot tips from market insiders have usually been fully discounted by the market by the time they are shared with outsiders. ("Fully discounted" means that most or all of the expected price rise/fall has already occurred.) There are basically only three ways to make money in the market.

One way is the cautious, plodding, persistent path of the patient and prudent investor who doesn't believe money grows on trees and therefore puts his or her money into more solid, sober investments than U.S. Mint seedlings. Over time, those AAA bonds, blue-chips, certificates of deposit, and other unglamorous but reliable investments, with interest, dividends, and capital gains reinvested, will grow to a rather impressive sum. This investor may never make the jet set, but his or her golden years should be very comfortable.

A second way is the "eggs in one basket" approach. Concentrate your investments in a few speculative areas—obscure stocks, commodities, comic books, off-the-beaten-track land, or a small business of your own. Your chances of losing your shirt on this approach far outweigh your likelihood of striking it rich, but this approach is one way that many people have made substantial amounts of money. It is not a path for the faint-of-heart, but there is some small chance of success.

The third path is to make an investment in time, money, and effort in being more educated and more attuned to market conditions than the average investor—whether the market is stocks, bonds, antique cars, baseball cards, autographs, 18th century paintings, vintage wine, or potato futures. This requires that you school yourself in the fundamentals of one or two types of investments (probably all you can manage in depth) and keep current, constantly updating your skills and information. General sources of investor information include *The Wall Street Journal, Business Week, Money* magazine, *Moody's, Fortune, Standard & Poor's,* and *Fundscope*. Sources of information for specific types of investments will be discussed in future chapters.

SUMMARY

Saving is the necessary first step on the road to investing. The process is easier to save if you tie saving to goals which could include an emergency fund, major purchases (car, boat, house, vacation), children's education, retirement, and an estate.

Techniques for forcing yourself to save include saving change, budgeting savings, automating savings, making saved funds inaccessible, buying whole life insurance, and becoming a compound interest watcher.

The investment outlets for saving are numerous, ranging from the ordinary—savings bonds and savings accounts—to the exotic—options, commodities, and rare coins. An investment medium should be chosen to match the goal for which it is earmarked and with reference to your preference among the various qualities of investment media. These qualities are yield, risk, liquidity/maturity, size, transaction costs, growth potential/ inflation hedge, and tax status.

Yield is the rate of return on an investment and can be high or low, fixed or uncertain. Some investments offer no yield other than the possibility of capital gain.

Risk is the possibility of a fall in yield or loss of principal. In general, risk varies inversely with yield.

Liquidity refers to the speed with which an asset can be converted to cash. *Maturity* is the length of time before a fixed-dollar asset can be redeemed at full face value. *Size* varies from a $10 minimum on a savings account to a recommended $10,000 minimum in a commodities account.

Transactions costs refer to sales commissions, transfer fees, and appraisal costs and can range from zero to substantial (especially on real estate). Management time can be considered a transactions cost.

Growth refers to the prospect of an increase in the price of the asset apart from the income yield. Assets with growth potential include common stocks, real estate, commodities, options, coins, stamps, and antiques. Assets with good growth potential can be used as an *inflation hedge* to compensate for the erosion of purchasing power in your investments as the price level rises.

Some forms of yield (dividends, rental income, interest on municipal bonds, and most forms of growth (long-term capital gains)) receive favorable *tax status,* resulting in a higher after-tax yield compared to investments with no special tax treatment.

The appropriate investment media for a particular investor depends on his or her goals, income/tax bracket, attitude toward risk, and liquidity preference. Most investors hold a variety of assets rather than concentrating on a single investment medium. The appropriate portfolio will change over your life cycle as your assets, income, dependents, tax brackets, and available time change.

Yield is affected by the market level of interest rates. Yields can be fixed in dollars (bonds, preferred stock), or percentage (savings accounts), or can be variable (common stocks). Bond yields are fixed in dollar amount but the percentage yield varies with the current price of the bond. The current yield is the dollar yield as a percentage of price paid. Yield to maturity includes both interest income and growth or reduction of principal if held to maturity.

Yield is also affected by frequency of compounding. Compound interest refers to payment of interest more often than annually, with the interest added to principal and also earning interest. Formulas are given in the chapter for computing compound interest on a lump sum investment. The appendix on the Mathematics of Finance contains an explanation for computing compound interest on an annual investment of a regular sum. Compound interest tables are provided for some common rates of return.

KEY WORDS

Capital gains
Compound interest
Discount
Diversification
Emergency fund
Fixed yield
Growth
Inflation hedge
Liquidity
Maturity
Minimum size
Portfolio
Premium
Risk
Savings goals
Tax status
Transactions cost
Variable yield
Yield
Yield to maturity

PROBLEMS

1. George and Henrietta Buyers, our friends in Chapter 3, have just inherited $20,000 from a wealthy uncle. Henrietta is willing to invest a moderate amount of time in research and portfolio management. Look carefully at their income statement and balance sheet and suggest an appropriate investment strategy.
2. Suggest suitable investment media for the following goals:
   a. Down payment on a house, $5,000, 3 years.
   b. College education for your five year old.
   c. A new sailboat, $2,500, date indefinite (as soon as possible).
   d. A supplementary retirement income for your aged and cautious mother with $30,000 to invest.

3. Using the compound interest tables in the appendix on Mathematics of Finance, solve the following problems:

a. You want to buy a new car in three years, cash. After trade in, you need $4,000. You have your money invested at 6 percent. How much do you need to set aside at the beginning of each year?

b. You have $2,000 invested in 8 percent bonds. In seven years, you plan to withdraw the money and spend it on a trip to Europe. How much will you have?

c. Your son wants a new ten-speed bicycle. He is saving $15 a month. You agree to pay him 8 percent a month on his savings as your contribution to the bicycle. The bicycle costs $150. How soon can he get it? (Note: Since the savings and interest are both monthly, you can use table B. Your answer will be in months instead of years.)

d. You inherit $20,000 which you set aside for your three children. They will receive it when the oldest turns 18 in ten years. You would like them to have $12,000 each. Approximately what yield would you require?

e. You win a lottery and have the choice of $50,000 now or $6,000 a year for ten years. Using the present value table (Table A–3, Appendix), which is the better deal?

Chapter 14

Assets for the small investor: Savings accounts and Series E and H bonds

The safest way to double your money is to fold it over once and put it in your pocket.

Frank McKenney Hubbard

INTRODUCTION

Now that you have talked yourself into a regular savings program and understand the reason for investing, the next step is to examine more thoroughly the various types of savings instruments available. This task will occupy the next several chapters. A group of safe, liquid, low-to-medium-yield, modest sized, widely available assets are considered in this chapter. Savings accounts, certificates of deposit, credit union accounts and Series E and H government bonds are all good places to keep your emergency fund and/or funds accumulating at interest for larger investments.

These financial instruments are all popular assets. Accumulated savings in these forms in October 1977 were as follows:

	Amount (billions)
Savings accounts (savings and loans)	$ 379.7
Savings accounts (mutual savings banks)	132.2
Savings accounts (commercial banks)	529.9
Credit union deposits	45.4
Series E and H bonds	76.0
Total	$1,163.2

This chapter describes

- Savings accounts.
- Certificates of deposit.
- Yields on savings accounts and certificates of deposit.
- Frequency of compounding.
- Methods of calculating principal.
    - Lifo.
    - Fifo.
    - Low balance.
    - Day of deposit to day of withdrawal.
- Credit union accounts.
- Series E and H bonds

SAVINGS ACCOUNTS

Savings accounts are available at commercial banks, savings and loan associations, building and loan associations, and mutual savings banks. Savings banks are all basically similar but go under different names in different states. Federally chartered savings and loan associations will usually have the word "federal" in their name and must belong to the *Federal Savings and Loan Insurance Corporation* (FSLIC). Savings accounts in commercial banks are usually insured by the *Federal Deposit Insurance Corporation* (FDIC). These two agencies insure accounts for up to $40,000 per account. State-chartered commercial and savings banks may choose to belong to one of the federal insurance programs but not all do; some participate in private or state-sponsored insurance programs. The safest place to stow your emergency fund is in a federally insured account. Within the commercial banks, national banks must and state-chartered banks may belong to the FDIC. (Check for deposit insurance before opening an account.) Recent losses suffered by depositors in failed, nonmember state-chartered banks have again brought the importance of deposit insurance to the public's attention.

The maximum yield on savings accounts is regulated by law. At present the ceiling on regular passbook accounts, which require very low minimum amounts, if any, and permit withdrawal virtually on demand, is 5¼ percent at savings banks and savings and loans, and 5 percent at commercial banks. Many banks pay lower than the permitted ceiling rate.

CERTIFICATES OF DEPOSIT

Higher yields are permitted on funds left for longer periods in larger amounts in special accounts, called *certificates of deposit*. These rates are also regulated by law. The maximum rate payable on a particular account depends on the minimum size and maturity, ranging from 5¾ percent on a 90-day, $100 minimum to 8 percent on an 8-year $1,000 minimum certificate. Very large certificates can be issued at negotiated rates.

A certificate of deposit may look like an ordinary passbook. But there are different withdrawal regulations for certificates of deposit. For example, early withdrawal carries an interest penalty, stated on the certificate. As much as three months' interest may be forfeited upon early withdrawal of funds from longer term certificates and the remaining balance will earn only the regular passbook rate. However, the certificates can still be considered liquid since funds can be withdrawn in a serious emergency. Nevertheless, some funds should be kept in passbook savings for occasional minor needs.

Certificates of deposit can be purchased at commercial banks, mutual savings banks, and savings and loan associations. In some cases, additional deposits can be made to certificates. Often these additional deposits must be made in specified minimum amounts or multiples of $50, $100, or $500, depending on the terms of the original certificate. An addition to a certificate of deposit reestablishes the maturity of the certificate. If, for example, you purchased a four-year certificate of deposit on July 1, 1977, and made an additional deposit on July 1, 1979, the certificate would mature in 1983 instead of on its original maturity date of July 1, 1981.

YIELDS ON SAVINGS ACCOUNTS AND CERTIFICATES OF DEPOSIT

Yields on savings accounts and certificates of deposit can be increased by special bonuses for opening or adding to an account, by frequency of compounding, and by the method of computing the balance on which interest is to be paid.

Bonuses include trading stamps, cash gifts, watches, calculators, blankets, and a variety of other items. When loan demand is strong and savings institutions need to attract funds, these special gifts will be offered free or at reduced prices. When lendable funds are ample and loan demand is weak, special offers will be withdrawn in preference to adjusting interest rates to levels below the legal ceiling. Bonuses allow banks to pay an effective rate of interest above the legal ceilings and also offer a convenient way of varying the effective yield on deposits without adjusting the interest rate. The depositor will have to determine the dollar value of the bonus to see the effect it has on yield.

FREQUENCY OF COMPOUNDING

Frequency of compounding ranges from continuous, hourly, daily, to quarterly, semiannually, and annually. More frequent compounding raises the *effective yield* because the interest is also earning interest. The effects of more frequent compounding on the interest paid on a $1,000 deposit and the effective yield is given in Table 14–1 for the passbook rate of 5½ percent and the four-year certificate rate of 7½ percent.

Table 14–1
Yields on a $1,000 deposit

	5¼%		*7½%*	
Frequency	***Dollar interest***	***Effective yield***	***Dollar interest***	***Effective yield***
Annually	52.50	5.25%	75.00	7.25%
Semiannually	53.19	5.32	76.41	7.64
Quarterly	53.54	5.35	77.13	7.71
Monthly	53.78	5.38	77.63	7.76
Weekly	53.87	5.39	77.83	7.78
Daily	53.90	5.39	77.88	7.79

To compute an effective yield for other rates of interest, use the formula

$$EY = (1 + r/N)^N - 1$$

where EY = effective yield, r = nominal annual interest rate, and N = number of times compounded per year.

Although compounding may be more frequent, most banks do not post interest more often than once a quarter. Check with your bank to see how often interest will be credited to your account.

The other factor in determining how much interest you actually receive is the *method of calculating the principal* on which to pay interest. There are more than 50 methods in use. The most common are first in, first out (Fifo); last in, first out (Lifo); low balance; and day of deposit to day of withdrawal (DD–DW). All four methods will be illustrated with compounding and crediting of interest on a quarterly basis. In addition, it is assumed that deposits must be made by the first of the month in order to earn interest for this month, except in the case of day of deposit to day of withdrawal.

Fifo assumes that funds withdrawn are those on deposit longest. In the example in Figure 14–1, the two withdrawals are assumed to be from the funds deposited on January 10 so that only the remaining $100 earns interest for February and March.

Under Fifo, $150 earns interest in January, $450 in February, and $450 in March, for an average interest earning balance of $350, although the actual average balance was $534. Interest at 5¼ percent is $4.59.

The *Lifo* method is a slight improvement. The two withdrawals are assumed to be from the most recent deposit. January's interest earning balance is $150, February's $550, and March's $550, for an average of $417 and interest of $5.47.

The *low balance* method would pay interest on the quarter's lowest balance of $150. Interest is $1.98. If the low balance is computed each month instead of quarterly, the quarter's interest would be $5.68 on a balance of $433.

Day of deposit to day of withdrawal is the most favorable method. All deposits earn interest for as many days as they are in the account. In the case given above, the balance on which interest is to be paid is computed as follows:

$$\frac{(\$150 \times 90 \text{ days} + \$450 \times 20 \text{ days} + \$650 \times 21 \text{ days} + \$550 \times 18 \text{ days} + \$700 \times 10 \text{ days} + \$600 \times 120 \text{ days})}{90 \text{ days}} = \$534$$

average daily balance. Interest is $7.01.

Figure 14–1
An illustrative deposit record

Date	*Activity*	*Amount*	*Balance*
1–1			$150
1–10	Deposit	$300	450
1–30	Deposit	200	650
2–20	Withdrawal	100	550
3–10	Deposit	150	700
3–20	Withdrawal	100	600

A variant in common use which increases the yield is to allow deposits made up to the tenth of the month (or the fifth) to earn interest from the first. In the example above, this would improve earnings under Fifo and Lifo as follows:

Fifo from $4.59 to $5.69
Lifo from $5.47 to $7.00.

Inquire at your bank about frequency of compounding and method of computation. If possible, find a bank which offers day of deposit to day of withdrawal with compounding at least quarterly. A second choice of method would be Lifo with deposits made up to the tenth of the month earning interest from the first.

Excessive amounts of funds should not be left on deposit for long periods in passbook savings accounts because of the low yield. Excess funds, over and above the emergency fund minimum, should be transferred to other, higher yielding investments.

Passbook savings accounts are popular because they are easy to open, add to, and withdraw from; the minimum is low (usually $10 will suffice); insured savings carry no risk; and passbook accounts can be used as collateral for low-interest loans. On the negative side, yields are low (though higher yields are available at some losses of liquidity and at higher required savings amounts in certificates of deposit); there is no inflation protection; and the interest is fully taxable in the year in which it is earned.

CREDIT UNION ACCOUNTS

Credit union accounts are similar to passbook savings accounts in many respects. They are readily accessible for withdrawal, provide collateral for a quick loan, and like savings accounts, lend themselves readily to automated savings. With an employer-based credit union, saving can be done by payroll deduction. But there are major differences, among which the principal ones are:

1. Credit unions are small. Almost two thirds of them have less than $500,000 in assets.
2. The interest rate on savings is not guaranteed. Most pay dividends in the 5 to 6 percent range. All earnings after expenses are paid in dividends. (Rates on loans, as indicated in Chapter 5, are usually limited to a maximum of 1 percent a month on the unpaid balance.)
3. Credit union membership is based on a common bond, with 55 percent of them being based on a common occupation or employer. Others are based on residence areas or membership in fraternal or professional associations.
4. Credit union loans are almost exclusively consumer loans, although recent trends indicate an expansion of the variety of their lending activities. Credit unions rank third (after commercial banks and finance companies) as a source of installment loans, with 14.2 percent of the total in 1974. In contrast, savings and loans, mutual savings banks, and savings banks have the vast bulk of their funds tied up in commercial and residential mortgages.

Credit unions are managed by their shareholders and belong to state leagues and a national association which provides guidelines and standards for operations. In addition, federally chartered credit unions have insurance features similar to those of banks and savings and loans.

SERIES E AND H BONDS

The last group of liquid assets we will consider in this chapter is *Series E and H bonds*. These are obligations of the federal government which can be bought and redeemed at commercial banks.

Series E bonds, also known as savings bonds, are available in denominations from $25 to $500. They are bought at 75 percent of face value and the interest accrues from purchase to maturity. At present they mature to face value in five years, which gives a compounded yield of 6 percent if held to maturity. An extension of the maturity period by the government to more than five years would be equivalent to a reduction in the interest rate, while a shortening of the maturity period is equivalent to an increase in the interest rate.

Series E bonds may be cashed in before maturity, after a two-month holding period, but the interest yield would be less than 6 percent. For example, $25 bond purchased for $18.75 in January 1975 would be redeemed for $19.61 in January 1976, $20.60 in January 1977, and $21.71 in January 1978. These represent annually compounded yields of 4.6 percent, 4.8 percent, and 5 percent respectively. Series E bonds may also be held past maturity and continue to earn interest at 6 percent.

Series E bonds are slightly less liquid than a savings account, but the yield is more attractive for small sums and the interest income need not be declared for tax purposes until they are redeemed, a definite plus compared to a savings account. There is no charge for redeeming or issuing Series E bonds. They are often available for purchase on an automatic payroll deduction plan.

While 6 percent is lower than the yield on many other assets, this is still an attractive yield for an asset available in such small denominations with only short-term lack of liquidity (two months), no transactions cost, and the advantage of tax deferral of interest.

A related but less popular government issue is the Series H bond, issued in $500 and $1,000 denominations and earning 6 percent interest. These bonds are sold at face value, not at discount. The interest is sent to the holder every six months. Like Series E bonds, they can be purchased at commercial banks with no transactions charge. The interest is taxable annually.

Series E and H bonds are registered in the owner's name, a protection against loss or theft. The owner is required to furnish proof of identification in order to cash these bonds. The bond may be registered in a single name, two names, or a single name with a designated beneficiary in case of death of the owner. Interest on bonds bought in a child's name will be taxable to the child, not to the parent. This clearly has the advantage of shifting taxable interest income from the parent's higher tax bracket to the child's lower tax bracket and is thus a convenient way to save for the child's education. The same advantage applies to a custodial savings account in the child's name with the parent as custodian. However, if funds are withdrawn from custodial accounts or bonds are cashed, these funds cannot be diverted to the parent's own use or to regular support items for the child (lodging, food, medical care, clothing, and so forth).

While married couples usually have joint ownership of passbook accounts, certificates of deposit, credit union accounts, and savings bonds, it is usually a wise practice for each partner to keep some funds in his or her own name. If one partner dies, joint accounts will be sealed for a brief time, the exact length varying from state to state. A small personal account will ensure each partner some funds to which he or she has ready access.

SUMMARY

All households need some funds in highly liquid forms for emergencies, as well as a medium in which to accumulate small sums at interest for larger investments. The usual forms in which such sums are kept are savings accounts, credit union deposits, and Series E bonds. Two closely related, slightly less liquid assets with higher minimums are also discussed in this chapter—certificates of deposit and Series H bonds. In general, this group of assets is low in yield, high in safety, liquid, and requires only very modest investments. None of them incurs a transaction cost.

Savings accounts are available at commercial banks and various types of savings institutions. Deposits in federally chartered institutions are insured up to $40,000 per account. The maximum yields are regulated by law. Certificates of deposit, which require higher minimum deposits and offer various maturities, are available at commercial banks and savings institutions. These offer higher yields than regular passbook accounts.

The yield on a savings account or certificate of deposit will depend not only on the stated yield but also on bonuses, frequency of compounding, and the method of calculating the principal balance on which interest is to be paid.

The credit union accounts are similar to passbook savings accounts. Credit unions are usually organized for employees of a common employer or members of a social, religious, civic, or professional organization.

Series E and H bonds are issued by the federal government and are sold and redeemed principally through commercial banks. Series E bonds are issued in denominations from $25 to $500. They currently yield 6 percent if held to maturity. These bonds are purchased at a discount and appreciate to maturity in five years. Series H bonds are sold at face value of $1,000 and also currently yield 6 percent.

KEY WORDS

Certificate of deposit
Credit union
Day of deposit to day of withdrawal
Effective yield
Federal Deposit Insurance Corporation (FDIC)
Federal Savings and Loan Insurance Corporation (FSLIC)
Fifo
Frequency of compounding
Lifo
Low balance method
Method of calculating principal
Savings account
Series E bond
Series H bond
Yield

PROBLEMS

1. The following is a quarter's entries in a savings account. Compute the interest at 5 percent using

a. Low balance, compound quarterly.
b. Day of deposit to day of withdrawal, compound quarterly.
c. Day of deposit to day of withdrawal, compound monthly.

Date	*Deposits*	*Withdrawals*	*Balance*
1–1–78			$3,380
1–4–78	$350		3,650
1–14–78		$ 80	3,570
1–28–78		100	3,470
2–15–78	140		3,610
2–19–78	50		3,660
3–6–78		300	3,360
3–17–78		100	3,260
3–27–78	50		3,310

2. Suggest some investment goals for which each of the types of investments described in this chapter would be appropriate.

3. Bank A offers a 5 percent savings account with no minimum and interest compounded quarterly, day of deposit to day of withdrawal. They also offer a 6 percent, 90-day maturity account, $100 minimum compounded quarterly, low balance. Which would be better for someone with $500 to deposit? For someone who wants to save $10 a week? Why?

APPENDIX: OTHER BANK SERVICES

A commercial bank—a bank which offers checking accounts, or "demand deposits"—is a veritable supermarket of financial services. Like supermarkets, commercial banks vary in size and in the number and variety of services they offer. Some of the most commonly available services are checking accounts, savings accounts, loans, safe-deposit boxes. In addition, there are Christmas clubs and vacation clubs, certified checks and cashier's checks, traveler's checks, foreign currency transactions, bank credit cards, trust and estate management, sales and redemption of Series E and H bonds, and bill-paying services.

The most popular and most useful consumer service of commercial banks is the *checking account.* Checking account deposits go back to 15th century Italy. They came into common use in the United States during the Civil War. Today about 80 percent of the U.S. money supply consists of demand deposits, or checking account money. The vast majority of transactions over ten dollars are made by check. Checking account money is easier to carry and less vulnerable to theft than cash. The check register offers a convenient record of income and outflow for taxes and for budgeting purposes. Main disadvantages are the need to produce identification to cash a check, the refusal of some establishments to accept checks, and the necessity of maintaining satisfactory check-register records and reconciling the monthly statement from the bank. There is also some slight risk of theft and forgery.

Checking accounts come in a bewildering variety of shapes, sizes, colors, terms, and service charges. You can have checkbooks with leather covers,

"But I don't *want* to know my bank balance instantly."

Reprinted by permission The Wall Street Journal

plastic covers, or cloth covers; plain brown checks, personalized checks, checks with sailboats or flowers or clouds. Personalized checks are a great convenience; having your name and address printed on the check not only saves time but often improves your chances of getting a check cashed. The other features—leather or plastic, boats or flowers—are among the many momentous decisions all consumers must deal with from time to time.

Check registers also come in various styles. Basically there are two. One is a continuous register of the type reproduced in Chapter 3. The second is an individual entry type of the sort illustrated in Figure 14A–1. A statement of

Figure 14A–1
Individual entry check register

Check 127	
Balance forwarded	$127.03
Amount of check/deposit to *Bugoff Exterminating Co.*	25.00
Balance	$102.03

this type will be attached to each check, which is perforated for tearing off. The individual entry method is more convenient for writing checks, since it is not necessary to flip back and forth between checks and check register to record each check. The check register shown in Chapter 3 is more useful in reconciling the monthly statement and in tracing tax and budget information.

Service charges on checking accounts vary widely from bank to bank. Generally, banks in urban areas are more competitive in terms of service charges and special services than are banks in smaller towns and cities. Banks usually charge for the service of imprinting personalized checks. They also charge for the service of processing checks and deposits and providing a monthly statement of your account. The service charge can be a flat fee, a charge per check and per deposit, or a combination—for example, one dollar per month plus ten cents per check or deposit. A flat fee is better for a highly active account, a per check charge for one which generates little volume of checks and deposits. Many banks offer a combination of service—checking account, personalized checks, safe-deposit box, and several others—for a single flat monthly fee. You will need to determine the value of these services to you and compare the value to the cost of those parts of the total package which you would choose to purchase separately.

Most banks also offer other special arrangements. A minimum balance of $100 or more may be good for free checking or reduced service charges at many banks. Other banks offer a low-cost *overdraft privilege* of a specified amount—in essence, a prearranged, automatic loan. If you write checks in excess of your actual balance, the bank would use your overdraft arrangement to credit your account with the necessary funds, at interest rates comparable to bankcard cash advances. If you are prone to carelessness in keeping your checking account balance current, this might be a useful service. The charges on "bounced" checks (checks returned because of insufficient funds) is usually quite high.

In order to reconcile a bank statement with your checkbook record, the following procedure should be followed:

1. Put the checks returned by the bank in the sequence in which they were written and check off those received in your check register. Check off deposits received by the bank for which they return a receipt.
2. Subtract any service charges and other debit memos from your current check-register balance.
3. Total all outstanding checks (those not returned by the bank).
4. Total deposits you have made which the bank has not yet included in the statement.
5. The balance shown by the bank minus any outstanding checks plus any unrecorded deposits should be equal to the balance in your check register. If not, check your arithmetic carefully for errors.
6. If the statements still do not agree, check with the bank.

Savings accounts can be opened at either a commercial bank, mutual savings bank, or a savings and loan association. These accounts were discussed in detail in this chapter. One of the advantages of having a savings account at a commercial bank is the easy transfer of funds between checking and savings, which can be done on a regular, automatic basis, or often by telephone. Presently the same privilege of transfer between savings and checking is available in some New England savings institutions, and there is a possibility that this right may eventually be extended to savings banks in other states—that is, the right to issue demand deposits and to transfer funds by telephone between savings and checking accounts in that bank. Allowing savings banks to issue demand deposits would eliminate the existing distinctions between commercial banks and savings banks.

Commercial *bank loans* to individuals were discussed in Chapter 5. It is usually easier to obtain a loan from a commercial bank in which you have a checking and/or savings account.

A *safe-deposit box* is rented on an annual basis. Two keys are required to open it—one held by the bank, and the other by the renter. Records and other valuable items requiring safe-deposit storage were discussed in Chapter 3.

Christmas clubs and vacation clubs are special savings accounts set up on an installment basis. Coupons are provided for 50 weekly installments in amounts from 50 cents to $20. Some interest is paid on sums on deposit, usually at a rate of 4 or 5 percent, sometimes only if all scheduled installments are met. The total is mailed to the owner shortly before the big date arrives.

Certified checks and cashier's checks are required for certain types of transactions for which a personal check is not acceptable. Moving companies, for example, require payment in cash or by certified check which can be purchased at a commercial bank. (A common alternative is a postal money order, purchased for cash at the post office; these are also used by people who have no checking account but occasionally need to mail money other than in cash.) A small fee is charged for this service. These checks are guaranteed not to "bounce" that is, not to have payment refused because of insufficient funds.

Traveler's checks are similar to cashier's checks but are issued in even denominations from $10 up. A record is maintained by the issuer and they can be replaced if lost or stolen. The two largest issuers are American Express and First National City Bank. The usual fee is 1 percent of the value of the checks. Traveler's checks are signed in the presence of the cashing party when they are cashed.

Foreign currency transactions are usually undertaken in most large banks at the current rate of exchange plus a small premium. Street or black market rates are often more favorable in some foreign countries, especially where the government practices exchange control, but there is a risk of counterfeit and sometimes a risk of arrest in dealing with the street market.

Bank credit cards were discussed in Chapter 5. They can be used for credit purchases and cash advances. Because bankcards are accepted by so many hotels, motels, restaurants, and service stations they are a great convenience for travelers. There is no fee for issue.

Trust services and estate management are discussed in Chapter 21. A trust is a separate legal entity, under the management of a trustee or trustees, in this instance a bank trust officer. A trust can be set up with an initial sum with or without subsequent additions, or it can be assigned some time of unearned income—interest, dividends, rents, royalties. Trusts can be used to provide an income for aged parents or other relatives, to manage an estate for surviving children, or for other purposes. Because the trust is a separate legal "person" which receives income and pays income taxes, it can often be used as a legal device to reduce income tax liability. The person who sets up the trust, however, relinquishes a great deal of control over the funds placed in trust. The bank, attorney, or individual serving as trustee assumes the obligation to invest the funds prudently, to preserve and enhance the capital, and to generate an income from the invested assets. A management fee is charged for this service.

Trust and estate management services are a complex legal and financial topic beyond the scope of this book. An attorney and/or bank trust officer can help you evaluate the potential usefulness of these services to you in the light of your assets, income, and responsibilities for support to others.

Sales and redemption of Series E and H bonds is another commercial bank service which was discussed in this chapter. Banks will issue individual bonds or send them to you on a regular monthly standing order. They also register the bonds for you and will redeem them at your request.

Bill-paying services are one of the newer bank services and are available in several forms. One approach is to have your account debited on a regular basis to pay a mortgage, life insurance premium, auto loan, and so forth—almost anything which is a fixed monthly amount. Regular bond purchases and regular monthly transfers to savings can be made in the same way. Instead of writing and mailing a check, you simply enter a debit memo in your checkbook at the appropriate date. If, for example, you pay $90 a month to General Motors Acceptance Corporation on the tenth of each month, and have arranged it with the creditor and your bank to be handled this way, your checkbook entry would read:

Check	***Date***	***To whom***	***Amount***	***Balance***
				$325.61
Debit memo	7–10–77	GMAC	$90	$235.61

Telephone payment of bills is now available from some banks, provided that the payee has an account in the same bank. In this case you would call the bank, giving them your account number, name of payee and amount, and the bank would transfer funds from your account to that of the telephone company, electric company, tax collector, and other designated creditors. Your checkbook entry would be the same as above. The telephone payment offers the same convenience of the debit memo but can be used for bills which vary in amount from month to month.

Many banks will, for a fee, take over all your bill-paying chores for you. You can arrange to have all your bills and deposits sent directly to the bank, which will furnish you with a monthly accounting of the flow of funds through your account. This can be a useful service for those who are very busy, very absentminded, or unable to handle the bill-paying chores for themselves.

Banks offer other services in addition to those mentioned. When you choose a bank, you are choosing a partner in a long-term, multifaceted financial relationship. Explore the variety of the services offered, the hours, the convenience of location, the prices of the various services, and the reputation for good and efficient service which a bank enjoys. A poorly run, limited service bank can make the task of managing personal, financial resources more difficult. A well-run, full service bank can make the management task easier, more pleasant, and more rewarding.

ADDITIONAL KEY WORDS

Cashier's check
Certified check
Checking account
Christmas club/vacation club
Overdraft privilege
Safe-deposit box
Service charge
Traveler's check

Chapter 15

Investing in stocks and bonds

There are two times in a man's life when he should not speculate: When he can't afford it and when he can.

Mark Twain

Perhaps everyone has had visions of some day calling a broker, investing a few hundred dollars in the stock of some fledgling firm, and watching the financial pages each day as we become richer, richer, and richer. Or maybe the dream is associated with the bonds of a troubled railroad which suddenly becomes solvent and later profitable because of new demand for coal.

Wall Street has always been a fascinating Mecca for dreamers. The street has also bankrupted quite a few! News from the street is a regular feature of the daily press and the 6:00 news. For example, this is typical: "The market was up today. The Dow Jones closing average was 950, up 2.5 points from yesterday's closing. The leading stock was Southern Company which was up ⅞ from its previous day's high for the year."

What does all this mean? Is there some safe middle ground between the bankrupt and the millionaires in the market? What exactly is a share of stock? A bond? The New York Stock Exchange? The Dow Jones Average? Points? How does one purchase stocks and bonds? How does one sell? Can I get rich or will I lose my shirt?

These are just some of the questions which spring forth when stocks, bonds, and financial markets are mentioned. There are many, many more questions.

In this chapter some of these questions and others will be answered. Later chapters will probe even further. Emphasis will be placed on the basic knowledge needed by the neophyte investor. That is, the discussions will provide a starting point for you, enough information to enable you to venture forth, gather information, call a broker, ask intelligent questions, and even make some purchases.

Two broad topics are taken up in this chapter:

- Stocks and their markets.
- Bonds and the investor.

STOCKS AND THEIR MARKETS

What are shares of stock?

Shares of stock form the basis of ownership for all corporations. For example, if you and two of your friends wanted to go into business, you could engage an attorney, have him or her draft a *corporate charter*—a document describing the venture, its legal name, address, purpose and scope, and other legal details, and then purchase all of the stock issued by the new firm. There would then be three shareholders or owners, and the proceeds from the sale of the stock would form part of the capital of the new corporation.

Your corporation would be a separate legal entity which would have many of the rights of an individual. It could buy, sell, produce, hold assets, go into debt, and sue and be sued. You and your friends would most likely be the *directors* and officers of the corporation. In fact, as the only stockholders you would vote yourselves into office as directors and the directors would hire the officers. Generally speaking, each share of stock would carry one vote for election of directors and deciding major questions affecting the corporation. As elected directors you would look after the interests of the owners of the firm, the shareholders who elected you to office.

If your corporation were successful and made a profit, the assets of the corporation would increase in value. In other words, your firm would have operated for a period of time, paid all its bills, including taxes, and earned a surplus. The surplus would be added to the capital paid in when the shares of stock were first sold. Thus, each of the original shares of stock owned by you and your two friends would be more valuable. That is, if you liquidated the corporation, which means selling all the assets and going out of business, each shareholder would redeem the shares of stock for more than they originally cost.

On the other hand, if the directors of the corporation (you and your friends) chose to remain in business, they could announce that *dividends* would be paid. The profits could then be divided by the number of shares outstanding and paid out on a per share basis. You might decide to keep part of the profits in the corporation and pay out a portion. In either case, each shareholder would receive a proportionate share of the paid-out earnings.

Suppose each share of stock had originally been sold at a par value of \$100. That is, each share of stock was arbitrarily assigned a value of \$100. If the first year's dividend were \$5 per share, you would have made 5 percent on your investment. If the earnings of the corporation had been kept in the

"He can't come to the phone now—he's crying."

Reprinted by permission The Wall Street Journal

firm, the value of your stock would have been $105. On that basis you would still have earned 5 percent on your investment. Of course, the value of your stock would be $105 if you could sell it for that price or liquidate the firm and still obtain the *book value* which is the value of all assets minus liabilities divided by the number of shares of stock outstanding.

Eventually, as your firm continued in business, the directors of the corporation might decide to sell more stock in order to obtain more capital for expanding the firm. Why would anyone want to buy the stock? The expectations of corporate profits would be their only logical reason. There could be other reasons. For example, your grandmother might buy some of your new shares in order to keep you off the streets. But sympathy purchases will not keep you in business long.

If prospective investors saw the opportunity of earning dividends or gaining value through the appreciation of the new stock and if this expected return on investment were attractive relative to other investment opportunities, then you might sell some stock. The price would be determined by market forces.

This illustration introduces the concept of stock, what it is, and how its value is determined. The details have been simplified in the discussion, but the principles involved are accurate. Now, the details need to be examined.

Three basic stock types

In practice there are three basic types of corporate stocks: *common, preferred,* and *convertible preferred.* Any one of these may be offered when a board of directors of a corporation decides to sell a new issue of stock. Common stock usually carries one vote for each share. This gives the shareholders a voice in the control of the corporation. There is no promise of dividends with common stock, although many corporations pay dividends to their common stock shareholders on a continual basis. Dividends are usually declared and paid on a quarterly basis. However, there is no guarantee of dividends with common stock ownership.

Preferred stock gets its name from the treatment of its owners with respect to the payment of dividends or the distribution of net assets in the event of liquidation. Usually, preferred stock receives a specified dividend from corporate earnings before dividends are paid to common stock shareholders. In some cases, preferred stock is also cumulative with respect to dividends. This means that dividends promised but not paid will be paid if and when profits allow payment. Thus, cumulative preferred shareholders would receive present and past dividends before any common stock dividends were paid.

Convertible preferred stock is usually issued as preferred with a stipulation that it can be converted to common stock on some specified basis or ratio. Conversion is at the option of the shareholder. For example, convertible preferred might have a dividend of $3.50 per share and a conversion ratio of 20 share of common for one share of convertible preferred. In this case, if the price of the common stock rises, the owner of the convertible stock might convert to common and enjoy even further increases in the growth value of the common stock.

When considering these three types of stock, you should recognize that preferred stock with a specified dividend is generally less risky than common stock from the same firm. That is, common stock may enjoy high dividends in some years and none in others. Common stock may also appreciate in value rapidly. On the other hand, preferred stock moves more slowly in price but pays a more regular income to its owners. Regular dividends and stable values mean security. This must be weighed against the loss of security but perhaps greater profits on common stock.

How to calculate your gains from stock

There are two components of return which investors seek when considering the purchase of stocks. As was mentioned earlier in the case of the three friends' corporation, you can receive dividends when a corporation earns a profit or you may obtain capital gains as the price of the stock rises. Preferred stock tends to grow in value less rapidly than common stock. It also tends to decline in value less rapidly. So, investors in preferred are generally seeking income from their investment. Common stock has generally a lower payout or yield, but under favorable conditions would produce greater growth in the original investment than preferred stock.

To compare the return on investment of $1,000 invested in 100 shares of preferred stock paying $0.50 per share annually in dividends with the same investment in common stock which pays no dividend, you would have to consider a rather long-time period, for example, two years.

Suppose that after two years the $1,000 in preferred stock has a market value of $1,100. That is, it has gained $100 in value since you purchased it. During those two years you also received $100 in dividends or $50 per year. On the basis of dividends alone you earned 5 percent per year on your investment. And on the basis of capital gains you earned another 5 percent ($100 across two years; or $50 per year). Thus, your total return would be 10 percent per year.

Now suppose that your $1,000 investment in common stocks rose in value to $1,175 over the two-year period. By dividing the purchase price into the final value, you have a compound growth factor of 1.175 over the two-year period. Table A–1 in the appendix on the Mathematics of Finance shows compound interest rates for lump sum investments. You will note there that a factor of 1.1664 is the equivalent of an 8 percent compounded rate of interest over a two-year period. The next factor below 1.1664 is 1.1881. Thus, you would have earned between 8 and 9 percent, roughly 8.5 percent on the common stock. Thus, in this illustration the preferred stock gave a higher total return or yield than the common stock. However, before reaching the conclusion that the preferred stock is truly preferred in this case, you must consider the tax treatment of the two components of income.

Dividends are ordinary income and will be taxed at the same marginal tax rate as your salary. (There is an exclusion of the first $100 in annual dividends for tax purposes.) Capital gains on the other hand, are taxed at one half the rate of your regular income, *if the capital gains are realized after having held an investment for one year.* The one year holding period defines long-term capital gains. If capital gains are realized in a period of less than one year, the resulting income is taxed at the same rate as your salary or other ordinary income.

The term realized capital gains refers to actual dollars which you obtain upon selling your stock (or any other asset for that matter). There are many occasions when an investor shows a paper profit. That is, stocks owned by an individual may increase in price above the amount paid for them. There are no taxes on unrealized income. A sale has to take place. Then the cash income which results is subject to taxation.

To illustrate capital gains versus ordinary income, consider Southern Company common stock. On August 1, 1977, Southern common sold at $17.25 per share. The company was paying an annual dividend of $1.46 per share at the time. Twelve months earlier Southern had sold for $15.25 per share. The dividend had still been $1.46 per share. Now, if you had bought 100 shares of Southern at $15.25, you would have paid $1,525 plus the cost of brokerage fees (about $38 in this particular case). Thus, your net cost would have been $1,563. If you sold the stock on August 2, 1977, you would have received $1,725 minus a brokerage fee of about $40 or $1,685. Thus, you would have realized a long-term capital gain of $160 ($1,685 minus $1,525) and dividends over the year of $146.

To determine your rate of return after tax on the transaction, let's assume that you are in the 30 percent marginal tax bracket. Furthermore, assume that you apply a dividend exclusion of $100 which leaves $46 of taxable dividend income. Your tax liability on the dividends is $13.80 (0.30 times $46) leaving a net gain of $132.20. The long-term capital gain is taxed at one half your marginal tax rate. Thus, the tax liability on that income is $24, which leaves a net gain of $136. The two components of gain are $268.20.

Now, since your original investment was $1,563 and your net gain was $268.20, you can calculate your annual rate of return after taxes. In this case, the return would be $268.20 divided by $1,563 or 17 percent.

The language of the stock market

In order to read the financial pages of *The Wall Street Journal* you must become familiar with some special terms. Consider the display in Figure 15–1 where a section of a financial page is shown. First, you will notice that the names of the firms are abbreviated. For example, General Motors Corporation is GnMot. You will also note that General Motors has three listings. The first is GM common stock; the second and third are preferred stocks as indicated by the lower case suffix "pf." Immediately to the right of the stock's name you find the current annual dividend which is based on the most recent payout of the corporation. Following the GM listing, you see $6.55 as the annual dividend for the common stock; $3.75 for the preferred stock listed first and $5.00 for the second.

Figure 15–1
Record of stock transactions

–1977– High	Low	Stocks	Div.	P-E Ratio	Sales 100s	High	Low	Close	Net Chg.
13⅝	9⅛	GAF	.60	..	187	10⅛	9⅝	10⅛	+ ½
19¾	15⅝	GAF pf	1.20	..	8	15⅞	15¾	15⅞	+ ⅛
34⅛	25⅞	GATX	1.80	11	30	27	26⅞	27	......
45	37½	GAT pf	2.50	..	11	37½	37½	37½	– ¼
10¼	7¼	GCA	.10e	10	23	7⅝	7⅜	7⅝	+ ⅜
6⅝	4⅝	GDV		5	98	4⅞	4¾	4⅞	......
7	5¼	GF Eqp	.08e	..	14	6⅛	6	6	......
7¾	4⅞	Gable		..	5	6	6	6	......
39¼	22½	GamSk	1.40	9	52	23½	d22	22⅛	– 1½
40¾	32⅜	Gannett	1.20	15	224	36⅞	36½	36½	+ ⅜
13	8¾	GapStr	.24	6	21	9¾	9½	9⅝	+ ⅛
22⅞	14½	GardDn	.76	13	67	15	14⅝	14⅝	......
15¾	13⅞	Garfink	1.04	6	41	15¼	14¾	14¾	+ ⅛
15⅝	13½	GasSvc	1.20	8	20	14¼	14	14⅛	......
11⅜	6¼	Gatewy	.45e	4	9	9⅜	9¼	9¼	– ⅛
38⅛	22	Gearhrt	.36	13	75	35¾	35½	35¾	+ ¼
21⅜	18⅜	Gelco	.46a	8	68	19⅜	19⅛	19⅜	+ ⅜
19⅝	16	GemCa		..	45	17¼	16⅝	17	+ ½
17⅛	14¾	GemIn	1.20a	..	6	16	16	16	......
12½	9⅝	GAInv	1.22e	..	13	10⅛	10	10⅛	......
69¾	52¾	GnAmO	1b	14	19	54½	54⅛	54¼	+ ⅛
14⅛	10⅝	GnBcsh	.80	6	10	11⅝	11½	11½	– ⅛
14¾	10⅜	GnCable	.82	9	31	12¼	12⅛	12¼	– ⅛
27⅝	20½	GCinma	.88	8	28	26⅝	25⅞	26½	+ ½
61¾	47	GenDyn		5	129	48⅞	48¼	48½	+ ½
57¼	47⅞	GenEl	2.20	11	791	51¼	50⅞	50⅞	+ ¼
36⅛	29	GnFds	1.64	9	154	30⅜	30	30¼	......
26⅛	21⅜	GnGth	1.42e	19	2	23	23	23	......
13⅛	9½	GenHost	.60	3	95	9½	d 9⅜	9⅜	– ¼
23⅛	17¼	GenInst	.40b	8	429	18⅛	17¾	18⅛	+ ¼
38½	35½	GnInstr	pf 3	..	2	36¼	36	36	......
20⅜	12⅞	GenMed	.40	8	37	15⅛	14¼	15	+ ⅞
34⅞	26¼	GnMills	1	11	395	28⅝	28⅛	28⅛	– ¼
78½	64¾	GnMot	6.55e	6	1413	70	69½	69⅝	– ¼
55	51½	GMot pf	3.75	..	1	52½	52½	52½	– ¼
73¼	69⅛	GMot pf	5	..	2	70⅝	70¼	70⅝	+ ⅛
10½	6¼	GenPort		44	361	10⅛	9⅝	9⅝	– ⅛
21⅜	18	GPU	1.76	8	253	21	20¾	20⅞	......
10⅜	7¼	GnRefr	.10e	..	10	7¾	7¾	7¾	......
28⅝	22¾	GnSignl	.68	11	49	24¼	24	24	– ¼
8⅛	5⅞	GenSteel	.29t	5	6	5⅞	5⅞	5⅞	......
33½	28½	GTelEl	2.24	8	434	31⅝	31⅜	31½	......
36⅜	31	GTE pf	2.50	..	4	34½	34½	34½	– ⅛
29⅝	27½	GTE pf	2.48	..	10	28⅝	28½	28½	......
16¾	15¼	GTFl pf	1.30		z100	16⅛	16⅛	16⅛	+ ⅛

Source: Reprinted with permission of *The Wall Street Journal,*

To the left of the stock name you see two numbers. The leftmost number is the high for the calendar year. The second is the lowest price at which the stock has traded. This gives you some idea of the stock's price range and how the current price compares with that range.

Now, consider the column of numbers to the right of the stock's name. The first gives the *price-earnings ratio* (P/E). This is one of the more important pieces of data for a particular stock. The P/E is found by dividing the current price of the stock by the earnings of the corporation on a per share basis. Notice the P/E does not reflect the dividends paid to the shareholder. For GM common the P/E is 6. That is, the earnings per share of stock were approximately \$11.60. (\$11.60 times 6 equals \$69.62, which is the closing price of the stock.)

The P/E reflects the strength of the market for a particular stock relative to the stock's earnings. At times, a P/E may be higher because investors expect future earnings to rise. Recall, the expected value of future earnings determines the value of an investment. But to have meaning P/Es must be compared through time for the same stock or among other similar stocks. Such comparisons can determine if a particular stock appears to be a bargain.

By examining the P/E column in Figure 15–1, you can see a large range of values. For example, General Telephone and Electronics, GTelEl common stock shows a P/E of 8. Some companies have no P/E. That is, they have no earnings.

Moving across the chart in Figure 15–1, you will see the price movement for the day's reported trading. The first figure, $70 for GM, is the price at which the first GM transaction traded. In other words, someone paid $70 per share for the stock. The second figure is the low price of the day and the next figure is the closing price, the last transaction of the day. Then the very last figure gives the net change in price from the closing price of the previous day. General Motors lost ¼ or $0.25 from the previous day's closing price.

More financial page nomenclature

Reading the financial pages will cause you to encounter other vocabulary problems. The terms used in following a transaction have already been described. There are also individual markets to consider. The discussion above came from a report of transactions on the *New York Stock Exchange* (NYSE). The NYSE is the major financial market in the United States and most of the larger corporations' stocks are found in that market. The *American Stock Exchange* (AMEX) is the second major market. In addition to these two national markets, there are regional markets—the Pacific Exchange, the Midwest Exchange and others. Each of these exchanges is actually a firm which is organized for the purpose of providing a market for their members. There is also the *over-the-counter* (*OTC*) *market,* a very active exchange where stocks are traded which are not listed on the major exchanges.

Your best introduction to the NYSE, Amex, and the OTC market is found in reading any issue of *The Wall Street Journal,* the major daily newspaper in the world of business and finance. A careful reading of the financial pages in that paper will bring you an astonishing amount of information. Such reading will also raise many questions which you will wish to pose to a broker.

Following the stocks

If you wish to keep abreast of activities on the stock exchanges, you will need to be familiar with some of the well-known indexes. The *Dow Jones Averages* are the most popular barometers of market activity. There are actually three Dow Jones Averages—Industrial, Utility, and Transportation.

The Dow Jones Industrial Average was begun in 1928 and was based on 30 stocks which reflected the major industrial firms and industries at that time. The firms in that first 30 industrial average are shown in Table 15–1. Two interesting points are illustrated by the list. First, many of the firms in that first average no longer exist. Second, there have been many changes in the financial structure of those first firms which have survived.

Table 15–1
Original Dow Jones 30 industrials

Allied Chemical	Nash Motors
American Can	North American
American Smelting	Paramount Publix
American Sugar	Postum, Inc.
American Tobacco	Radio Corp.
Atlantic Refining	Sears, Roebuck
Bethlehem Steel	Standard Oil (N.J.)
Chrysler	Texas Corp.
General Electric	Texas Gulf Sulphur
General Motors	Union Carbide
General Railway Signal	U.S. Steel
Goodrich	Victor Talking Machine
International Harvester	Westinghouse Electric
International Nickel	Woolworth
Mack Truck	Wright Aeronautical

Source: *The Dow Jones Investor's Handbook* (Princeton: Dow Jones Books, 1973), p. 13.

Because of the many changes which have occurred in our economy, the Dow Jones Industrial Average has been modified many times. In addition to replacing firms which go out of business, when a firm issues new stock or splits its stock (issues a certain number of new shares for each share outstanding) the Average must be modified. That is, the Dow Jones Industrial Average is an index number, a uniform measure which can be used for comparisons through time.

The current composition of the Dow Jones Industrial stocks is listed each Monday in *The Wall Street Journal*. You might find it interesting to compare the latest list with that shown in Table 15–1.

In addition to the 30 industrial stocks, there is a Dow Jones Utility Average composed of 15 utility stocks, which are firms which produce electricity, telephone, water, and gas services. There is also a Transportation index which includes 20 stocks from firms in that sector of the economy.

The movement of the Dow Jones Averages is recorded daily in *The Wall Street Journal*. Figure 15–1 illustrates the standard format used each day. This information is found in the inside back page of the *Journal*. In examining Figure 15–2, you will note that bars have been used to show the daily

Figure 15–2

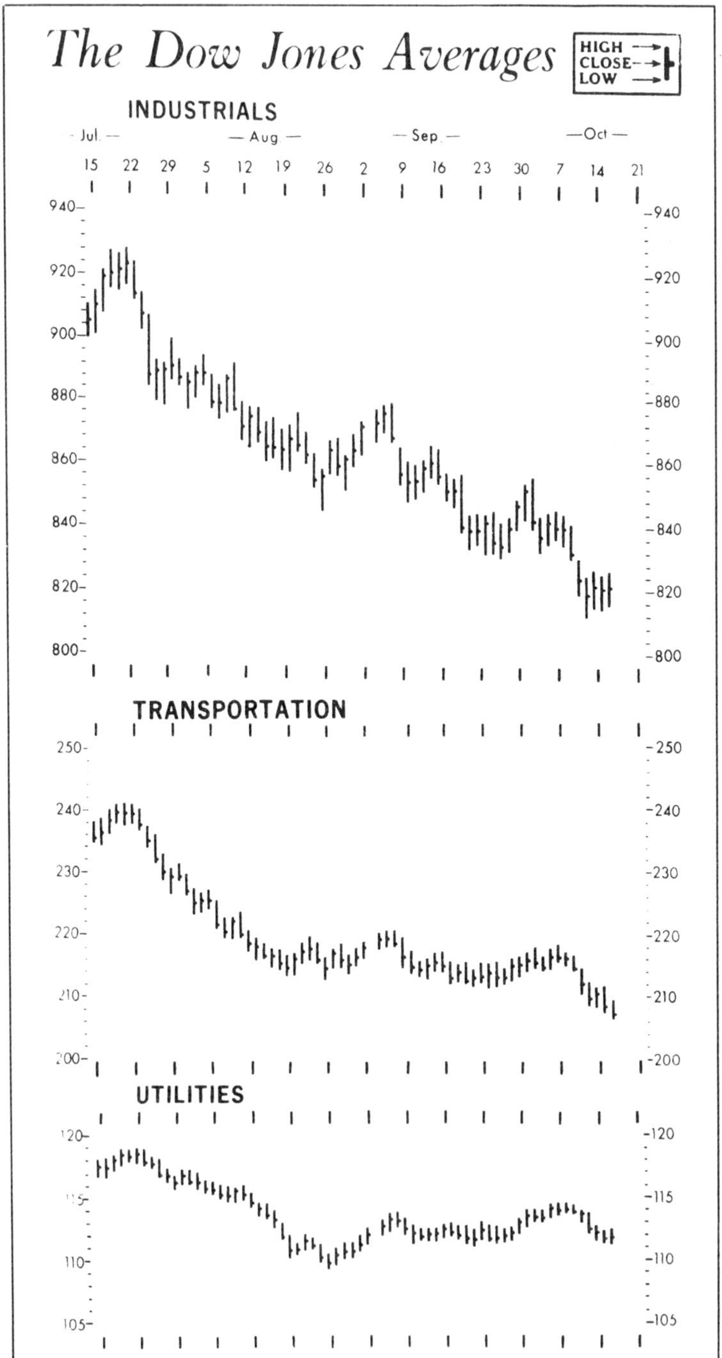

Source: Reprinted with permission of *The Wall Street Journal*, © Dow Jones & Company, Inc. (1977). All Rights Reserved.

averages. The length of the bars reflects the movement of the average for that day.

In addition to the Dow Jones Averages, there are other closely followed barometers of the stock market. *Standard & Poor's 400 Industrials* is obviously a much broader index than the Dow Jones Industrial Average. There is also a *Standard & Poor's Utility* and a *Transportation* index. The *New York Stock Exchange Index* is based on all common stocks listed on the New York Stock Exchange. How much broader can one get?

STOCKHOLDERS' PAYOFF

Some people purchase shares of stock just to say they have ventured into the market. But investing on a continuing basis comes about because of an expected payoff, a return which exceeds other alternative investments.

You have already learned how to calculate your return from owning and selling shares of stock. The components of the return were gains in the value of your stock from the time of purchase and dividends received while you owned the stock.

While the discussion of return on investment covered the basic concepts there are some particulars which you need to recognize. The payout to shareholders can take the forms of *cash dividends* and *stock dividends.*

Cash dividends are the most common. These are paid to owners of common or preferred stock on a quarterly basis. The payout comes in the form of a check made payable to the owner of record. For example, if you had owned 50 shares of General Motors common stock in 1977, you would have received $6.55 per share or $327.50 during that calendar year. This amount would have been paid in four equal payments of $1.6375 per share each quarter. In some cases you can arrange to have your dividends designated to purchase more shares of the paying firm's stock. Shareholders may receive a discount on the shares purchased this way and also avoid the brokerage costs associated with market purchases.

Stock dividends are often paid when a firm desires to conserve its cash. For example, during a time of tight credit, a firm may need to pay off debts. Instead of paying cash dividends the firm may choose to issue more stock to its present owners. In such a case, the Board of Directors of the firm might declare a 10 percent stock dividend. If you already owned 100 shares of the stock, you would receive 10 additional shares. However, if the earnings and outlook of the firm do not change, the dollar value of each share of stock will adjust in the market so that your 110 shares have the same value as your original 100 shares.

Stock splits also occur and are closely related to stock dividends. A split may occur for totally different reasons, however. There seem to be dollar ranges which attract a broader number of investors. That is, General Motors common stock may trade better in the $50 to $90 range than in a $500 to

$900 range. So, if the firm had one million shares outstanding and the stock was selling for $900 per share, the firm might issue ten shares for each share outstanding. This would change the total number of shares outstanding to 10 million and the price would fall to $90. Everyone would have the same total investment as before. Even so, it is possible that new interest would be attracted to the stock. If demand increased, the price could rise. Furthermore, firms sometimes split their stock when they anticipate higher earnings. The higher earnings cause the split stock to increase in value, maybe to the presplit value.

WHAT DETERMINES THE OUTLOOK FOR STOCKS?

The movement of stock prices reflects general economic conditions, specific industry trends, and the basic condition of specific firms. For example, the Dow Jones Industrial Average may be falling because of rising interest rates. When the yields on alternative investments rises and the dividends of stocks are not rising, investment funds will move to the higher yields. This results in there being more sellers of stocks than there are buyers. So, the prices of stocks tend to fall. At some point, the price of a given stock will fall to the point where its return is equal to the new higher interest rate. The movement of funds begins to stabilize at that time. Such activity would affect generally all stocks. An example may illustrate the point.

Southern Company common stock has been mentioned in several examples in this chapter. Southern is a public utility firm which has its stock listed on the New York Stock Exchange. In 1977, Southern paid $1.54 in dividends. The price of stock on October 18, 1977, was $17.50. This gave a yield of 8.8 percent to the purchaser ($1.54 divided by $17.50 equals 0.088). At that time, long-term interest rates were beginning to rise. This meant that new investors could expect higher yields. Suppose that investors found opportunities to invest which had the same risk as Southern stock but the expected yield from the alternative was 10 percent. More people would sell Southern stock in order to invest in the higher yield opportunity. Fewer people would buy Southern common stock. Eventually the price of Southern stock would fall to $15.40, unless something happened to offset the trend. If the price fell to $15.40, the dividend of $1.54 would give a 10 percent yield.

When the general outlook of the economy is uncertain, but not optimistic, general activity in the stock market will reflect that also. News from Washington about unemployment, government policies regarding tax reform, new pollution standards, an upcoming presidential election with inexperienced candidates seeking office, even unexpected surgery on the President can affect the general outlook of the market. Since common stocks are very sensitive to any information about the economy, particular industries or firms, the activities of government, and international events, common stock prices can be quite volatile. Even the safest, most stable stocks, the so-called *blue-chip* stocks, can be impacted by unusual news.

For example, practically all stocks suffered declines during the early days of the Arab oil boycott. As the market sorted out the full meaning of this event some stocks began to recover, others fell even lower.

Common stocks may be classified as *cyclical,* meaning that the basic conditions of their industry causes them to follow regular patterns reflective of the national economy. Other stocks are termed *growth stocks* because they are a part of an industry which is expected to outperform the overall economy. Still other stocks are labeled *speculative,* suggesting that there is a broad range of positive and negative possibilities for those firms or industries. An untested, but significant, technological breakthrough in the research and development stages might cause a particular firm's stock to be classified as speculative. Such stocks may exhibit erratic prices with accompanying large profits and large losses for their owners.

BONDS AS AN INVESTMENT

Types of bonds

In the early discussion of the three friends' corporation, it was noted that the firm raised its initial capital by selling shares of stock. The ownership of stock represented the owners' equity in the firm. That is, all the three friends could look forward to was either dividends or higher priced stock. The firm owed them nothing. Firms have another way of raising capital. They can go into debt. Debt usually provides a way for raising long-term funds needed for capital improvements—plant, machinery, and land. Furthermore, municipalities, states, national governments, and other political jurisdictions also go into debt. In each case, bonds are the promissory notes used to borrow money. Unlike shares of stock, bonds will be paid off. That is, bonds are sold initially for a specific face amount, have a stipulated rate of interest which, barring bankruptcy, must be paid, and have a specific maturity date.

Once bonds are sold by the issuer they can be traded among buyers. The issuer sends interest payments to the owner and ultimately redeems the bond and pays the face value to the final owner.

Bonds usually have long-range maturity dates. Twenty-to-thirty-year maturities are not uncommon. Even so, a buyer of bonds can find a complete array of maturity dates in the market. Some bonds may be just months from maturity, others five years, while some mature after the year 2000.

Bonds may be *secured* or *unsecured*. That is, there may be specific assets pledged by the issuer or the bonds may rely on the issuer's general financial strength. Whether secured or unsecured, interest must still be paid on time.

Unsecured bonds are also called *debentures.* If a corporation, for example, has both secured bonds, sometimes called mortgage bonds, and debentures outstanding, the debentures will be subordinated to a position below the secured debt in the event of bankruptcy proceedings. In such a case, the holders of the secured debt would be paid first. Holders of *subordinated debentures* would follow later in the distribution of proceeds from the firm's assets. Of course, one would expect the interest or yield on subordinated debentures to be higher than that of secured bonds for the same corporation.

Convertible bonds are set up so that the owner may convert them to the common stock of the firm at a specific rate of exchange. For example, a corporation's convertible bonds which sold for $1,000 each may be exchanged for ten shares of common stock. The effective conversion value of the stock is $100 per share. The price of the bond will fluctuate since the value of the bond is related to the market value of the common stock. However, if the price of the stock fell below $100, the bond would still tend to keep its maturity value of $1,000, since bonds are a debt instrument.

Callable bonds may be redeemed by the issuer before their maturity date. Interest rates generally determine if and when an issuer may decide to call its bonds. A corporation, for example, may have sold its bonds when interest rates were high. The firm would then have a heavy interest cost to cover in subsequent years. By having callable bonds, the firm could refinance its debt if interest rates fell. Generally speaking, the issuing firm has to pay a premium to bondowners when it calls its bonds for redemption. You should look for this feature when considering callable bonds as an investment.

Tax-exempt and other government bonds

In addition to the characteristics of bonds mentioned thus far, there are bonds issued by public sector organizations which offer some other features which you should recognize. These bonds represent the debt of municipalities, sewer and water districts, universities, state governments, state authorities, federal government agencies, and federal government itself.

Agencies closely related to the federal government have slightly higher risk. The debt of states and municipalities comes in all gradations of risk. Bonds issued by public sector organizations are by no means uniform in quality.

Municipal bonds (a catch-all term for bonds issued by state and local government agencies) offer an advantage to investors which cannot be found elsewhere. The interest paid to the bondholder is exempt from federal income taxes. In certain cases, there are also exemptions from state and local taxes. This is certainly an important consideration for people who have high marginal tax rates since the effective yield of the bond, the return after taxes, is the basis for investing. Consider what the tax exempt feature might mean to you. To calculate the return after taxes (R.A.T.), you must know your marginal tax rate. The formula is simple:

$$\frac{\text{R.A.T.}}{1.00 - \text{Marginal tax rate}} = \text{Taxable yield.}$$

To illustrate, assume that you are in the 30 percent tax bracket and purchase a municipal bond which has a yield of 6 percent. How does that yield compare with 8.5 percent before taxes?

$$\frac{0.06}{1.00 - 0.30} = \frac{0.06}{0.7} = 0.0857 = 8.57\%$$

The municipal bond has a slight advantage.

Municipal bonds are available in denominations of $1,000 to $5,000 and may be issued in 5-, 10-, 15-, and 20-year maturity dates or even longer. You can purchase municipals through a broker.

U.S. government and federal agency bonds

In addition to the savings bonds discussed in Chapter 14, the federal government issues many other debt instruments. There are *U.S. treasury bills* which are issued for maturity periods of one year or less to cover the treasury's need for short-term cash. These are sold at a discount from their face value of $10,000 so that the buyer receives his yield when the bill is redeemed. Bills pay the lowest of all rates of return since they are practically money.

U.S. bonds are also sold in minimum lots of $10,000 and specify an interest rate at the time of issue which is less than the highest quality corporate bond. Since, the U.S. government can print money, holders of U.S. bonds can be said to have assumed no risk.

Federal agency bonds are many in number and the number of agencies issuing them is growing. These bonds are not backed by the full faith and security of the U.S. government, but nonetheless enjoy the risk reducing benefit of close affiliation with the U.S. Treasury. Bonds of agencies such as the Federal Land Bank, Federal Home Loan Bank, Production Credit Association, Export–Import Bank, and Tennessee Valley Authority may be found in denominations of $1,000, $5,000, and $10,000. Agency bonds outstanding may be purchased through a broker, whereas new issues must be purchased from the fiscal agent of the agency itself.

The owners of these bonds have the responsibility of redeeming the bonds and may have to turn in coupons for interest. Bankers and brokers can describe the process of purchase to you.

Calculating the total return on bonds

In addition to effective yield, you will want to know the total return on an investment in bonds, which includes both interest and capital gains and losses. Even though the interest payment is set and does not vary, bond prices rise and fall because of financial conditions. Bonds are very sensitive to interest rate changes in the general economy. Just like stock market investors, owners of bonds are searching for the highest return on their dollars. When the return on other investments goes up, the price of bonds must adjust so that their yield stays competitive.

A corporation may sell its new bonds for $1,000 each and pay 7 percent interest annually. The yield to the initial owner is 7 percent. Now, suppose financial conditions in the economy change and the interest rate on comparable debt goes down to 6 percent. Firms selling their new bonds at $1,000 would pay 6 percent to their bond buyers. This would cause people to become more interested in the 7 percent bonds which were already sold. Their price would subsequently be bid up above the $1,000 face value. In fact, the price of the 7 percent bonds would tend to rise toward $1,167. At that price a bond paying $70 per year (7 percent of $1,000) would yield 6 percent. The reverse occurs when interest rates go up. In that case, the price of the bonds would go down.

Estimating yield to maturity

When a bond's price rises above its face value it is said to be selling at a *premium*. When being sold below face value, a bond is said to be sold at a *discount*. The premium or discount must be considered in calculating the yield if a bond is held to maturity, since the issuing firm will pay the face value to the owner of the bond at maturity.

To determine the *yield to maturity,* the return you will receive by holding a bond from the time of purchase to its redemption, you must estimate the equivalent return which results from the discount or premium and add to (or subtract it from) the interest you are paid while holding the bond.

Suppose you paid $950 for a bond which matures in five years. The bond has a face value of $1,000 and pays you $90 per year in interest. If you hold the bond for five years, you will receive $1,000, which represents a capital gain of $50 at the maturity date. This gain of $50 must be considered along with the $90 per year in interest when calculating yield to maturity.

Since the interest is paid annually,

$$\text{Yield to maturity} = \frac{\text{Average income per year}}{\text{Average value per year}}$$

The average value is the average of the purchase price and the face value at maturity. Average income consists of total interest earned across the five years plus the capital gained at maturity.

In this example, average value is:

$$\frac{\$950 + \$1{,}000}{2} = \$975.$$

Average income is:

$$\frac{\$90 \times 5 \text{ yrs.} + \$50 \text{ gain at maturity}}{5} = \$100$$

Thus the yield to maturity is:

$$\frac{\$100}{\$975} = 10.2 \text{ percent.}$$

Bond rating agencies

In addition to general financial conditions which affect the price of bonds, two other fundamental factors must be considered. What is the financial strength of the issuing firm or agency? What is the likelihood that interest payments will be made on schedule or that the bond will be paid at maturity?

Since bonds are debt instruments the answers to these questions require a careful analysis of the balance sheets and economic outlook of the issuing firms or agencies. Because of the large number of bonds issued and the demand for information, several firms have emerged which make a business of rating bonds. The best known ratings are *Moody's* and *Standard & Poor's*. Both of these rating agencies publish material which is sold to subscribers. You will find publications from each of the rating services in most college and public libraries.

The rating agencies have developed symbols which capture the credit quality of the issuing firm or agency. A section of the symbols (which run from triple A to D) are shown below:

Moody	*S&P*
Aaa	AAA
Aa	AA
A	A
Baa	BBB

Triple A ratings are reserved for those bonds which have a very low risk of default. This is the highest quality rating available. Generally speaking, bonds rated below triple B are felt to have significant risk of default.

Following the bond market

Bonds, like stocks, are sold in the major financial markets. There are daily listings in *The Wall Street Journal* for bonds on both the New York Exchange and the American Exchange. Figure 15–3 shows a section from the New York Exchange listing which appeared in *The Wall Street Journal*. The listing is very similar to that described for stocks in Figure 15–1. Consider the bond

Figure 15–3
Record of bond transactions

Bonds	Cur Yld	Vol	High	Low	Close	Net Chg
DPF 5½87	cv	5	68	68	68	– ⅝
Dart 4¼97	cv	145	76	75½	75½	– ½
Dayc 6¼96	cv	32	87	87	87	–1⅞
Deere 5½01	cv	10	92⅛	92⅛	92⅛	– ⅞
DetEd 9s99	9.0	20	100	99⅞	100	– ¼
DetEd 9.15s	9.1	10	100⅞	100⅞	100⅞	.....
DetEd 8⅛01	9.0	2	91⅞	90½	90½	–1⅝
DetEd 7½03	9.0	17	85	83½	83½	–1½
DetEd 9⅞04	9.4	38	105¼	104⅝	105¼	+ ⅝
DetEd 12¾82	11.	4	113¾	113¾	113¾	+1¾
Digit 4½02	cv	38	98¾	97⅝	97⅝	– ⅜
Dilling 5½94	cv	10	64	64	64	–1
Dilling 9¾99	cv	3	103	103	103	.....
Divers 9⅞91	15.	7	68½	68	68	.....
Dow 8⅞2000	8.5	1	104	104	104	+1
Dow 8.92000	8.6	28	104	104	104	.....
Dow 7⅝s03	8.0	20	95⅛	95⅛	95⅛	–1⅞
Dresr 8.65s85	8.4	10	102½	102½	102½	–1¾
duPnt 8s86	7.8	15	102¼	102¼	102¼	– ¾
duPnt 8½06	8.1	1	105	105	105	+ ¼
DukeP 6.85s78	6.9	30	99½	99⅜	99½	– ⅛
DukeP 7¾02	8.3	34	93⅝	93½	93½	.....
DukeP 7⅜02	8.3	8	88¾	87¾	88¾	+1⅛
DukeP 8⅛03	8.5	5	95⅞	95⅞	95⅞	–1⅛
DukeP 13s79	12.	9	107¾	107¾	107¾	.....
DukeP 8⅜06	8.4	7	99⅜	99⅜	99⅜	– ⅛
DukeP 8⅛07	8.4	100	96¼	96	96¼	.....
DuqL 8¾00	8.5	1	103	103	103	.....
ESys 4½s92	cv	15	86	85¼	85¼	–1¼
EasAir 5s92	cv	30	55	55	55	+ ¾
EasAir 4¾93	cv	23	50	49	49	–1
EasAir 10s02	cv	41	99½	99	99⅛	.....
EatnCr 8½84	8.3	35	102	102	102	+ ⅛
ElPas 6s93	cv	5	96½	96½	96½	.....
ElPas 6s93A	cv	17	96¾	96	96½	+ ¼

Note: The symbol cv indicates convertible bond.

Source: Reprinted with permission of *The Wall Street Journal,* © Dow Jones & Company, Inc. (1977). All Rights Reserved.

listings for Duke Power Company bonds (DukeP). There are seven issues listed. Immediately following the first listing of the company's name you will see 6.85s 78. That issue pays 6.85 percent of the face value ($1,000) and matures in 1978. Following the identification of the issue you will see the current before-tax yield for the issue, which is the yield based on that day's closing price. Duke's 6.85s had a yield of 6.9 percent (6.85/995 = 6.89 percent). The next column gives the number of bonds traded that day.

The remaining columns show the high for the day, the low, and the closing price. The values shown are 10 percent of face value. For example, Duke's 6.85s 85 closed at $995 on the day recorded.

SUMMARY

Stocks and bonds are two of the most popular investment media. A stock is an ownership share in a corporation. Common stockholders elect the directors who run the corporation. Stock shares increase in value if the corporation is successful. These shares also earn dividends on a per share basis which are paid out of profits. The book value of a share is the value of the corporation's net assets divided by the number of shares outstanding.

There are three types of stock: common, preferred, and convertible preferred. Common stock is voting stock with no guaranteed dividend. Preferred stock is nonvoting but has a prior claim on dividends; the dividends are fixed but not guaranteed. Convertible preferred is preferred stock which can be converted to common at some fixed ratio.

The return on stock consists of capital gains and dividends. Capital gains receive favorable tax treatment. The first $100 of dividends ($200 on a joint return) is excluded from income for federal tax purposes.

The financial pages provide information on dividends, volume of shares traded, the price—earnings ratio, and the price of the stock—high and low for the year, and high, low and, closing prices for the day. Stocks may be traded on the New York Stock Exchange, the American Stock Exchange, the Pacific and Midwest exchanges, other local exchanges and on the over-the-counter market (OTC).

Overall ups and downs of the market are measured by the Dow Jones Averages, the Standard & Poor's Indexes, and the New York Stock Exchange Index.

Dividends can be paid in stock or in additional shares of stock. In addition, a company may wish to have more shares outstanding at a lower price per share, so they will split the stock, exchanging three shares for two or five shares for three.

Stock prices reflect general economic conditions, specific industry conditions, and the performance and prospects of the firm itself. Interest rates, unemployment, tax changes, elections, and general uncertainty are among many broad economic influences on stock prices.

Blue-chip stocks are stocks which are safe, stable, and pay regular dividends. Cyclical stocks go up and down with the economy. Growth stocks are those expected to outpace the economy as a whole. Speculative stocks are subject to more than average uncertainty about price and earnings.

Bonds are debt rather than ownership shares, with a specified (usually long-term) maturity date. Secured bonds have specific assets pledged to payments of interest and principal. Unsecured bonds are called debentures. Subordinated debentures have a secondary claim on the firm's assets after secured bonds. Convertible bonds may be exchanged for common stock. Callable bonds may be redeemed before the maturity date. Municipal bonds are issued by state and local governments; the interest is exempt from federal income tax, a substantial advantage to high tax bracket investors.

High denomination U.S. government obligations include treasury bills (one year or less) and bonds (more than one year), issued in denominations of $10,000. They are virtually riskless.

Bond prices and yields are very sensitive to interest rates. The price of outstanding bonds falls when interest rates rise and rises when interest rates fall. Bonds selling for above face value are sold at a premium, below face value at discount. Yield to maturity includes not only interest but also the increase or decrease in price from purchase until it matures at face value.

Bonds are rated from Aaa to Baa (Moody) or AAA to BBB (Standard & Poor's) reflecting risk. Bond market information is found in the financial pages of major newspapers.

KEY WORDS

American Stock Exchange (AMEX)
Blue-chip stock
Book value
Callable bond
Common stock
Convertible bond
Convertible preferred stock
Corporate charter
Cyclical stock
Director
Discount
Dividend
Dow Jones Industrial Average
Growth stock
Moody's
Municipal bond
New York Stock Exchange
Over-the-counter market (OTC)
Preferred stock
Premium
Price-earnings ratio (P/E)
Secured bond
Speculative stock
Standard & Poor's
Standard & Poor's 400
Stock dividend
Stock split
Subordinated debenture
Tax-exempt bond
Treasury bill
Unsecured bond (debenture)
U.S. bond
Yield to maturity

PROBLEMS

1. Explain the difference between common and preferred stock. What considerations are relevant to investors when choosing between these two basic types of stock?
2. If a particular stock is selling for $100 per share and the firm has 3 million shares outstanding, and annual earnings of $1 million, what is the price-earning ratio of the stock?
3. Explain how the level of interest rates in the economy affects the price of common stocks and bonds.

4. Suppose you are in the 25 percent tax bracket and can purchase a tax-exempt bond for $1,000 which pays 12 percent in interest. What is your equivalent pretax return?
5. You have purchased a corporate bond which will mature in six years. You paid $900 for the bond, and it has a face value of $1,000. The bond pays $100 per year in interest. What is your yield to maturity?
6. Compare the stocks which comprise today's Dow Jones Industrial Average with those listed in this chapter. What might explain the changes in the list?

Chapter 16

Buying and selling stocks and bonds

Anyone who thinks there is safety in numbers hasn't looked at the stock market pages.

Irene Peter

With the background of Chapter 15, you are now in a better position to understand trading in the securities markets. Of course, these two chapters only scratch the surface. There are entire courses, degree programs, and thousands of books devoted to the study of investments and financial markets. But one has to start somewhere.

In this chapter the process of buying and selling securities will be discussed. The discussion will provide answers to the following questions:

- What must I do to buy stocks and bonds?
- What is a broker and what does he or she do for me?
- What investment techniques should I be aware of?
- Where do I get more information on stocks and bonds?

WHAT MUST YOU DO TO BUY OR SELL SECURITIES?

Practically speaking, all securities transactions take place through a stockbroker, an individual who specializes in bringing buyers and sellers together. The broker is an intermediary who earns his or her living on commissions paid by both parties to a securities transaction. To earn his or her commission, a stockbroker must supply information to clients, assist them in making choices among the many stocks and bonds available in the market, and advise clients when their investment needs change.

All transactions on the major exchanges discussed in Chapter 15 are generally carried out by a member of the exchange. Members are actually brokerage firms which have bought a seat on the exchange. The seat is membership and membership cost is not trivial. The price of a seat on the

New York Stock Exchange has recently been as high as $515,000.[1] Even so, there were 1,366 memberships in the New York Stock Exchange in 1976. With this many members, there is a great amount of competition among firms. And this competition assists buyers and sellers in gaining information and service at low costs.

The securities transaction

Suppose that you have studied several alternative investments and decided that you wish to purchase some common stock. You look in the Yellow Pages and get the names of brokerage firms in your area. You then ask some of your neighbors or family for recommendations regarding the various firms. Finally you decide on a firm and have the name of an individual broker. You telephone the broker and inquire about opening an account with the firm.

You must have an account in order to carry out transactions, and the broker will ask for the predictable information from you—name, address, Social Security number, and credit references including the bank with which you do business. Since the broker will be buying securities for you, he or she will need to know that you pay your bills.

Your transactions generally follow this sequence. You place the order; the broker executes the order; you receive or send the securities involved; you receive a bill (if you are buying); and if you owe the broker money, you send a check.

Types of orders

There are several types of orders which you might place with a broker. *At the market* orders tell your broker to buy or sell at the best price he or she can obtain. When this order is executed by your broker, a message is sent to the floor of the exchange which lists the stock. If the stock is not listed, the order goes to a specialist who deals in the stock. Then the order goes at the best price offered by another buyer or seller at the time.

Limit orders specify a particular price. Suppose that you want to buy 100 shares of Bearings Incorporated common stock and you tell your broker to buy at $31 per share. You have limited the broker's flexibility in handling your order. The broker will not purchase at a price above $31.

In buying stocks, you can also buy on *margin*. That is, you can buy more stocks than you can pay for with cash. The margin requirement is set by the Federal Reserve Board and varies with economic conditions. In October 1977, for example, the margin requirement was 50 percent for stocks. This means that your broker can actually arrange a loan for you to cover one half

[1] See The New York Stock Exchange, *You and the Investment World*, December 1976, p. 15.

of the amount of your purchase. The brokerage firm then charges you interest on the loan.

Although margin trading is not recommended for the beginning investor, you can increase your *leverage* by buying on margin. For example, you might purchase 100 shares of Bearings Incorporated common stock at $31 each and pay your broker $1,550 plus the expenses of handling the transaction, borrowing the other $1,550 from the brokerage house. This is buying on margin. The broker keeps the shares in your account and awaits your instructions. If the stock rises in price to $35 per share or $3,500 in total value, you could sell, pay off your broker, and earn approximately $400 on a $1,550 investment. If you had not waited too long for the sale, it is possible that the expense of your loan would be quite small. But, what if the stock goes down in value, contrary to your expectations? In that event, your broker would be holding shares which might not even cover the value of your loan—the margin the broker had paid. At that point, you would get a call from your broker asking for more cash, which could force you to sell your stock at a loss in order to cover the loan. Sooner or later all bills must be paid. You must be prepared to handle either a rise or a fall in the price of a stock.

Selling short enables you to make money on a decline in the price of a stock. Once again you must borrow from your broker, but this time you will be borrowing stock, not cash. Suppose you believe that the General Motors common stock is in for a fall. You have no GM stock, but call your broker and ask him or her to sell 100 shares at the present price. The broker must either own the stock or be in a position to borrow it from someone. Now, after having sold the borrowed stock, the price of GM does in fact go down. You now ask your broker to buy 100 shares at the lower price and you return the purchased shares to the lender, making a profit in the process.

Of course it is also possible that the price of the borrowed stock could go up. Then you would have to cover your *short sale* with higher priced stocks.

Stocks are usually purchased in lots of 100 shares which are called *round lot* orders. Orders for fewer than 100 shares are referred to as *odd lot*. Brokers will accommodate transactions regardless of size, but there is generally a premium of 12½ cents per share to cover the cost of odd-lot transactions.

Stop orders can be used to protect the value of stocks which you already own. The stop sets a lower limit on the price at which you sell. For example, suppose you owned 100 shares of Southern Company common stock which you purchased for $14.50 per share. The price has risen as high as $17.75 but in recent days has fallen to $16.50. You hope that the decline is temporary but wish to hold on to some of your gain. In this case, you might enter a stop order at $16, which is a valid standing order until you cancel it. Thus, if the stock falls to $16 it would be sold automatically.

BROKERAGE FEES AND TRANSACTIONS EXPENSES

The brokerage firm with which you do business will charge you a fee each time you buy or sell securities. These fees are determined by competition between firms and their customers. There is no set schedule, but fees actually paid on several transactions are listed in Table 16–1.

Table 16–1
Brokerage fees for actual transactions

Amount of transaction	*Fee or commission*	*Fee as a percent of transaction*
$ 759.00	$ 24.46	3.2
1037.50	28.89	2.7
2650.00	57.20	2.1
6487.50	128.31	1.9

The fees charged relate to the dollar value of the transaction. The larger the purchase or sale, the smaller the percentage fee. Fees also vary among brokerage firms. You will want to check this cost with your broker. Since you will be charged each time you buy or sell, you may want to avoid frequent trades. While you might become your broker's best friend, as a steady customer, it is possible that all your profits will be eaten up by brokerage fees.

In addition to broker's fees or commission, you will also have to pay a transfer tax on your transactions and a federal registration fee when you do business with either of the two major exchanges. These fees are quite small. For example, the fee on a $750 transaction is $1.00 and $1.22 on a $6,600 transaction.

All fees and commissions are deductible from earnings for tax purposes. You should keep records on all of your investment expenses since these are a cost of doing business which will be deducted from your earnings before determining capital gains.

RECORDS AND FORMS

You will receive a written statement for each transaction you make with your broker. If you have made a purchase, you will have seven days in which to make payment. You need to retain the record of your transactions so as to report your earnings and transactions costs when filing your tax returns.

In addition to records of individual transactions, you will receive a monthly statement from your broker, recording all the activity which has taken place in your account. Many people leave their stocks and bonds with their broker, which ensures safekeeping and convenience for trading. If your broker keeps your securities, your monthly statement will list each stock and bond being held in your account, any dividends and interest which have accumulated during the period, the status of any margin transactions, and any charges of interest for funds borrowed from your broker to cover margin requirements. Your broker will also send you an annual statement of dividends and interest earned which you can use for income tax purposes.

When your securities are kept by your broker you will still receive all reports and communications from the firms in which you have an investment. You can expect a regular flow of annual reports, quarterly statements of earnings, and other items of business requiring a vote by stockholders.

SOME INVESTMENT STRATEGIES

There are literally hundreds of strategies, rules of thumb, and techniques which have been developed and tried by investors who hope to strike it rich with stocks and bonds. Some of the strategies relate to short run changes in stock prices where the investor hopes to identify the peaks and valleys of a particular stock's price. Other strategies are long term, with the investor hoping to outperform the overall market averages. In the latter case, an

"Ed, you're the only person I know who *always* makes money in the Stock Market. What's your secret?"

Reprinted by permission The Wall Street Journal

investor might use the Dow Jones Industrial Average or Standard & Poor's 400 as a target. By earning more than the target average, the investor would be "swimming upstream." That is, the investor would be shooting for a return which would outperform the overall economy.

Regardless of the strategy chosen, investors are always interested in *bull* and *bear markets*. Bull markets occur in periods when most investors are optimistic about future economic events. Information on investment outlook appears favorable in such periods. The prospect for earnings is generally good, and the total economy appears to be moving into a period of real growth. Under these circumstances, the majority of investors are buying. This pushes up the broad averages and, of course, reflects a rise in price of most stocks. When expectations become pessimistic and these expectations become reflected in sell decisions, the broad averages begin a trend in the opposite direction. That is, the Dow Jones and Standard & Poor's indexes begin to move generally downward. Even in the bull and bear markets there will be fluctuations against the general trend. One can find some rising prices in a bear market and some falling prices during a bull market. There are no magic formulas which can tell the investor when a bull market has reached its peak or when a bear market is at its trough.

Figure 16–1 illustrates bull and bear markets. By examining the three indexes shown you can identify the bull and bear markets since 1968. In the Dow Jones Industrials series you can see the bull market of 1968; the bear market of 1969 and early 1970; and then the bull market of 1970–71. By following the cyclical behavior of the index, other bulls and bears can be found. However, you will find fluctuations during the broadly defined periods. Knowing when to buy or when to sell is of course the most sought after information. Timing is the problem for the investor who wishes to make the most out of each turn in the market.

Dollar averaging

You can avoid the concern for peaks and valleys, bull and bear markets, by consistently investing a fixed sum of money in a group of sound stocks. Finding the sound stocks is a problem, but your broker can assist you in the selection process. Once you have a portfolio of satisfactory stocks identified, you then determine the amount of money which you can budget for stocks. Each stock in the portfolio is assigned a dollar amount which will be invested in it without respect to the price of the stock at a given time. Then you would decide upon the number of times each year when you would make your purchases. These decisions set into place an automatic strategy.

To illustrate dollar averaging, suppose you decide to invest $1,000 every four months in a single stock. Table 16–2 illustrates this case. Notice that the table contains six transactions, and in each case, the price of the stock has changed. In some cases, you will have to invest slightly less than $1,000. By

Figure 16–1
Stock market indexes: 1968–1976

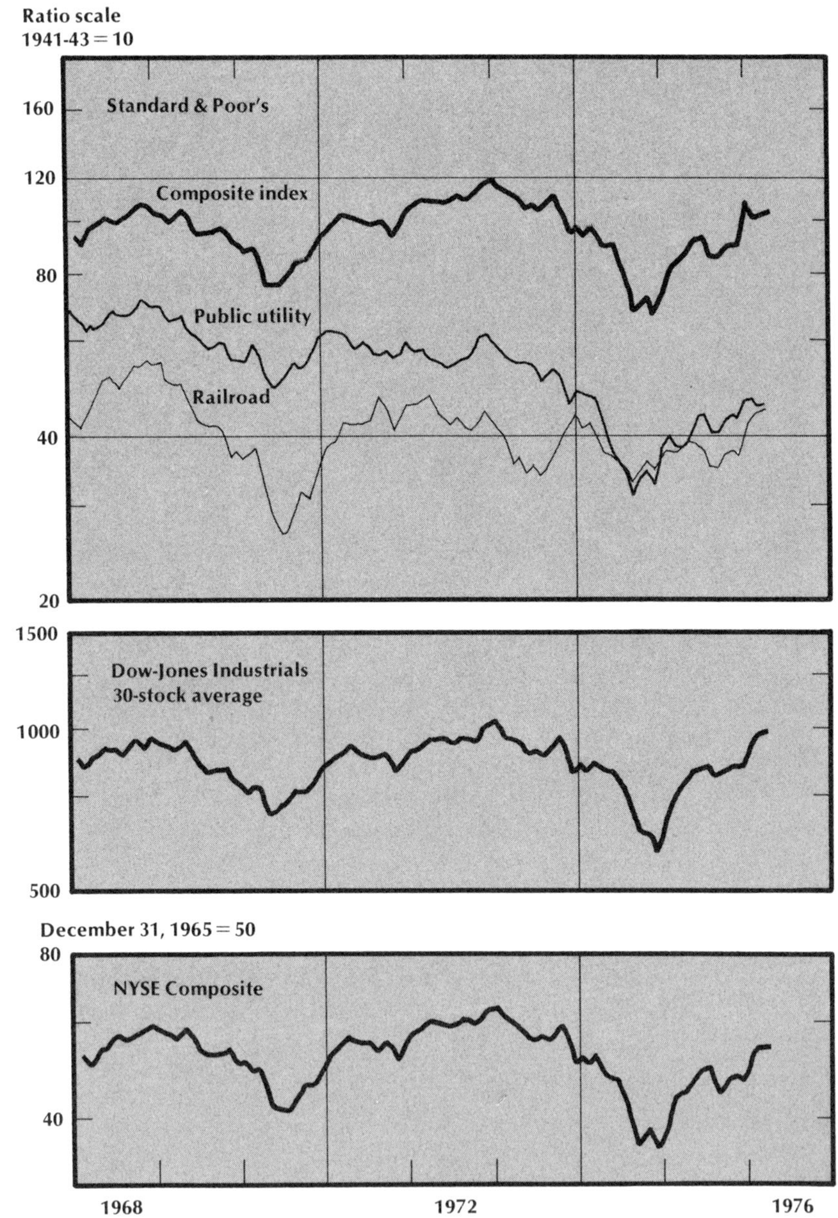

Source: *Federal Reserve Monthly Chart Book*, May 1976, p. 70.

Table 16–2
Illustration of dollar averaging

Transaction	Price of stock	No. of shares purchased	No. of shares owned	Total value of shares	Total invested	Average cost per share owned
1	$100	10	10	$1,000	$1,000	$100.00
2	125	8	18	2,250	2,000	111.10
3	90	11	29	2,610	2,990	103.10
4	95	10	39	3,705	3,940	101.02
5	140	7	46	6,440	4,920	106.95
6	150	6	52	7,800	5,820	111.92

the end of the sixth transaction, you would have invested approximately $6,000. Since the price of the stock has been different for each transaction, the average value of the stock in your portfolio has changed with each transaction. This is seen in the last column of the table. You can also determine the yield on your portfolio by referring to Table A–2 in the appendix on the Mathematics of Finance at the end of the book. You have invested approximately $1,000 per year for six years, or a total of $6,000. Your portfolio is worth $7,800. By dividing $7,800 by $1,000 you have a factor of 7.8 for a six-year recurring investment of $1,000. Table A–2 contains a factor of 7.7873 for a 7.5 percent yield.

This example illustrates the concept of dollar averaging with a profitable result. It is much easier to show a profit on paper than to earn a profit in the market. Another series of transactions could have shown a constantly declining price for the stock. The average price of the stock would have continued to fall giving you more shares per $1,000 purchase but the total value of your portfolio would be steadily falling also.

To follow the dollar averaging approach successfully, some writers recommend that you should set up a long-range program of 10 to 15 years, and that you stay with the program through thick and thin. One must be willing to weather fluctuations in price in order to gain through dollar averaging.

Stock-bond averaging

You can modify a dollar averaging approach by setting a fixed number of dollars to be invested so as to keep a fixed percentage of dollars in stocks and the balance in bonds. Setting the ratio is the problem, but the approach is as follows.

Suppose that you decide to invest $5,000 every year and that you wish to keep 20 percent of your portfolio's value in bonds and the balance in stocks.

You might begin by putting the first $4,000 in your preselected list of stocks. You would put $1,000 in bonds. Then if the value of your stock portfolio became greater than 80 percent of your total portfolio, you would sell some stocks and put the proceeds in bonds. The 80–20 balance would be maintained.

The advantage of making such switches between stocks and bonds and back again when the value of the bonds begins to rise comes about because of the general relationship between the two securities. Bond prices tend to rise when stock prices are falling, and vice versa. This reverse or inverse relationship is caused by interest rates movements. When the economy is in a boom period, stocks will tend to be rising. At the same time, the demand for investment funds pushes up the interest rates. And when interest rates rise, those securities with a fixed yield, such as bonds, tend to fall in value. When interest rates fall because of a slack demand for investment funds, stocks tend to be falling in value and bonds tend to be increasing in value.

There are other variations of the dollar averaging concept which might be interesting to you. But, once again, you should talk with brokers and study other more detailed materials before embarking on such a program on your own.

Efficient markets and the fundamentals

Outperforming the market or the rate of growth of the overall economy is difficult because of a very fundamental phenomenon known as the *law of efficient markets*. The law states that information, once announced, has zero value in the market. That is, an active market processes information so quickly that the price of an item almost instantly reflects all of the information available. In terms of stocks and bonds, this suggests that you cannot learn valuable information quickly enough to make money. Suppose you learn that a particular defense firm is to be awarded a gigantic government contract. By the time you get the information, an efficient market would have likely already processed the information. The price of stock would have been bid up so that the expected value of the assumed future profits would be zero. In other words, you would have to own the stock before any of the information was made known in order to gain the full value of the information.

People who believe in the law of efficient markets suggest that an individual investor can do no better than the overall market. In fact, some suggest that you might as well pin the pages of *The Wall Street Journal* to the wall and throw darts to determine which stock to buy or sell. You could, of course, use that strategy as a dollar averaging technique. Taking such an approach would take some of the fun out of buying and selling, but you might become good at throwing darts.

The law of efficient markets is very persuasive. That's why it is called a law. Nonetheless there is something to be said for studying the fundamental positions of firms and industries. Most people are in a position to know something extra about the firm where they are employed, the major industries in their region, or companies with which they do business. This information can be fortified by studying materials on the firms which are provided by a number of financial services as well as by brokers. By searching for firms which offer strength in particular markets, one can obviously make long-run plans which could outperform the market averages. But, remember, many others are playing the same game. For this reason, you will want to consider the advantages and the disadvantages of using an investment service or buying into a mutual fund. These alternatives are discussed in the next chapter.

A word on investor psychology

No matter what strategy you follow in buying stocks or bonds there is one difficult lesson which should be learned as early as possible. It's tough, but you must be willing to get rid of losers. When you purchase a stock or bond it is easy to become emotionally attached to it. After all, you have sunk your hard-earned cash in it. But that is the point—your money is sunk. If the price of the stock or bond begins to sink and sinks even further, you must be willing to take your losses, recover as much cash as you can and search for a winner. Of course, losses can be deducted from your taxable income, which offers some consolation. To reduce losses, you may want to consider the use of limit orders as a way to cover the risk of sinking stock values.

INVESTOR INFORMATION

As indicated, your broker is the major source of investment information. Each of the leading brokerage firms has publications and reports which are available to customers. Among the major brokerage firms are:

Bache Halsey Stuart Shields.
Blythe Eastman Dillon.
J. C. Bradford.
Dean Witter.
Dillon Read.
Hornblower Weekes Noyes Trask.
E. F. Hutton.
Kidder Peabody.
Kuhn Loeb.
Lehman Brothers.
Merrill Lynch, Pierce, Fenner, & Smith.
Paine Webber Jackson Curtis.
Reynolds Securities.
Robinson Humphreys.

You may find other local, regional, and national firms listed in the telephone directory of the nearest major city.

In addition to the special reports and other brochures available from brokerage firms, you will find the much-mentioned *The Wall Street Journal* a most valuable source of information. *Barron's* and *Forbes* are excellent magazines for the investor as are the more general *Money, Fortune, Changing Times,* and *Business Week*.

REPORTING SERVICES

There are three major investor reporting services which deserve your attention. These are: *Moody's Investor Service, Standard & Poor's,* and *Value Line Investment Survey*. Both *Moody's* and *Standard & Poor's* publish manuals which have individual sheets on major corporations. These services also publish a variety of handbooks with detailed information on individual stocks and bonds. *Value Line* provides a weekly and quarterly analysis of a particular group of stocks selected from 60 industries.

You will want to familiarize yourself with these reports. They should be available in your college and city library. Of course, your broker will have these services available in his office.

SUMMARY

In this chapter you have been introduced to some of the basics of buying and selling securities. The information in this chapter has only scratched the surface. But you should be prepared to call a broker, gather information, and possibly take a first step toward investing in securities. Money does not grow on trees or in the stock market. If you are to earn a return which exceeds the interest on a savings account, you will have to study and manage your investments on a regular basis. Luck will help, but even the best of luck can not last year in and year out. Long-term gains require long hours of attention.

KEY WORDS

At the market
Bear market
Brokerage fee
Bull market
Dollar averaging
Law of efficient markets
Leverage
Limit orders
Margin
Odd lot
Round lot
Short sale
Stock-bond averaging
Stop order

PROBLEMS

1. Explain the purpose and advantage of selling short.
2. You have advised a friend to use dollar averaging as an investment strategy. He follows your advice and invests $5,000 every year for ten years. The stocks he has chosen have the following composite purchase price each time he buys (1) $500, (2) $750, (3) $900, (4) $400, (5) $700, (6) $1,100, (7) $900, (8) $1,000, (9) $1,200, (10) $1,300. Prepare a table similar to Table 16–2 for your friend.

Chapter 17

Investing in mutual funds

We must all hang together or we will most assuredly all hang separately.

Benjamin Franklin

Many people find that they can earn a better total return on their effort and time by working in their regular occupation than by using their time to manage an investment portfolio. As we have indicated, earning a consistently high return on stocks and bonds requires consistent study and decision making.

There is an alternative. You can devote your energies to earning an income and saving some of it and pay someone else to make investments for you. By specializing in this way, it is certainly possible that your total earnings will be maximized. After all, there is more to your total earnings picture than getting a high yield on a portfolio.

In this chapter we will introduce this alternative by discussing:

- Mutual funds.
- The language of mutual funds.
- Common features of mutual funds.
- Tax treatment of mutual fund earnings.
- How have mutual funds performed?
- Sources of information.

MUTUAL FUNDS AND INVESTMENT COMPANIES

A *mutual fund* is a portfolio managed by an *investment company* for individuals who own shares in the investment company. In other words, investment companies are firms which invest money for their owners. You might think of the investment company as another intermediary which brings together savers and sellers of securities.

The investment companies develop portfolios of investments which may include stocks, bonds, and mortgages. The portfolios are then managed by full-time professionals who earn their living by earning a return for the owners of the fund.

There is as much variety in the offerings of investment companies as there is in the demands from those who seek investment alternatives. For example, there are funds which specialize in:

- The protection of capital.
- Growth in capital consistent with prudent management.
- Speculative opportunities where the rate of return is highest.
- Particular industries such as chemicals.
- Tax-exempt municipal bonds.
- Corporate bonds.
- Government bonds and treasury bills.
- Guaranteed or insured mortgages.

Once an investment company develops its objectives and states them to the public in the form of a *prospectus,* a detailed offer to sell, no change can be made in the objectives without the approval of the owners.

The language of mutual funds

Investment companies can be organized along two lines. First, there are true mutual funds, the so-called *open-end* investment company. Open-end companies are able to sell new shares of stock at any time. In other words, there isn't a fixed number of shares in the fund that are traded among buyers and sellers.

A second type of investment company is called *closed end* and operates on the basis of a single issue of stock. That is, these firms develop a portfolio and make a one-time offering of shares with no guarantee of repurchase. Buying and selling takes place among the shareholders with no expansion or contraction of shares.

The shares in the closed-end companies are listed on the New York and American Stock exchanges or in the Over-the-Counter market. These shares are listed along with other corporate securities. Adams Express and Lehman Corporation are examples of closed-end funds listed on the New York Stock Exchange. The prices of these shares are determined by the interaction in the market, whereas the guaranteed repurchase provision of the open-end companies sets the price of those shares.

When new shares are sold by open-end companies, the price is determined by the *net asset value* (NAV) of the shares already outstanding. The

NAV on a per share basis becomes the going price for new and old shares. Open-end companies also redeem their shares at any time. Thus, there can be continual buying and selling of shares with the price always reflecting the NAV of the fund.

NAV is determined by the price of the actual securities in the open-end fund's portfolio. In other words, a given mutual fund has a specific number of shares of stock for various companies at any particular moment in time. There could be bonds and other securities as well. If the closing price of all securities in the fund are determined for a particular day and then multiplied by the number of shares of each stock, one would have the gross asset value of the fund. From this, you would subtract any of the fund's liabilities. Then, the net value remaining would be divided by the number of mutual fund shares outstanding. This would give NAV.

Fees and load charges must be paid when purchasing the shares of many open-end investment companies. Load charges may run as high as 8.5 percent of the net asset value of the shares. Table 17–1 shows a typical load charge schedule. You will notice the declining rate as the amount of shares increases. The load charge represents a commission paid to the fund's sales agents and the operating cost of the investment company. These charges can represent a significant load on your expected earnings.

Table 17–1
Example of mutual fund load charge

Amount of purchase	*Sales charge as percentage of the net amount invested*	*Sales charge as percentage of the offering price*
Less than $15,000	9.3%	8.5%
$15,000 but less than $25,000	8.1	7.5
$25,000 but less than $50,000	6.4	6.0
$50,000 but less than $100,000	4.7	4.5
$100,000 but less than $250,000	3.6	3.5
$250,000 but less than $500,000	2.6	2.5
$500,000 but less than $1,000,000	2.0	2.0
$1,000,000 but less than $2,000,000	1.5	1.5
$2,000,000 and over	1.0	1.0

Source: Washington Mutual Investors Fund, *Prospectus,* August 20, 1976, p. 5.

No-load funds charge no commission since these funds sell their shares directly to the investor. Still, there is a management fee which must be paid by the buyer, but the cost is small, falling in the range of 1 to 2 percent of NAV.

The prices of mutual funds are listed each day in *The Wall Street Journal.* A sample listing is shown in Figure 17–1. You will note that no-load funds

Figure 17–1
Mutual fund prices

Mutual Funds

Friday, October 21, 1977

Price ranges for investment companies, as quoted by the National Association of Securities Dealers. NAV stands for net asset value per share; the offering includes net asset value plus maximum sales charge, if any.

	NAV	Offer Price	NAV Chg.
Acorn Fnd	14.84	N.L.	...
Adv Invest	9.30	N.L.	−.03
Aetna Fnd	7.06	7.72	+.01
Aetna InSh	12.95	14.15	...
Afuture Fd	8.98	N.L.	+.01
AGE Fund	5.56	5.67	−.01
Allstate	8.29	N.L.	−.01
Alpha Fnd	10.09	N.L.	−.02
Am Birthrt	9.56	10.45	−.01
Am Equity	4.65	5.08	...
American Funds Group:			
Am Bal	7.91	8.64	−.01
Amcap F	5.69	6.22	−.01
Am Mutl	9.00	9.84	−.02
Bnd FdA	14.87	16.25	+.01
Cap FdA	6.46	7.06	+.02
Gth FdA	4.89	5.34	+.03
IncF Am	15.42	16.85	−.03
I C A	13.12	14.34	−.02
Nw Prsp	14.94	16.33	−.01
Wash Mt	6.20	6.78	−.01
American General Group:			
A GnCBd	8.94	9.77	...
A GC Gr	3.77	4.12	...
A Gn Inc	6.35	6.94	−.01
A GnVen	12.41	13.56	−.02
Eqty Gth	6.31	6.90	...
Fd Amer	6.18	6.75	−.01
Prov Inc	3.85	4.15	−.01
Am Grwth	5.52	5.95	−.04
Am Ins Ind	5.11	5.58	−.01
Am Invest	5.24	N.L.	+.02
AmInv Inc	11.92	N.L.	+.04
AmNat Gw	2.89	3.16	...
Anchor Group:			
Daily Inc	1.00	N.L.	...
Growth	6.10	6.58	...
Income	7.23	7.80	−.02
Spectm	4.19	4.52	...
Fund Inv	6.29	6.78	−.02
Wa Natl	9.52	10.26	−.02
Audax Fnd	7.96	8.70	+.03
Axe-Houghton:			
Fund B	7.43	8.08	−.01
Income	5.01	5.45	...
Stock Fd	5.43	5.93	−.01
BLC Gwth	10.24	11.20	−.02
Babsn Inc	1.77	N.L.	...
Babsn Inv	8.74	N.L.	−.03
Beacon Hll	8.34	N.L.	−.02
Beacon Inv	8.91	N.L.	−.03
Berger Group Funds:			
100 Fund	7.15	N.L.	−.01
101 Fund	8.80	N.L.	−.03
Brksh Cap	7.33	8.01	−.05
Bondsk Cp	4.54	4.96	−.02
Bos Found	9.28	10.14	−.04
Calvin Bullock Funds:			
Bullock	11.87	12.97	...
Canadn	7.01	7.66	−.03
Div Shrs	2.68	2.92	...
Income	14.66	16.02	...
Ntwide	9.29	10.15	−.02
NY Vent	10.74	11.74	+.01
C G Fund	9.09	9.83	−.02
CG Inc Fd	8.57	9.26	−.01
Cap Presv	1.00	N.L.	...
Century Sh	10.79	11.63	−.04
Chalng Inv	9.49	10.37	−.03
Charter Fd	13.52	14.78	+.08
Chase Group of Boston:			
Fnd Bost	5.83	6.37	−.03
Front Cp	3.60	3.93	+.01
ShTr Bos	6.96	7.61	−.03

	NAV	Offer Price	NAV Chg.
Commonwealth Trust:			
A & B	.96	1.04	...
C	1.42	1.53	...
Comp BdSt	8.45	9.09	−.02
Composit	6.87	7.39	−.02
Concord F	12.31	N.L.	+.03
Consol Inv	9.00	9.37	...
Constlatn	5.39	N.L.	−.01
Cont Mtlv	6.03	N.L.	+.01
Coutry Cap	10.93	11.82	−.02
Daily Incm	1.00	N.L.	...
Davidg Fd	7.18	N.L.	...
Delaware Group:			
Decatr	11.63	12.71	−.03
Delchs F	9.23	9.66	+.01
Delw Fd	10.38	11.34	−.02
Delta Td	4.65	5.08	−.01
DeVegh M	29.49	N.L.	−.07
Direct Cap	3.78	4.13	−.01
DodgC Bal	20.95	N.L.	−.04
DodgC Stk	14.82	N.L.	−.01
Drx Burnh	9.18	N.L.	+.01
Dreyfus Group:			
Dreyf Fd	11.22	12.28	−.03
Dreyf Lv	15.60	17.05	−.06
Dryf LAs	9.98	N.L.	
Numbr 9	5.24	N.L.	−.02
Spl Incm	7.20	N.L.	
Tax ExB	15.91	N.L.	
Third Cn	12.27	N.L.	
Eagle Gth	10.24	11.19	−.0[illegible]
Eaton & Howard:			
Balncd F	7.76	8.37	−.02
Foursq	7.57	N.L.	−.03
Growth	8.69	9.37	...
Income	6.03	6.50	+.01
Spec Fnd	6.20	6.68	...
Stock Fd	8.41	9.07	−.02
Edie Spec'l	16.80	N.L.	+.09
Edson Gld	8.52	N.L.	...
Egret Fnd	10.11	10.99	−.03
Elfun Trst	13.75	(z)	−.03
Fairfld Fd	8.80	9.57	+.02
Federated Group:			
Am Lead	7.60	7.72	
Empire	18.15	(z)	−.10
4th Emp	17.16	(z)	−.09
Optn Inc	13.28	14.51	−.02
Tax Free	13.27	N.L.	...
Fidelity Group Funds:			
Bd Corp	8.74	N.L.	−.01
Capital	7.78	8.50	−.04
Contra	9.56	N.L.	−.02
Daily Inc	1.00	N.L.	
Destiny	7.70	(z)	−.01
Eq Incm	14.81	N.L.	−.06
Fidel Fd	14.99	16.38	−.04
Mageln	22.29	(z)	−.02
Muncpl	10.58	N.L.	...
Puritan	10.04	10.97	−.03
Salem	4.58	5.01	−.02
Thrift Tr	10.33	N.L.	−.01
Trend	19.88	21.73	−.03
Financial Programs:			
Dynam	4.68	N.L.	+.01
Industl	4.03	N.L.	...
Income	7.19	N.L.	...
First Investors Fund:			
Discovr	5.11	5.58	−.02
Growth	6.41	7.01	−.01
Income	8.69	9.50	...
Stock Fd	8.13	8.89	−.01
1st MultiA	7.76	N.L.	−.06
1stMult Inc	10.00	N.L.	...
44 Wall St	16.14	N.L.	−.01
Fnd Grwth	3.70	4.04	+.01

Source: Reprinted with permission of *The Wall Street Journal*,

are identified by the symbol N.L. which follows the NAV of the stock. For example, Acorn Fund, a no-load fund, has a NAV of $14.84 in the table and shows an increase in NAV of $0.03 from the previous day. Aetna Fund, on the other hand, has a load charge. If you subtract its price of $14.15 from the NAV of $12.95, there is a balance of $1.20 which is approximately 8.5 percent of the price. You can examine other funds in the listing and identify their load charges. In each case, you would buy at the offer price and sell at NAV.

Common features of mutual funds

The owners of shares in mutual funds may exercise several options to assist them in meeting their investment objectives. *Automatic investment* enables owners to issue drafts on their banks to the mutual fund, enabling the fund to make regular purchases in their behalf of a set amount of money. You get the benefits of dollar averaging in a managed portfolio and the elimination of the bother of making purchases.

Reinvestment of dividends and gains allows the fund manager to reinvest your share of the funds profits. You would normally receive a quarterly check for any dividends and capital gains which related to your shares. Under this option, you would have additional shares purchased automatically.

Systematic withdrawal of share values is offered by some funds. This option enables you to receive regular payments as you liquidate your shares over time. This might help you in using a mutual fund to supplement a retirement program. On the other hand, you have some flexibility in taking your gains which could help in tax planning.

TAX TREATMENT OF MUTUAL FUND EARNINGS

Your earnings from mutual funds can take two forms: dividends and capital gains. These income forms receive the same tax treatment as their counterparts from other investments. Dividends would be treated as ordinary income and would benefit from any exclusion of dividends which is permitted a taxpayer. Capital gains can occur as a result of action by the management of the fund when they buy and sell securities in the fund and when you sell your shares in the fund itself. In the case of capital gains generated by management, you will receive your share of these along with your share of dividends paid into the fund. Of course, it is your responsibility to determine and report for tax purposes any capital gains which occur when you sell your mutual fund shares.

In the case of tax-exempt mutual funds, your share of interest earned on the municipal bonds in the fund will not be subject to federal taxes. That is, the tax-exempt status of the securities in the fund is passed on to the owners of the fund. Capital gains generated by the fund are subject to taxation, however.

HOW HAVE THE MUTUAL FUNDS PERFORMED?

When considering the performance of alternative investments, you must realize that history is all there is to offer. No one knows what the future holds. Sylvia Porter in her *Money Book* has an interesting chart which is highly recommended. Some of the elements of that chart are included in Table 17–2. The continuously compounded rate of return on the various investments is added to her figures in column 4.[1]

Table 17–2
Relative performance of mutual funds after an original investment of $10,000: 1960–1970

Investment vehicle	*Value 10 years later*	*Compounded yield (percent)*
Growth mutual fund average	$25,022	9.1
All mutual funds	21,255	7.5
Standard & Poor's 500	20,950	6.9
Dow Jones Industrial Average	16,450	4.7
5 Percent compounded annually	16,436	4.7
Series E government bond	14,580	3.3

Source: Sylvia Porter, *Sylvia Porter's Money Book,* vol. 2 (Garden City, N.Y.: Doubleday & Company, Inc., 1975), p. 1013.

On the basis of Table 17–2, you might accept mutual funds as the logical way to invest your savings. Their performance for the period shown looks good. But remember, you still must select the "right" mutual fund. The values in the table are averages. In reading the table, bear in mind also that 1960–70 was a very good decade for investments.

A careful examination of Table 17–2 also offers another interesting point. Across 1960–70 you would have done as well as the Dow Jones Industrial Average stocks, if you had left your money in a savings account earning 5 percent interest. It is difficult to make a high return continuously over a long period of time.

In the more recent period 1967–77, the best funds have outperformed this record. With reinvestment of dividends, the top ten mutual funds had continuously compounded rates of return from 7.62 percent to over 17 percent.

SOURCES OF INFORMATION

The search for information on mutual funds should start with the brokerage firms. They sell many funds and will gladly provide a range of literature including announcements of new funds. From there you can watch for adver-

[1] Continuously compounding means that the principal invested is growing continuously, rather than on the basis of monthly or daily compounding.

tisements in *The Wall Street Journal, Forbes,* and *Barron's.* Beyond the well known sources are the associations which represent mutual funds. Two of these are:

No Load Fund Association, Inc.
475 Park Avenue South
New York, N.Y. 10016.

The Investment Institute
1775 K Street, N.W.
Washington, D.C. 20006.

You will also want to become familiar with these publications:

Mutual Fund Scoreboard.
FundScope.

SUMMARY

Mutual funds are portfolios of investment assets professionally managed for individual investors. There is a great variety of funds with different goals and types of portfolios. The offer to sell is conveyed in a prospectus. Open-end funds continue to issue new shares, while closed-end funds have a limited number of shares. The selling price of an open-ended fund is determined by net asset value per share plus fees and load charges (commissions). No-load funds charge no commissions. Prices are listed daily in the financial pages.

Mutual funds often offer automatic investment plans, reinvestment of dividends and gains, and systematic withdrawal. Dividends and capital gains are treated the same way for tax purposes as regular stock ownership.

KEY WORDS

Automatic investment
Closed-end investment company
Investment company
Load charge
Mutual fund
Net asset value
No-load fund
Open-end investment company
Reinvestment of dividends
Systematic withdrawal

PROBLEMS

1. Discuss some of the advantages offered the investor by mutual funds.
2. Identify the differences between open-end and closed-end mutual funds; load and no-load funds.
3. Examine Figure 17–1 and calculate the load charge for American Equity and Century Shares.

Chapter 18

Other investments

All . . . that glitters is not gold.
Dryden

Investing hard-earned money in stocks and bonds is unappealing to some people, especially during times of inflation. They may want to know exactly where their money is, or to invest in things they can see and hold. Or, they may be interested in commodities, another alternative reported in the *The Wall Street Journal.* They also want to get a real return on their investment. For these people either buying or investing in a futures contract for corn or sugar, gold and silver bullion and coins, and any number of collector's items is an attractive route. In fact, you might even have fun while making money.

Consider your hobby. Do you collect coins, or stamps, or even baseball cards? One amateur baseball card collector turned his hobby into a profitable business, selling to other collectors. Mechanically minded individuals who tinker with old cars sometimes make sound investments in automobiles which appreciate significantly in a few years.

This chapter is concerned with all sorts of alternative investments and will perhaps set you thinking of a few new ones. At the outset, it must be emphasized that you should never invest in anything—be it books, broilers, bullion, or baseball cards—before acquiring a sound background in the area. Bankrupt speculators, phony first edition books and fly-by-night gold dealers are a dime a dozen.

To introduce you to these alternative, real investments, this chapter deals with the following questions:

- What is the commodity market?
- How do investors operate in commodities?
- What about gold and silver?
- How can I make money from my hobby?
- What are the problems with collectibles?

INVESTING IN COMMODITY FUTURES

Investing in commodity futures is not recommended for the timid soul or the typical investor who has only a few hours each week to devote to following the market. Commodities futures are a demanding investment in many ways.

A *commodities future* is a contract to accept future delivery or make future delivery of a specified amount of grain, lumber, copper, pork bellies, or any one of the more than 20 items traded at the *Chicago Board of Trade,* Chicago Mercantile Exchange, Kansas City Board of Trade, and in the commodities markets. In other words, a person who sells 5,000 bushels of wheat on August 15, 1979, to be delivered in December 1979, has actually entered into a legal contract for delivery of wheat which may be stored somewhere or about to be harvested in some farmer's field. In a similar way, if you purchase a contract to accept future delivery of wheat, you have set in motion a process which could lead to your ownership of 5,000 bushels of grain.

The investor is usually speculating on price movements. He or she does not expect to hold the purchased contract to the date of its completion. Instead, the contract will be sold to someone else. The timing of such action is crucial.

Speculating in futures contracts and the rise of the Chicago Board of Trade came about because of uncertainty faced by producers of commodities and manufacturers who actually used the commodities in their final product. Back in the early 1800s, for example, most wheat would be harvested, carried to various markets, and then sold or stored. There were surpluses which led to rapidly falling prices and shortages which caused prices to rise just as quickly.

To smooth these price changes and to gain certainty, some buyers began to make contracts at a firm price for future delivery. Wheat farmers, for example, might sell an entire crop to a miller well before harvest time. Sometimes the price in the future contract ended up higher than the ultimate market price. The farmer was better off. In other seasons, bad weather reduced crops generally and the price in the market for immediate delivery—the *spot price*—went above the contract price. In that case, the farmer didn't do as well. But in each case, both the buyer and seller gained certainty by having a binding futures contract. They had a *hedge* against an undesirable price change. In other words, the farmer hedged, protected himself, against a fall in price; the miller who bought the future contract had a hedge against a rise in price. In this case, the farmer would sell his wheat to the owner of the contract, who would take final delivery.

Speculators enter this picture when the owner of a futures contract has reason to think that he can better himself by selling his present contract and doing something else with the money. Suppose the miller believed that a bumper crop of wheat would be harvested which would lead to a lower price than that in his futures contract. In that case, he would want to sell the contract. Suppose you were a speculator who believed the opposite—the crop would be short and prices were going to rise. You would then be willing to buy the miller's contract.

Now suppose the speculator buys the contract, and the short harvest begins to materialize. The value of the futures contract begins to rise as the delivery date approaches. The speculator sells the contract and makes a profit. Of course, the speculator could be wrong. He could lose his shirt. He would never see the wheat, however.

By pursuing profits, the speculator searches for information and bids on that basis. As a result, price movements are smoothed by the many speculators in the market who bid against one another.

The Chicago Board of Trade is the major commodity exchange in the United States. It is a business governed by a board of directors who oversee the operation for some 1,400 members of the Board of Trade who have purchased the right to buy and sell contracts on the floor of the exchange. If you enter into a commodities transaction—futures contract or spot purchase—one of the members will handle your order.

The typical commodity trader places orders through a brokerage firm, the same firms which handle stocks and bonds. In effect, a broker offers a commodity trader the same services which are offered other investment customers and a commission will be charged. However, since commodities are fast moving and require highly specialized knowledge, brokerage firms usually have specialists who work primarily with commodity traders.

There are a wide range of instructions which you can give your broker in placing a commodities order:

1. *Price limit:* sets a price limitation below (above) which the order cannot be executed.
2. *Fill or kill:* must be executed immediately as given.
3. *Stop:* filled by selling or buying when a specified price is reached.
4. *Stop limit:* filled at specified price or better.
5. *Board:* filled by buying or selling a specified price.
6. *Day:* must be filled at specified price in a given trading day.
7. *Time limit:* good until cancelled by time specified.
8. *Intramarket spread:* filled by buying in one futures contract month and selling in another. Example: "Buy July wheat and sell March wheat."
9. *Inter-commodity spread:* Example: "Buy Kansas City March wheat; sell Chicago March corn."
10. *Cancel:* cancel previous order.

While most of the order types mentioned above are fairly easy to understand, the spread order may be something new. An illustration developed from *Changing Times* may help to make the spread transaction clear.[1]

[1] *Changing Times* (February 1978), p. 32.

Suppose the May delivery of corn is selling for $3.50 per bushel; the December price for the same commodity is $4.25. Through much trading experience and study, you are aware that the normal difference between these two prices is $0.50 instead of $0.75. Thus you think the typical spread of $0.50 will soon be reestablished. You sell December corn at $4.25 and buy May at $3.50. As predicted, the spread converges. December declines to $3.90 and May to $3.40. You then sell a May contract and buy a December contract. This offsets your earlier transaction.

What are the results? You lost $0.10 on the May contract, but gained $0.35 on the December contract. That gives you a profit of $0.25 per bushel.

The example is based on a successful spread. You could have misjudged and gotten another result. May could have held at $3.50, and December might have risen to $5.00. You would have lost $0.75 per bushel.

As with stocks, you may purchase commodities on margin. The margins are slim. For example, you can enter into a $10,000 contract with $500 of your own money. The margins are fixed dollar amounts, but can involve loans from your broker of up to 95 percent of a contract price. Of course, you must have some net worth to back such loans. In any case, you can make or lose a great deal because of the leverage available through margin accounts.

You can follow commodity prices by referring to *The Wall Street Journal*. Figure 18–1 gives a sample of the daily listing for commodities. There you will see both futures prices and cash (spot) prices. The entries are self-explanatory. In addition to daily prices, you will also find a Dow Jones Commodities Futures Index and a Dow Jones Spot Commodity Index published daily in *The Wall Street Journal*. These indexes give a reading of broad commodity price movements.

As with other major financial markets, the commodities markets are regulated by the federal government. In their case, the agency is the Commodities Futures Trading Commission.

BUYING A HEDGE AGAINST INFLATION: THE GOLDBUGS

Until December 31, 1974, Americans could not own gold *bullion* (bars of wafers of pure gold). President Gerald Ford signed the legislation making this legal for the first time since 1933 when Franklin Roosevelt took the dollar off the gold standard.

Now gold is available from commercial American banks and professional dealers as well as the traditional source, Swiss banks. Some Swiss banks insist on a minimum purchase of a 400-ounce bar of gold. At the March 1977 price of $150 an ounce, that represents a $60,000 investment. American dealers and some Swiss banks sell smaller "wafers" of 10 to 1,000 grams, however.

There is a dealer's charge for the sale of the gold, usually 6 to 8 percent of

Figure 18–1
Commodity prices

Futures Price

	Open	High	Low	Close	Change	Season's High	Season's Low
–FOODS AND FIBER–							
FRESH EGGS (CME)–22,500 doz.; cents per doz.							
June	41.80	42.55	41.65	41.65-42.4	– .15to+.60	50.40	41.50
July	46.90	47.60	46.90	47.30	+ .25	52.75	45.10
Sept	57.10	58.10	57.00	58.-57.70	+ .90to.60	59.40	47 20
Nov	....	....	..	60.00n	....	60.75	59.40
Dec	61.00	61.50	60.90	61.50	+ .50	62.00	59.50
Est. sales 614; sales Thurs : 296 contracts.							
MAINE POTATOES (NYM)–50,000 lbs.; cts. per lb.-s							
Nov	5.07	5.15	5.02	5.15	+ .09	5.68	4.75
Mar79	5.87	6.00	5.87	6.00	+ .12	6.77	5.71
Apr	6.45	6.45	6.45	6.45	+ .12	7.19	6.28
May	7.23	7.45	7.22	7.40	+ .17	8.59	6.90
Est. sales 611; sales Thurs.: 457 contracts.							
COFFEE (CSE)–37,500 lbs.; cents per lb.							
July	167.50	169.25	166.75	168.50	+1.50	238.00	128.00
Sept	160.50	163.25	159.75	162.50-163.	+2.25to3.75	243.00	126.75
Dec	154.50	157.00	154.25	156.00b	+2.80	165.00	115.00
Mar79	149.00	150.25	147.50	150.25b	+4.00	160.00	113.00
May	146.50	146.50	146.50	146.50	+4.00	146.50	111.00
July	143.00	143.00	142.50	143.00	+4.00	143.00	110.50
Sept	140.00	140.00	140.00	140.00b	+4.00	140.00	109.50
Est sales 795; sales Thurs.: 1.068 contracts.							
–GRAINS AND FEEDS–							
WHEAT (CBT)–5,000 bu.; cents per bu.							
July	334½	334½	330¼	332½-333	–1to½	337	243½
Sept	338¾	339	334	336	....	339	248½
Dec	345½	346½	340½	343-343¾	–½to+¼	346½	273¾
Mar 79	347	347	342	345-344½	–½to1	348½	280¾
May	344	344	340	343½	+1	349	310½
July	338	338	335½	337¾	–¾	338½	333
Sales Thurs.: 9,423 contracts.							
WHEAT (K.C.)–5,000 bu.; cents per bu.							
July	313	314½	312½	314¼-313¾	+¼to–¼	325	242¾
Sept	318	319½	316¾	318½-317¾	Unch to–¾	327½	263½
Dec	325	326	322¾	324½-323½	+½to–½	331½	269
Mar 79	332	332	327½	329	....	335	274½
May	331	331	329	330	....	333	309
Sales Thurs.: 3,801 contracts.							
WHEAT (MPLS)–5,000 bu.; cents per bu.							
July	319	320½	318½	320¼-½	+¼to½	326¾	256¾
Sept	323	324¼	322¾	324	....	330½	270½
Dec	328¼	328¾	326¾	328	+¼	333	277¾
Mar 79	331	331½	330	331	–1	339	306
Sales Thurs.: 1,040 contracts.							

Spot (cash) Prices

	Fri.	Thurs.	Yr. Ago
FOODS			
Flour, hard winter KC cwt	$7.55	$7.55	$6.00
Coffee, Brazilian, NY lb	n1.65	1.65	3.00
Cocoa, Accra NY lb	z	z	z
Potatoes, rnd wht, 50 lb, NY del	y3.25	3.25	4.85
Sugar, cane, raw NY lb del	z	z	.1092
Sugar, cane, ref NY lb fob	.2015	.2015	.1710
Sugar, beet, ref Chgo-W lb fob	.1865	.1865	.1525
Orange Juice, frz con, NY lb ...	b1.0400	1.100	.9050
Butter, AA, Chgo., lb.	1.05¼	1.05¼	.99¼
Eggs, Lge white, Chgo doz. ...	.49	.49	.53
Broilers, Dressed "A" NY lb ...	x.4913	.4931	.4356
Beef, 700-900 lbs, Midw lb fob ..	n.94½	.94½	.63¾
Pork Loins, 14 down Mdw lb fob	n.99¾	.99¾	.83½
Hams, 14-17 lbs, Midw lb fob	n.80	.80	.73½
Pork Bellies, 12-14lbMdw lb fob	n.67	.68½	.54
Hogs, Sioux City avg cwt	e50.80	50.30	43.25
Hogs, Omaha avg cwt	e50.75	49.60	42.85
Steers, Omaha choice avg cwt	60.25	60.25	40.90
Steers, Sioux City ch avg cwt ..	60.75	60.75	41.10
Feeder Cattle, Okl Cty, av cwt	e65.75	65.75	42.50
Pepper, black NY lb	a1.18	1.18	1 [illegible]
GRAINS AND FEEDS			
Wheat, No. 2 ord hard KC bu	3.20½	3.25½	2.31½
Wht,No.1 dk Nthn 14%-pro Mpls	3.36½	3.36	2.72½
Wheat, No. 2 soft red Chgo bu	n3.35¾	3.36½	2.31¾
Milo, No. 2 KC cwt	4.42	4.25	3.78
Corn, No. 2 yellow Chgo. bu ..	h2.69	2.69½	2.43
Oats, No. 2 milling, Mpls bu ...	1.48	1.48	1.56
Rye, No. 2 Mpls bu	3.12	3.12	2.80
Barley, top-qlty. Mpls bu	2.50-2.55	2.50-2.55	3.10
Soybeans, No. 1 yellow Chgo bu	n7.23	7.34½	9.32
Flaxseed, Mpls bu	6.50	6.35	7.50
Bran, KC ton	69.00	70.00	78.00
Linseed Meal, Mpls ton	137.00	137.00	190.00
Cottonseed Meal, Memphis ton	n126.50	125.00	210.00
Soybean Meal, Decatur, Ill. ton	182.50	184.00	252.00
Corn Gluten Feed, Chgo ton ..	88.00	88.00	118.00
Hominy Feed, Ill. ton	79.00	78.00	77.00
Meat-Bonemeal 50%-pro, Ill ton	210.00	207.50	249.00
Brewer's Grains, Milw ton	84.00	83.00	124.00
Alfalfa Pellets, dehy, Neb., ton	63.00	63.00	78.00

Source: Reprinted with permission of *The Wall Street Journal,* © Dow Jones & Company, Inc. (1978). *All Rights Reserved.*

the price. The smaller bars and wafers tend to have the higher charge imposed on them. There may also be a mark-up from the wholesale to the retail price—sometimes as much as 30 percent. In addition, banks will charge you for storing your gold, if that is your preference. There is nothing illegal about storing bullion in a home safe, but gold is heavy and bulky to store, and there is always a risk of theft.

The price of gold fluctuates, depending for the most part on confidence in world currency and particularly in the American dollar. When confidence in the dollar is low, gold prices are high. This is because people buy gold to protect themselves from economic disasters. If buyers see a depression or currency devaluation coming on, their demand for gold increases, driving up its price. Some consider gold to be the ultimate inflation hedge. The price of gold shot from an official price of $36 to $197.50 an ounce in the 1970s, reflecting partially the declining value of world currencies.

The current gold price is listed daily in *The Wall Street Journal* under "Cash Prices." Look at Figure 18–2. Under Precious Metals, you see that

Figure 18–2
Precious metal prices

PRECIOUS METALS

Platinum, NY troy oz		p220.00	220.00	162.00
Silver, troy ounce				
London, spot (in pence)		287.75	285.45	268.20
3-Month		294.55	291.85	273.65
6-Month		302.20	299.35	280.40
One year		319.25	316.30	295.40
(The U.S. equivalent for spot was $5.208 based on the $1.8098 London rate for sterling Friday.)				
Handy & Harman base price		5.245	5.155	4.58
Engelhard Minerals & Chemicals				
Industrial bullion		5.245	5.155	4.58
Fabricated products		5.376	5.284	4.695
Gold, troy ounce				
Engelhard Minerals & Chemicals				
Industrial bullion		179.95	179.10	144.90
Fabricated products		184.45	183.58	148.52
Handy & Harman base price		179.80	178.95	144.40
	– –Fixings– –		Prev.	Year
	Morn.	Aftn.	Aftn.	Ago
London	178.95	179.45	178.60	144.40

a-Asked. b-Bid. c-Corrected. d-Dealer market. e-Estimated. f-Near-term shipment, C.I.F. delivered U.S. ports. h-In hopper railroad cars. k-Represents dealer selling price in lots of 40,000 pounds or more, f.o.b. buyer's works. Smaller lots can command lower prices. n-Nominal p-Producer price. s-Source. Metals Week. x-Less than truckloads. y-Maine origin; varies seasonally. z-Not quoted.

Source: Reprinted with permission of *The Wall Street Journal,*

industrial bullion cost $179.95 on May 30, 1978. The price has jumped considerably from a year earlier when gold sold for $144.90.

The greatest advantage of gold bullion is its ability to rise in value with inflation. Gold bullion has disadvantages, though. It does not earn dividends or interest like other investments do. It simply sits in a vault. In addition, gold is especially susceptible to political upheavals in South Africa because 60 percent of the world's gold is mined there.

There are other ways of investing in gold besides bullion. Some people prefer gold coins. In addition to the gold content, some coins are valuable for their rarity. The coin's market value above its intrinsic value (its percentage content of gold) is called the *premium.* Coins can sell for 10 to 50 percent above the intrinsic value.

U.S. laws allow American investors to own U.S. gold coins minted before 1933 and foreign coins minted before 1960. The American coins are, of course, rarer. Favorite gold coins are the American Double Eagle, originally a $20 gold piece, the British sovereign, and the Mexican 50 peso. The South African Krugerrand, a coin minted specially for investors, is also popular. The

Mexican peso's premium in 1974 was about 13 percent. Sovereigns had a 30 percent premium, and the Double Eagle, reflecting its rarity, had a 100 percent premium. A 1907 Double Eagle in very good condition brought $200,000 at a 1974 auction.

Gold coins are bought from a coin dealer, who will charge a broker's fee. The coins are priced in lots of perhaps 20, but you need not buy an entire lot.

Gold coins have advantages over bullion in that they can represent a less expensive investment and are portable. In an economic crisis, they do not hold up as well as bullion, however. Rare coins would lose their high premiums, although coins with high gold content would not suffer as much.

To compute a gold coin's value:

$$(\text{Gold weight} \times \text{Current world gold price}) + \text{Premium} = \text{Value.}$$

Fledgling coin collectors are advised to buy only from reputable dealers, and avoid ordering coins through the mail.

A final way to invest in gold is by buying shares in gold mines. Appreciation is faster for gold mining stocks than for bullion, but gold stock is no different from stock of any other company in its volatility. In addition, gold stock is very susceptible to labor disputes and the South African political situation. As you have had a chapter on stock market investment, mining stocks need not be discussed further here.

AND THE SILVERBUGS

The price of silver is on the rise, and for good reason. All known silver mines are being worked, and new sources of the precious metal have yet to be found. Any bride-to-be can attest to the skyrocketing price of sterling flatware, and the fixed supply plus increasing demand is the culprit.

In early 1973, silver cost $1.96 an ounce. By 1978, it was up to $5.20, and silver watchers expect this to jump a few more dollars by 1979. Industrial use of silver is up, and the U.S. government is also a big user. U.S. coinage uses 50 million ounces of the metal a year, while industries use 400 million ounces. The government has a small supply, and some 300 million ounces of silver are produced a year, but this is not sufficient to satisfy all demands at the current price.

Silver, like gold, can be purchased in several forms, including bullion and coins. Silver bars may be purchased from refiners like Handy and Harman and Englehard Minerals & Chemical Company. Buying straight from *refiners* saves the middleman costs which you pay when buying from coin dealers.

These refiners supply industrial purchasers with silver, and usually sell minimum lots of 5,000 ounces. However, Englehard's New York office sells single 100-ounce bars.

The pre–1965 U.S. coins are being hoarded these days because their melt-down value, the worth of their silver content, is much higher than their face value. In addition, unusual coins sometimes bring high prices. A 1940 quarter brought its owner $7.50, while a 1950 nickel was appraised at $10.

Still, these gains are just pocket money compared to what might be made by investing in *silver futures*. Investors buy bags of silver coins weighing 55 pounds. The bags contain 720 ounces of pure silver. Investors can buy their bags outright or on margin, paying 35 percent of the current market price. They also pay interest on the unpaid balance, storage costs for their bags, and a 2 percent brokerage fee.

"Hello, Howard? The dividend from your feedlot investment arrived today."

Reprinted by permission The Wall Street Journal

JOINING THE NUMISMATISTS

Numismatists are not exercise freaks or members of a strange religious cult. They collect rare coins. There are about ten million coin collectors in the United States, and their hobby often brings in big money.

Tips from professional coin collectors include:

- Specialize in certain coins or areas, and learn all you can about them. Some people stick with the "lowly" penny, with impressive results. A penny struck in San Francisco in 1894 was worth $50,000 in 1972. This is because only 24 pennies with the 1894–S mark were struck that year. Of course, an 1895 or 1893 penny would be worth relatively little, because over a million of each of these were struck.

- Buy the very best examples. Coins are valued according to their rarity, condition, current demand for them among collectors, and their legitimacy.
- Order from established dealers, and never through the mail. Coins, like anything else, need to be examined before purchasing.
- Employ only reasonable time and effort in procuring your specimens.

DIAMONDS ARE FOREVER

Diamonds and other precious and semiprecious stones are riding on the wave of a gem explosion which began in the early 1970s. Their value is increasing as much as 50 percent a year. For example, a diamond ring purchased for $5,500 in 1974 was appriased at $13,500 in early 1977.

Like gold and silver bullion, gems—diamonds, emeralds, rubies, topazes, jade, and opals—are an inflation hedge. Since diamond supplies are limited, their value is not hurt by inflation, but rather enhanced.

These tips are offered by the experts on diamond buying:

- Buy only from an established jeweler or dealer.
- Look for the "four Cs" in your gem: color, clarity, cut, and carats. A flawless, colorless, round, one-carat diamond is the best buy and commands from $9,000 to over $17,000 from a retailer.
- Avoid fancy settings when buying jewelry.
- Hold on to your gem for about ten years before considering a sale.

There is a liquidity problem in the diamond and gem market, and investors must figure out a way around the professional wholesalers to make their profit. Unless a buyer in the private market can be found, the sellers will suffer from the 100 percent mark-up imposed by retailers.

ART APPRECIATION AND THE INVESTOR

Someone has said that a thing of beauty is a joy forever, and this is certainly true of fine artwork. A good piece of art is a source of pride to a collector while its value increases.

Some background in art is necessary before you rush out to your nearest gallery and start picking out paintings. As in coin collecting, one is advised to specialize in a certain field, such as American primitives or nautical scenes.

Perhaps you took an art history or art appreciation course in college. That's a good beginning background for an art collector, and it may give you some ideas for your area of concentration. Did you fall in love with the works of Matisse or another impressionist? How about 19th century French works? Those of the Barbizon school—J. F. Millet, who painted landscapes was a member—are favorites among collectors and a good investment.

Right now, limited edition prints are a good place for a beginner to start. They are not too expensive for a buyer on a limited budget.

Other best bets include the timeless works of the "old masters"—Rubens, Raphael, and Vermeer. These paintings and drawings are comparable to the very best blue-chip stock and can cost upward from $50,000. African primitives (50–$100 and up) and classical antiquities—such as Greek statuary—are other promising investments.

Works associated with prominent owners, such as the William Randolph Hearst family, can yield surprising revenues, so watch for estate auctions from the homes of celebrities.

A word of warning—forgeries run rampant in the art world, and seasoned collectors as well as amateurs can fall prey to good copies. French master forger Elmyr de Hory fooled many a pro with his fakes of impressionist works by Matisse and Chagall.

Before sinking a large sum into a piece of art, it is wise to get a list of previous owners, called a *provenance* from your dealer. You can check on the work's authenticity by contacting the people on the list and thus assure yourself of the pedigree.

RARE BOOKS

The most popular books on the auction circuit these days are those on natural history, such as John Audubon's *The Birds of America*. Sought for its fabulous prints, copies of the Audubon book are bringing up to $352,000 each at auction. Buyers usually sell the book's 435 engravings separately for $850 to $18,000 a piece.

A collection of rare books, like an art collection, can be a source of pride as well as profit. The interest in rare books is evidenced by such magazines as *Book Collector's Market,* which serves as an exchange of information about auctions and shops for collectors.

A book's value is based on its rarity, condition, importance, and aesthetic appeal. First editions are the most sought after books, and they can become even more valuable with an author's autograph or inscription inside. Signed first editions by younger authors, like John Updike, are bringing $20 to $25 today, but their value will increase with time.

As with stocks, there are "fashions" in the book market. When the remake of *The Great Gatsby* came out in 1974, first editions of books by F. Scott Fitzgerald, *Gatsby* in particular, were auctioned for several hundred dollars.

Collectors often specialize in a certain subject area. The recent deluge of books on Watergate are worth speculating on, according to some experts. Also, collections of related books like this are worth more than the separately sold volumes.

Another area for the amateur to consider is old editions of children's book classics like the Beatrix Potter series (*Peter Rabbit* and others).

Certain presses, like the British Doves Press operated in the early 1900s, produced books which are now in great demand. The Doves Bible has brought as much as $2,000. Because the publishers threw their presses into the Thames River in 1916, books of the Doves quality were never reproduced, making the existing ones all the more rare.

Amateurs need to get a solid background in their area of special interest and in book collecting in general before attempting to compete with the pros. There are several books written for amateurs every year. (See the information at the end of the chapter.)

Liquidity is a problem in profitable book investing, as the retailer's mark-up is high. However, books donated to a school represent a tax deduction to a collector, should he or she decide not to sell.

PHOTOGRAPHS

One of the newest and fastest growing areas for collectors is old and new photographs. The fact that major corporations like Philip Morris, Atlantic Richfield, and J. C. Penney are investing in collections of photographs is an indication of their promise. Copies of Gardner's *Photographic Sketchbook of the War,* a book of Civil War prints, jumped from a 1967 auction price of $1,300 to $12,000 and up ten years later.

Sets of photographs, like book and art collections, should be built around a certain theme or artist. The works of female photographers have aroused much interest of late, and the Smithsonian even developed a traveling exhibit of photographs of women by women. The great naturalist photographer, Edward Steichen, is a perennial favorite among collectors.

In addition to old works, photographs by promising new artists can grow valuable with time. The Seagram company in 1976 launched a dozen photographers on picture-taking trips focused on old county courthouses. The resulting collection was of significant historical and architectural interest, not to mention what it did for Seagram's public image.

Owning a collection of a contemporary photographer's work, like owning a pleasing print, can be satisfying even if it does not reap great rewards.

CARS

Cars as investments do not refer to new Cadillacs or those old jalopies the Shriners drive in Christmas parades. Classic cars in mint condition, such as 1920s Packards, are appreciating as much as 10 and 15 percent a year. One lucky car enthusiast bought a Dusenberg in 1955 for $1,560 and spent $35,000 on its restoration. It was appraised at $175,000 in 1977.

A seasoned collector warns that it is "risky" to enter the antique car market with only a profit motive. Fakes are rampant, and investing is tricky. Amateurs are advised to spend $550–$3,500 on their first unrestored cars and to pour over the enthusiast's "bible," *Hemmings Motor News,* to develop a feel for the market.

There are three kinds of collector's cars:

- *Classic Cars.* These are chosen by the Classic Car Club of America and include Cadillacs, Lincolns, Mercedes, Packards, and Rolls of the 1920s and 1930s. They were the luxury cars of their times and are still costly, upwards from $20,000.
- *Milestone Models.* The Milestone Car Society designates these models. Included are 1946–48 Lincoln Continentals, the 1948 Chrysler Town and Country convertible, and the 1953–54 Studebaker Starliners. Priced at $5,000–$20,000, these automobiles may appreciate 50 percent in the next five years.
- *Antique Cars.* The older cars are cheaper, but they are not the best investments. A 1915 Model T Ford can be had for the price of a new Mustang. A better investment would be the luxury cars of the same period, like the 1910 brass-fitted Stutz Bearcat raceabout. It sells at the $40,000–plus level and shows good appreciation promise.

Note that these prices do not include the cost of restoration, which can be sizable. Unless you are intimate with the workings of old machinery and have good facilities—a garage and old tools—you must hire a professional to do the job for you. His or her services can cost from $10,000 to $40,000.

ANTIQUES

Just about everything left worth collecting could fall into this category. The continuing popularity of antiques is evidenced by the presence of an "antique" store in every sleepy town in the country. An area of specialization is an absolute must here, and the narrower the better.

Buying antiques is similar to buying art in many ways. You look for rare, beautiful, or unusual pieces which show promise for appreciation. As with art, you are vulnerable to hoax. When buying an expensive piece, a provenance is a good safeguard against fraud.

Areas of interest to collectors include:

- *Americana.* An ever-popular field for collectors. Weathervanes, wooden decoys, cooking utensils (especially pre–Civil War utensils), handmade furniture, and all sorts of other goodies fall into this category. Pennsylvania toleware and colors on black lacquer are bringing prices in the $500 range. Old whale oil lamps with blown glass globes go at $75. For the collector on a shoestring, Americana is a good area to investigate.
- *Clocks.* Just about every home has an old clock, probably inoperative, sitting on a shelf or standing in a corner. To settlers and uprooted families, the clock was cherished as a symbol of stability. Old clocks are sure to be found at country auctions and every hole-in-the-wall antique store.
- *Furniture.* A useful investment. You will probably want to pick a certain period as your area of specialization. Right now the cheapest antiques are the heavy

Victorian pieces, which go in and out of vogue regularly. Right now they are out, but the cycle is sure to change in their favor.

The *Chippendale* name is highly respected in furniture. American and European Chippendales are different, but both are based on the principles of Thomas Chippendale, set into a book in 1754. A Philadelphia Chippendale highboy sold for $60,000 in 1969, but cheaper pieces crop up. An American mahogany Chippendale chest of drawers was listed at $600 in 1977.

- *Glass*. The most popular area for collectors. Handblown glass is the oldest, as the machine pressing process wasn't perfected until 1825. "Sandwich glass," manufactured by the American Sandwich Glass Company, is highly prized.

  The colored Favrile glass of Louis Comfort Tiffany, produced in the late 1800s, is much sought after. Tiffany also made the famous stained glass windows and lamps.

  The more recent Depression glass, dirt cheap when it was first sold, command high prices today. Iridescent carnival glass is also popular.
- *Jewelry*. Art Nouveau is enjoying a vogue today. First created in the 1890s, it used few jewels but imaginative naturalistic settings. The names Fouquet and Lalique are the ones to watch for on this jewelry.
- *Silver*. The earliest pieces with the Paul Revere mark are of course very valuable, but certain other American and English marks rival these. (See information at chapter's end.)
- *Textiles*. Quilts, the most genuine of the American folk arts, are very popular as decorator items today. The oldest ones were done in geometric designs, usually diamonds and squares. Appliqué came later. Tapestries and samplers are other collectible pieces often with patriotic themes on the oldest ones.

  Country auctions are a good source for old quilts. They represent a small investment—about $100.
- *Antiques of the future*. An enterprising man has set up a mail-order antique service which publishes a catalog of "21st century antiques." Included are art deco figurines of the 1920s and 1930s which were commonly found in homes. One porcelain piece by Rosenthal of Selb, Bavaria, brings $300 today.

Margaret Brunner, author of *Collecting Anything—For Fun and Profit,* advises novices to buy anything of "voting age" if they really like it. Brunner lists treadle sewing machines, first issues of magazines, kitchen utensils, bottles and decorative hair combs as possibilities. Coca-cola memorabilia is a big item also. A tray featuring Johnny Weissmuller and Maureen O'Sullivan is worth $100.

Political buttons are another sleeper to be found in most households. Because buttons are too expensive to be made in large numbers like they once were, certain specimens may bring $300 in 30 years.

Don't tease kid brothers and sisters about their baseball card collections anymore. Those little cardboard pictures may be priceless in time. A 1910 card of Honus Wagner brought $1,500 in 1974 because the athlete was chewing tobacco in the picture. Wagner ordered it off the market because he didn't want his younger fans to know he chewed.

Navaho rugs are becoming scarce because few Indian women take up the ancient craft of making them. Those rugs with the mark of a well known artist, such as Daisy Togelchee or Julia Jumbo, are the most expensive. These rugs cost well over the starting figure ($600). However, they are appreciating at the rate of 20 percent a year and are a beautiful addition to any home.

PROBLEMS WITH COLLECTIBLES

Insurance

Once you have some rare piece in your possession, it is imperative that you buy proper insurance. Artwork and antiques should be appraised every few years, and if their value exceeds $1,000, a certificate should be procured from the appraiser for insurance purposes. The names of good appraisers may be obtained from the Appraisers Association of America. All-risk insurance generally runs about $5 per $1,000 of possessions.

Both appraised and unappraised objects should be photographed as they appear in your home. Store these pictures with a list of the dates of purchase, prices paid for them, and current appraisals in your safe or a bank strongbox.

Selling out

The liquidation problem with collectibles can be managed but not easily or cheaply. One way is to have dealers sell your goods on consignment. They will not pay you for them until they have a buyer, but they will charge a smaller commission for their services.

Auctions are another way. Fifteen percent is the commission usually taken by auctioneers. Again, a novice should not enter this area without good advice and guidance.

SUMMARY

This chapter was devoted to some of the more common commodity type investments. Commodity futures are interesting, complex, and exciting. Thus, a rather detailed discussion was given to them. Gold and silver are perennial favorites, but costs of buying, selling, and storage can be high. Both are popular as a hedge against inflation. Both gold and silver can be purchased either as bullion or coins.

Rare coins, diamonds, works of art, and rare books are all popular investments which have been appreciating rapidly in price. The would-be investor should do some homework on what to look for, how long to hold it, and how to buy or sell before investing. Photographs, classic cars, and antiques are among the many types of investments which can be enjoyed by the owner while they appreciate in value.

Popular types of antiques include a variety of Americana, furniture, glass, jewelry, silver pieces, and quilts.

Newer items becoming popular with collectors and appreciating rapidly include political buttons, baseball cards, and Navaho rugs.

KEY WORDS

Appraiser
Bullion
Chicago Board of Trade
Chippendale
Classic car
Commodities future
Hedge
Milestone model
Numismatist
Premium
Provenance
Refiner
Silver futures
Spot price

FOR MORE INFORMATION

Commodities:

Chicago Board of Trade. *Commodity Trading Manual.*

The Dow Jones Commodities Handbook. Princeton, N.J.: Dow Jones Books (published annually).

Money. New York: Time Inc. (monthly).

Changing Times. Washington, D.C.: The Kiplinger Magazine (monthly).

The Wall Street Journal.

Coins:

Bowers, Q. David. *High Profits from Rare Coin Investment.* Los Angeles: Bowers and Ruddy Galleries, Inc.

Yeoman, R. S. *A Guidebook of United States Coins.* Book lists retail prices of coins.

Art:

Rush, Richard. *Art as an Investment.* Englewood Cliffs, N.J.: Prentice-Hall, Inc.

Loria, J. H. *Collecting Original Art.* New York: Harper Press.

Wraight, Robert. *The Art Game.* New York: Simon & Schuster, Inc.

International Art Market. A monthly survey of art and antique prices. Write to: Interart, 115 Central Park West, New York, N.Y.

Books:

Carter, John. *ABC for Book Collectors.* New York: Alfred A. Knopf, Inc.

Dunbar, Maurice. *Fundamentals of Book Collecting.* Hermes Pub. Aimed at collecting to profit.

Photographs:

Welling, William. *Collector's Guide to 19th Century Photographs.* Collier Pub. Co.

Cars:

Hemmings Motor News. 75¢ per copy, $5.75 a year. Box 380. Bennington, Vt. 05201.

Antiques:

Brunner, Margaret. *Collecting Anything—For Fun and Profit.*

Hammond, Dorothy. *Pictorial Price Guide to American Antiques.* New York: E. P. Dutton. Illustrations of over 5,000 pieces, most of 19th and 20th century, and recent prices.

Appraisers Association of America. 663 Fifth Ave., New York, N.Y.

Twenty-first Century Antiques. c/o Peter Rakelbusch. Hadley, Mass. Second Collection catalog. $2.50.

Marks of American Silversmiths. c/o Robert Alan Green. 8 Shawnee Trail, Harrison, N.Y. 10528. $25.00

Political buttons and memorabilia:

American Political Items Collectors. c/o Donald B. Coney. 66 Golf St., Newington, Conn. 06111. $10 membership fee includes the association's quarterly, *The Keynoter.*

PROBLEMS

1. Why do individuals purchase futures contracts?
2. What is a hedge? Who uses them?
3. What is an intramarket spread order?
4. Why does the value of gold climb with inflation?
5. What are the advantages of good bullion over rare gold coins?
6. What are two universal pieces of advice when making alternative investments like the ones in this chapter?
7. Why is it necessary to get a provenance when buying an expensive piece of art or an antique?
8. What are two ways to prepare your valuable objects for insurance purposes?
9. What are some liquidation problems on the book, antique, and art markets?
10. Find out where you can buy gold bullion locally and see in what amounts the dealer sells it.

PART IV

This section consists of one lengthy chapter on taxes, most of which is devoted to the federal income tax. Other taxes, including the variety of state taxes and a brief discussion of property taxes, conclude the chapter.

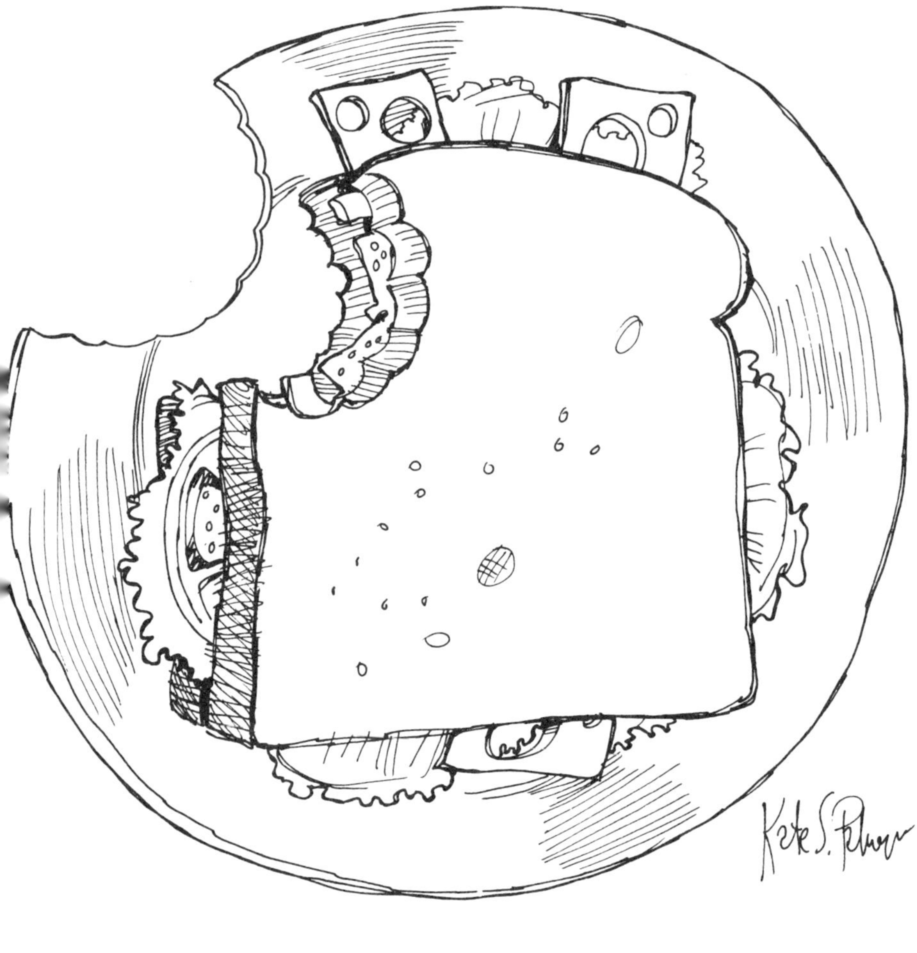

THE GOVERNMENT AND YOUR LIFESTYLE

Chapter 19

Federal and state taxes

The reward of energy, enterprise, and thrift—is taxes.
William Feather

INTRODUCTION

Taxes are the prices paid for the services of government. Government is not cheap. If the "average" American family of four, income $15,000, house worth $25,000, car worth $3,000, were to total their major taxes the list would look like this:

Federal	Income tax	$1,204
	FICA (Social Security)	$ 720
State*	Income tax	$ 0 to $ 690
	Sales tax	$ 0 to $ 272
Property tax	(Approximate)	$ 280 to $1,400
Total taxes $2,404 to $4,486		
Percent of income 16.03 to 29.9		

* Seven states have no general income tax, five have no sales tax.

In addition to the major taxes, there are federal and state excise taxes on tobacco, alcohol, and gasoline; occasional local income and sales taxes; license fees; tariffs; and other minor taxes.

The amount you pay is largely unrelated to your use of government services. The amount paid is a function of your family composition, business and occupation, expenditure patterns, income level and sources, property owned, and creativity in legal tax avoidance. Congress has made some attempt to give equal treatment to people in equal economic situations instead of merely equal treatment to people of equal income. Much of the complexity of the federal individual income tax code derives from attempts to define exactly what are equal economic situations for different households.

This chapter will examine:

- The general process of determining tax due.
- What forms are required.
- What is considered income.
- What are adjustments to income.
- Who counts as an exemption.
- Itemized deductions versus zero bracket amount (standard deduction).
- Keeping records.
- Special problems: capital gains and losses, income averaging, estimated tax.
- Where to go for help.
- Tax planning.
- Being audited.

While the primary focus is on the federal income tax, the last section of the chapter takes a brief look at the other taxes paid—state income and sales taxes, gasoline taxes, and property taxes.

HOW MUCH TAX DO YOU OWE?

Underlying the complex personal tax return, Form 1040, is a simple equation:

Income
Less adjustments and exclusions
Equals adjusted gross income
Less exemptions and deductions (in excess of zero bracket amount)
Equals taxable income (also called tax table income).

Tax table income determines tax due:

Tax due
Less withholding
Less credits
Equals refund or balance due.

It is easy to lose track of this simple sequence of relationships of income → tax table income → tax due → refund or balance due among the numerous individual pieces of information required to fill out the two sides of Form 1040 (the most basic form), Schedule A itemized deductions (the next most basic form), and Schedule TC (tax computation). Nor is the procedure purely straightforward or without discretionary decisions. It is true that two families of the same gross income, derived from wages and salaries only, with the same clearly established number of exemptions and not itemizing deductions, will usually come up with the same tax bill. But once the family embarks in the thicket of allowable exclusions, adjustments, itemized deductions, and nonwage sources of income, there are differences in interpretation leading to vastly different estimates of tax liability on the same set of facts. Even the Internal Revenue Service (IRS) tax advisors have been known to come up with different results from the same set of tax information.

Once you have crossed the mountains and forded the rivers of Form 1040 to arrive at taxable income, the determination of tax due is fairly easy. Ninety percent of taxpayers can—most must—use a tax table. *Tax schedules* X, Y, and Z (amounts of tax due for various incomes and filing statuses) are provided for incomes over $20,000. A small minority may combine the tax schedule with Schedule G (income averaging) to determine their tax liability. *Averaging* is a special procedure for families with highly volatile incomes, designed to keep them in a tax bracket which reflects their average income rather than their peak income. (Averaging is discussed later in the chapter under the heading of *special problems*.)

A tax table or tax schedule is needed because the federal income tax, like many state income taxes, is *progressive*—which means higher rates for higher incomes. In other words, the percentage of your income paid in tax is lower for lower incomes and higher for higher incomes. There are two features that make the federal income tax progressive. One is the combination of personal exemptions and the *zero bracket amount* (formerly standard deduction). This alone would make the federal income tax moderately progressive. The other is the rate structure itself.

The *personal exemption* is $1,000 per dependent including yourself and your spouse if you file jointly, with an extra exemption if over 65 or blind. In addition, a zero bracket amount of $2,300 for singles and $3,400 for a couple or family is exempt from taxation. This means that a single person with an income of up to $2,950 or a family of four with an income of up to $6,400 pays no federal income tax at all.

Suppose that the federal income tax were a flat 10 percent of taxable income (total income less exemptions and deductions). Then the *effective rate* (tax as a percent of total income) for a family of four not itemizing deductions would be as indicated in Table 19–1. The progressiveness results from the fact that the exemptions and deductions become smaller and smaller percentages of a rising gross income. Turned around, this means that taxable income becomes a larger and larger percentage of gross income.

The rate schedule reinforces the progressiveness. Rates range from 14 percent of the first $2,100 in excess of the zero bracket amount on joint returns ($1,000 for singles) to 70 percent of income in excess of $215,400 ($108,700 for singles). However, there is a ceiling of 50 percent on earned

Table 19–1
Hypothetical taxes for a family of four, no itemized deductions and $1,000 personal exemption, flat 10 percent rate

Gross income	*Taxable income**	*Tax*	*Tax as percent of gross*
$ 5000	$ 0	$ 0	0
10,000	2,600	260	2.6
15,000	7,600	760	5.1
20,000	12,600	1260	6.3

* Zero bracket amount has been subtracted.

income such as wages and salaries. Even the 70 percent maximum rate on unearned income does *not* mean that a person with a taxable income of $215,400 (joint return) pays 70 percent of his or her income or $140,000 in taxes.[1] The person pays 70 percent only on those dollars in excess of $215,400. Like everyone else, he or she pays

14% of the first $2,100
15% of the next $2,100, etc.

For example, a gross income of $100,000 (joint) would, after exemptions and itemized deduction of 23 percent of income, be in the 54 percent bracket. That is, 54 percent is the rate paid on the last dollar of income. But the actual tax due of $26,698 is only 26.7 percent of gross income and 37 percent of taxable income.

WHAT FORMS WILL YOU REQUIRE?

If you have income only from wages and salaries, no other tax complications, and do not choose to itemize your deductions, you can complete your tax return using only Form 1040 (or Form 1040A). Once you start itemizing and/or earning more than $400 a year in interest and dividends, you will add the one page Schedules A and B form (A for itemized deductions, B for iterest and dividends) and Schedule TC for tax computations. Among the other commonly used forms are:

Schedule D— for capital gains.

Schedule G—for income averaging.

Form 2106—for employee business expenses.

Form 3903—for moving expenses.

Form 2441—for child care expenses.

[1] Unearned income consists of interest, dividends, rents, royalties, and other property income.

Once you have filed your first return, the IRS will mail you a packet of Form 1040 and Schedules A, B, and TC (two of each) in future years, along with instructions and a mail-order blank for additional forms and schedules and various information booklets. Additional forms are also available at local Internal Revenue Service offices, banks, and other locations.

"—and I used the simplified form."

Reprinted by permission The Wall Street Journal

WHAT IS INCOME?

This question can be harder to answer than it appears. Wages, salaries, interest, tips, dividends, rent payments to you, alimony, and many other items are considered *income* for tax purposes. But insurance benefits, gifts, child support, scholarships, inheritances, and many other items which represent a real cash inflow that buys groceries and pays bills are not counted as income for tax purposes. The instructions accompanying Form 1040 and any good tax guide can help resolve most areas of doubt. There is a logic of sorts to the definition of income. Child support, for example, is not taxed because it is paid out of income which has already been taxed to the paying ex-spouse. But alimony is deductible to the payers, so it has not yet been taxed, and is therefore taxed to recipients. Social Security benefits, not taxed, are paid out of trust funds built up with Social Security taxes, and those taxes are not deductible. So the money you paid into the system was taxed, and therefore the money you take out is not taxed. It would seem unfair to tax it again when you get it back, although in fact most Social Security recipients receive far more dollars in benefits than they paid into the system in taxes. Dividends, likewise, are taxable to the corporation that pays them, so the first $100 in dividends is excluded from taxable income in partial correction for double taxation.

Table 19–2
Examples of taxable and nontaxable income*

Some kinds to report	*Some kinds to ignore*
Wages and salaries	Veterans' benefits
Dividends	Insurance dividends
Interest on savings	Life insurance death benefits
Interest on tax refunds	Interest on state and local bonds
Interest on bonds (including savings bonds)	Social Security benefits
Profits from business, partnership, etc.	Workers' compensation
Pension, annuities, endowments	Gifts and inheritances
Profits from sale of capital assets	Scholarships and fellowships
Rents	Most group fringe benefits
Alimony	Rental value of parsonage or rent allowance to ministers
Trust income	Child support
Jury fees	
Illegal income	
Fees, commissions, tips, bonuses	

* For more detail, consult IRS publication 525 *Taxable and Nontaxable Income.*

Logic, however, is no sure guide for what is taxable income and what is not. A listing of the most common categories of taxable and nontaxable income is given in Table 19–2.

ADJUSTMENTS

Adjustments consist of corrections to taxable income for special expenses, capital gains and losses, and a few other items. It is important to distinguish between adjustments and itemized deductions because there are items which are subtracted before arriving at adjusted gross income and which can be subtracted regardless of whether you itemize or take the standard deduction. Also, by reducing your adjusted gross income, you increase your potential medical expense deduction if you do itemize deductions. Medical expenses are deductible only to the extent that they exceed 3 percent of adjusted gross income.

Adjustments are listed on the front of From 1040. They include capital gains and losses, contributions to self-employed retirement plans or Individual Retirement Accounts (see Chapter 20), sick pay, moving expenses, employee business expenses for travel and entertainment, alimony, and forfeited interest from premature withdrawal from a savings account.

Most but not all of these require separate forms to explain or calculate the amount which is then listed on Form 1040. Disability income (sick pay) is to be explained on Form 2440; moving expenses (for travel, house-hunting, transporting household goods, and so forth) on Form 3903; capital losses are documented on Schedule D and Forms 4797 and 4798; and employee business expenses on Form 2106. Each of these is subject to strict rules, eligibility requirements, and record-keeping regulations. Moving expenses, for example, are only deductible if your old home is at least 35 miles farther from your new job location than your new home is and if you work at the new location at least 39 of the following 52 weeks. At present, there is a ceiling of $3,000 on the amount of deductible moving expenses. Any reimbursement from your employer is subtracted from that amount.

Gross income plus and/or minus adjustments determines *adjusted gross income.*

EXEMPTIONS

An *exemption* is a set amount ($1,000 at present) per person or dependent to be subtracted from adjusted gross income as your progress toward taxable income. In effect, exemptions allow a minimal amount of income to escape tax, makes the rate structure more progressive, as previously noted. Exemptions also adjust the tax bill for family size, old age, and blindness. You and your spouse are each entitled to one exemption for yourselves and an extra exemption if you are over 65 and/or blind. Thus, a blind couple over 65 would have 6 exemptions.

Each child under 19 (22 if a full-time student who gets at least half his or her support from you) is another exemption. Divorced partents will have to resolve who is entitled to the exemption each year based on relative support contributions (including housing, clothing, schooling, food, and so forth). Aged parents, stepchildren, brothers, sisters and even some nonrelatives can qualify as dependents if they meet the 50 percent support test. The IRS lists five criteria for exemptions: income, support, did not file a joint return with someone else, citizenship, and relationship. These are explained in Table 19–3.

TABLE 19–3
Criteria for exemptions for dependents

Income	Under $1,000 *or* your child (natural, adopted, step, or foster) who is either under 19 or a full-time student.
Support	Received at least half of support from you (food, shelter, clothing, medical care, education).
Did not file a joint return with someone else	
Citizenship	U.S., Canadian, Mexican, Panamanian/Canal Zone *or* alien child adopted by and living with U.S. citizen.
Relationship	Blood relatives, steprelations of most kinds, *or* persons who lived with you the entire year.

Most difficulties in determining who is an allowable exemption revolve around college students, children of separated or divorced parents, and aged relatives supported by several families. In the last case, a joint support agreement can be reached by the contributing relatives to assign the exemption to one taxpayer.

Exemptions are checked on the front of Form 1040. Those exemptions which require elaboration must be explained on the back of that form. The total (exemptions ×$1,000) is subtracted on Form TC, if you need to use that form. Otherwise, exemptions are built into the tax tables.

DEDUCTIONS

Most *deductions* are expenditures that the government either wishes to encourage (for example, contributions) or regards as special hardships (for example, medical expenses in excess of 3 percent of adjusted gross income).

"You certainly make a lot of contributions."

Reprinted by permission The Wall Street Journal

Partly for historical/political reasons and partly because of large differences in the level of state and local taxes in different parts of the country, state and local taxes (income, sales, property) are deductible. But *no* federal taxes (excise, Social Security, telephone, gasoline, and so forth) are deductible on the federal income tax, although many can be deducted on state income tax returns. Most states with income taxes reciprocate with at least partial deductions for federal taxes on state income tax forms.

Interest on most kinds of loans is deductible, a curious carryover from British income tax. In England, if you own a house, you are treated as a "business" renting the house to yourself. The estimated value of the rental income you are "earning" by renting the house to yourself is therefore taxable income. But you are allowed to subtract the costs of earning that income—repairs, depreciation, property tax, and interest. In the United States, the same is true if you own property which you rent to others. But if you rent to yourself, you subtract only part of the cost—property taxes and interest on the mortgage—and are not taxed on the implicit rental income. This is the source of the tax incentives to home ownership noted in Chapter 6. Interest on other loans is also deductible on the same logic. The effect of this deduction has been to encourage consumers to borrow by reducing their after-tax interest cost, much to the delight of the homebuilding, automobile, and banking industries.

Another major category of deductible expenditures is charitable contributions. Be sure that the charity is, in fact, certified as deductible before claiming a deduction. Contributions for which you have a cancelled check or other receipt can be entered in total; gifts in cash must be itemized by recipient. Because of this requirement and also for your own record-keeping

Table 19–4
Commonly deducted items, Schedule A

Medical	Professional services of doctors and dentists (except cosmetic plastic surgery, nursing for healthy persons). Medical equipment and supplies. Hospital services. Laboratory tests. Premiums for medical insurance. Medicines and drugs. Braille books, seeing eye dogs.
Contributions	To: Government units or agencies. Religious, scientific, charitable and educational groups. Veteran's organizations. Fraternal groups (for charitable purposes). (Note: organizations which lobby are generally not deductible.) Of: Cash. Checks. Property. Life insurance. Purchase of benefit ticket in excess of market price. Unreimbursed expenses of volunteer works (excludes time and babysitter).
Interest	Mortgages. Personal loans. Bank loans. Margin accounts. Installment purchases. Revolving charge accounts. Bank credit cards. Insurance loans. Points on mortgages. (Note: interest on funds borrowed to buy tax-exempt securities is not deductible.)
Taxes	Gasoline (state and local). Income (state, local, foreign). Real and personal property. School tax. Sales and use. Most other taxes are *not* deductible.
Miscellaneous	Job costs (unreimbursed). Association and union dues. Uniforms and tools. Job search costs. Investment expenses. Some educational costs. Tax preparation costs. Political contributions.

convenience, it is a good practice to make most contributions by check. Contributions in kind (things other than money) may also be deducted—used clothing, furniture, stocks, works of art, and so forth—but you will need a written statement of the fair market value to include with your tax return. Driving for charitable causes is also deductible at seven cents a mile. Again, you need to keep adequate records of dates, purpose, and distance. There is a ceiling on the amount of contributions you can deduct in any one year of 50 percent of adjusted gross income (less for in-kind contributions).

In addition to medical expenses, taxes, interest, and contributions, there are two other categories you may require—casualty and theft losses in excess of insurance reimbursement, and a catchall category of miscellaneous deductions. Major items here are educational expenses and employee business expenses other than travel and entertainment (tools, association membership, uniforms, and other costs of earning an income). Child care expenses, formerly in this category, have been converted to a tax credit which will be considered later.

A listing of the most common items deducted in each of the five major categories is given in Table 19–4. Itemized deductions are entered and totaled on Schedule A and on the reverse of Form 1040.

You may choose not to itemize. If your income is low, or your contributions are modest, your health inexpensive to maintain, your outstanding loans few (particularly no mortgage), your itemized deductions may be less than the zero bracket amount. The regular increases in the standard deduction (now zero bracket amount) have steadily reduced the percentage of taxpayers whose itemized deductions exceed that sum. Only about 15 percent of taxpayers now list itemized deductions. One result of this gradual increase in standard deduction, or zero bracket amount, is to reduce the tax incentive to borrow money, contribute to charity, or incur other deductible expenses.

The combined effect of personal exemptions and the zero bracket amount is that a family of two pays no tax on an income less than $5,400; a family of six, no tax on an income up to $9,400, and so forth.

DETERMINING TAX DUE

Having accounted for exemptions and deductions or zero bracket amount, you are now ready to determine your tax due. A tax table will now give you the tax bill if your taxable income is $20,000 or less and you are not able to use income averaging. The tables have separate columns for single, married filing separately, head of household, and married filing jointly, as well as columns for the number of exemptions. If your taxable income is greater than $20,000 or if you are income averaging, you will have to compute your own tax from the *tax rate schedules*. The tables, Schedule TC and the rate schedule are included with your package of forms and information from the IRS.

Your tax bill depends not only on your income, adjustments, exemptions, and deductions, but also on one other important factor; your *filing status*. In order of favored treatment, you can be:

Married, filing jointly.

Unmarried head of household (widowed, separated, divorced, and so forth with a least one dependent living with you).

Single.

Married filing separately.

The rates range from 14 percent to 70 percent of taxable income in all cases but the size of the *brackets* (range of dollars subject to a given rate) is much larger for married filing jointly than for singles. For example, on a joint return, the rate is 14 percent of the first $2,100, 16 percent of the next $2,100, and so forth; for singles it is 14 percent of the first $1,100, 16 percent of the next $1,100. Heads of households pay rates which are in between. Some examples of the amounts paid on different levels of income by filing status are given in Table 19–5, based on 1977 tax schedules.

Table 19–5
Tax due by filing status
(no itemized deductions)

Income of $10,000 after adjustments:	
Couple, two children	$ 450
Couple, no children	765
Head of household, one dependent	985
Single	1,227
Married filing separately	1,514
Income of $15,000 after adjustments:	
Couple, two children	$1,375
Couple, no children	1,701
Head of household, one dependent	2,091
Single	2,457
Married filing separately	3,038
Income of $20,000 after adjustments:	
Couple, two children	$2,524
Couple no children	2,899
Head of household, one dependent	3,445
Single	3,999
Married, filing separately	4,978

Finally, tax due must be weighed against *tax credits* to determine the net amount owed to you (refund) or by you (balance due). These include:

1. *Withholding*. This should cover most of your tax bill. If not, you should ask your employer to increase the amount he or she withholds for income tax from your paycheck in the future.

2. *Overpayment of Social Security taxes.* This only occurs if your income exceeds the current Social Security ceiling of $22,900 (1979) *and* was paid by more than one employer.
3. *Child care.* This is a credit of 20 percent of expenditures for the care of children while both parents work. There is no longer an income ceiling for individuals who use the deduction, but there are dollar limitations and other regulations on the deduction itself.
4. *Credit for political contributions.* Half the amount, up to $50 ($100 on a joint return).
5. *Earned income credit.* Only on incomes under $10,000, all from wages and salaries, households must contain one dependent other than spouse.
6. *Retirement income credit.* For incomes from taxable pensions and other non–Social Security sources.

Credits are used in place of deductions for some items because a credit treats all taxpayers equally and can be used whether or not the taxpayer itemized. An itemized deduction for child care expenses, as was the case prior to 1976, would only benefit taxpayers who itemized, and the size of the benefit would vary with the tax bracket. A $100 child care deduction would save $39 to someone in the 39 percent bracket, and only $19 to someone in the 19 percent bracket. Those who did not itemize would save nothing. The change to 20 percent tax credit meant that a $100 child care expense would save $20 in taxes to all three of these taxpayers.

Most of these credits are entered on the back of Form 1040 and subtracted from tax due. The difference between tax due and credits brings you to the bottom line. You are ready to write your check or send for a refund.

Before examining some special problems one might encounter in filling out these forms, there is a universal problem for taxpayers which needs to be considered—finding your own tax information to fill out the form and meeting the IRS record-keeping requirements.

TAX RECORD KEEPING

When you sit down each spring to file your income tax, you will need a set of forms, a calculator, a good tax guide, your W–2 forms, budget, check registers for the entire previous year, loan statements from all loans on which payments were made during the last year, and a statement or account of income not reported on the W–2 (for example, interest, dividends). Income is not difficult to determine if it is all from wages, salaries, interest, and dividends. If you regularly receive royalties, rental income, tips, business income, or other special kinds of income, record should have been made of this in your financial accounts. Interest and dividend payers usually supply statements of amounts and dates of payments to you which should be kept with other tax records. If you acquire assets with capital gain or loss potential, you need to record the date and price of purchase, transactions cost, holding and other expenses, and sales date and price. This applies to stocks, bonds, land, real estate, stamps, coins, antiques, and any other asset with significant capital gain potential.

Exemptions may require support records—especially in cases of divorce or separation, college students, and aged relatives. A diary form with dates, amounts, and purposes of expenditure may be called for in case of audit.

Adjustments, exclusions, and itemized deductions generate the most record-keeping problems. Taxes and interest are usually not difficult. Sales tax can be determined from tables supplied with your return (plus tax on purchases of new boats, cars, and a few other big ticket items), income tax from the state tax return you are required to file, and property tax from the assessor's notice. Interest information is usually supplied by the lender or can be apportioned on installment loans by the Rule of 78s (see Chapter 5), with information drawn from the original lender's statement. Some charge account lenders (including bank cards) list interest each month, so a set of statements will supply the interest total. Cancelled checks, receipts, and your personal written record for charitable contributions and medical expenses should be kept in separate files. The check register and old budgets will be your most valuable sources, but receipts and written records may prove necessary in case of audit. Specific, dated, itemized records are especially needed for employee business expenses for travel and entertainment and also casualty and theft losses. In the record-keeping system described in Chapter 3, a tax record section of your file with headings of income, employee business expenses, medical expenses, taxes, interest paid, contributions, miscellaneous deductions, credits against tax due, and other would be essential if you expect to itemize or have adjustments to income.

In order to be certain that your record keeping will satisfy the tax auditor, you can request a free pamphlet on the subject (552, *Record-Keeping Requirements*) from the Internal Revenue Service.

SPECIAL PROBLEMS

The federal income tax is enormously complex. Almost every taxpayer's situation is unique, and volumes of law, decisions, and interpretations have been written about the Internal Revenue Code. Courses and even degrees in federal income tax are offered, and tax and accounting specialists devote their careers to it. A single chapter in a personal finance text can only scratch the surface. We will therefore examine only those special problems which most people can expect to encounter, not every year, but at some point during their lifetime. These are:

1. The treatment of capital gains and losses.
2. Income averaging.
3. Declaration of estimated tax.

A *capital gain* is taxable when realized, that is, when an asset is sold at a profit. The capital gain is the difference between the selling price and the cost of the asset including original price, sales commission and other transactions costs, and any improvements. Capital gains are most often realized on land, houses, and stock market investments, and other securities. If you sell the house you live in and buy another, more expensive one, you can defer the tax on the capital gain on your house until you sell the new one, and still defer if you again invest in another, more expensive one within a year. If you hold an asset less than 12 months, the capital gain is considered short term and is fully taxable as ordinary income. If you hold it for more than 12 months, it is considered long term and receives more favorable treatment. Only 40 percent of the capital gain is reported as income on Form 1040. This means that the effective tax rate on capital gains ranges from 5.6 percent to 28 percent.

Short-term *capital losses* on the sale or exchange of assets up to $3,000 can be deducted from income, with losses in excess of $3,000 carried forward to be subtracted in future years. One half of long-term capital losses can be deducted in the income section of Form 1040 and Form 4797, up to $1,000 in deductions ($2,000 in losses). If you have both gains and losses, you can offset the losses against gains in the same time category (long- or short-term) and still deduct excess losses. Losses in excess of both gains and the $1,000 limitation can only be carried forward.

Income averaging is an alternative method of computing your tax if your income rises sharply. If you had an adjusted gross income of $20,000 a year for five years, your tax each year (joint return, no itemized deductions) would be $2,899, or a total of $14,495 over the five years. But if your adjusted gross incomes were $5,000, $15,000, $20,000, $25,000 and $35,000, your taxes without averaging would be zero, $1,701, $2,899, $4,288 and $7,807—a total of $19,695 and an average of $3,939 although total income over the five-year span was the same. In other words, people with highly variable income are penalized relative to people with more stable incomes under a progressive tax system. Income averaging was designed to correct this by taxing some of the extra income in the higher income years as if part of it had been earned in the earlier, lower income, lower tax bracket years. If you have just graduated from school, you are not eligible to average unless you and/or your spouse provided more than half your own support during the four preceding years. There are a few exceptions to this rule, but generally averaging is *not* designed for the 22 year old fresh out of college.

Averaging is particularly useful if your spouse goes back to work after a long period out of the labor market, if your salary is substantially upgraded, or if you are in a business or profession (such as acting, professional sports, salesman on commission) where your income varies greatly from year to year.

To determine whether you can average, add up your taxable (not adjusted gross) income plus the zero bracket amount of $3,400 for the four preceding tax years, and multiply the total by 30 percent. Subtract this from current year's tax table income. If the difference is $3,000 or more, you can average. A simple averaging example is worked out in Table 19–6. Averaging requires Schedule G plus the tax rate schedule to compute your tax liability.

Table 19–6
Income averaging*

1. 1978 tax table income: $34,000
2. a. Taxable income, 1977. . . . . $20,000 + $3,400 (zero bracket amount)
   b. Taxable income,1976 . . . . 18,000 + 3,400
   c. Taxable income, 1975. . . . . 16,000 + 3,400
   d. Taxable income, 1974. . . . . 14,000 + 3,400
3. Sum of 2a–d = $81,600
4. 30% of line 3 = $24,480
5. Averageable income (line 1–line 4) = $9,520.
   Since this exceeds $3,000, you may average.
6. Line 4 plus 20% of averageable income (line 5):
   $24,480 + $1,952 = $26,384.
7. Tax on line 6 from tax schedule $6,179.
8. Tax on line 4 $5,555.
9. Difference (line 6 – line 4) $624.
10. Line 9 times 4 $2,496.
11. Line 7 plus line 10 = your tax = $8,051.
    The tax on $34,000 without averaging would have been $9,128.
    Averaging reduced taxes by $977.

* This simplified example assumes a joint return and no capital gains. When years after 1978 are included in item 2, use tax table income and do not add in zero bracket amount.

A *declaration of estimated tax* is supposed to be filed each quarter if your gross income is $20,000 or more (10,000 if married and your spouse also has wages) *or* if you have earnings of $500 or more not subject to withholding. If you meet either of these tests, you should file form 1040–ES each quarter, estimating your income, tax due, and withholding for the year and paying 25 percent more of the estimated additional tax due each time. Two working spouses can quickly find themselves meeting the income test for estimated tax. If you fail to file a declaration when you meet either test, or if you do file but seriously underestimate your tax, a penalty of 7 percent will be applied. The penalty only applies to the underpayment and/or underwithholding to the extent that the total received by the IRS is less than 80 percent of the tax due. For example, if your tax liability is $8,000 and withholding plus amounts sent in with the declaration of estimated tax only amount to $6,000, the penalty is 7 percent of $400 or $28. The $400 is the shortfall under 80 percent of tax liability. If you had paid the IRS $6,400 or more, there would be no penalty.

TAX PLANNING

Complying with the Internal Revenue Code is a time-consuming chore. Federal income taxes require record keeping and an inordinate amount of time early in the calendar year to fill out the necessary forms to file a return. An alert taxpayer must keep abreast of tax developments as they occur to

Table 19–7
Tax calendar

Quarter	*File*	*Records*	*Planning*
First	4th declaration of estimated tax. (January 15) Prepare 1040 for filing (file now if a refund is due).	File and store last year's records. Set up and begin this year's records.	Estimate this year's income, tax due, and withholding. Increase withholding if necessary.
Second	1st declaration of estimated tax. (April 15) File 1040 by April 15.	Make sure records are current.	Review investments for tax status. Revise current year estimates.
Third	2d declaration of estimated tax (July 15)	From records, determine whether you expect to itemize or take the standard deduction this year.	Readjust withholding if necessary. Review medical bills to consider shifting expenditures. Watch Congress; this is usually a major quarter for tax legislation.
Fourth	3d declaration of estimated tax. (October 15)	Make sure records are complete and in order. Do a December 1 tax estimate for year end.	Decide which expenditures to make and which to postpone to January based on whether you will itemize or take standard deduction. Make last minute capital gains and losses transactions. Pay any bills for itemized deductions Make final withholding adjustment if needed to avoid underpayment penalty

Note: If medical expenses are shiftable (much dental work, minor elective surgery, routine physicals) between one year and another, try to bunch them in a single year to bring medical expenses over the 3 percent minimum. (Only medical expenses in excess of 3 percent of adjusted gross income can be deducted on Schedule A.) This can also be helpful if you alternate standard and itemized deductions. Payment can often be postponed until January 1 if you want to add to an anticipated "big deduction" year.

adjust expenditures and investments so as to legally minimize his tax liability. Although the spring quarter is the peak period of activity, taxes require year-round attention. A suggested tax calendar for the average middle-income taxpayer is given in Table 19–7.

Where to go for help

Many taxpayers have thrown up their hands in despair and gone to a tax preparation service to get their forms in order and ready to file. This is one of several sources of help with your federal income tax. Another is the free information and assistance supplied by IRS pamphlets and IRS district offices around the country. These two sources can answer most of your specific questions. A step up in cost from the free help at the IRS is one of the popular tax annuals in the $3 to $4 price range sold on newsstands and in stores. The best known are those by J. K. Lasser, Sylvia Porter, and the government's own "Your Federal Income Tax." Armed with one of these and considerable patience, taxpayers can prepare their own returns with a reasonable degree of accuracy. A trip to a tax preparation service, at a cost from $5 up, can often come up with overlooked deductions and suggestions on improving your records in the future. Make sure the service has adequately trained personnel.

Complex problems, especially those resulting from investment income, rental income, and ownership of small businesses, may call for an accountant and/or a tax lawyer.

Being audited

Audit is a word which strikes fear in the heart of even the most conscientious and meticulous taxpayer. Audits can result from questionable items on your tax return, or can be the result of a random selection of your return by the computer for closer scrutiny. Generally you will be asked to provide verification (cancelled checks, receipts) for a few questionable items. Errors in arithmetic or other minor matters generally do not require audit. These will be corrected in processing and the Internal Revenue Service will notify you about the change in your refund or balance due. About 2 percent of all returns are audited each year, with some variations from year to year and region to region. Your chances of being audited go up sharply as your income rises, if you claim unusual exemptions or if your itemized deductions are substantially above what is typical for your income and family size.

The federal audit cycle (other than for fraud) is three years. Since time must be allowed for carrying out the audit, most audits are initiated within 26 months of the April 15 filing date. If you have not heard about your 1977 return (filed April 15, 1978) by June 15, 1980, you may assume that the chances of being audited on that return are quite small.

Most audits are settled in the district office, but an established appeals procedure is provided which may carry you all the way to tax court. The IRS wins over half of its cases. Taxpayers win about 10 percent, and an intermediate decision is arrived at in about one third of the cases.

OTHER TAXES

The federal government's main source of general revenue is the individual income tax, followed by the corporate income tax. Social Security tax leads the list of special taxes which are not included in general revenue. (For a further discussion of Social Security, see Chapter 11.)

Less obvious are the *federal excise taxes* on alcohol, tobacco, gasoline, telephone service, and a few other items, and tariffs on selected imports. Inheritance and gift taxes are discussed in Chapter 20.

Forty-three states and the District of Columbia impose income taxes. Connecticut, New Hampshire, and Tennessee tax only certain kinds of investment income (interest, dividends, and/or capital gains). Wyoming, Nevada, South Dakota, and Florida have no income tax whatever as of 1977. Alaska, Nebraska, and Vermont calculate tax as a percentage of federal income tax. Several states—Illinois, Indiana, Michigan, and Pennsylvania—charge a single flat rate ranging from 2 percent to 4.6 percent of income (net, adjusted gross, or taxable) with varying credits. The other 36 states and the District of Columbia have federal-type progressive taxes, generally at much lower rates. These have personal exemptions varying from $600 to $4,500, heavily concentrated in the $800 to $1,200 range. Ten states use tax credits in place of a personal exemption.

Thirty-six states offer some form of standard deduction. These taxes are deductible on Schedule A of federal income tax. Fourteen states reciprocate with at least partial deductibility of federal income taxes on state income tax returns. In the progressive tax states, the range of rates is from Alabama's 1.5 to 5 percent to Delaware's 1.6 to 19.8 percent. Top rates generally fall in the 6 to 11 percent range.

Local income taxes are also in use in 21 major cities and a number of smaller ones, depending on what the state permits. Rates for local income taxes range from 1 to 4 percent.

If you have any discretion in residence, state and local income taxes should certainly be considered in choosing where to live. However, they should be considered in conjunction with other state and local taxes and with the level and variety of services provided by state and local government.

Sales taxes are collected in 45 states and the District of Columbia at rates from 3 to 7½ percent. Items covered make a big difference in the burden. Some states exempt food, prescriptions, children's clothing, and other items to reduce the burden of the tax on low-income taxpayers. Colorado gives a credit for part of sales tax paid on their state income tax. If you make out-of-state purchases, you are supposed to pay your state (and local, if any) sales tax on the purchase, not that of the state of sale. Many smaller mail-order houses only collect taxes from in-state residents, but the larger ones collect and remit to each state. The same rules are intended to apply to in-person purchases but are widely ignored except for large purchases, for example automobiles which must be registered in the home state. Efforts are also made to collect the tax on large volume purchases of items subject to widely varying state excise taxes, notably alcohol and tobacco. Other state excises are levied on specific items such as soft drinks and disposable bottles. The most universal state excise tax is on gasoline, at 6 to 11 cents a gallon.

Property taxes are generally local and show little uniformity even within states. These taxes are assessed on real estate (land, buildings, other improvements) and personal property (usually cars and boats, but some states include jewelry, stocks, bonds, savings accounts, and other assets). The property is assessed or evaluated by a tax assessor.

It is customary to list items on the tax rolls at some percentage of the fair market value. This percentage rate is called the *assessment rate*. In some areas there is a single assessment rate for all classes of property; in other states the assessment rate may be different for different classes—one rate for residential, another for cars, still another for inventories, or farmland, or commercial and industrial property.

The tax rate is known as the *mil rate* from the old English coin (mil) which equals one tenth of a cent. Thus, a mil rate of 50 mils per dollar of assessed valuation would be $^{50}/_{10}$ or 5 cents—5 percent in more usual language.

The *effective tax rate* (tax as a percentage of fair market value) is the product of the assessment rate and the mil rate. A 20 percent assessment and a 40 mil rate would be $0.20 \times 0.04 = 0.008$ or 0.8 percent. A 50 percent assessment at 30 mils would come to 1.5 percent of the fair market value. A $40,000 home would pay $320 in the first case and $900 in the second case. Effective rates presently range from less than 1 percent to more than 5 percent. As a general rule, property taxes are lowest in the southeast, highest in the northeast.

SUMMARY

This chapter has followed basic tax preparation through the process from income through exclusions and adjustments, exemptions, and deductions to tax table income. Tax table income determines tax due. Tax due less withholding and credits equals refund or balance due.

The complexity of the tax is a result of its progressivity combined with the attempt to extract equal tax from people in equal economic situations rather than people of equal dollar income. Progressivity means higher rates on additional dollars of income.

The basic forms required are Form 1040 plus Schedules A and B if you itemize and/or have interest and dividend income. Other forms may be required to explain adjustments and credits and to deal with additional income sources or other special circumstances.

Income includes most sources of money inflow but there is a long list of exclusions and kinds of income subject to special treatment, given in Table 19–2.

Adjustments are corrections for capital gains and losses, contributions to self-employed retirement plans, employee business expenses, alimony, moving expenses, and sick pay. Exemptions of $1,000 per person are allowed for each person you support, subject to tests of relationship, residence, and the dependent's own income. Deductions are allowed for medical expenses, state and local taxes, interest paid, contributions, casualty and theft losses, and a few other items. A zero bracket amount of $3,400 ($2,300 for singles) is taken by all taxpayers. Those who have deductions in excess of $3,400 itemize on Schedule A.

Tax due is determined from a tax table or tax schedule or by averaging. Tax due on a certain income depends on your filing status—single, head of household, married filing separately, or married filing jointly. Subtracted from tax due are credits for withholding, overpayment of social security taxes, child care expenses, political contributions, earned income credit, and a variable per-exemption credit.

Record keeping is a demanding chore which requires year-long attention if you are to have the information you require at filing time.

Special problems include the treatment of capital gains and losses on the sale or exchange of assets; income averaging for people whose income rises suddenly or sharply; and the obligation of many taxpayers to file a declaration of estimated tax in order to avoid an underpayment penalty.

Tax planning can save not only headaches at filing time but also dollars in taxes. A suggested quarterly calendar of tax planning and filing is given in Table 19–7.

Sources of help in preparing tax returns include the IRS, commercial tax guides, tax preparation services, and accountants and tax attorneys.

State taxes consist mainly of income, sales, excise, and gasoline taxes. Local government relies mainly on taxes on real estate and personal property. The effective tax rate on property is the product of the assessment rate and the mil rate.

KEY WORDS

Adjusted gross income
Adjustments
Assessment rate
Audit
Income
Income averaging
Mil rate
Progressive tax

Capital gains
Capital losses
Declaration of estimated tax
Deductions
Effective tax rate
Exemptions
Federal excise taxes
Filing status
Property tax
Tax bracket (marginal tax rate)
Tax calendar
Tax credits
Tax schedules
Tax table income
Withholding
Zero bracket amount

PROBLEMS

1. The Jones household has computed their taxable income for 1979 at $24,000. Looking through their past tax records, they find that their taxable income (after adding in a $3,400 zero bracket amount for 1974–76) was as follows: 1974–$7,900; 1975—8,500; 1976—$10,000; 1977—$15,000; and 1978—$16,000. Can they income average? Using the rate schedule below, compute their tax bill with and without averaging. How much do they save?

Taxable income for married couple filing jointly (1977 rates)

Taxable income	Tax		
$ 0–$ 1,000	14%		
1,001– 2,000	$ 140 plus 15%	of excess over $	1,000
2,001– 3,000	290 plus 16	of excess over	2,000
3,001– 4,000	450 plus 17	of excess over	3,000
4,001– 8,000	620 plus 19	of excess over	4,000
8,001– 12,000	1,380 plus 22	of excess over	8,000
12,001– 16,000	2,260 plus 25	of excess over	12,000
16,001– 20,000	3,260 plus 28	of excess over	16,000
20,001– 24,000	4,380 plus 32	of excess over	20,000

2. Referring back to the income statement for George and Henrietta in Chapter 3, answer the following questions:

a. What is their income for tax purposes?

b. What is their filing status?

c. List their itemized deductions. (Estimate those you cannot determine precisely.)

3. It is October 1 and George and Henrietta are thinking about next year's tax return. What should they have done already in preparation? What should they be doing right now?

PART V

The final two chapters consider retirement income and activities, planning your funeral, drawing up a will, and arranging your affairs so as to minimize taxes and make settling your accounts as simple as possible for your survivors.

LATER IN YOUR LIFESTYLE

Chapter 20

Looking ahead to retirement

Will you still need me,
Will you still feed me,
When I'm sixty-four?
Lennon—McCartney

INTRODUCTION

Even the Beatles, riding high on the wave of the 60s youth culture, sang about retirement. The picture they painted in "When I'm Sixty-Four" was a charming one: enjoying grandchildren, puttering around in the garden, and spending summers on the English coat.

Many people think of retirement in just those terms—a far distant period of leisure and relaxation with the bill footed by Social Security.

"By itself, Social Security is not sufficient to support any retired American in dignity and comfort," warns consumer economist Sylvia Porter.[1] The Social Security system was not intended to provide full retirement benefits, so to avoid spending the last years of your life in the poverty that claims one fourth of all Americans over 65, it is necessary to plan.[2]

Obviously, a person just entering the job market has more important things on their mind—like finding employment in the first place—but they are sure to know someone who has retirement looking over a shoulder. Chances are your parents will be retiring within the next 20 years.

This chapter contains answers to several major retirement questions:

- At what age do I wish to retire, and how many years after that should I expect to live?

[1] Sylvia Porter, *Money Book,* vol. 2 (Garden City, N.Y.: Doubleday & Company, Inc., 1975), p. 883.

[2] Ibid., p. 873.

- What kind of lifestyle do I wish to have after I retire?
- What are some sources of retirement income?
- What do I do with my time?

WHEN DO I WISH TO RETIRE?

Early retirement is becoming more and more popular. In 1900, three out of every four men over 65 worked. Today, only one in four works. Mandatory retirement from many jobs and reduction or loss of Social Security benefits for working after 65 enforce the early retirement trend.

The expected life span for people who live to age 65 is 15 years. Another ten years are added once a person lives to be 75. Fifteen to 25 years is a long time to depend on savings and Social Security.

WHAT KIND OF LIFESTYLE WILL I HAVE?

In 1973, the U.S. Bureau of Labor Statistics set the cost of a moderate annual standard of living for a retired couple at $4,500 to $6,400. Obviously, this allowed little money for travel or entertainment. But the problem reflected in the budget is even more serious than that. The actual per capita income for people over 65 is only $4,100. Obviously, many retired persons must have some savings upon which to draw.

A person facing retirement would expect certain expenses to increase. For example, doctor bills and other medical expenses will likely increase. On the other hand, income taxes and insurance premiums will likely diminish. Dependent children will probably have completed their educations and be financially independent. Furthermore, a person retiring is likely to own his or her home—three fourths of all older people do.

However, many people find the large homes they maintained while raising children unnecessary after retirement. The sale of a home can guarantee cash and free the owners to move into cheaper, more convenient housing.

Not everyone stops working after retirement. Second careers often lead to greater success than primary ones. For example, a retired telephone lineman took up painting, selling his first work at age 66. Today his paintings command up to $10,000 each and are included in the collections of 15 major American museums.

Similar success stories dispel the myth that most retirees ride off into the Florida sunset in their econoline vans, although retirement to Florida is the dream of many. Retirement is a time to do all the things one didn't have the time to do while working, and the working years are when one must provide for retirement.

WHAT ARE SOME RETIREMENT INCOME SOURCES?

Whatever your lifestyle choice, you will have to balance its cost with your retirement income. There are two general sources of retirement income to consider.

1. Social Security. In chapter 11, you learned how to calculate your benefits from Social Security upon retirement. To receive your benefits, you must apply to your local Social Security Office about three months before you stop working.

2. Pensions. Many organizations and major companies have pension plans. If you belong to a union, part of your dues goes into such a program. The Civil Service Commission, Veterans Administration (VA), armed forces, and the railroad industry have pension plans. Pensions received from the VA and railroad are tax free, as is Social Security.

Within this broad category of pensions, there are five types of retirement under Civil Service. First there is optional retirement for employees who have achieved one of the following combinations of age and length of service:

Age 55, with 30 years of service.

Age 60, with 20 years of service.

Age 62, with 5 years of service.

Second, there is disability retirement. After five years of civilian service and the Civil Service Commissions' approval, a disabled employee can qualify.

The discontinued-service retirement plan is for employees 50 or over who have been laid off after 20 or more years of service. The National Association of Retired Federal Employees (NARFE) calls it separation "because of reduction-in-force." People who have completed 25 years of service, regardless of age, also fit into this category, but benefits are reduced for each year under age 55.

Deferred retirement benefits are payable at age 62 to anyone with five years of Civil Service behind them.

Civil Service benefits are determined on the basis of average salary over the three highest paying years.

The following example was developed by NARFE for a 62-year-old worker with 30 years of service who retires. His "high three" average is $12,000:

1½% × $12,000 × first 5 years of service	$ 900
1¾% × $12,000 × next 5 years of service	1,050
2% × $12,000 × last 20 years of service	4,800
Total annuity	$6,750

Annuities can also be transferred to widows or widowers. Fifty-five percent of the annuity, plus any cost-of-living increases (there are two a year), is paid to a survivor. To provide for this, the employee's annuity is reduced during his or her retired lifetime. For example, the $6,750 annuity derived above would be reduced to $6,345.

For people employed in the private sector, there are two types of company pension plans. The first type involves company management. Of course, if the company goes bankrupt, the pension plan faces difficulty. However, those having claims to the retirement income are partially compensated by the government's *Pension Benefit Guaranty Corporation,* which is supported by compulsory funds from companies with retirement plans. Furthermore, the strict regulation of retirement funds minimizes the likelihood of bankruptcy losses.

The second type of pension is a funded plan maintained by either a trustee or an insurance company. It is far more common than the first type plan, although it can be susceptible to mismanagement, as has sometimes been the case with union pension plans.

Usually an employee must work for his or her company a certain number of years to be eligible for retirement benefits. Questions about this coming from a young person being interviewed for a company job can be a real turn-off to an employer, however. For this reason, it may be helpful to know that the government regulates private pension plans to safeguard employee interests. The government sets a maximum time period for an employee's acceptance into a retirement plan.

Private pension plans are partly tax free. In some cases, the money contributed to the pension fund by the worker is exempted from taxation, while the company-contributed portion is taxed.

Pensions are payable in monthly installments, but employees can sometimes have part of their pensions deferred to be paid to their survivors in a lump sum on their deaths. Payment choices depend on the options offered by the company.

Railroad Retirement Benefits are available after ten years of railroad service. An individual is eligible for monthly cash benefits, which are tax free, as well as survivor's benefits.

Disabled veterans may receive monthly pensions, and those over 65 with limited incomes also may receive pensions. Admission to hospitals and other health care facilities is guaranteed, as well as burial in national cemetaries, when space is available. The VA will also pay up to $400 in burial and cemetery plot costs.

3. Keough plans. Created by Congress in 1962, *Keough plans* make it possible for self-employed individuals to provide their own tax-sheltered retirement funds. Professional people, doctors, lawyers, and actors, for example, farmers, and people who own their own businesses are eligible for Keough Plans.

The fund money can be invested in several federally approved ways, including bank, trust company-administered trusts, annuities and endowment life insurance, mutual funds, and mixtures of several investments. Banks can pay up to 7¾ percent interest on Keough plans.

Although income drawn from this personal pension plan is taxable after retirement, contributions of up to 15 percent of earned income or $7,500 a year, whichever is less, can be listed as a tax deduction before retirement. Also, interest earned on the fund and capital appreciation are tax free until benefits are paid.

Payments can be drawn from the Keough Plan fund after age 59½ and must begin to be distributed no later than age 70½.

4. Individual Retirement Accounts (IRAs). Similar to Keough plans, IRAs are aimed at persons employed by companies with no retirement plans. Up to $1,500 a year can be contributed to the fund. Joint IRA accounts can also be established, provided one of the account creators does not work. For example, a man contributes up to $1,750 a year into a joint account for himself and his housewife spouse.

Like the Keough plans, IRAs can't be used before age 59½ and must begin to be distributed by age 70½.

Another advantage of the IRA over a conventional savings account, in addition to the tax shelter, is that a significant sum of retirement benefits from your employer can be transferred tax free into the IRA if done within 60 days of receipt. That way if your company terminates its pension program and distributes earned benefits or stock, they will be tax sheltered. Also, banks can pay up to 7¾ percent interest on IRAs.

5. Other savings accounts and investments. Most people keep savings accounts all their lives. Retirement is a good reason for saving.

6. Supplemental security income (SSI). These payments were established in 1974 and are available to aged, blind, or disabled people, based on their incomes and assets. To qualify, a single person can have cash assets up to $1,500 and a couple may have $2,250. You may own a home and a car as well as other possessions, if they are of moderate value. Your life insurance policy must have a face value below $1,500.

Payments are $146 a month for single people over 65, $219 for couples. Qualification for SSI usually guarantees eligibility for Medicare and food stamps as well.

More information on Supplemental Security Income is available from Social Security Offices.

7. Sale of home. The sale of a home can bring in considerable cash which can be invested to generate an income. The government gives a generous tax break to people over 65 who sell their homes.

If you have owned your home for at least eight years and lived in it the five years before selling it for $35,000 or less, none of the money you receive for the sale is taxable. Part of the revenue derived from more valuable homes is taxable, but there is some tax saving for everyone.

If you decide to keep your home and want to make improvements on it, low-interest loans are available from the Department of Housing and Urban Development (HUD). For small town homes and farms, you might contact the U.S. Department of Agriculture's Farmer's Home Administration.

Property taxes can mount up when you are on a limited budget. Fortunately, many states and localities will reduce these taxes for older home owners living on small incomes. Illinois, for example, bases its property taxes on income, not property value, for those over 65. The city of Philadelphia even gives its older residents 20 percent discounts on gas, water, and sewage bills.

A move to an apartment does not preclude financial aid. The government will pay part of your rent in a decent building under several HUD programs if you qualify for assistance.

8. Other tax breaks. After you turn 65, you can claim an additional $1,000 exemption on your tax returns. Your spouse can also, for a total possible exemption of $4,000 on a joint return. Furthermore, many states give special tax treatment to the income of people over 65.

9. Medicare and health benefits. Spiraling health care costs will be partially offset by Medicare as you grow older, but not completely. Medicare covers less than one half the cost of health care for the ailing elderly. Many of the elderly suffer from degenerative diseases, which require regular medical care. And older Americans account for 20 percent of all dollars spent on nonprescription drugs.

Medicare is a two-part program. Part A, available to anyone who gets Social Security, covers food, drugs, equipment, supplies, and normal services in a semiprivate hospital room for 60 days. There is a $124 deductible fee. After the first 60 days of the hospital stay, you must pay $31 per day of your hospital charges. After the 90th day of hospitalization, you can opt for more Medicare coverage. This comes from your "lifetime reserve days" coverage. There are 60 of these days of partial cost payment, and once used they cannot be replaced.

The services of a nurse, therapist, or health aide in the home can be covered by Medicare in some cases. Doctor bills, private duty nurses, and convenience items (such as televisions) aren't included in Medicare Part A.

Part B of Medicare is optional medical insurance. A $7.70 monthly premium is charged for insurance that pays 80 percent of your bills over $60 for a doctor's diagnostic and surgical procedures, physical therapy, emergency room and outpatient care, and necessary ambulance service.

If you want to join the Medicare program and are not old enough, you can pay a $45 monthly premium and be included.

Retired federal employees can enroll in the Federal Employees Health Benefits Program for health and accident protection. *NARFE* also has a group insurance program for its members.

10. Inflation. And now for the bad news. When the Beatles added "we shall scrimp and save" to their song about retirement, they were not joking. The annual inflation rate can eat up life savings faster than interest can accumulate on it. For example, a 5 percent annual inflation rate would boost the price of a $3,000 item to $7,950 in 20 years.

One bright spot in the inflation cloud is the 1974 amendment to the Social Security Act which provides for a cost-of-living increase in benefits and recent changes indexing the wage base. Benefits rose 70 percent between 1969 and 1974. Even so, there are serious questions regarding the long-run ability of Social Security to keep up with inflation. Someone has to pay for it.

RETIREMENT: THE GOLDEN YEARS

The phrase is hackneyed, but the word "golden" can apply to many things—money, time, opportunities, happiness. Your retirement lifestyle choices are many and varied, especially if you have provided for yourself financially.

Finding a second job

Fully a third of all retirees embark on second careers. Because the job market is restrictive for older people, there are several nonprofit organizations which serve as information clearinghouses on employment. One of these, 40–Plus, consists of people over 40 who help each other find jobs in a cooperative fashion.

A profit-making organization, Mature Temps, Inc., specializes in finding temporary jobs for skilled and unskilled older workers. Mature Temps has offices in 11 states and the District of Columbia.

The U.S. Department of Labor sponsors several employment programs for low-income senior workers which pay at least the minimum wage. Included are the Senior Aides, urban workers 55 or older who are employed in schools, hospitals, and other health-care facilities. The rural counterpart to Senior Aides is called Green Thumb Green Light.

The federal government operates two "employment agencies"—Government Employment Services and Federal Job Information Centers. Although full-time federal employees must retire at 70, plenty of older people are hired after that age on a part-time basis. Listings for these and other agencies are included in the telephone book.

Stereotypes of older workers would have us believe that people over 50 are more accident prone and more susceptible to depression and psychiatric disturbances. Actually, older workers have less absenteeism and fewer on-the-job accidents. They are no more susceptible to mental problems than their younger co-workers.

These stereotypes extend beyond the employer-employee relationship. A poll taken by the National Council on Aging and Louis Harris found that only

"Now that I've retired, I have time for all the things I dreamed of doing, but I forget what they were!"

Reprinted by permission The Wall Street Journal

29 percent of the public age 18 to 64 viewed older people as "very bright and alert" and only 35 percent saw them as "very good at getting things done."

Those retirees who move into successful second careers dispel such myths. A case in point is a 69-year-old woman who developed a method of canning boiled shelled peanuts, which had been commercially impractical. Her method was sold to a Florida food company which now profitably markets her peanuts in the Southeast.

A return to the books

Besides establishing second careers, many retirees return to school. One out of every eight adults in the United States is participating in some form of adult education and over 500 colleges now offer special programs for older people. An 82-year-old student enrolled in one such program was named to *Who's Who in American Universities and Colleges,* having served with distinction on his university's debate team.

Many large colleges and universities have continuing education programs. Night courses are inexpensive and cover an amazing range of subjects, from bread baking and macrame to conversational German and beginning guitar. In addition, many community technical centers offer regular college curriculums as well as vocational programs.

Giving your time away

Extra hours can be devoted to volunteer and semivolunteer work in your community and abroad. As exemplified by President Jimmy Carter's indomitable mother, Miss Lillian, older people may find a place in the Peace Corps. The Corps' oldest couple, an 81-year-old man and his 77-year-old wife, adopted a wildly different lifestyle when they began teaching school in a remote village in Samoa.

A similar program in the United States is VISTA, Volunteers in Service to America, which dispatches its members to impoverished urban and rural communities throughout the country.

On the local home front there is the Foster Grandparent Program, part of the government's *ACTION* agency. Foster Grandparents work 20 hours a week for a minimum wage, visiting lonely children in hospitals.

The Retired Senior Volunteer Program (RSVP), another ACTION project, is for people 60 and over. They do a variety of community service work under ACTION guidelines.

Retired businessmen can put their experience to work as consultants to small businesses as members of SCORE, the Service Corps of Retired Executives. SCORE is run by the government's Small Business Administration.

Hospitals, schools, and churches often appreciate volunteer help. Many communities have a Local Volunteer Coordination Service to match people to needs. If your community has no such service, contact the government's National Center for Voluntary Action which dispatches information about local programs and needs on request.

Hobbies and leisure activities

An occasional game of tennis after work can become a full-time passion after retirement, as a group of men known as the "Super-Seniors" illustrates.

These worthy athletes, ranging in age from 55 to 81, play each other in tennis tournaments in America and Britain. A quartet of octogenarians played in a sideline tournament at Wimbledon in 1977.

Tennis equipment costs money and so does a lot of equipment needed to keep your hobby going. Be sure this expense is in your retirement plan, if your hobby is one which does not pay for iteslf.

Many people look forward to travel, and if your health and bank account are in good shape, travel can be a rewarding experience. Cost discounts for older people are offered by several large hotel chains, including Holiday Inn, Days Inn, Quality Inns and Howard Johnson's. Days Inn also runs a "September Days Club" for senior travelers. The club publishes a magazine, organizes trips to Jamaica, Hawaii, and other resort areas, and gives discounts on renting cars.

The National Retired Teachers Association and American Association of Retired Persons have a travel service which tailors tours to the older traveler's "taste and pace."

Walt Disney World offers cut-rate prices for senior tourists during two weeks in May and two in November every year.

Those who seek entertainment within their own cities can take advantage of reduced fares offered by mass transit systems. New York, Milwaukee, and Philadelphia are among the cities offering discounts. Senior citizens are also eligible for cheaper theater tickets in some places, such as the New York State Theater in New York City. The same discount is offered to students!

Getting away from it all

If your home town pales next to a spot you have visited, you might consider pulling up roots. Be aware that the most expensive areas in the United States to live are in the Northeast. The cheapest are in the South, including Texas. However, New York offers more benefits for the elderly than most states. New York, Michigan, Minnesota, Wisconsin, and Florida lead the nation in legislation benefiting senior citizens.

Before leaving for good, however, it is advisable to live in your would-be adopted home for a few months. A good testing period should cover a season change. That Florida sunshine may prove too much after just one summer.

SUMMARY

Retirement can be an exciting new phase of life if some careful planning of income and lifestyle is done ahead of time.

Retirement income sources include Social Security, pension plans (including Civil Service), annuities, railroad and VA benefits, Keough plans, Individual Retirement accounts, and supplemental security income. Other sources to tap are the sale of a house (a move to smaller quarters may be advisable in any case) and Medicare benefits. Inflation can be expected to continue to eat away at the income and assets of retired people.

Activities which can be part of a changed lifestyle might include a second job, returning to school, volunteer work, hobbies and leisure activities, and travel.

Advance planning is the key to a comfortable and rewarding last stage of life.

KEY WORDS

ACTION
Annuity
Individual Retirement Account (IRA)
Keough plan
NARFE
Pension Benefit Guaranty Corporation
Supplemental security income (SSI)

FOR MORE INFORMATION

Education:

"Alternatives for Later Life and Learning." Available for $1.50 from American Association of State Colleges and Universities, One Dupont Circle, Suite 700, Washington, D.C. 20036.

Housing:

"A Guide for Selection of Retirement Housing." Available for $1.95 from National Council on Aging, 1828 L St., Washington, D.C. 20036.

Booklets on housing from Publication Service Center, Dept. of Housing and Urban Development, Room B258, 451 Seventh St. SW, Washington, D.C. 20410.

Jobs:

Mature Temps, 1114 Avenue of the Americas, 26th Floor, New York, N.Y. 10036.

AARP–NRTA Senior Community Service Employment Program, P.O. Box 19269, Washington, D.C. 20036.

Law:

"You, the Law and Retirement." From Administration on Aging, Dept. of Health, Education, and Welfare, Washington, D.C. 20201.

Medicare:

Information on this and many other subjects from your nearest Social Security office.

Pensions:

"Know Your Pension Plan." From U.S. Dept. of Labor, Washington, D.C.

Taxes:

"Tax Facts 1977" from AARP–NRTA, P.O. Box 2400, Long Beach, Calif. 90801.

Tax-Aide Program, 1909 K St., Washington, D.C. 20049 for specific questions and advice.

Volunteers:

SCORE, Small Business Administration, 1441 L St. NW, Washington, D.C. 20416.

ACTION, 806 Connecticut Ave. NW, Washington, D.C. 20525.

National Center for Voluntary Action, 1785 Massachusetts Ave. NW, Washington, D.C. 20036.

American Association of Retired Persons (AARP) with the National Retired Teachers Association (NRTA) publishes several free Better Retirement guides on health, housing, money, jobs, taxes and overall planning. Write to them at 215 Long Beach Blvd., Long Beach, Calif. 90801.

PROBLEMS

1. A civil service worker, age 65, is retiring after 20 years of government employment. The highest salaried years of her career average out to $10,000. What will her pension be?
2. What are the advantages and disadvantages of advance funded pension plans?
3. Who is eligible to set up a Keough Plan? An IRA?
4. What are some tax breaks aimed at people over 65?
5. Find out what programs are available for older people at your college or university.

Chapter 21

Wills, estates, and funerals

And my advice to those who die,
Beware the pennies on your eyes,
'Cause I'm the taxman.
Lennon–McCartney

INTRODUCTION

People today hold a rather different view of death than the one held by the ancients. Our "civilized" burial customs are much more elaborate than the simple placing of coins on the dead man's eyes to pay for his ferry ride over the river Styx to the underworld. Funerals today are more formal, perhaps more civilized, and, without a doubt, more expensive.

The cost of living isn't the only thing on the rise today. The cost of dying is skyrocketing, and the snarl of taxes and estate distribution to be unraveled after a death are enough to keep the greediest heirs from murdering rich Uncle Albert. As in retirement, the key to a prosperous future for your heirs is good planning.

In this process, called estate planning, you figure how to avoid as many taxes after your death as possible without seriously restricting your lifestyle. Samuel Johnson, an 18th century writer and critic, said that it is better to live rich than to die rich. While this is worth keeping in mind, many widows have come to rude awakenings about the state of their "prosperous" husbands' financial affairs.

To complete the life cycle planning process, this chapter contains discussion on the following topics:

- Records for estate planning.
- The will—its form and purpose.
- The role of executor.

- Estate taxes and reducing them.
- Funerals and their costs.

KEEPING GOOD RECORDS

First of all, it is important that you keep good records of your financial dealings. Besides financial records, your files should include your Social Security number, military discharge (if you have one), a marriage certificate, your spouse's birth certificate, the birth certificates of dependent children, and your latest W–2 form. These are all necessary to apply for survivor's benefits from Social Security.

If you are a railroad employee, be aware that your surviving spouse must file within a year of his or her 60th birthday to get benefits. Include in your files the address of your nearest Railroad Board Office, where application must be made.

Your family must know where your records are kept in order to gain access to them. Be sure your family understands your investment and money management methods. Otherwise your careful work will go to waste once you are no longer there.

WRITING A WILL

Next, you should write a will. Wills are not just for old people on their last legs. Anyone of legal age—18 or 21, depending on the state—can write a will. Although there is no law requiring an attorney to draw up your will, it would be rather like taking out your own tonsils to do it yourself.

The will has five sections:

1. **Opening recitation.** This states your name and address, including county and state, and revokes any previous wills you might have made. It tells how you want your debts and funeral expenses to be settled, usually as soon after death as possible.

2. **Disposition clause.** This tells who gets what parts of your estate—probably the most important part of your will. Correctly identify each person and/or organization (your beneficiaries) by giving full name and address. Also state whether inheritance taxes are to be paid out of your estate or by the recipient.

3. **Administration clause.** Here you explain how your will's instructions are to be carried out. You name the manager of your estate, called an executor (or executrix, if the person is a woman), in this clause.

4. **Testimonium clause.** Your signature of approval goes here. You again declare the document to be your "last will and testament."

5. **Attestation clause.** The circumstances under which the will was signed are described here and the witnesses (two or three, depending on the

state) place their signatures at the bottom of the document, along with their addresses.

You may make a *mutual* or *joint will* with your wife or husband. The joint will is a single document. Persons choosing to have mutual wills put the same instructions in two separate documents.

YOUR EXECUTOR AND HIS DUTIES

One of the most crucial decisions made in your will is the person you choose to be your *executor.* Often a close family friend or relative is selected. However, the executor should also be a shrewd business manager and knowledgeable in tax law. Even the most well-meaning executor can ruin an estate if incompetent.

The executor's duties are:

1. Submit a copy of your will to a *probate* court to ascertain its validity. Your heirs and beneficiaries cannot receive any part of your estate until your will has been probated or "proven."
2. Provide *beneficiaries* and the U.S. Treasury Department with valuations for each of the estate's assets. These include property, real estate, stocks, bonds, and life insurance. An appraiser may have to be hired to do this. The executor, since the 1976 revision of the tax code, is personally liable for incorrect information about your estate.
3. Take title to all your property.
4. Collect all money owed to you and pay all creditors who file claims against your estate within the time period the executor sets.
5. File estate tax returns with the federal and state tax authorities if your estate is worth over $60,000
6. Manage the estate's business concerns and pay out bequests to beneficiaries. The executor must get a receipt from each beneficiary and file the receipt in court.
7. Finally, submit to the court an account upon the completion of all the will's instructions.

The executor receives a salary, sometimes fixed by state law. This, along with attorney, probate, and appraisal fees, adds to the cost of dying.

OTHER TYPES OF WILLS

Besides the formal will drafted by an attorney, there are other legal wills. Oral or *nuncupative wills* are made by people in contemplation of eminent death, but may still be binding. Large estates cannot be disposed of in this fashion. A witness to an oral will must put it in writing and submit it to a court within a specified time limit, often as short as 30 days.

A handwritten or *holographic will* is also legal, but may be invalidated if it is undated, includes any typewritten data, or fails to mention a surviving spouse or children.

WHAT ABOUT AFTER I WRITE MY WILL?

You should remember to revise your will from time to time as your estate and beneficiaries change. You need not completely rewrite the will. A legal instrument called a *codicil* serves as an amendment to the original document.

Also, any time you move, even within the same state, you must rewrite or revise your will.

A copy of your will should be kept with your funeral instructions and other personal records. Be sure your family knows where to find a copy of it. The plight of the estate left by reclusive multimillionaire Howard Hughes clearly shows what can happen when a will is not kept in an appropriate place.

THE PERILS OF DYING INTESTATE

If you should die *intestate* (without writing a will) or fail to name an executor, the court will name an *administrator* to perform the duties involved. Having an unknown individual take control of your business affairs is just one of the pitfalls of dying intestate. You also forfeit some opportunities to reduce your estate taxes, and the people who benefit the most from your leavings may be the ones you would have cut off without a cent.

In some states, a widow receives one third of her intestate husband's estate, and her children share the rest. But what if you and your wife are separated or if you have some other preferences for distributing your assets? Writing a will is a very small thing to do for those dearest to you.

HOW MUCH WILL I PAY IN ESTATE TAXES?

As the old saying goes, the only things you can be sure of are death and taxes. And the taxes continue after death. They are called estate taxes, and are applicable to any estate with gross assets over $60,000.

This *gross estate* can include cash, business interests (a law partnership, for example), real estate, stocks and bonds, and taxable gifts made in the three years before your death. Taxable gifts are any in excess of $3,000 per person per year. Your spouse can receive up to $100,000 in gifts per year from you, tax free.

Your gross estate is reduced through various deductions to derive your taxable estate. Depending on the state involved, these deductions may include a marital deduction of $250,000 or half your assets, whichever is greater, as well as funeral expenses, payment of debts, contributions to charities, attorney, appraiser and executor fees, and uninsured losses incurred on your estate after your death.

A *unified tax credit,* part of the revised tax laws of 1976, is subtracted from the gross estate. The credit is applicable only to estates worth more than $40,000. (See Table 21–1.) This unified tax credit replaces a $60,000 personal exemption and a $30,000 lifetime gift exemption formerly allowed. Thus, it is hard to escape taxes by giving your estate away before you die.

Table 21–1
Unified credit against estate tax

a. **General rule.** A credit of $47,000 shall be allowed to the estate of every decedent against the tax imposed by section 2001.

b. **Phase-in of $47,000 credit.**

In the case of decedents dying in:	Subsection (a) shall be applied by substituting for "$47,000" the following amount:
1977	$30,000
1978	34,000
1979	38,000
1980	42,500

c. **Adjustment to credit for certain gifts made before 1977.** The amount of the credit allowable under subsection (a) shall be reduced by an amount equal to 20 percent of the aggregate amount allowed as a specific exemption under section 2521.

Source: *Prentice–Hall Internal Revenue Code,* p. 25,868.

Another tax credit is allowed against state taxes on estates worth over $40,000. The exemption is based on Table 21–2.

Just how high are estate taxes? Table 21–3 shows you. To take one example, an estate valued at $60,000 would have tentative taxes of $13,000—more than 20 percent. However, the tax credit of $34,000 (in 1978), described in Table 21–1, would more than cover the $13,000.

HOW DO I AVOID ESTATE TAXES?

As you can see, estate taxes bite a big chunk out of the money you leave behind. To avoid them, many people set up *living trusts,* funds which are invested to generate income before their creators die.

Trusts. The person creating a trust is called a trustor or grantor. He or she specifies beneficiaries who will get the income from his or her trust. The assets of the trust, or *principal,* go to *remaindermen* upon dissolution of the fund.

A person called a *trustee* manages the trust. A trustee can be a friend, like

Table 21–2
Credit for state death taxes

a. **In general.** The tax imposed by section 2001 shall be credited with the amount of any estate inheritance, legacy, or succession taxes actually paid to any State or the District of Columbia, in respect of any property included in the gross estate (not including any such taxes paid with respect to the estate of a person other than the decedent).

Prior amendment.—Sec. 201(a) was amended by Sec. 102(c)(1) of Public Law 85-866. Sept 2, 1958 (qualified effective date rule in Sec. 102(d) of P.L. 85-866). Sec. 2011(a) as so amended is in P-H Cumulative Changes.

b. **Amount of credit.** The credit allowed by this section shall not exceed the appropriate amount stated in the following table:

If the adjusted taxable estate is:	The maximum tax credit shall be:
Not over $90,000	8/10ths of 1% of the amount by which the adjusted taxable estate exceeds $40,000.
Over $90,000 but not over $140,000	$400 plus 1.6% of the excess over $90,000.
Over $140,000 but not over $240,000	$1,200 plus 2.4% of the excess over $140,000.
Over $240,000 but not over $440,000	$3,600 plus 3.2% of the excess over $240,000.
Over $440,000 but not over $640,000	$10,000 plus 4% of the excess over $440,000.
Over $640,000 but not over $840,000	$18,000 plus 4.8% of the excess over $640,000.
Over $840,000 but not over $1,040,000	$27,600 plus 5.6% of the excess over $840,000.
Over $1,040,000 but not over $1,540,000	$38,800 plus 6.4% of the excess over $1,040,000.
Over $1,540,000 but not over $2,040,000	$70,800 plus 7.2% of the excess over $1,540,000.
Over $2,040,000 but not over $2,540,000	$106,800 plus 8% of the excess over $2,040,000.
Over $2,540,000 but not over $3,040,000	$146,800 plus 8.8% of the excess over $2,540,000.
Over $3,040,000 but not over $3,540,000	$190,800 plus 9.6% of the excess over $3,040,000.
Over $3,540,000 but not over $4,040,000	$238,800 plus 10.4% of the excess over $3,540,000.
Over $4,040,000 but not over $5,040,000	$290,800 plus 11.2% of the excess over $4,040,000.
Over $5,040,000 but not over $6,040,000	$402,800 plus 12% of the excess over $5,040,000.
Over $6,040,000 but not over $7,040,000	$522,800 plus 12.8% of the excess over $6,040,000.
Over $7,040,000 but not over $8,040,000	$650,800 plus 13.6% of the excess over $7,040,000.
Over $8,040,000 but not over $9,040,000	$786,800 plus 14.4% of the excess over $8,040,000.
Over $9,040,000 but not over $10,040,000	$930,800 plus 15.2% of the excess over $9,040,000.
Over $10,040,000	$1,082,800 plus 16% of the excess over $10,040,000.

For purposes of this section, the term "adjusted taxable estate" means the taxable estate reduced by $60,000.

Source: *Prentice–Hall Internal Revenue Code,* p. 25,869.

Table 21–3
Imposition and rate of tax

***a.* Imposition.** A tax is hereby imposed on the transfer of the taxable estate of every decedent who is a citizen or resident of the United States.

***b.* Computation of tax.** The tax imposed by this section shall be the amount equal to the excess (if any) of

1. a tentative tax computed in accordance with the rate schedule set forth in subsection (e) on the sum of
   A. the amount of the taxable estate, and
   B. the amount of the adjusted taxable gifts, over

2. the aggregate amount of tax payable under chapter 12 with respect to gifts made by the decedent after December 31, 1976.

For purposes of paragraph (1)(B), the term "adjusted taxable gifts" means the total amount of the taxable gifts (within the meaning of section 2503) made by the decedent after December 31, 1976, other than gifts which are includible in the gross estate of the decedent.

c. Rate schedule.

If the amount with respect to which the tentative tax to be computed is:	The tentative tax is:
Not over $10,000	18 percent of such amount.
Over $10,000 but not over $20,000	$1,800, plus 20 percent of the excess of such amount over $10,000.
Over $20,000 but not over $40,000	$3,800, plus 22 percent of the excess of such amount over $20,000.
Over $40,000 but not over $60,000	$8,200, plus 24 percent of the excess of such amount over $40,000.
Over $60,000 but not over $80,000	$13,000, plus 26 percent of the excess of such amount over $60,000.
Over $80,000 but not over $100,000	$18,200, plus 28 percent of the excess of such amount over $80,000.
Over $100,000 but not over $150,000	$23,800, plus 30 percent of the excess of such amount over $100,000.
Over $150,000 but not over $250,000	$38,800, plus 32 percent of the excess of such amount over $150,000.
Over $250,000 but not over $500,000	$70,800, plus 34 percent of the excess of such amount over $250,000.
Over $500,000 but not over $750,000	$155,800, plus 37 percent of the excess of such amount over $500,000.
Over $750,000 but not over $1,000,000	$248,300, plus 39 percent of the excess of such amount over $750,000.
Over $1,000,000 but not over $1,250,000	$345,800 plus 41 percent of the excess of such amount over $1,000,000.
Over $1,250,000 but not over $1,500,000	$448,300, plus 43 percent of the excess of such amount over $1,250,000.
Over $1,500,000 but not over $2,000,000	$555,800, plus 45 percent of the excess of such amount over $1,500,000.
Over $2,000,000 but not over $2,500,000	$780,800, plus 49 percent of the excess of such amount over $2,000,000.
Over $2,500,000 but not over $3,000,000	$1,025,800, plus 53 percent of the excess of such amount over $2,500,000.
Over $3,000,000 but not over $3,500,000	$1,290,800, plus 57 percent of the excess of such amount over $3,000,000.
Over $3,500,000 but not over $4,000,000	$1,575,800, plus 61 percent of the excess of such amount over $3,500,000.
Over $4,000,000 but not over $4,500,000	$1,880,800, plus 65 percent over the excess of such amount over $4,000,000.
Over $4,500,000 but not over $5,000,000	$2,205,800, plus 69 percent of the excess of such amount over $4,500,000.
Over $5,000,000	$2,550,800, plus 70 percent of the excess of such amount over $5,000,000

Source: *Prentice–Hall Internal Revenue Code,* p. 25,867-8.

an executor, or a professional employed by a trust company. A trustee's job is to preserve the principal and invest it wisely, so it will yield interest or other income.

The professional trustee may not take a personal interest in your trust, like a family friend would, but he or she could probably manage it more effectively. Should your trustee prove unsatisfactory, he or she can be removed from his or her position in court.

There are three types of living trusts: *revocable, irrevocable,* and *reversionary*.

Revocable. This trust agreement can be cancelled by the trustor at any time. The trust's earnings are passed to the beneficiaries in the form of an annuity. For the person trying to avoid probate, it is important to know that a revocable trust is not included in probate. However, it can easily be converted into a *testamentary,* or willed, trust which would be included in probate.

Irrevocable. Once this type of trust is set up, it can never be cancelled except by agreement of all parties mentioned in the trust—trustor, beneficiaries, and remaindermen. This type of trust also reduces the size of the taxable estate. However, the trustor loses all control of the principal once the trust is established.

Reversionary. A combination of revocable and irrevocable, the reversionary trust cannot be cancelled for a certain time period, say ten years or before the occurrence of an unplanned event, such as a marriage or birth. The trust is being built up for a beneficiary during this time period. After the trust is terminated, the principal will revert to the trustor, so estate taxes are not avoided. The tax advantage of this type trust comes if the trustor is in a higher income tax bracket than the beneficiary. Then the income would be taxed at a lower rate.

You could set up a trust for a grandchild or another person, for a charity, or an organization, such as your college. Before you create a trust for the old alma mater, however, consult your alumni association, which probably has a trust expert on hand who could save you even more money with good advice.

State law sets a time limit on trusts (except charitable ones). The most common period is 21 years and 9 months after the deaths of all people mentioned by name in the trust agreement who were living when it was written. Thus unborn beneficiaries, such as grandchildren, will not have their annuities cut short.

Of course you can set up a trust in your will, but you do not avoid estate taxes that way, as a testamentary trust is included in probate. However, you do keep control over the money intended for the trust during your lifetime.

Gifts. Another way to avoid some taxes on your estate is by making outright gifts before you die. Gifts made within three years of death, however, are taxable under your estate. As mentioned earlier in the chapter, you can give an individual up to $3,000 in gifts per year without paying income tax (or estate tax, if within that three-year limit) and you can give your spouse up to $100,000 in gifts a year. Half of any money you give your spouse over $200,000 is also tax free. Of course all charitable gifts are tax deductible.

You can transfer your life insurance policy to someone else to avoid paying estate taxes on it. For example, you could give it to your wife, which also gives her the power to change beneficiaries and other rights. She would also have to take over the payment of premiums. Before you do this, it would be wise to consult an attorney.

IS THERE A LAWYER IN THE HOUSE?

We talk a lot about attorneys in this chapter. How do you find one? You could go on the recommendations of a friend, or let your fingers do the walking through the Yellow Pages until you find an honest-sounding name.

The American Bar Association has a lawyer referral service which will guarantee you a consultation of a certain time period for a certain fee. (See information section at the end of this chapter.)

Your local library may have a copy of a lawyer directory listing every attorney in the country, where they got their degrees, their areas of specialization, and how long they have been practicing. Ask for the *Martindale-Hubbell Lawyer's Dictionary, Best's Recommended Insurance Attorneys,* and *Sullivan's Probate Directory*.

If you are on a limited budget, you can apply for free help from a chapter of the Legal Aid Society. Usually you must earn less than $100 a week to be eligible. University law schools are another source of inexpensive legal aid, as some operate law clinics. Check with the one nearest you.

THE FINAL EXIT: PLANNING YOUR OWN FUNERAL

It is said that funerals are planned for the living, not the dead. They are a time for mourners to comfort each other. It's called "grief therapy" and morticians make a mint on it—they run a $4 billion industry, annually. The theory is that giving a big funeral is the last thing mourners can do for the deceased. And of course, the person is beyond knowing or caring.

If you want your family to save the money you will them for their own living expenses, you must plan your funeral before your death. The form included in this chapter has a section for listing funeral preferences. You might want to include some of these on your funeral checklist, as well.

- How much to spend on the casket, if you want to be buried. If you would rather be cremated, specify this. Some casket pricing will be necessary on your part, but this will involve a simple phone call to a funeral director—not nearly as morbid a procedure as it sounds.

- Location of your cemetery plot, if you have one. Where you wish to be buried should be indicated if you don't own a plot.
- Type of service to be performed. Include whether you want a church or funeral home chapel service. Use of the chapel would add $200 to $300 to your bill, while a church is free. Also indicate preferences in music to be played, and whether a graveside service should be held.
- Whether you desire participation by your lodge, veteran's group, or other organization.
- The names and addresses of friends and relatives who should be notified of your death.
- The names and addresses of officers of clubs and associations of which you are a member and should be notified.
- Your serial number if you are a war veteran and are eligible for burial benefits.

Your family should know to get six to ten copies of your death certificate to be sent to your life insurance company, banks where you hold a joint checking, or savings account, and others to make claims for benefits.

Because savings and checking accounts in your name cannot be used until probate proceedings on your estate have begun, it is wise to keep some cash on hand for your survivors. However, you should check your state's laws on this. If funds can be set aside, a safety-deposit box at the bank, in your spouse's name, would be a good place.

THE HIGH COST OF DYING

What about the actual cost of funerals? The cheapest kind is cremation, which can cost as little as $100, although state laws requiring burial of ashes or cremation in coffins can send this price up several hundred dollars. Also, not all funeral homes have the facilities to cremate bodies. In that case, the corpse must be shipped to a crematorium, and the shipping costs are added to the bill.

Most funeral homes charge a combined fee for their services and casket. A random sampling of parlors showed the rock-bottom cost to be $750–800. From there, the cost can climb to $2,500 and up. One small town mortuary cited its average fee at $1,800. The Federal Trade Commission estimates the cost of an average "traditional" funeral and burial at $2,000, and cremation at $250 to $350.

Prefinanced funerals are not unusual today. You can join a "memorial society" which arranges simple funeral services for its members, who pay $5 to $20 for a lifetime membership. These societies shop around at various morticians, arranging package deals costing $150 to $350 for burials and about $190 for cremations.

There are 140 such organizations in 137 U.S. cities, and if you move, you can transfer your membership. (See information section at end of this chapter.)

You can also prearrange your funeral with a mortician and pay after your death by placing the necessary funds in a trust.

Burial benefits come from two of the same government agencies which provide pensions, Social Security and the Veterans Administration. A $255 lump sum is paid by Social Security to all those who have worked at least 18 months in the three years before death. Veterans can get up to $400 in burial and cemetery plot costs. If there is no free cemetery space available, a veteran is entitled to $250 for burial costs.

SUMMARY

In preparing for your own inevitable demise, you need to be concerned with the disposition of your assets and your mortal remains. Assets are disposed of by estate planning, which includes keeping records, writing a will, and minimizing estate taxes.

The will provides for disposition of assets and names an estate manager (executor or executrix) to carry out your final wishes. The executor (executrix) will submit your will to probate, have the estate's assets valued, collect money owed your estate, settle debts, pay bequests, and render a final accounting. Wills may be formal, oral (nuncupative), or handwritten (holographic). A codicil can be used to revise a will. If you die intestate (without a will), the state will provide for the disposition of your assets.

Your estate will be subject to federal and state taxes, which may be reduced through trusts and/or gifts before death. A trust is managed by a third party for the benefit of named beneficiary. Gifts within limits can avoid some estate taxes. Legal help is recommended for wills and estate planning.

You would be well advised to specify your funeral preferences in advance to save money and simplify planning for your survivors. Funerals can be prearranged and prefinanced.

KEY WORDS

Administrator
Beneficiary
Codicil
Executor
Gross estate
Holographic will
Intestate
Irrevocable trust
Joint will
Living trust
Mutual will
Nuncupative will
Principal
Probate
Remaindermen
Reversionary trust
Revocable trust
Testamentary trust
Trustee
Unified tax credit

FOR MORE INFORMATION

Lawyers:

"A Shopper's Guide to Lawyers." Herbert S. Denenberg. $1 from Consumer News, Inc., 813 National Press Bldg., Washington, D.C. 20045.

Ask about lawyer referral service in your area by writing to American Bar Association, 1155 E. 60th St., Chicago, Ill. 60637.

Funerals:

A Manual of Death Education and Simple Burial. Ernest Morgan. $1.50 from Celo Press, Burnsville, N.C. 28714.

For address of memorial societies near you, write Rebecca Cohen, Executive Secretary, Continental Association of Funeral and Memorial Services, Suite 1100, 1828 L St. NW, Washington, D.C. 20036.

PROBLEMS

1. Call three lawyers and get estimates on the cost of writing a simple will. Find out how the cost increases with the complexity of the will.
2. What are the advantages of testamentary trusts over living trusts?
3. What are the advantages and disadvantages of naming a close friend to be your executor or executrix?
4. In which section of the will do you name your beneficiaries?
5. What are some of the problems of dying intestate?
6. Get an estimate from three funeral homes on their price ranges for burials, from simple to elaborate, and cremation.

Appendix:

Mathematics of finance

The mathematics of finance for personal use does not require any more background in mathematics than high school algebra plus a working knowledge of a calculator which can perform the basic four functions and powers and roots. A reader who is interested in some of the more sophisticated aspects of the mathematics of finance can find many useful texts. A good place to start might be the Schaum's Outline Series *Theory and Problems of Mathematics of Finance,* by Frank Ayres, Jr. (New York: McGraw–Hill, 1963).

The following topics covered in this book require mathematical techniques beyond elementary arithmetic but well within the limits of the skills mentioned above:

Credit:	The Rule of 78s
	Computing the APR
	Estimating the monthly payment
Investments:	Compound interest
	lump sum
	annual sum
	Present value (discounting)

There are other areas covered in this text which are also mathematically based but which involve a level of complexity beyond the scope of this book. These would include generating an amortization table for loan repayments, determining the allocation of mortgage payments between interest and principal at various points during the life of a mortgage, determining net level premium for life insurance on the basis of a mortality table, and determining annuity schedules. Most of this information is readily available in published tables or from the lender or insurer.

CREDIT

The rule of 78s

The following is a general formula for the procedure described in Chapter 5. The proportion of interest charged to the kth installment of a debt repaid in n equal installments is

$$T \sum_{i=1}^{n+1-k} \qquad (1)$$

where n = total number of payments, k = number of this payment, and T = total interest charge. The accumulated interest charged to payments on a debt through month k is given by

$$\frac{\sum_{i=1}^{k} (n + 1 - i)}{\sum_{i=1}^{n} (i)} \cdot T \qquad (2)$$

For example, a 48-month loan with total interest of \$900 is repaid at the end of 20 months. How much interest does the lender get to keep, and how much does the borrower save by repaying early?

Answer: $n = 48$, $k = 20$, $T = \$900$.

$$\frac{\sum_{i=0}^{k+1} (n + 1 - i)}{\sum_{i=1}^{n} (i)} \cdot T = \frac{48 + 47 + 46 + \cdots + 21 + 20}{48 + 57 + 46 + \cdots + 2 + 1} \cdot \$900$$

$$= \frac{986}{1176} \cdot \$900 = 0.831 \times \$900 = \$747.90.$$

The lender keeps \$747.90 of the interest, and the borrower saves \$152.10 by repaying early.

A shortcut formula for the sum of the digits from n to k is as follows:

$$(n + 1) + n + (n - 1) + (n - 2) + \cdots + (n - k)$$
$$= \frac{n + n - k + 1}{2}(k + 1) = \frac{(2n - k + 1)}{2}(k + 1) \qquad (3)$$

When the series goes all the way to $n = k$, this simplifies to

$$\frac{n + 1}{2} \cdot n \qquad (4)$$

Computing the APR

The formula used in Chapter 5 for the APR was similar to the one below:

$$i = \frac{2TN}{p(NY + 1)} \tag{5}$$

where T = interest charge in dollars, N = number of payments per year, P = principal (amount borrowed), and Y = number of years. This formula (5) assumes that each payment is divided equally between interest and principal. If instead we attribute interest and principal to each payment on the present value principle, we find a more accurate formula is

$$i = \frac{2TN}{SNY(NY + 1)} \tag{6}$$

where S = monthly payment.

Example. Suppose that you purchased a $5,000 car, $1,000 down, paid for in 36 monthly installments of $140 each. What is the APR?

Answer: I = total payments − cash balance financed = 136(140)4,000 = $1,040.

Under formula (5),

$$i = \frac{2(1{,}040)12}{(4{,}000)37} = 0.169 \text{ or } 16.9\%$$

Under formula (6), the APR is

$$i = \frac{2(1{,}040)12}{140(36)37} = 0.134 \text{ or } 13.4\%$$

Estimating the monthly payment

Formula (5) may also be used indirectly to estimate the monthly payment if the amount, duration, and approximate interest rate are known. Solving (5) for T, yields

$$T = \frac{iP(NY + 1)}{2N} \tag{7}$$

and the monthly payment, M, is

$$M = \frac{P + T}{NY} \tag{8}$$

Suppose, for example, you wish to borrow $2,500 for three years and you expect to pay 12 percent interest (APR). Then using (7)

$$T = \frac{0.12(2{,}500)37}{2(12)} = \$412.50$$

$$M = \frac{2{,}500 + 412.50}{36} = \$80.90 \text{ per month.}$$

INVESTMENTS

Compound interest can be determined using the formula developed in Chapter 13,

$$A = P(1 + r)^n \tag{9}$$

where A = final amount, P = initial investment, r = rate of interest, and n = number of years. Table A–1 gives the value of $(1 + r)^n$ for some commonly available yields and various values of n. If compounding occurs more than once a year, the formula can be modified. Suppose that $r = 0.06$ (6%) but compounding is monthly. Then

$$A = P\left(1 + \frac{0.06}{12}\right)^{12n}$$

If T = \$1,500 and n = 5 years, then

$$A = \$1{,}500\ (1.005)^{60} = \$2{,}023.28$$

This compares to annual compounding for the same rate, amount, and period of

$$P = \$1{,}500(1.3382) = \$2{,}007.30$$

The figure in parentheses, 1.3382, was obtained from Table A–1 and is the value of $(1.06)^5$, or the factor for five years and 6 percent interest.

In general, if k is the frequency of compounding per years, then the expression for the value after n years at interest r of a known sum P is

$$A = P\left(1 + \frac{r}{k}\right)^{nk} \tag{10}$$

Equations (9) and (10) can be solved with a calculator and equation (9) can be solved with Table A–1 for any of the four variables—initial investment, final amount, yield, and number of years—when the other three are given.

To find years not given, use a combination. For example 13 years = 3 + 10. Compute the amount at the end of ten years. Using that amount as a new principal, compute the amount at the end of three years.

Example. Sue and John have three daughters, aged 11, 8, and 5. They want to educate them. They have just inherited \$16,000 to divide and invest for that purpose.

Table A–1
Compound interest table
(lump sum investment)

Yield (%)	Years									
	1	*2*	*3*	*4*	*5*	*6*	*7*	*10*	*15*	*20*
1	1.01	1.0201	1.0303	1.0406	1.0510	1.0615	1.0721	1.1046	1.1609	1.2201
2	1.02	1.0404	1.0612	1.0824	1.1041	1.1262	1.1487	1.2190	1.3459	1.4860
3	1.03	1.0609	1.0927	1.1255	1.1593	1.1941	1.2299	1.3439	1.5580	1.8061
4	1.04	1.0816	1.1249	1.1699	1.2167	1.2653	1.3159	1.4803	1.8009	2.1911
5	1.05	1.1025	1.1576	1.2155	1.2763	1.3401	1.4071	1.6289	2.0789	2.6533
5¼	1.0525	1.1078	1.1659	1.2271	1.2915	2.3594	1.4307	1.6681	2.1544	2.7825
5¾	1.0575	1.1183	1.1826	1.2506	1.3225	1.3986	1.4790	1.7491	2.3132	3.0592
6	1.06	1.1236	1.1910	1.2625	1.3382	1.4185	1.5036	1.7908	2.3964	3.2070
6½	1.065	1.1342	1.2079	1.2865	1.3701	1.4591	1.5540	1.8771	2.5718	3.5236
7	1.07	1.1449	1.2250	1.3108	1.4026	1.5007	1.6058	1.9672	2.7590	3.8697
7½	1.075	1.1556	1.2423	1.3356	1.4356	1.5433	1.6590	2.0610	2.9589	4.2479
8	1.08	1.1664	1.2597	1.3605	1.4693	1.5869	1.7138	2.1589	3.1722	4.6610
9	1.09	1.1881	1.2950	1.4116	1.5386	1.6771	1.8280	2.3674	3.6425	5.6044

1. The oldest needs \$8,000 in seven years. They are investing her money in a 6½ percent savings account. How much do they need to put in her account?
   Answer: 6½ percent for 7 years gives a factor from Table A–1 of 1.5540.
   \$8,000 = 1.5540 × Sum invested
   Sum = \$8,000/1.5540 = \$5,148.
2. The second daughter needs \$8,200 (allowing for inflation), but in ten years. They have agreed to set aside \$5,000 for her. What yield do they need to get to \$8,200 in ten years?
   Answer: 8,200/5,000 gives a factor of 1.64. Looking down the ten-year column, we see that this falls between 5 and 5¼ percent. A yield of about 5⅛ percent would do.
3. Their third daughter is only 5. If they invest \$3,500 for her at 7 percent, how much will she have at age 18?
   Answer: The factor for 13 years and 7 percent is the product of the factor for 10 years and 3 years.
   1.9672 × 1.2250 = 2.4098.
   2.4098 × \$3,500 = \$8,434.30.
4. This leaves them \$2,352 out of their original \$16,000. They want to take a trip around the world which will cost \$10,000 for five people. They have the money invested at 8 percent. How soon can they go?
   Answer: \$10,000/2,352 = 4.2517. At 8 percent, the factor for 20 years is 4.6610, so about 19 years is the answer.

The problem of compounding becomes a little more complex when you consider a regular annual investment of a fixed sum. The following example illustrates this type of problem.

How much do I need to invest at the beginning of each year for 10 years at 6.5 percent in order to provide my child with \$8,000 for her education? Let P = annual amount invested.

$$P(1.065)^{10} + P(1.065)^{9} + P(1.065)^{8} + P(1.065)^{7} + \cdots + P(1.065) = \$8{,}000. \quad (11)$$

This computation is cumbersome, although a calculator with one or two memories can do it fairly easily.

$$P[(1.065)^{10} + (1.065)^{9} + (1.065)^{8} + (1.065)^{7} + \cdots + 1.065] = \$8{,}000.$$

or

$$14.3716\,P = \$8{,}000$$

$$P = \frac{\$8{,}000}{14.3716} = \$556.65 \text{ per year.}$$

Similar computations can be made to determine number of years, final amount, or rate required. With either lump sum or regular periodic investments, you need to know three of the four variables—amount invested, amount at end, number of years, and interest rate. Either a table of commound interest values or a calculator will enable you to compute the missing number. for those who wish to use a calculator to compute yield on regular annual investments, the expression is

$$P(1 + r)\left[\frac{(1 + r)^n - 1}{r}\right] = A \tag{12}$$

where P = principal invested per year, A = final amount, r = interest rate, and n = number of years.

Formula (12) can be used directly on a calculator if you are given r and n, and know one of the two variables A or P. You can then substitute for the three known variables to find the fourth. If you are seeking n, however, the procedure is a bit more complex; and if you are looking for r, the procedure is extremely difficult. In that case, the use of approximations of Table A–2 is recommended.

For n, we return to equation (11), substituting k for $1 + r$:

$$A = P(k^n + k^{n-1} + \cdot \cdot \cdot + k) = P(k)\left[\frac{1 - k^n}{1 - k}\right].$$

Solving for n, we get

$$n = \frac{\ln\left[1 + \frac{A}{P}\left(\frac{k - 1}{k}\right)\right]}{\ln K} \tag{13}$$

For example, suppose you are investing $200 a year at 5 percent interest, and you want to know how long it will take to reach $3,500. $R = 0.05$, $k = 1.05$, A = $3,500, and P = $200.

Solving (13) for n, we see that $n = 12.4$. The derivation above assumes that n is an integer, so the next greatest integer is 13 years. Because of the difficulty of these computations, Table A–2 supplies a table of factors for recurring annual investments for yields from 5 to 9 percent and periods from 1 to 20 years. These factors are the value of the expression

$$(1 + r)\left[\frac{(1 + r)^n - 1}{r}\right] \tag{14}$$

for various values of r and n. The following examples illustrate the use of Table A–2.

Sue and John do not have an inheritance, so they are going to provide for their children's education through regular annual investments.

1. The oldest needs $8,000 in seven years. They are investing her money in 6½ percent savings account. How much do they need to save each year?
   Answer: $8,000 = Factor from table × Annual sum invested = 9.0769 A. $A \doteq$ $8,000/9.0769 = $881.36 per year.

Table A–2
Compound interest on recurring investments

Yield	*Years*									
(%)	*1*	*2*	*3*	*4*	*5*	*6*	*7*	*10*	*15*	*20*
1	1.01	2.0301	3.0604	4.1010	5.1520	6.2135	7.2857	10.5668	16.259	22.2392
2	1.02	2.0604	3.1216	4.2040	5.3081	6.4343	7.5830	11.1687	17.6393	24.7833
3	1.03	2.0909	3.1836	4.3091	5.4684	6.6623	7.8923	11.8078	19.1569	27.6765
4	1.04	2.1216	3.2465	4.4163	5.6330	6.8983	8.2142	12.4864	20.8245	30.9692
5	1.05	2.1525	3.3101	4.5256	5.8019	7.1420	8.5491	13.2068	22.6575	34.7193
5¼	1.0525	2.1603	3.3262	4.5533	5.8448	7.2042	8.6144	13.3937	32.1435	35.7358
5¾	1.0575	2.1758	3.3584	4.6090	5.9315	7.3301	8.8091	13.7761	24.1507	37.8713
6	1.06	2.1836	3.3476	4.6371	4.9753	7.3938	8.8975	13.9716	24.6725	38.9927
6½	1.065	2.3713	3.3912	4.6936	6.0637	7.5229	9.0769	14.4716	25,7540	41.3490
7	1.07	2.2149	3.4399	4.7507	6.1533	7.6540	9.2598	14.7836	26.8880	43.8652
7½	1.075	2.2306	3.4729	4.8084	7.2440	7.7873	9.4464	15.2081	27.0772	46.5525
8	1.08	2.2464	3.5061	4.8666	6.3359	7.9228	9.6366	15.6455	29.3243	49,4229
9	1.09	2.2781	3.5731	4.9847	6.5233	8.2004	10.0284	16.5603	32.0034	55.7645

2. The second daughter needs \$8,200 in ten years. They plan to set aside \$600 per year for her. What yield do they require?
   Answer: \$8,200 = Factor from table × \$600.
   Factor = \$8,200/\$600 = 13.6667. Under the ten-year column, the yield falls between 5¼ and 5¾ percent.
3. Their third daughter is only five. If they invest \$400 a year for her at 7 percent, how much will she have at age 18?
   Answer: To get a sum for 13 years, a number not given in the table, compute the sum at the end of 10 years and multiply it by the 3-year factor from the table to get the additional interest that sum will earn after 10 years. The last 3 years' investment will use the 3-year factor from Table A–2.
   10 years @ 7% (Table A–2) = 14.7836.
   3 years @ 7% (Table A–1) = 1.2250.
   14.7836 × 1.2250 = 18.1099.
   18.1099 × \$400 = \$7,244.
   Plus three years at 7%; factor from Table A–2 is 3.4399.
   3.4399 × \$400 = \$1,376.
   \$7,244 + \$1,376 = \$8,620.
4. They want to take a trip around the world which will cost \$10,000 for five people. They are investing \$1,000 a year at 8 percent. When do they leave?
   Answer: \$10,000 = Factor from table × \$1,000.
   Factor = 10.

In the 8 percent row, this is slightly more than seven years.

Present value computations are compounding in reverse (also known as *discounting*). Instead of asking, "how much will my dollar grow to in five years at 4 percent?" (\$1.22), the question is restated as "How much is a dollar which is to be repaid or delivered to me five years hence at 4 percent worth right now?"

In equation form, instead of

$$\$1(1.04)^5 = x$$

where x = \$1.22, or in general,

$$P(1 + r)^n = A,$$

we are now asking,

$$x(1.04)^5 = \$1.00$$

where x = \$0.82, which is the same as

$$x = \frac{\$1.00}{(1.04)^5}$$

or in general,

$$P = \frac{A}{(1 + r)^n}. \qquad (15)$$

Since Table A–1 gives values of $(1 + r)^n$ for various values of r and n, this table can be used for both compounding and discounting. The same is true of Table A–2. If the question is in the form, "If I invest $1 a year for five years at 4 percent, how much will I have?" then it is a question of compounding

$$\$1(1.04)\,\frac{(1.04)^5 - 1}{0.04} = x$$

where $x = \$5.63$.

If instead the question is "how much must I invest per year for five years at 4 percent to have $1 at the end, then the question is

$$x(1.04)\,\frac{(1.04)^5 - 1}{0.04} = \$1$$

where $x = \$0.18$, then you are dealing with discounting.

Again, a table of factors for various combinations of r and n can answer this question. Table A–3 is a table of annuity factors for various common

Table A–3
Annuity factors

Interest (%)	Years 1	2	3	4	5	10	15	20
1	0.9901	1.9704	2.9410	3.9020	4.8534	9.4713	13.8651	18.0456
2	0.9804	1.9416	2.8839	3.8077	4.7136	9.9826	12.8493	16.3514
3	0.9708	1.9135	2.8286	3.7171	4.5797	8.5302	11.9379	14.8775
4	0.9615	1.8861	2.7751	3.6299	4.4518	8.1109	11.1184	13.5903
5	0.9524	1.8594	2.7232	3.5460	4.3295	7.7217	10.3797	12.4622
6	0.9434	1.8334	2.2694	3.4651	4.2124	7.3601	9.7122	11.4699
7	0.9346	1.8080	2.6243	3.3872	4.1002	7.0236	9.1079	10.5940
8	0.9259	1.7833	2.5771	3.3121	3.9927	6.7101	8.5595	9.8181
9	0.9174	1.7591	2.5313	3.2397	3.8897	6.4177	8.0607	9.1285

interest rates and time periods which can be used to solve present value problems. The equation on which it is based is

$$P = A\,\frac{1 - (1 - r)^{-n}}{r} \qquad (16)$$

where P = present value, A = annual amount, r = the rate of interest, and n = number of years.

The following examples illustrate some of the uses of such a table, which can occur in insurance, credit, tax planning, housing, and other decision-making areas.

1. Suppose you won a lottery which will pay either $10,000 now, or $600 a year for 20 years. At 6 percent interest, which is the better deal?
   Answer: The present value, *P*, of the 20 future payments is *P* = $600 × 11.4699 = $6,881.94. The cash $10,000 is a better deal.
   At what interest rate would the two be equivalent?
   Answer: $10,000/$600 = 16.6667. Under the 20-year column in the table, just under 2 percent. If you can earn more than 2 percent on the $10,000, take the cash.
2. You anticipate inflation of 6 percent a year for the next five years. If you are making $10,000 a year, what is the present value of your anticipated five-year income stream?
   Answer: *P* = $10,000 × 4.2124 = $42,124, which is less than the actual $50,000 you will receive over five years.
3. You are contemplating buying a new car. You estimate that the better gas mileage and lower maintenance cost will save you $800 a year for the next five years. Using a 7 percent rate of discount, how much will these savings contribute to this year's cash outlay for the new car?
   Answer: *P* = $800 × 4.1002 = $3,280. Thus if your net cost after trade-in is less than $3,280, you should buy the new car. It may still be a wise decision even at a higher net cost if there are other benefits in the new car—size, performance, comfort, and so forth—to offset any excess net cost over and above $3,280.
4. You are trying to decide whether to buy a dishwasher or hire your eight-year-old to do it instead. The dishwasher costs $400 and should be good for ten years. Your eight-year-old will contract for $1 a week for the next ten years. Discounting future payments to your child at 5 percent and ignoring other costs, which is the cheaper? For simplicity, we reduce the weekly payment to an annual payment of $52 a year.
   Answer: Total payments to child are $520.
   Using Table A–3 and discounting at 7 percent, we see that *P* = $52 × 7.7217 = $401.53.
   They are nearly equivalent; the dishwasher has a negligible cost advantage.

Glossary

Acceleration clause a clause in some installment contracts which provides that if one or more payments is missed, the entire balance becomes immediately due and payable; collateral can be repossessed if the balance is not paid.

ACTION an agency of the federal government which is responsible for a broad range of service programs including the Peace Corps, VISTA, and RSVP.

Actual cash value (automobile insurance) the value of the loss for collision or comprehensive, which is what the owner receives; the cost of repairing or replacing the car.

Add-on clause a clause in installment loans whereby new purchases are added to the original loan. If the borrower defaults, all of the collateral (all items successively purchased under the contract) can be repossessed.

Adjusted balance one of several methods for determining the balance on which charge account interest is to be computed; subtracts payments from previous balance but does not add in new purchases.

Adjusted gross income total income (excluding nontaxable income sources, such as municipal bond interest) less adjustments and exclusions (q.v.).

Adjustments and exclusions items subtracted from gross income on federal income tax to arrive at adjusted gross income. Includes sick pay, some pension fund contributions, capital losses, moving expenses, and other items.

Administrator an individual named by a court to manage the estate of an individual who dies without leaving a will.

All risks (property insurance) policy covering all possible sources of damage or loss to property except certain named exclusions.

American Stock Exchange (AMEX) The AMEX is the second major stock exchange in the United States. The AMEX is a firm whose owners have access to the market where shares of stock listed on the exchange are purchased and sold.

Annual percentage rate (APR) the true annual interest rate on a loan; makes interest rates expressed in different ways easier to compare.

Annuity in general, an annual stream of payments. Specifically, an insurance-type policy which provides for regular monthly or annual payments of a specified amount to the insured or a designated beneficiary.

Antitrust laws federal and state laws designed to reduce the extent and power of monopoly enterprise in the economy. Antitrust laws prohibit such behavior as collusion and price discrimination.

Appraiser an individual who specializes in estimating the market value of items traded infrequently. Appraisers are commonly found for such items as land, housing, antiques, and art.

Assessment rate the percentage of fair market value at which property is recorded for property tax books. This amount is called the *assessed valuation*.

Asset anything you own which has market value, including financial claims (cash, stocks, bonds, and so forth), physical property (real estate, cars, personal possessions), and money owed to you.

At the market an order to a stockbroker to purchase a stock at whatever the market price is at the time the order is executed.

Attractive nuisance a feature of your property which attracts trespassers and uninvited guests, for example, a swimming pool.

Audit a review of your income tax return by the Internal Revenue Service when they dispute the amount of tax due you have computed for reasons other than errors in arithmetic.

Automatic investment an agreement with a mutual fund made by an investor in the fund, which automatically invests into new shares dividends earned by investor.

Average daily balance one of several methods for determining the balance on which charge account interest is to be determined; adds in charges as they come in and subtracts payments as they come in to determine average amount owed during the period.

Balance sheet a summary of your assets, liabilities, and net worth at a point in time.

Balloon clause installment loan clause with a large final payment which frequently requires refinancing at additional interest.

Bank card a multipurpose credit card issued by a commercial bank and honored by a great variety of businesses all over the United States and in some foreign countries.

Bankruptcy the value of debts exceeds the value of assets to the point where one is no longer able to pay debts. Declaring bankruptcy requires legal assistance.

Bear market a generally falling stock market where more shares decline in value than increase in value.

Beneficiary a person named in a will or insurance contract who is to receive certain proceeds of the policy or estate.

Better Business Bureau local organizations supported by merchants and civic organizations for the purpose of maintaining ethical dealing by business firms in a community.

Binder check a payment made to bind a contract or offer of a contract. Sometimes called earnest money, the binder check serves to close negotiations between a seller and buyer. The buyer provides the binder.

Blue-chip stocks a category of stocks which include the top quality stocks at a given time. Blue-chip stocks are not defined, but may be called by the term because of their generally recognized quality.

Blue Cross–Blue Shield a pair of nonprofit organizations offering hospitalization and medical/surgical insurance; the largest single source of private health insurance.

Bodily injury (automobile insurance) coverage of injury to others resulting from the operation of your automobile when you are at fault.

Book value the dollar value of corporate stock, determined by dividing the total number of shares of stock outstanding into the total value of the corporations assets as listed in the accounting records of the corporation.

Brokerage fee a charge paid by buyers and sellers of stock or bonds to a broker for the services involved with stock or bond transactions.

Budget a statement of expected income and planned expenditures and savings for a specific period.

Budget period the subdivisions of the year for which budgets are made; a planning period, usually a week or month.

Bull market a generally rising stock market where more shares increase in price than fall in price.

Bullion refined gold or silver in bar form.

Cafeteria plan a fringe benefit program which offers flexibility and choice from a range of options for each employee. An individual can custom tailor his own package of fringe benefits by selecting a limited number of items from the "cafeteria."

Callable bonds a category of corporate debt which may be redeemed, or paid off, at will by the issuer.

Capital gains increase in the value of an asset over original purchase price. Capital gains are only taxable when realized by selling the asset.

Capital losses decrease in the value of an asset between purchase and sale.

Cash dividends money payments made on a per share basis to owners of common and preferred stocks.

Cash value insurance insurance which builds up a savings account which can be borrowed or exchanged for cash, paid-up insurance, or extended term insurance when the policy is discontinued.

Cashier's check a check issued by a bank and signed by a bank agent which is guaranteed by the issuing bank; can be purchased with cash, usually requires a small fee.

Caveat emptor let the buyer beware. An ancient doctrine which recognized the power of the consumer and placed the responsibility of the consumer's actions on the consumer.

Certificate of deposit a savings account with a minimum amount and a specified maturity bearing higher interest rates than ordinary (passbook) accounts; issued by commercial banks and savings banks.

Certificate of eligibility a certification that an individual is entitled to veteran's benefits associated with home financing.

Certified check a check issued by a bank which guarantees payment of the face amount.

Chamber of Commerce local organizations supported by businesses for the purpose of enhancing the economic outlook of the community.

Checking account an account in a commercial bank on which checks can be written, bears no interest, usually has service charges.

Chicago Board of Trade the principal exchange on which commodity futures (q.v.) are traded.

Chippendale furniture designed by the principles set forth by Thomas Chippendale in 1754.

Christmas club/vacation club a special savings account with fixed weekly or monthly deposits of small amounts and a one-year (or less) maturity, pays modest interest.

Civil Service retirement completion of a specified period of service with an agency of the federal government giving entitlement to retirement benefits offered by the Civil Service.

Class action suit a legal suit brought by one individual in behalf of himself or herself and a larger group of people who fall into a class of interested or damaged parties. The person bringing the suit represents that class of people who are damaged or interested by or in the subject of the suit.

Classic car automobiles designated as collectors items by the Classic Car Club of America.

Clayton Act an amendment to the Sherman Antitrust Act, passed in 1914. The Clayton Act outlawed specific actions such as charging different prices for the same service and thus made the Sherman Act a more operational law.

Closed-end investment company a company organized to manage investments. Shares of stock in a closed-end company are sold on a once-and-for-all-time basis. These shares are then traded among buyers and sellers.

Closing the time at which title to real estate is transferred from seller to buyer. Usually this involves the two parties plus the mortgage lender and one or more attorneys.

Closing costs the costs associated with closing a mortgage contract. The costs may include the cost of title search, transfer of deed, lawyer's services, and special taxes on the mortgage itself.

Codicil a legal instrument which amends an original will. A codicil is used to make changes which do not require a completely rewritten will.

Coinsurance (health insurance) a provision requiring that the insurer and insured share insured medical expenses in excess of deductible; most commonly 80/20 percent. Designed to reduce overuse.

Coinsurance (homeowners insurance) a provision requiring that the owner carry insurance on the dwelling equal to at least 80 percent of fair market value; failure to do so will result in only partial recovery on partial losses.

Collision hazard to automobiles, any damage source which is due to the car running into other physical property (cars, stop signs, houses, bridges, and so forth).

Commodities futures contracts for delivery of a specified amount of goods at a specified future date. Commodities futures are most often in metals, minerals, and agricultural products.

Common carrier a carrier of freight or people which offers its services to the general public on a scheduled basis. A common carrier is said to offer services to any and all who might wish to ship freight or ride on the carrier. The common carrier is contrasted with the contract carrier which does not offer scheduled services to the general public.

Common stock shares of ownership in a corporation which are sold to individuals. Common stock is the most popular and extensively owned category of corporate stock. Owners of common stock are not assured dividends.

Compound interest interest is added to principal and also earns interest in subsequent periods.

Comprehensive (auto insurance) physical damage covering hazards to the automobile other than collision (q.v.).

Comprehensive health insurance a combination policy covering both hospital/medical/surgical expense and major medical.

Comprehensive personal liability a part of homeowner's insurance covering liability arising from sources other than operating an automobile or practicing your business or profession.

Constant dollars current dollar values which have been adjusted for inflation by using a particular price index. That is, constant dollars are expressed in terms of a particular year, for example, 1970 dollars.

Consumer price index an index compiled by the U.S. Department of Labor based on a basket of goods purchased by a typical urban family.

Consumer sovereignty the concept that consumers determine ultimately what will be produced in a market economy. Since the consumer has choices and producers cannot force a person to make a purchase, the consumer is said to be sovereign.

Conventional loan a home loan made between a lender and borrower which is not associated with government subsidies or guarantees.

Convertible bonds a category of corporate debt instruments which can be converted to shares of stock on a specified basis.

Convertible preferred stock shares of preferred stock which may be converted to common stock.

Corporate charter a legal form which establishes a corporation. The charter describes the legal name, place, nature of responsibilities of officers, directors, stock to be issued, and purpose of the corporation.

Cosigner a third party who insures the debt of a borrower by signing with the borrower. The lender may then turn to either the borrower or the cosigner to gain payment of the debt.

Credit counselling service agencies available in many areas which will help you work off an excessive debt load and put your finances in order without resorting to more drastic measures, such as bankruptcy.

Credit union a cooperative savings and lending agency, organized among a group with a common bond, most often the employees of a single employer.

Cyclical stocks shares of stock which have a pronounced price behavior that follows a cycle. These may be compared with stocks which have a very stable pricing pattern.

Day of deposit to day of withdrawal a method of computing the balance on which interest is to be paid on a savings account; all funds earn interest for the number of days they are on deposit.

Debt capacity the amount of debt you can afford to owe and service (meet monthly payments) based on your income, assets, and other expenses.

Declaration of estimated tax a form filed quarterly in which your income and tax due for the current quarter (three-month period) is estimated and any tax due in excess of withholding is paid. Persons with high incomes or large amounts of income not subject to withholding are most likely to need to file a declaration of estimated tax.

Decreasing term term insurance with a level premium but a face value which decreases each year.

Deductible the amount that the insured must pay before insurance begins to cover part or all of the loss.

Deductions subtractions from adjusted gross income to arrive at tax table income. Includes medical expenses, state and local taxes, interest paid, charitable contributions, casualty and theft losses, and miscellaneous. Deductions in excess of a zero bracket amount only are subtracted.

Demand for labor the amounts of salary or wage which a firm will pay for various quantities of labor in a given time period.

Dental care insurance insurance to cover dental care expenses; most commonly offered on a group basis.

Depreciation the decline in the value of an asset due to wear and tear, obsolescence, and age.

Directors individuals elected by shareholders in a corporation to oversee the operation of the corporation and guide the officers of the corporation in managing the firm.

Disability income policies policies designed to replace part or all of income lost while disabled (unable to work).

Discount *a.* selling for less than face value (for example, bonds); *b.* interest which is subtracted before loan or scale; *c.* with bonds, a reduction in the face value of a bond which accounts for an adjustment in the stated interest yield, making the yield competitive with other comparable investments.

Discount rate an interest rate used to find the present value of some future payment or cost.

Discounted note a loan repayable in a single installment; interest is subtracted from the amount borrowed at the beginning.

Discounted present value the dollar equivalent right now of a sum to be paid at some specific future date.

Discretionary income income available after covering the basics of rent (or mortgage), utilities, food, and insurance.

Diversification spreading your assets among a variety of investment media to minimize the loss from any particular investment.

Dividends (life insurance) refunds to mutual company policyholders of overpayment of premiums, as a result of better-than-expected claims and/or expense experience.

Dividends (investments) cash or stock payments to owners of stock in a corporation. Dividends are a partial component of the return obtained by those who own stock in a corporation.

Dollar averaging an investment strategy which requires a fixed dollar investment in a specific portfolio of stocks to be made on a scheduled basis. While the price of the stocks may rise or fall, the number of dollars invested remains constant. Thus, the average price paid for particular stocks changes through time.

Double indemnity an endorsement (q.v.) to your life insurance policy which provides double the face value of the policy in case of accidental death.

Dow Jones Averages indexes of activity for stocks on the New York Stock Exchange. There are Dow Jones Industrial, Transportation, and Utility indexes. Each index has a defined set of stocks as a basis. The prices of these stocks are then recorded and developed into indexes for each day's trading on the NYSE.

Down payment on a house or credit purchase, the amount of the actual cash you put up; the difference between the sales price and the amount borrowed.

Dread disease insurance medical insurance designed to cover expenses/income losses associated with specific diseases, such as cancer.

Early payoff payment of a debt before the due date, usually associated with long-term debts such as mortgages where a borrower pays the full balance of the debt and completes the contract.

Effective tax rate total tax as a percentage of the base, which is usually gross income. For property tax, tax as a percentage of market value of the property.

Effective yield the annual interest as a percentage of amount saved or invested; in a savings account, as a percentage of average balance.

Emergency fund a sum of money set aside to cover unexpected expenses, insurance deductibles or waiting periods, and other items. Should be kept in liquid form (for example, a savings account).

Endorsements additions to the life insurance policy which modify the basic contract; for example, waiver of premium benefit, guaranteed insurability, double indemnity (qq.v.).

Endowment policy a life insurance policy which guarantees payment of face value at the end of a specific period (for example, 20 years) or upon death if it occurs before that date.

Equilibrium wage level that wage at which the quantity of labor demanded by employers is exactly equal to the quantity of labor offered by workers.

Escrow account an account maintained by a lender to provide for the accumulation of funds which will then be used to pay property taxes, insurance, or other loan-related expenses. The escrow account is the property of the borrower and serves as a convenience for the borrower.

Exclusive agent a property/liability insurance seller who represents only one company.

Executor an individual named in a will who is responsible for carrying out the instructions of the will.

Exemptions a subtraction from adjusted gross income of $1,000 per person claimed. Exemptions include self, spouse, dependent children, and others supported by the person(s) filing.

Expected value in insurance, probability of loss times value of property insured.

Externality an economic concept which relates to the effects of a transaction between two parties which impacts a third unrelated party. External effects can be positive or negative, but the third party does not pay for the benefits or receive compensation for costs.

Family income needs insurance needs to cover the expense of maintaining the family's standard of living when one of the income earners dies.

Farmers Home Administration an administrative unit of the U.S. Department of Agriculture which makes subsidized loans for housing in rural areas.

Federal Deposit Insurance Corporation (FDIC) a federal agency insuring deposits in commercial banks up to $40,000 per account.

Federal excise tax taxes on specific goods and services such as telephone service, automobile tires, gasoline, and a few other items. Not deductible for federal income tax purposes.

Federal Land Bank a financial intermediary which specializes in long term lending associated with farming. The federal land banks have regional offices throughout the United States and make loans for farmland and equipment as well as for homes in rural farming locations.

Federal Savings and Loan Insurance Corporation (FSLIC) a federal agency insuring deposits in member savings banks for up to $40,000 per account.

Federal Trade Commission Act federal legislation passed in 1914 which established the Federal Trade Commission and charged it with the responsibility of administering certain antimonopoly legislation.

Fees and load charges the cost associated with purchasing shares of stock in certain mutual funds. The fees and load charges represent commissions to sales agents.

FHA-insured mortgage home loans between a borrower and mortgage lender wherein the borrower purchases insurance from the Federal Housing Administration which insures that payment of the mortgage will be made. If the borrower defaults, the insurer pays off the mortgage.

Fifo a method of computing the balance on which interest is to be paid on a savings account, in which withdrawals are assumed to be made from the first funds deposited in the period.

Filing status classification of taxpayer as married filing jointly, married filing separately, single, or head of household. Determines which tax rate schedule applies.

Final expenses expenses of funerals, estate taxes, medical expenses incurred immediately before death, and similar items.

Fixed expenses predictable expenses in regular amounts, such as rent or mortgage and installment payments.

Fixed yield a dollar yield which will be the same each year regardless of asset's current selling price.

Floater an addition to a homeowner's policy covering specific excluded items such as jewelry, antiques, boats, silver, works of art, and so forth.

Fly-by-night operator sellers which have no long-term interests in a market. The seller which is only interested in making one sale and then vanishes from the scene is often described as "fly-by-night."

Food and Drug Administration an administrative unit of the Department of Health, Education, and Welfare which has broad regulatory responsibilities regarding the safety and effectiveness of medicines and the quality of foods.

40–plus an organization which assists individuals who are over 40 years in age to obtain employment.

Frequency of compounding the number of times per year that interest is credited to an account or asset, to be added to principal and earn more interest.

Fringe benefits payments from your employer other than wages, salary, bonuses, and commissions, which are not in cash but rather in goods and services purchased for all employees or a specific group of employees.

Goals broad categories of achievements which one hopes to accomplish.

Gross estate the total dollar value of an estate prior to the deduction of tax exemption. The gross estate can be thought of as the value of an estate before any considerations are given to taxes.

Group insurance insurance issued to a group, such as employees of a common employer, with a single master contract instead of individual policies; usually less costly than individual policies.

Group life insurance life insurance sold to employees of a common employer or members of an association of some kind; usually term, usually much less costly than individual policies.

Growth increase in the value (market price) of an asset.

Growth stocks those shares of stock in a corporation which appears to be headed toward a long period of increasing profits. Growth stocks relate to growth firms which cause the shares of stock to have good prospects for increased value.

Guaranteed insurability an endorsement (q.v.) to a life insurance policy which provides that the insured may purchase specified additional amounts of additional insurance at specified future dates regardless or health or other conditions.

Health maintenance organization a prepayment health care plan, providing a variety of group practice health care services for a regular monthly fee.

Hedge reducing risk by covering a purchase or sale with another purchase or sale in the opposite direction for example, sell April wheat, buy June wheat. Used in commodity futures and also in the stock market.

Heterogeneity of products a characteristic of goods and services produced in a market economy. The heterogeneity or wide variety of products reflects the many preferences and skills of individuals who make up the economic system.

Holographic will a handwritten will.

Homeowner's insurance a package policy covering physical damage to property (including dwelling, contents, attached private structt .es, and landscaping), additional living expense, and personal liability.

Hospital expense insurance medical insurance covering costs of hospitalization (X rays, nursing care, room and board, operating room, and so forth) on a per day basis plus flat reimbursements for specific extra charges, usually with a low deductible.

Human capital the investment made in acquiring specialized knowledge and skills which offer future benefits or earnings.

Income averaging an alternate method of computing tax due when your income has risen sharply in relation to the past four years, which will shift some of the additional income into lower tax brackets and thereby reduce your tax due.

Income statement a summary of income and expenditures over a period of time, usually a year.

Independent agent a property/liability insurance seller who represents two or more companies.

Individual Retirement Account (IRA) a retirement plan for individuals who are employed by firms which offer no retirement benefits. Pretax income can be invested in an IRA thereby avoiding income tax.

Inflation the erosion of the purchasing power of money caused when more dollars are created than there are goods produced.

Inflation hedge an asset which is purchased because its market value is expected to rise at least as rapidly as the rate of inflation, and hopefully faster.

Infrequent expenses expenses which do not occur in every budget period, such as vacations, organization dues, and auto insurance.

Insatiable wants the human trait which causes one to recognize an ever-growing array of expenditure opportunities.

Insurable risk any threat of loss or damage which can be transferred through insurance. Generally risks which involve only the possibility of loss and not gain, have low probabilities, and are not subject to catastrophe are insurable.

Insurance a system of pooling and spreading risk; any system of sharing risk equally or proportionally among a group of individuals.

Interest amortization tables a schedule which shows the monthly payment required to pay off interest and principal on a loan for various amounts borrowed, interest rates, and lengths of time to repay.

Intestate the condition of an estate when an individual dies without leaving a legal will.

Investment company an investment company offers stock in it on a one-time basis. From the revenues received the company makes subsequent investments in securities. After the initial sale of stock in an investment company, shares outstanding continue to be traded between buyers and sellers.

Invisible costs those costs which might be paid by someone else, thus not recognized by an individual decision maker, or unseen or unrecognized costs.

Irrevocable trust an amount of money established as principal by a trustor, the individual setting aside the assets, for a specific purpose which cannot be altered without agreement by all parties named in the trust.

Joint will see mutual will.

Keough plan a retirement plan which enables self-employed people to invest pretax dollars in specified investments for future payment. A portion of invested dollars can be deducted for tax purposes as a cost of business expense.

Large loss principle the losses which could create severe financial distress for a family deserves first priority; smaller losses can be covered through deductibles and/or budgeting expected expenses.

Law of efficient markets an economic law which states that information is immediately captured in the prices of any information-related investments.

Leverage using a relatively small amount of cash to obtain a larger amount of cash. For example, a 10 percent down payment provides 90 percent borrowed money. The smaller the amount of cash required, the greater is the leverage.

Liability any debt owed to other persons.

Liability insurance insurance covering you for damages payable to others as a result of your negligence.

Life insurance a sum to be paid to designated survivors upon death of the insured.

Lifestyle the sum total of your personality, possessions, tastes and preferences, hobbies, income, expenditures, marital status, career, and so forth, which are the basis for your financial decision making.

Lifetime earnings profile a graphic presentation of annual income which depicts the total earnings for each year of a person's life.

Lifo a method of computing the principal on which interest is to be paid on a savings account, in which withdrawals are assumed to have been made from the most recently deposited funds.

Limit orders a sell or buy order for stock or bonds which is placed with a broker and which limits the price at which the transaction can be made. A limit order sets a specific price for the broker as opposed to an "at market" order.

Liquidity a measure of the amount of cash one has on hand or can raise quickly by turning assets into cash. Liquidity on a balance sheet is liquid assets (those which can be quickly and easily turned into cash) less short-term liabilities (due within six months).

Living trust an amount of assets set aside by a trustor who specifies that the income from the assets be used for a specific purpose while the trustor is still living.

Load charge (mutual funds) the difference between the net asset value per share and the selling price of a share of a mutual fund. This difference is the sales commission.

Load factor the part of the insurance premium to cover the insurer's expenses, including claims adjustment, sales commission, collection costs, addition to reserves and profit.

Low balance a method of computing the balance on which interest is to be paid on a savings account; the lowest balance for the accounting period is used.

Major medical insurance all purpose medical insurance with a large deductible, coinsurance (q.v.), and a high limit of liability.

Management fee a payment to a realty firm by an owner of rental property for managing the property. The services provided by the realty or management firm include collecting rent, making repairs, and obtaining occupants for the rental property.

Margin A down payment on the purchase of stock from a broker. The broker lends money to the buyer to cover the full cost of the stock purchase.

Marginal analysis comparing additional benefits to additional costs in making financial decisions.

Marginal product of labor the amount of production added to the output of a firm by an additional worker.

Market system an economic system characterized by private ownership of property, including labor, and voluntary exchange between buyers and sellers.

Marine insurance policy covers property damage to boat and contents and liability arising from ownership and use of a boat.

Maturity the length of time before an asset can be redeemed for face value.

Medical/surgical expense insurance insurance to cover doctor's charges for surgery and in-hospital care based on a fixed-fee schedule.

Medicare a federal program provided under the Social Security Administration which provides repayment of medical expenses for participants.

Method of calculating principal alternative methods of computing the principal on which interest is to be paid; methods include low balance, FIFO, LIFO, and day of deposit to day of withdrawal (q.q.v.).

Mil rate the rate at which property tax is levied on assessed value. One mil equals one tenth of one cent (per dollar of assessed value).

Milestone model automobile models designated as collectors items by the Milestone Car Society.

Minimum size the smallest amount acceptable for investing in a particular type of asset.

Moody's a rating service which examines the debt issue of corporations and municipalities and assigns a qualitative evaluation to the bonds. Other investor services are also provided by Moody's.

Moral hazard any temptation to create a loss to collect insurance or to overuse insurance because it is available.

Multipurpose credit card credit cards which can be used at businesses other than the issuing business or chain of businesses, such as American Express or Carte Blanche.

Municipal bonds the debt issue of cities, counties, or other political jurisdictions such as school districts.

Mutual company in insurance, a company which is owned by the policyholders, whose dividends go up and down with the company's loss experience.

Mutual fund an investment management fund in which individuals buy shares which provides the funds for investment into stocks and bonds. The managers of mutual funds make all investment decisions. Shares in mutual funds are offered for sale on a continuous basis.

Mutual (joint) will a document prepared by husband and wife which may have instructions in separate documents (mutual) or in one document (joint).

Named perils (homeowner's insurance) a type of coverage which protects real and personal property only from loss or damage caused by perils specifically listed in the contract.

NARFE (National Association of Retired Federal Employees) An organization which provides opportunities for activities for former civil service employees.

Needs approach measuring the amount of life insurance required by computing final expenses, debt resolution, contingency fund, college education, and supplementary income needs for surviving dependents.

Negligence failure to exert reasonable precautions in protecting others from damage or injury resulting from your automobile, real and personal property, children, dogs, servants, and so forth.

Net asset value the basis for determining the value of shares in a mutual fund. The total value of securities owned by the mutual fund are calculated daily. From this asset value are subtracted all outstanding liabilities. Then the net asset value is divided by the number of shares outstanding in the mutual fund. This gives the net asset value.

Net level premium the premium required to meet losses and expenses for a life insurance policy written over a long period of time (usually to age 65 or life); will be higher in early years and lower in later years than an equivalent policy, written on an annual or other renewable basis where the premium is raised periodically.

Net worth the excess of the value of your assets over the value of your liabilities.

New York Stock Exchange (NYSE) the major market for corporate stock in the United States. The NYSE is a firm whose members own "seats" on the exchange giving them the right to buy and sell shares of stock which are listed on the exchange.

No-fault insurance (automobile insurance) covers injury and damage to your car, contents, and occupants regardless of which driver is at fault.

No-load funds mutual funds which sell their shares at net asset value with no further charge for fees or load charges.

Nominal income the amount of income expressed in today's dollars as opposed to income expressed in constant dollars.

Nonforfeiture options the uses of the cash value of life insurance when the policy is discontinued; includes cash, paid-up life insurance, or extended-term insurance.

Nonstandard families families other than the typical family of two adults and two or three children—singles, divorcées, childless or retired couples.

Numismatists collectors of coins.

Nuncupative will a will prepared by an individual in contemplation of imminent death. There are restrictions as to the size of an estate which can be disposed of with this type will.

Nursing care insurance insurance to cover out-of-hospital nursing care, usually for a limited number of days.

Objectives highly specific accomplishments which may lead to the achievement of a longer term goal.

Occupancy risk the unpredictable element in estimating the number of rental units which might be occupied for a given period of time. A landlord or manager of homes or apartments being rented must earn enough rent to cover the cost of empty units.

Odd lot less than 100 shares of stock. Odd lots of stock are sold at a slight price premium.

Old Age, Survivors', and Disability Insurance the correct title for Social Security. See, Social Security.

Old master a term used to identify a large group of outstanding painters of earlier periods. These include Rubens, Raphael, and others.

Open-end investment company a company organized to manage investments. An open-end investment company offers new shares of stock on a continuous basis. The revenue received may be invested in shares of corporate securities, bonds, gold, or other investments.

Opportunity cost the cost forgone when an individual or any other economic resource is used in a particular way. The value given up when another opportunity is taken.

Over-the-counter market (OTC) the OTC market is an informal stock exchange where stock not listed on the AMEX or NYSE is listed. Individual dealers and brokers make up the actual market for OTC stocks and report their prices for listing on the OTC exchange.

Overdraft privilege the right to draw checks on your account in excess of the balance on deposit up to a prearranged amount; an automatic loan privilege.

Participating policy a life insurance policy which is entitled to receive dividends (q.v.).

Pension retirement income provided by an employer to qualified employees.

Pension Benefit Guaranty Corporation a government corporation which insures pension plans in the private sector. Private firms with retirement programs are required to contribute funds to the corporation to provide a reserve for bankrupt pension programs

Personal property (homeowner's insurance) any personal possessions other than cars, boats, airplanes, or other items requiring separate coverage.

Points a method for charging additional costs on home loans which are being financed by VA- or FHA-guaranteed or insured loans. When the maximum interest allowed by VA or FHA is less than the cost of money to the lender, the borrower may have to pay a percentage "point" of the total amount borrowed.

Portfolio the array of assets owned by an individual investor.

Preferred stock shares of ownership in a corporation which are sold to individuals. Preferred stock usually pays a stated dividend to owners and will do so in preference to common stock. Preferred stock may also give preference to its owners in the distribution of assets should a corporation cease to do business.

Premium *a*. the excess of the market price over the face value of an investment; in particular, the excess of the dollar amount paid for gold or silver coins over the precious metal content of the coins. *b*. an amount in excess of the face value of a bond which is paid when the bond is purchased. The premium represents an adjustment to the interest rate paid on the bond so as to make the interest yield comparable to returns on similar investments. *c*. the price of insurance.

Present value the value today of some future payment or future cost.

Previous balance one of several methods for determining the balance on which charge account interest is to be determined; the balance forwarded from previous month with no adjustment for payments or charges made during the month.

Price-earnings ratio the market price of a stock divided by the earnings per share of that stock. The P/E ratio is found by taking the last closing price of a stock and then finding the amount of profit earned by the corporation per share of stock. The profit per share is divided into the closing price to obtain the P/E ratio.

Principal an amount of dollar assets set aside as an investment or designated for a trust. The principal is the earning asset which yields interest or proceeds.

Probate the legal process which tests the validity of a will and gives a hearing to all parties interested in the will or the estate of a deceased. The probate process is conducted by a probate court.

Product liability the legal obligation of the seller to make reparations for losses or injury caused by his or her product.

Productivity the ability to contribute to the production or output of a firm or organization.

Professional liability insurance insurance covering damage claims by others resulting from the practice of your business or profession.

Progressive tax a tax which takes a higher percentage of your income as your income increases.

Property damage (automobile insurance) damage done to your car and/or contents; includes collision and comprehensive.

Property insurance insurance covering damage to or loss of real estate and personal possessions of all kinds.

Property tax tax on capital assets levied by most local governments and some state governments. Most commonly on real estate, commercial and industrial peroperty, automobiles, and boats.

Prospectus a legal instrument used to announce the availability and details of a new offering of stocks. The prospectus represents the firm's initial sale of securities and provides information on how shares may be purchased.

Provenance a list of the previous owners of a piece of art; much like a title for a parcel of land.

Pure premium that part of the premium which covers average expected losses or claims.

Real income money income corrected for changes in purchasing power. Money income is divided by a price index to arrive at real income.

Refiner an industrial firm which purchases precious metal ore and processes the ore into refined metal of uniform quality.

Registration fee the cost of listing shares of stock in the name of an owner. Every share of outstanding stock is registered in the name of an owner. When stock is sold it must be transferred and registered in the new owner's name.

Regulatory commissions governmental units—local, state, and federal—which establish prices, standards of quality, and rules and procedures to be followed by private individuals and firms which are the subjects of the commissions' authority. Zoning boards, state public service commissions, and the Interstate Commerce Commission are examples of regulatory bodies.

Reinvestment of dividends and gains a provision in a mutual fund contract which establishes a procedure for purchasing additional mutual fund shares with all earnings which might accrue to an owner of shares in the mutual fund.

Remaindermen those individuals who receive the assets of a trust once the trust is dissolved or completed.

Renewable term term insurance which is issued for short periods of one, five, or ten years but which can be renewed at a guaranteed rate which increases with age at renewal.

Renter's insurance a package policy for tenants covering personal property, additional living expenses, and personal liability.

Reserve(s) the amount an insurance company must keep on hand to meet expected losses each year, plus some funds to cover the possibility of above-average losses.

Restoration (health insurance) the amount of your maximum health care insurance restored every year after the limit has been depleted by claims.

Retaining risk choosing to take a chance on suffering a loss by not insuring an insurable risk.

Reversionary trust a trust which cannot be cancelled for a specified period of time. Upon completion of that time period the principal of the trust reverts to the originator of the trust.

Revocable trust a trust contract which can be cancelled by the originator at any time.

Risk the possibility of increase or decrease in interest, dividends, and/or market value of a financial asset.

Robinson–Patman Act one of the primary federal antitrust laws, passed in 1936, which, rather oddly, reduced the ability of larger firms to offer lower prices to consumers.

Round lot an even block or round lot of stock is usually defined to be 100 shares. This is the standard order quantity. Smaller or odd lots carry a slight price premium.

RSVP (Retired Senior Volunteer Program) a program organized by ACTION, a federal agency, which is directed to community service activities.

Rule of 78s a method of allocating interest among the monthly payments on an installment loan which credits more of the interest to the earlier months and less to the later months.

Safe-deposit box a place to store valuables securely, usually in a commercial bank.

Sales tax taxes by most states and some local governments on the purchase of goods and services expressed as a percentage of selling price. Rates and items included vary from state to state.

Savings account highly liquid interest-bearing bank deposits, low minimum, immediate access; available at commercial banks and savings banks.

Savings goal any financial goal for which you need to set aside funds over and above current expenses. Savings goals are usually tied to specific invested sums and specific investment media.

SCORE (Service Corps of Retired Executives) a program operated by the Small Business Administration which is designed to use the talents of retired business executives in consulting activities with small businesses.

Search costs the expense in time and money paid when seeking an economic opportunity.

Secured bonds corporate or other debt instruments which are related to certain specific assets.

Self-insurance providing a fund to cover expected losses yourself rather than insurance. Deductibles are a limited form of self-insurance.

Selling short the sale of stock which is borrowed from a banker. The seller anticipates being able to purchase the same stock later at a lower price and would then replace the borrowed shares.

Series E bonds government bonds issued through commercial banks, sold at 75 percent of face value and maturing in five years, in amounts of $25–$500.

Series H bonds government bonds issued in denominations of $500 and $1,000, sold at face value, can be purchased and redeemed at commercial banks. The interest rate is usually competitive with 90-day certificates of deposit.

Service charge fees for the use of a checking account; may include flat monthly fee, charge per check or deposit, and/or charge for personalized checks.

Sherman Antitrust Act the first federal antitrust law, which was passed in 1890, that outlawed actions leading to monopoly. The act was designed to reduce the perceived power of certain large organizations known as "trusts."

Short sale selling stock you do not actually own but borrow from your broker in anticipation of a fall in price. When the price falls you buy at the lower price, replace the borrowed stock, and make a profit.

Silver futures the contract price paid for the future delivery of silver of a specified quality. Futures contract prices take into account the expected changes in supply which occur prior to the contract delivery date.

Social Security social insurance paid for through required contributions by workers and employers. Social Security is designed primarily for retirement benefit purposes. However, there is a broad range of benefits available. Social Security is the common term for Old Age, Survivors' and Disability Insurance.

Solvency market value of one's assets is greater than market value of one's liabilities: positive net worth.

Speculative stocks shares of stock in corporations which have a heavy risk element. Where there are uncertainties with respect to profit shares of stock may change value on the basis of minute items of information.

Spot-price the price for immediate delivery of commodities or foreign exchange.

Standard & Poor's a major bond-rating agency (see Moody's).

Standard & Poor's 400 an index of 400 common stocks listed on the NYSE. The 400 stocks are defined and followed each day so that the index can be computed and reported each day.

Standard risk a person who pays the normal (lowest) rate for life insurance because his or her health, occupation, and so forth give no cause for expecting him/her to die earlier than the average.

Stock bond averaging an investment strategy which requires a fixed ratio of dollars to be invested in stocks and bonds. The total dollars to be invested each time are fixed.

Stock company in insurance, a company which is owned by stockholders, who receive dividends in good years and bear excess losses in bad years.

Stock dividends payments to owners of common stock which payments are made in the form of additional shares of the same stock.

Stock split a change in the number of shares outstanding by issuing more than one share to stockholders for each outstanding share they already own. Usually this is done to bring the price of a share back down into a more satisfactory trading range.

Stop order an order given by a seller of stock to his or her broker. The stop order sets a lower limit on price and causes a sale of stock to occur automatically if the price of the stock reaches the stop order level.

Subordinated debentures a category of debt instruments which would be paid after other debts of the corporation are paid in the event of bankruptcy or liquidation.

Supplemental security income a benefit offered under Social Security for blind, aged, and disabled individuals who qualify on the basis of maximum assets.

Supply of labor the number of workers who are willing to work for various amounts of pay.

Systematic withdrawal a provision in a mutual fund which allows for the payment of funds to the investor. The investor's holdings in the mutual fund are liquidated through time and the proceeds from liquidation are paid systematically to the owner of the mutual fund shares.

Tax bracket in federal or state income tax, the marginal tax rate or rate on the *last* (or next) dollar of taxable income.

Tax calendar a schedule of tax planning, record keeping, and filing activities to be done throughout the tax year.

Tax credits amounts subtracted from tax due to find balance due or refund. Includes tax withholding, 20 percent of child care expenses, Social Security overpayments, and other items.

Tax-exempt bonds the debt issue of certain public bodies, particularly municipalities, whose owners enjoy a tax exemption on bond interest payments.

Tax schedules a listing of tax amounts and percentage tax rates for the various fractions of taxable income (first $2,000, second $2,000) used to compute federal income tax due.

Tax status the way that interest, dividends, capital gains and losses, and depreciation of assets are treated for income tax purposes.

Taxable income the amount of income on which federal income tax is paid; equals gross income less adjustments and exclusions, exemptions, and itemized deductions in excess of zero bracket amount. Also called tax table income.

Term insurance insurance which builds no cash value and expires at the end of a specified time.

Term-to-65 a life insurance policy which expires at age 65.

Testamentary trust an established trust which becomes a part of an individual's estate by specification in a will.

Time distribution of income and expenditures the pattern of when your income comes in and at what times during the year expenditures have to be made.

Tracking following expenditures in a certain category for a short period in order to estimate variable expenses for your income statement.

Trade associations Organizations formed by individuals who have common business interests and problems associated with their interests. These organizations provide technical, political, and public relations support to their members.

Transactions costs the costs associated with buying, selling, storing, evaluating, and maintaining assets.

Transfer tax a tax on the transfer of shares of stock from one owner to another.

Traveler's checks special checks purchased through banks in even denominations for cash plus a 1 percent fee, usually as acceptable as money, can be replaced if lost or stolen.

Treasury bill short-term, large denomination ($10,000 or more) obligations of the U.S. Treasury.

Trustee an individual named in a trust to oversee the operation of the trust.

Truth in Lending popular name of federal legislation regulating information which must be provided to borrowers at the time a loan is arranged.

Twenty-pay life life insurance which is paid for in 20 equal annual (or 240 monthly) installments but whose cash value does not reach face value until age 100.

Umbrella policy a broad liability insurance policy, usually covering both personal and professional liability (exception—automobile liability) which is written with very high limits of liability. Limits of $1 million are not uncommon.

Unemployment insurance benefits provided for workers who are temporarily out of work and seeking employment. Unemployment insurance is funded by contributions required of employers.

Unified tax credit a deduction from a gross estate which reduces the taxable estate.

Uniform Commercial Code a standard component of contract law which relates to commercial contracts.

Uninsured motorist coverage a part of many automobile policies, covers you for damages caused by hit-and-run drivers and uninsured drivers.

Unscheduled personal property personal possessions in the house or apartment not covered by separate floater additions to the policy.

Unsecured bonds corporate or other debt instruments which relate to the general financial strength of the issuer. These bonds are not related to or backed by specific assets.

U.S. bonds the long-term debt instruments of the U.S. Treasury.

Usury laws state laws which limit the maximum rate of interest which can be charged by a lender or paid to a saver.

VA-guaranteed loan home loans between a borrower and a mortgage lender wherein the VA guarantees that the loan will be paid. The Veterans Administration will pay off guaranteed mortgages should the borrower default on his payment.

Variable expenses those living expenses which are higher in some periods and lower in others, such as food, recreation, clothing, and gifts.

Variable yield a return on invested assets which is not guaranteed but can rise or fall depending on market conditions.

VISTA (Volunteers in Service to America) an organization which matches the abilities of volunteers to needed service areas in the United States.

Wage-earner plan title 13 of the Bankruptcy Act which arranges for extended payment of debts without bankruptcy.

Waiting period (disability insurance) the time period that elapses between onset of disability and payment of benefits, takes the place of a deductible.

Waiver of premium benefit (life insurance) no premium need be paid during periods of substantiated disability. A slight extra charge is made for this provision.

Whole life (ordinary life) a life insurance policy equivalent to endowment at age 100; builds cash value premiums payable to age 100.

Withholding amount withheld from your paycheck by your employer and sent to the Internal Revenue Service to be credited against your federal income tax bill.

Worker's compensation insurance state insurance plans which provide reimbursement of the costs of medical treatment for job-related injuries or disability. The benefits are funded by required payments of employers.

Yield the rate of return on an asset, expressed as a percentage of the asset's purchase price.

Yield to maturity the average annual rate of return on an investment between purchase date and maturity date, taking into account not only interest or dividends but also capital gains and losses measured by the difference between purchase price and face value.

Zero bracket amount a sum, currently $3,400 on joint returns and $2,300 on a single, which is subtracted from adjusted gross income to find tax table income. Itemized deductions in excess of this amount can also be deducted.

Index

C

T

This book has been set in 10 point and 9 point Optima, leaded 2 points. Part numbers and titles and chapter numbers and titles are in 36 point Optima. The size of the type page is 27 × 46½ picas.